George C. Wallace and the Politics of Powerlessness

George C. Wallace and the Politics of Powerlessness

The Wallace Campaigns for the Presidency, 1964-1976

Jody Carlson

Transaction Books
New Brunswick (U.S.A.) and London (U.K.)

Library of Congress Catalog Number: 79-65225
ISBN: 0-87855-344-4
Printed in the United States of America

Library of Congress Cataloging in Publication Data
Carlson, Jody, 1938—
    George C. Wallace and the politics of powerlessness.

    Bibliography: p.
    Includes index.
    1. Wallace, George Corley, 1919- 2. United
States—Politics and government—1945- 3. Voting
—United States. 4. Presidents—United States—
Election. 5. Southern States—Politics and
government—1951-   I. Title.
F330.W3C37   324.973′092 [B]   79-65225
ISBN 0-87855-344-4

For Kim and Margot

Contents

List of Tables and Figures   viii
Preface   xi
Acknowledgments   xiv
Prologue: Wallace's South   1
1. The Politics of Powerlessness   5
2. Voting Theories and the Wallace Voter   9
3. Public Office 1945-1963: Wallace's Move Toward
    Segregation and National Notoriety   19
4. The 1964 Presidential Primaries: Breaking in on the
    National Scene   27
5. Wallace Support in 1964: Building a Constituency   45
6. Analysis of 1964 Speeches: "George C. Wallace for President"   61
7. 1968: The Third Party   67
8. Wallace Support in 1968: From Southern to National Politics   85
9. Analysis of 1968 Speeches: "Stand Up for America"   127
10. 1972: Going After the Democratic Nomination   133
11. Wallace Support in 1972: The Florida Primary   157
12. Analysis of 1972 Speeches: "Send Them a Message"   173
13. 1976: The Last Hurrah   181
14. Wallace Support in 1976: Into the Mainstream   221
15. Analysis of 1976 Speeches: "Trust the People"   247
16. Wallace Support: Demographic and Attitudinal Changes,
    1964 to 1976   253
Epilogue   269
Conclusion   275
Appendix: Methods   281
Bibliography   287
Index   319

List of Tables and Figures

Tables		Page
5.1	Selected Demographic Characteristics	46
5.2	Position on Civil Rights	48
5.3	Respondent's Definition of His/Her Own Ideology	49
5.4	Selected Status Characteristics	53
5.5	Proportions Against Civil Rights by Number of Ascribed Social Characteristics	55
5.6	Proportions Against Civil Rights by Percentage in Each SES Group	55
5.7	Proportions Against Reapportionment by Attitudes on Civil Rights	57
8.1	Selected Demographic Characteristics	88
8.2	Selected Domestic Policy Issues	92
8.3	Selected Foreign Policy Issues	93
8.4	Selected Attitudes Toward Law and Order	95
8.5	Selected Racial Attitudes	96
8.6	Authoritarian Measures	100
8.7	Marginal Voter Measures	101
8.8	Selected Status Characteristics	104
8.9	Measures of Mobility	106
8.10	Measures of Status Anxiety	108
8.11	Status and Racial Attitudes	110
8.12	Selected Attitudes Toward the Federal Government	112
8.13	Measures of Personal and Political Anomie and Powerlessness	118
8.14	Position on Race by Degree of Power	122
11.1	Selected Demographic Characteristics	159
11.2	Position on Selected Issues	161
11.3	Attitudes Toward Busing and Integration	162

11.4	Proportions in Each Cell of Figure 11.1 by Voter Groups	164
11.5	Attitude Toward Withdrawing from Vietnam	165
11.6	Selected Status Characteristics	168
11.7	Measures of Status Deprivation	169
11.8	Measure of Political Anomie	171
14.1	Selected Demographic Characteristics	224
14.2	Affective Issues	228
14.3	Campaign Issues — Domestic Policy	230
14.4	Campaign Issues — Foreign Policy	233
14.5	Racial Attitudes	235
14.6	Marginal Voter Measures	236
14.7	Selected Status Variables	238
14.8	Selected Power Variables	241
14.9	Which of These Qualities Best Describe Why You Voted for Your Candidate Today?	242
14.10	Which Issues Were Most Important in Deciding Which Person to Vote For?	244
14.11	Selected Campaign Issues	245
16.1	Actual Vote of Those Who Are Pro-Wallace in 1968, 1972, and 1976	255
16.2	Pro/Anti-Wallace Samples	255
16.3	Selected Demographic Characteristics	259
16.4	Ideological Positions	260
16.5	Selected Racial Attitudes	261
16.6	Measures of Political Marginality	263
16.7	Selected Authoritarian Measures	264
16.8	Selected Status Attributes	266
16.9	Selected Power Measures	268

Figure

11.1	Crosstabulation of Questions on Busing with Explanation of Significance of Each Cell	163

Preface

The aim of this book is to explore systematically and substantively the political appeal of George C. Wallace, who as candidate for president of the United States four times, got almost enough votes to throw both the 1968 and the 1972 elections into the House of Representatives. Not only that, his presence had such a profound influence on American politics that it pushed not only Nixon but every other presidential hopeful to the right and was subsequently responsible for the election of Jimmy Carter as well as the direction of American politics for a great many years.

Until now there has been no systematic attempt to examine Wallace and his appeal from the point of view of his politics. This study is unique because it employs both qualitative and quantitative methodology. I have employed a multimethodological approach using history as reported by journalists, social scientists, and the participants, including Wallace himself; official documents, speeches, and other materials from the Wallace campaigns; and demographic and attitudinal data on Wallace supporters to explore one essential question: What were the Wallace politics?

This question, however, is inextricably tied up with another—that of Wallace's cultural context and the tenor of the times—and the answer, no matter what methodology is used, keeps coming up powerlessness.

It is a long and complex story, and my interest in it is personal as well as intellectual. I grew up in the segregated South, a product of upper-middle-class white parents and the folklore of southern womanhood. Life was riddled with contradictions: black/white, South/North, federal government/states' rights, male/female.

Much of the violence of southern politics and the brutality of black/white relations was kept a secret from southern women in general—we were to be protected at all costs from the realities of southern life and the

xi

power interests of men. In many ways, growing up in that kind of South was like growing up before the Civil War, or as southerners put it, the War between the States. When the twentieth century finally burst into my consciousness and I had acquired scholarly and intellectual skills, I wanted to go back to the past and unmask every myth, to finally and fully understand the intricacies of the culture from which I had emerged. I was particularly interested because it is a culture and polity which has had such a great—even disproportionate—impact on American society. In many ways the South, like presidential candidate Wallace, has been the tail wagging the dog, and as such, needs to be better understood.

This book began in a graduate class in political sociology taught by Irving Louis Horowitz at Rutgers University. Horowitz had been talking about the 1968 general election and mentioned that the Arkansas elections were particularly curious—American Independent Party presidential candidate George Wallace, Senator William Fulbright and Governor Winthrop Rockefeller had all captured a plurality of the same voting populace. I was immediately intrigued. They were such different politicians; how could this be? I decided to find out.

A close scrutiny of voting data led nowhere. The Fulbright vote was most definitely not related to Fulbright's position on Vietnam; most Arkansans were hawks. Voting theory was no help. The Wallace vote was not related to the number of blacks in a county, as V.O. Key had suggested, and the Rockefeller vote had nothing to do with economic indicators. Rockefeller, as chair of the Arkansas Industrial Development Board, had brought in many new jobs and was responsible for improved economic conditions in general.

Only one thing could explain these contradictions: all three candidates projected the same image—that of a David fighting Goliath: Wallace and Fulbright railing against the federal government, and Rockefeller fighting crime and corruption.

Wallace's stance was the most dramatic. His speeches were fiery personifications of the South's resistance to the federal government's policy of integration. I got a picture of the South being dragged, kicking and screaming, into the twentieth century. Wallace represented his constituency as proud, powerless, and fiercely resistant. At once he captured the South of my girlhood—the pride, the agony, the boisterousness, the insecurity, the violence. I wanted to know more, and this book is what I found out.

This is a book for those interested in sociology, political sociology, political science and government, history, social research, and communications. As such, it is organized by campaigns—1964, 1968, 1972, 1976. Within each campaign there is a chapter on the historical events of the campaign, a chapter that compares Wallace supporters with supporters of other candidates, and a chapter that analyzes the content of the candidate's most revealing public utterances.

If your interest is history, you may want to read the narratives straight through (Prologue, Chs. 1, 3, 4, 7, 10, 13, and Epilogue). And students of research will be interested in the data analyses of Wallace supporters (Chs. 5, 8, 11, 14, and 16) and the content analysis of the speeches (Chs. 6, 9, 12, and 15).

You will find that this study is not only about Wallace, it is also about the South and southerners and Wallace supporters everywhere. Most of all, however, it is about social change and the reaction of one faction of the voting populace to the most revolutionary social structural changes that have yet taken place in this century.

Acknowledgments

The process of doing and completing any work of this sort involves the stimulation of brief conversations as well as continued dialogue with friends and colleagues. Many people have contributed toward my understanding of the subject as well as involved themselves in the process of production through listening, questioning, and encouraging. My thanks go to all of them.

Those to whom I owe an intellectual debt and who have been particularly supportive during the process of my research and writing have been Irving Louis Horowitz and Marc Rice. I am also grateful for the help and support of Lee Kirby and Lynn Donovan.

My gratitude also goes to Matilda White Riley, Harry C. Bredemeier, John Leggett, and Marty Oppenheimer, each of whom in their own ways made me feel that the project was possible and that my efforts might make a contribution. Gerald Pomper, Joe Conforti, and Kathy Frankovic also deserve special thanks.

I appreciate the intellectual and emotional sustenance given me by Mildred Antonelli, Michael Edison, Leslie Freeman, Judy Lilleston, Leah Margulies, John Raymond, Julie Schneider, Bob Spiegelman, and George Vickers.

And I am most grateful for the support and encouragement of my daughters, Kim Carlson and Margot Carlson, and of my friends Richard Ackerman, Leslie Allan, John Amato, Nancy Attas, Michael Fogarty, Nina Kowaloff, Brian McBain, Woody Mackintosh, Eleanor Richman, Claudia Rosenhouse, and Susan Zilbering. A very special thanks goes to Barbara Siviglia for her help in the actual production of the work.

This is a much better book because of the generous contributions of time and information from George Wallace, Joe Azbell, Mark Bablin, Billy Joe Camp, Alton Dauphin, Michael Griffin, Milo Howard, Robert Kendall, Pete Mathews, Mable Pirtle, Jean Robinson, and Charles Snider.

The data used in the writing of this book were made available by the Inter-University Consortium for Political and Social Research, Roper Public Opinion Research Center, and the CBS News/*New York Times* Poll. The data for the Center for Political Studies American National Election Studies were originally collected by the Center for Political Studies of the Institute for Social Research, the University of Michigan, under a grant from the National Science Foundation. Philip Meyer of Knight Newspapers directed the study of the 1972 Florida Primary, and Warren Mitofsky directed the 1976 CBS News/*New York Times* Polls. Neither the original collectors of the data, nor the Consortium, nor Roper, nor CBS News bears any responsibility for the analyses or interpretations presented here.

Prologue: Wallace's South

In imagination and in fact, the South has been set apart from the North since the 1860s. The feeling that it is somehow different from the rest of the United States, resulting at first from its participation and defeat in the Civil War, has been fueled by both the memories and myths of Reconstruction and reinforced by the behavior of the rest of the United States toward the South. I.F. Stone (Middleton 1973, p. 106) portrays the white South as feeling that it is "a victim of injustice, misunderstanding, and brute force." Such feelings allow little recourse. The resulting resentment and rage at being made to feel so powerless are apparent as both psychological and cultural themes throughout all of Wallace's speeches.

Feelings of resentment and separateness continue, as shown by the presence in southern souvenir shops of "Forget, Hell!" captioned-pictures of an old Civil War soldier carrying a Confederate flag, as well as the strong feelings expressed by southerners that "Yankees" are somehow different from them. It is a view not limited to southerners; most Americans in the rest of the United States also think that southerners are different from other people.

Wallace's South was primarily agricultural and comparatively more poverty-stricken than the rest of the United States (Havard 1972, ch. 1). But the white South had one thing that made it feel powerful: superiority over the black South, a set of power relations which had been salvaged and reinforced in the years since the Reconstruction period (Woodward 1966). That one thing above all else was to be preserved.

Also of great cultural importance was the bravado with which the white southern male lived his life. Bravado can be understood as a way of dealing with life that allows one to hide feelings of pain and inadequacy. Having less of the education and income valued by the larger society, the southerner was obliged to outdistance the northerner through devious

1

means: by manipulating thought and logic and by projecting the threat of violence. Politically, this kind of style had great power. The gentlemen of the North could not easily deal with the southerner's style—seemingly genteel while deliberately misleading the other and promoting a mood of unpredictability.

As a result of such "games," southerners came to be perceived by others as primitive and dangerous, a reputation which they welcomed and cultivated and which served them well in their games of power. Wallace's vast talents of this style of political manipulation can be seen in Frady's (1968, pp. 150-170) account of Robert Kennedy's futile attempt to avert the stand in the schoolhouse door at a meeting with Wallace in Montgomery in April 1963.

In discussing Southern politics, V.O. Key makes many valuable observations along these lines. He suggests that the Civil War left a much higher degree of southern unity against the rest of the nation than had existed before. The experience of that war and the reconstruction following it purged any integral differences which had been present in the South (Key 1949, p. 7), and the resulting unity came about primarily to "oppose external intervention in matters of race relations" (Key 1949, p. 352). A strong and united front was presented in Congress as well as in the voting in national elections (Key 1949, p. 8), but the consequences were a growing isolation coupled with a very strong resistance to any kind of federal intervention. Having to produce such a strong united front in the face of feared national intervention led to the dimunition of democratic politics and the rise of a one-party system.

In such a situation, it is not surprising that no real understanding of civil rights would develop. The absence of dissident groups and the political dynamics which would have resulted from such groups tend to make the norm one of conformity rather than democratic discussion. While Democratic primaries functioned somewhat as forums for the settlement of interest group differences, the main raison d'etre of southern politics—to keep the Negro in his place—remained secure, whatever the political infighting might have been.

In protecting that power interest, the southern politician spent most of his time dealing with issues which distracted others from his true purpose of keeping black/white power relations intact; he worked tirelessly to entrench himself into positions of control in national politics. As an underdog relative to the general American political system (his region did not share equally in the distribution of goods and services, perhaps a trade-off for leaving the southern social system untouched), he spent most of his time operating solely by the use of threat and bravado.

During the decade of the 1960s, the South was the location of social-structural changes that reached back to the beginnings of Southern history and involved the deepest social cleavage in the United States. These changes were substantial ones and it is quite remarkable that something so revolutionary took place with a minimum of bloodshed. Part of the reason that it was relatively peaceful is that the South found itself in a position (due to the rise of federalism [Elazar 1972] as well as the preponderance of the industrial and agricultural market networks) of little choice. To fight federal orders would have been sheer economic suicide. Frederick M. Wirt, in *The Politics of Southern Equality* (1970) shows how federal money was used as threat and was the deciding factor in accomplishing desegregation of the school system and other public agencies in Panola County, Mississippi. Such institutions had been dependent for years on federal funds, and a pragmatic assessment on the part of local citizens of what they would lose financially if they chose to defy orders made the crucial difference. Wirt emphasizes that "without Title VI [of the 1964 Civil Rights Act] and its guidelines, no school integration whatever would have taken place" (Wirt 1970, p. 221). Local businessmen, eager to get federal funds and to attract industry from the North, also served to smooth the move towards integration (Wirt 1970, p. 304; Cramer 1963, p. 384). Although most Panolians greatly opposed the changes, Wirt remarks that those questioned said that they would support the law "because it was the law." Not once did anyone say that he agreed with what the law was trying to do (Wirt 1970, p. 136). There was also the threat of federal force if they did not comply. The option of noncompliance was simply not possible, but delay tactics and the exercise of temporary defiance were. And this is where Wallace came in.

Chapter One

The Politics of Powerlessness

George Wallace ran for president of the United States four times—in 1964, 1968, 1972, and 1976. In 1968, as the candidate of the newly formed American Independent Party, he came close to throwing the election into the House of Representatives, getting over nine million popular votes and forty-six electoral votes. In 1972, he ran as a Democrat. "In the fourteen primaries that he entered before he was shot, he got 1.5 million more votes than any other Democrat . . . won five of the contests and was second in five others" (Ayres 1974b).

Because he had such widespread support, his candidacies caused a great deal of consternation among politicians, journalists, and scholars. While almost everyone had an opinion about George Wallace, few people stopped to examine his politics and those of his supporters closely. Those who did usually termed Wallace a racist and tended to classify both him and his supporters as right wing.

That Wallace was a racist is not in doubt, although he did make a pragmatic reappraisal of his segregationist position after the 1970 gubernatorial election and began to focus on busing, dropping all references to race relations from his rhetoric altogether. The views of his supporters also shifted, but there is no conclusive evidence that either he or they were right wing. In fact, Wallace supporters were virtually indistinguishable from supporters of other candidates on measures traditionally considered right wing. Moreover, in terms of demographics, they looked like Republicans.

A reading of the Wallace speeches provides some insight. In his attacks on the federal government in regard to its continuing interference in

5

people's lives, Wallace gives precise expression to something that his supporters seem to respond to overwhelmingly: that they have lost power relative to the growing power of "Washington." Supporters of Wallace have certain identifiable attitudes toward power which serve to distinguish them from supporters for other candidates.

The data show that Wallace supporters are politically alienated and feel powerless in relation to the American political system. In demanding power, they are also demanding that the system operate in a legitimate fashion, rewarding effort and faithfulness, distributing goods and services equitably. In the general scheme of things their bid for power is conceived of as "getting one's share." The model is one of scarcity—there is only so much to go around, and governmental response to civil rights demands means that one's "share" has to be jealously guarded, as blacks are perceived as getting more than what rightfully belongs to them. Further, blacks and other minorities ("and welfare loafers" in the mid-1970s) are getting their demands met in ways that, to the Wallace supporter, are illegal and un-American. This means that "good Americans" are getting left out of the distribution process and this calls for action, but the only action available to them is defiance masquerading as power.

Wallace is a master at knowing how to feel out and exploit discontent:

> They've looked down their noses at the average man on the street too long. They've looked at the bus driver, the truck driver, the beautician, the fireman, the policeman, and the steelworker, the plumber, and the communication worker, and the oil worker and the little businessman and they say, "We've gotta write a guideline, We've gotta tell you when to get up in the morning, We've gotta tell you when to go to bed at night. And we gonna tell both national parties the average man on the street in Tennessee and Alabama and California don't need anybody to write him a guideline to tell him when to get up. (Armstrong 1970, pp. 184–85)

Wallace puts on a show of power. It attracts certain kinds of people, people who feel essentially powerless and whose understanding of power is very limited. As Lurleen Wallace once said of her husband: "When he's on 'Meet the Press' they can listen to George and think, 'That's what I would say if I were up there.'" The reporter adds that to these people, "In a sense, hearing it said matters more than the fact that saying it accomplishes little" (Wicker 1972). Frady echoes this in his remark that "it has not mattered to most Alabamians that in his series of confrontations with the federal government Wallace had met with consistent failure. What matters is that he fought, and continues to fight" (Frady 1968, p. 149).

Wallace's supporters, like Wallace, believe that defiance is all that is necessary. Their sense of powerlessness is so ingrained that they do not understand that a show of outrage is nothing more than an exercise which brings them nothing.

Central to Wallace's posturing is the presence of an enemy to rail against. Joe Azbell, the Wallace campaign's public relations man in 1972 and 1976, tells the following anecdote to explain Wallace's politics. Azbell postulates that if two men fall in love with the same woman, they will both be jealous. There is no possibility of a friendship between them; the only possibility is being enemies, as they would both want the same thing. He maintains that the two men could be friends only if they both hated the woman. Azbell summarized bluntly that hatred is the prime motivator in politics. A successful politician is one who has figured out what people's "devils" are, and focuses on them in order to gain support and excite the imagination. And that, Azbell contends, is the secret of Wallace's politics (Azbell 1974c).

The assumptions of Azbell's parable are that there is a limited piece of the pie which must be fought for and it is necessary to have an enemy. These assumptions breed a strange politics. While the clamor is for power, there is a lack of understanding of the nature of politics. Power is perceived only as power over or power against, never power with. The concept of participation, kept to a minimum by the candidate in his organization and in his enumeration of the possibilities (limited mainly to protest through the ballot box or by the drama of defiance), is likewise limited.

Consider the political activities of those who belong to the John Birch Society and other right-wing organizations. Their activities consist essentially of isolated, individual actions: letter writing, petition signing, conferences about the evils of communism. In almost no case is there any real participation—a making something happen, a reaching goals through working with others. Instead, one is concerned with exercising his individual power against an unseen but certainly conspiratorial enemy. There is no joint feeling, no exercise of creative politics dedicated to meeting the needs of fellow human beings, only an exercise which perpetuates isolation.

The same is true of Wallace supporters. Wallace strikes chords of discontent in those who support him, but they participate only by attending rallies, contributing funds, or watching his gyrations on television.

In the end the Wallace supporters' discontents and agonies remain private, individual ones exploited by the candidate. If these disgruntlements were shared, they would become "public troubles," as Mills calls them (1959). Pateman (1970) also expresses the thought that if people participated in the decisions which affect them, then they would begin to feel responsible not only for themselves, but also for others. In an exercise of true politics, the nihilistic quality exhibited here would vanish.

Wallace supporters have chosen to remain in the same kind of lonely, individual struggles that Wallace dramatizes rather than participate in the kinds of actions that would solve real human problems as well as dispel feeling of powerlessness. They cannot picture life without enemies to fight, and they, like Wallace, remain shadow boxers—the ultimate product of a twentieth century that has put its emphasis on individualism, on competition and winning, and on the necessity of fighting to get what one needs.

Chapter Two

Voting Theories and the Wallace Voter

In the early campaigns, Wallace supporters were referred to as "kooks," racial bigots, and right-wingers. However, their numbers grew; from 1968 on, a full twenty to twenty-five percent of voters were considered hardcore Wallace supporters. They could no longer be dismissed as crazies. This was a faction that, combined with others, could make a politician a winner, and politicians in the mainstream knew it. They began to acknowledge Wallace's presence and note his appeal, and one by one the politicians of the mainstream moved to the right: Nixon touting law and order in 1968 and 1972, Jackson stressing antibusing in 1972 and 1976. Campaign issues gradually grew more conservative, away from the so-called excesses of the Johnson years. By 1976, Wallace was complaining that the others had stolen his issues.

Social scientists have been as concerned with Wallace supporters as politicians have been. In general, they see them as dangerous—representative of the darker side of human nature, as being "that element" in society from which mass politics and fascism spring. They scrutinize them carefully, using theories which have been developed before to explain politics outside of the mainstream: the authoritarian personality (Adorno 1950), marginal voting (Campbell 1960; Converse 1967), and status politics (Bell 1963; Rohter 1969).

Never mind that these theories raise more questions than they answer about support for Senator Joseph McCarthy, the John Birch Society and other right-wing groups; the old pigeonholes would do.

The Authoritarian Personality

Among the first explanations offered was that Wallace supporters might perhaps be explained in terms of personality traits—specifically those

9

associated with the authoritarian personality (Adorno 1950). People with authoritarian personalities are described as rigidly adhering to conventional middle-class values and condemning, rejecting and/or punishing people who violate those values. They are recognized further by their belief that one's fate is determined by mystical forces and by their generalized hostility (Adorno 1950, p. 228). In their political behavior, they tend to adopt a submissive, uncritical attitude toward moral authorities idealized by those close to them, and to focus on considerations of power and toughness. In being so focused, they are preoccupied with questions of strength and weakness, domination and subservience, superiority and inferiority (Janowitz and Marvick 1953, p. 186).

The theory had been used before, with mixed results. (Polsby 1963; Lipset 1963; Rohter 1969; see McEvoy 1971, p. 35 for criticism.) Only Lipset (1963) had found an unequivocable relationship between authoritarianism and right-wing ideas: in this case, support for McCarthy. Moreover, one social scientist (McClosky 1958) had found evidence that conservatives also had characteristics associated with authoritarianism.

The research was inconsistent in yet another way. Definitions of authoritarianism differed; rarely would items from Adorno's original F (authoritarianism) Scale be used. In many cases, tests for the authoritarian personality employed instead the intermediate variable of political intolerance, often defined as hostility toward civil rights (Trow 1957; Wolfinger 1964).

One can see immediately that this line of reasoning does not work in explaining Wallace supporters. For Wallace supporters, being racist, are undeniably hostile toward civil rights. Thus, here the argument is circular: any racist would automatically be classified as authoritarian. Adorno himself had been careful to separate authoritarianism from what he called ethnocentrism. They are not the same thing, and they should be kept conceptually apart.

McEvoy tried another tack in studying Wallace supporters. He used three items from Adorno's F Scale and three from McClosky and Scharr's anomie scale to measure psychological, or anomic authoritarianism. It does not distinguish Wallace's 1968 supporters from the supporters of other candidates (McEvoy 1971, p. 140). McEvoy did, however, find that Wallace supporters have higher scores on political vengeance, a measure of "verbal support for violent actions against political elites and extreme distrust of government" (McEvoy 1971, p. 136). While the items which constitute this index are not directly related to those on the F Scale, it is evident that McEvoy was making an important observation about Wallace supporters. They are extremely angry at the federal government, and their attitudes toward government set them apart from supporters for other candidates.

While McEvoy's findings give little evidence of an authoritarian personality among Wallace supporters, this study will demonstrate that there is evidence of such a personality among Wallace supporters, as described both by items on the F Scale and their attitudes toward concerns of strength and weakness.

Marginal Voter Theory

Marginal voters (Campbell et al. 1960; Converse 1967; McEvoy 1971) are defined as voters for third parties in general, and can also be characterized by a history of almost no participation in the democratic process. They have voted with little regularity, belong to few if any voluntary associations, and are more likely to call themselves Independents rather than profess interest in one particular political party. Their marginality is defined relative to the political behavior of the majority of voters in the United States; they are outside that mainstream.

In exploring the Wallace support, it seems immediately clear that in this case third-party considerations are inadequate in measuring true marginality, for by definition, all voters for third-party candidate Wallace in 1968 would be classified as marginal. The model has further problems. Ever since the 1966 election, growing numbers of voters have classified themselves as Independents. By 1976, the percent of persons who identified themselves as Independents outnumbered those who said they were Republicans—party identification figures in 1976 were: Democrats 39%, Independents 36%, and Republicans 23% (Flanigan and Zingal 1979, p. 54). Under such conditions, one wonders if the continued designation of the Democratic and Republican parties as mainstream is correct.

McEvoy found conflicting evidence of political marginality among Wallace supporters in 1968. They have average rates of political interest and political activity but are less likely than others to have voted in previous elections (McEvoy 1971, p. 124). They also are much more likely than supporters of other candidates to doubt the legitimacy of government and to reject political institutions. McEvoy considered this "evidence of disproportionate political marginality" (McEvoy 1971, p. 119). Pettigrew and Riley (Pettigrew 1971) noted the same finding as well as the same conclusion.

McEvoy clinched his argument for political marginality among Wallace supporters with questionable assumptions. He noted a demographic fact about southern Wallace supporters: they are more likely than others to have been born on farms. That is apparently enough of a finding for McEvoy to insist that since

> previous research (reported in *The American Voter*) shows that low levels of involvement and participation persist in persons of farm origin, even though they may move later to an urban environment ... we might, on the basis of previous evidence, infer that this [Wallace supporters' average rates of political activity and involvement] is possibly an abnormal condition and that political quiescence among these persons is the usual state of affairs. (McEvoy 1971, p. 117)

Wallace supporters can in no way be classified as marginal voters, as subsequent analysis will demonstrate. Feeling that the system isn't working the way it should does not mean that one is politically marginal. While an assessment that one does not have any power to influence government may be an indication of political marginality, the fact that the Wallace supporters' political activity is above average (Pettigrew 1971) questions that interpretation. I shall argue (in agreement with those who originally devised the measures) that the indices which these studies described as indicative of marginality are more specifically measures of political anomie and political powerlessness.

The Theory of Status Politics

Most research efforts have used status politics to explain support for the radical right (Bell 1963; Rohter 1969). Often social scientists use the concept of status discrepancy (Lenski 1954), a condition which exists when one or more of the three concomitants of status (income, occupation, and education) is mismatched, or discrepant with another. If even one status component is mismatched, then it can be expected that a person with such discrepancy might well manifest certain predictable political attitudes (Geschwender 1967, 1971; Lipset 1963). If, for instance, one has a high income and a low education, then he most likely has right-wing attitudes. Although touted as a productive theory, few empirical studies show clear connection between status discrepancy and a right-wing political consciousness (Olsen and Tully 1972).

McEvoy looked for status discrepancy among Wallace supporters by correlating income and education. He found very little difference among them and supporters of Humphrey and Nixon in 1968 (McEvoy 1971, p. 127).

Another aspect of status politics involves status frustration. It can be explained in these terms: an individual must, first of all, "place himself in society." That is, he must see himself and others like him as part of a group which can be identified according to certain characteristics that the individual members of the group have in common. For instance, an individual may perceive "that he and others belong to specific racial groups and that the different groups occupy a complex hierarchy of positions vis-a-vis his own group." In such an instance, Herbert Blumer contends, racial prejudice may "be viewed 'fundamentally [as] a matter of relationship between racial groups.'" (Blumer in Lyman 1972, p. 138). Blumer goes on to say that this consciousness of group position is forged and reinforced by institutions such as legislatures, public meetings, and the mass media (Lyman 1972, p. 140).

An awareness of where one's own group stands in relation to other groups in society may give rise to status anxiety of a particular sort—here status frustration. Some groups are more subject to status frustrations than are others, particularly those

> groups which feel themselves to be "dispossessed," to be declining in status as a result of the rise of other types of communities, occupations, or ethnic groups, and groups which have recently risen, but find themselves barred from being able to claim the concomitant of success. (Lipset and Raab 1970, p. 306)

Pettigrew, Riley, and Vanneman (1972) noted that the motivating factor for "participants in the black ghetto riots of the late 1960s" as well as for 1968 supporters of Wallace in the cities of Boston, Cleveland, and Gary, seemed to be "a psychological mechanism called relative deprivation." Because relative status deprivation is status anxiety resulting from a feeling of deprivation, which comes when one compares himself to those in another reference group of which he is not a part (Sherif 1953), this would seem to be confirmation of Lipset and Raab's (1970) view of status politics.

As indicated above, status anxiety or status frustration arises when one compares his own group with another group. The reference group may be above his in a position that he and the others in his group would like to attain, or below his and perceived to be gaining on his group's position, thereby threatening a loss of status. In the first case, he has a deficiency of status in comparison with the other group which is almost impossible to rectify; in the second case, he is threatened with a loss of status, the magnitude of which cannot be calculated. In either case, there is wholesale status anxiety.

Of most interest here are the groups which feel that others are gaining on them and/or they are in imminent danger of losing status. Such people, the theoretical argument goes, are deeply concerned over their decline in influence (either real or imagined) in American society. If they respond politically, it is considered a move toward preservation. The expectation is that old "in" groups, when threatened by displacement because of social change, will seek to protect their values and status. This thrust toward preservationism, when accompanied by gestures of repression or exclusion, is at the heart of most definitions of extremist politics.

McEvoy viewed the Wallace movement as a preservationist response to social change. He argued that Wallace supporters are experiencing a "withdrawal of social support" (McEvoy 1971, p. 148). What is going on is that they have lost status relative to that which they enjoyed in the past. Lipset and Raab (1970) also make this argument.

Further, McEvoy felt that Wallace supporters are motivated by threats they perceived to originate from blacks (McEvoy 1971, p. 145). Lipset and Raab described this phenomenon as "blacklash," and define it as a "displacement of hostility toward the designated source of change" (Lipset and Raab 1970, p. 488).

McEvoy, in fact, saw the racism of Wallace supporters as a key component of their status politics.

> In the Wallace movement, ... racism [is] ... a desire to maintain an increasingly threatened traditional status-deference pattern upon which southerners and the white urban working classes have depended as one important component of their prestige. (McEvoy 1971, p. 149)

To see racism as a matter of status, or to understand the concept of relative deprivation as solely representative of status politics, is completely missing the mark.

In actuality neither McEvoy (1971), or Pettigrew (1971) or Lipset and Raab (1970), or Pettigrew, Riley or Vanneman (1972) ever came up with any clear evidence of status discrepancy or status anxiety among Wallace supporters. What they portrayed as comparisons of one group relative to another, and what they term relative status deprivation, are not really a matter of status politics at all. It is power politics.

The Power Theory

Wallace supporters have status. As Gary Wills once described the audience at a Wallace rally: "They are not hungry or underprivileged or deprived in material ways. Each has, in some minor way, 'made it,' and it all means nothing. Washington does not care" (Wills 1970, p. 58).

Wallace supporters do feel anger and frustration toward blacks, but status anxiety is not a part of it. In 1968

> over half of the Wallace supporters were *not* willing to say that Negro progress was "too fast." Presumably, many who are disturbed by integration

> may still feel that as a group Negroes are underprivileged and favor their
> moving ahead. (Lipset and Raab 1970, p. 402)

Thus it is not the upward mobility of blacks as such that bothers Wallace
supporters, and threats to status are felt by these Wallace supporters to be
either nonexistent or of little consequence.

The real appeal is to their proportionate sense of power. Power to
influence the government is seen in zero-sum terms (Parsons 1967): the
more some other group gains, the more their own group loses (Coles in
Barnicle 1974). Wallace supporters feel that they have a very low place on
the list of interests with which the government is concerned and their
appraisal of the situation is accurate.

In the first place, the locus of responsibility has shifted in the last twenty
years from the state and local level to the federal level. Federal government
priorities do tend to ignore the white working class, and this is the group
that in 1968 was proportionately more responsive to Wallace than to any
other candidate. Jerome Rosow, assistant secretary of labor in the Nixon
Administration, wrote a memorandum in 1970 calling attention to the
federal government's lack of aid to the lower middle class. The abuses
vary—some are in the tax structure (federal, state, and local); in the lack of
services available to the blue-collar worker (for instance, his payment of
taxes is used in financing welfare programs which do not provide these
same services for him); in the lack of low-cost housing; in the worker's
inability to pay for proper medical care and to attain proper legal services
because of the expenses involved. "Washington," Rosow admitted, "has
been definitely unresponsive to the blue-collar worker" (Rosow 1970).

Moreover, Washington, Wallace supporters think, is giving preferential
treatment to blacks.

> ... in the minds of the blue-collar worker the black citizen had "gotten to" the
> effective centers of cultural change ... "they" were giving the Negro the
> decision-making power and personal recognition [the blue-collar worker] so
> desperately craved. (Fackre 1969, p. 646)

The resentment extends toward other groups as well. Ransford (1972)
found that white working-class people who felt politically powerless are the
people who expect public officials to be unresponsive to their needs and are
antagonistic toward student activists as well as black militants. The
Wallace supporters appear to feel particular resentment toward any group
that attempts to gain political advantages through the threat of force. This
is seen as a most "un-American" way of accomplishing a social goal.

Wallace supporters are furious at the federal government for what they
perceive as capitulation to the demands of such groups. They view

themselves as upstanding citizens and cannot understand the disinterest or the refusal of government to relate to their needs. Where there once was no federal government, they now see federal policy as influencing every aspect of their lives—the economy, their access to jobs, the kinds of houses they can afford to live in, and the kinds of schools their children can go to. In short, governmental decisions affect them greatly, and they have no input. Few politicians represent their interests. The American dream is getting them nowhere.

Consider this letter from a Wallace supporter, written in 1972 on the back of a Wallace solicitation poll and returned to campaign headquarters:

> Dear Governor Wallace, I will send you a donation later on if this country isn't bankrupt by then. It's just getting harder and harder to make an honest living. What I really don't understand is why we pour billions of dollars to Israel when they are responsible for all of our oil cutoff from the Arab countries? As much aid as we give them, they should pay U.S. income tax. Why do we keep on exporting more crude oil than ever when there is a shortage in this country? Shouldn't we be taking care of the U.S. first? The federal government is cutting and cutting service with the U.S. mail, but there is plenty of money for foreign aid. Every citizen benefits from the postal service, it never was intended to break even. Why not use some of the money they waste to improve the postal service? The U.S. Senators and Congressmen are already overpaid and they want another raise. The President's salary should be cut. There is supposed to be a gasoline shortage, yet the federal government refuses to put an end to forced busing. Why is there enough gas for such foolishness? I'm getting sick of hearing people holler minority and get all the breaks in jobs and everything. What about all these auto workers that already have been laid off due to the manufactured energy crisis? The time has come for new leadership in Washington and you are the only man that can do it.

Scholars have rarely dealt with the question of a loss of power as a motivating factor in politics. One exception is Horowitz (1968, p. 10), who remarked that "the so-called radical right is in fact reacting to a genuine diminution of local power by federal authorities."

Seeman's definition of powerlessness is most relevant here. He defined loss of power as "... the expression or probability held by the individual that his own behavior cannot determine the occurrence of the outcomes, or reinforcements he seeks" (Seeman 1959, p. 784).

This study will demonstrate unequivocally that the Wallace supporter feels precisely this kind of powerlessness relative to his ability to influence the federal government. Such feelings are intrinsically related to perceptions of change over the last twenty years and are related directly to the perceived actions and the consequent inactions of the federal government,

Racism and the Power Theory

The powerlessness, frustration, and anger that the Wallace supporter feels toward the federal government is also directed toward blacks, but it differs in very important ways from the ways in which racism is traditionally defined.

In this instance, racism can be viewed not as a "feeling or set of feelings lodged within an individual ... (but as) a matter of relationship between racial groups" (Lyman 1972, p. 138). It arises from the competition inherent in power relations (Blumer in Lyman 1972; Brown 1971; Carlson 1976a) not from competition for status position (Dye 1971; Pettigrew 1971; Lipset and Raab 1970; Pettigrew, Riley and Vanneman 1972). Recalling for a moment the discussion on reference groups, consciousness of group position serves to place one's group relative to others in a hierarchy of positions. Racism thus functions as a means of clarifying that hierarchy, thereby defining power relationships and justifying in ideological terms the specific power relationships of the groups vis-a-vis one another.

Cox maintained that racial groups are power groups and that the relationships between them are relationships of power rather than of social status (1948, pp. 318, 332, 335). Robert Coles gave data to support this theoretical approach through his observations on busing in Boston.

> "The ultimate reality," Coles states, "is the reality of class. And it's around this issue of having and not having—and social and economic vulnerability versus social and economic power—that's where the real issue is."
> "That's the real struggle that's going on," Coles says. "And to talk about it only in terms of racism is to miss the point. It's working-class people who happen to be white and working-class people who happen to be black ... poor people ... both of whom are very hard pressed; neither of whom have got much leverage on anything. They are both competing for a very limited piece of pie, the limits of which are being set by the larger limits of class which allow them damn little if anything." (Barnicle, 1974)

To summarize, the response to Wallace represents a bid for power that is felt to be the inherent right of every citizen, a power which the Wallace supporter feels was once there and is now felt to be either slipping away or lost altogether. Specifically, the support for Wallace represents a protest against the erosion of that power by the federal government, the proof of which is seen by the Wallace supporters through the government's increasing involvement in areas of decision making and influence that originally were thought to lie within the domain of individual or local power.

Changes in the workplace and in the schools, bolstered by the revelations of television newscasts—desegregation, Vietnam, black protest, student power, Watergate—over the same time period have served to stir the political awareness of most Americans. The Wallace voter has responded to these things in a particular way. Unwilling to give up the belief in the "American Dream," still hoping that hard work and being a good citizen will pay off, he is very angry at student protestors who are disparaging of that dream and those who are getting what they want without going through the "proper channels"—black protestors, "welfare loafers," etc. He is aware, however, that some groups are getting some of what they need, and he wants to be able to do that, too. Disagreeing with the means that these people are using, he continues to try to work within the system by casting a vote for Wallace, whose politics may be seen as a kind of symbolic protest. But he has very little hope, given those particular government priorities which he feels do not include him in their considerations. He feels virtually powerless.

Chapter Three

Public Office 1945–1963: Wallace's Move Toward Segregationism and National Notoriety

George Wallace got out of the Army Air Corps in 1945 shortly before V-J Day, returned home and "hitchhiked to Montgomery to see the governor, himself a native of Barbour County (Wallace's home county), and got a 175-dollar-a-month job as one of the state's assistant attorneys general" (Frady 1968, p. 88). A few months later Wallace ran successfully for the state legislature and served two terms. Most sources agree that he was effective (Dorman 1976, p. 20); his legislative actions were generally humanistic and designed to upgrade conditions within the state. Wallace was viewed by his fellows as "the leading liberal in the legislature, . . . a dangerous left-winger. A lot of people looked on him as downright pink" (quoted in Frady 1968, p. 98).

Not only was the legislation he introduced regarded as liberal, he was also considered liberal on the race issue. As one of his first acts, Wallace had Folsom, the governor during his first term, appoint him to the Tuskegee Institute Board of Trustees. Further, both Folsom and Kohn, who wrote Wallace's first inaugural speech ("Segregation now . . . segregation tomorrow . . . segregation forever") told Marshall Frady (1968, pp. 116, 144) in interviews that Wallace was not originally a racist. Frady also reports:

> Shortly after returning from the war, Wallace had confided to a Sunday school teacher in his church in Clayton, "You know, we just can't keep the colored folks down like we been doin' around here for years and years. We got to quit. We got to start treatin' 'em right. They just like everybody else." (Frady 1968, p. 141)

19

Wallace may have been considered liberal by his cronies, and he may have been liberal compared to them, but when campaigning as an alternate delegate to the 1948 Democratic national convention, he presented himself as being opposed to the idea of civil rights. At the convention, Wallace made his presence known by speaking against the civil rights plank, but when several southern delegations left in protest, Wallace stayed behind. He kept up his vociferous opposition to the convention's racial position and proceeded to nominate Senator Russell of Georgia for vice-president (Jones 1966, p. 6). Some did not view Wallace's behavior as positive, interpreting it as a refusal ". . . to walk out with other delegates in protest to the racial politics of . . . Harry Truman" (*Montgomery Advertiser* 1956b). Wallace, however, gained notoriety and "strengthened his political position back home" (Dorman 1976, p. 20).

For a while Wallace seems to have been undecided as to which position on the race issue would most pay off politically. As one of Folsom's campaign aides in his second contest (1953), Wallace wrote most of the speeches and Folsom was notably liberal on the race issue. But when Adam Clayton Powell, present in Montgomery to address a group of blacks at the Coliseum, revealed to his audience that he and Governor Folsom had just spent the afternoon talking over a few drinks (Mathews 1974), Wallace showed distress. The public was in a furor, and " 'when Wallace heard about the Powell thing,' says an Alabama newsman, 'that was the day he knew he had to break with Folsom' " (Frady 1968, p. 108). To his colleagues, who supported this move, he began to express the predominant racial attitudes of the other legislators.

In 1953, Wallace was elected to a circuit court judgeship and served in that capacity until 1959. After his election to the bench, it wasn't long before he began to eye the governorship, and his approach toward it seems deliberate. It was evident to Wallace that he had to change his racial views and to inform the public of that change. Kohn said that Wallace "had enough practical political sense to know cussin' nigras was popular" (Frady 1968, p. 144). And in Frady's interview with Patterson, the man who defeated Wallace for the governorship in 1958, Patterson said:

> In fifty-eight, now, I was the champion of segregation, because there just isn't any way to run as a liberal in this state and get elected. That's all there is to it. I couldn't be what I wanted to be. You were either for the white folks or the nigras. If you didn't appeal to prejudices, you'd get beat. (Frady 1968, p. 207)

Wallace soon began to make his new racial views public. In 1953 he was the first southern judge "to issue an injunction against the removal of segregation signs in railroad terminals" (Dorman 1976, p. 21). An incident which provided the opportunity to generate more publicity for his posture was a federal investigation of the racial makeup of grand juries in Cobb

County, Georgia. Wallace's circuit had not been threatened in any way, but he took the chance to get some attention. He "accused government investigators of 'Gestapo methods' . . . and threatened to jail any federal officers engaged in 'deliberate invasion of state sovereignty' "(*Montgomery Advertiser* 1956b).

Two days later the current grand jury pledged to support Wallace: "The jurors agreed that if federal officers can dictate the makeup of grand juries of any county 'then local government is forever dead in this nation'" (*Montgomery Advertiser* 1956a). The words, even though they came from the grand jury, are most probably Wallace's. Included in them is the embryonic issue of local government control which later evolved as the smokescreen covering Wallace's real issue, that of maintaining segregation. It is some time before a stratagem of interposing each issue as a constitutional question appears.

In the summer of 1956, Wallace was again a delegate to the Democratic National Convention, this time as Alabama's representative on the platform committee. Jones states:

> Again, his work impressed southerners: he succeeded in watering down the civil rights plank which originally included endorsement of the 1954 Supreme Court decision ending segregation in public schools and the adoption of a federally enforced Fair Employment Practices Commission. (Jones 1966, p. 6)

For these accomplishments, he got favorable publicity throughout the state.

In 1957, Wallace stated in a speech to the Anniston Rotary Club, reported in *The Birmingham News* (1957), that

> when the Supreme Court declared segregation unconstitutional and referred the matter to the district courts to enforce through their power to punish for contempt, there was a total and alarming departure from all the basic principles of criminal prosecutions.

Here the idea of forced government by contempt proceeding was born.

Later that year Wallace testified in Washington against the civil rights bill then being considered by Congress. A clash with Rep. Emanuel Celler resulted, and Wallace received some national press attention. All in all, Wallace seems to have made several such trips while a circuit court judge to testify against the impending civil rights legislation (Crass 1976, p. 49).

Adopting a Stance for Segregation and Defiance

Wallace's first gubernatorial contest took place in 1958. The race was between Wallace and John Patterson in the runoff for the Democratic primary. Patterson had two advantages: years before, his father had been assassinated in Phenix City, Alabama, just after winning the Democratic primary for attorney general of Alabama with a campaign promise to clean up Phenix City. After the murder, the state Democratic Executive Committee had nominated the younger Patterson to take his father's place. Jones maintains that a "guilt complex" and continuing public sympathy for Patterson was the main cause of Wallace's loss; he barely mentions the second advantage, that of the segregation issue. Frady, however, says that Patterson reacted to the temper of the times and captured the prize issue quickly. He "established himself as the stridently irreconcilable segregationist, while Wallace, more by default than anything else, became the muted and circumspect segregationist" (Frady 1968, p. 125). Patterson subsequently was endorsed by the Ku Klux Klan, and Wallace found himself in the doubtfully favorable position of being endorsed by both the Jewish population of Alabama and the NAACP.

Wallace lost the election by 64,902 votes. He later put his finger squarely on the reason for the defeat in one of his most memorable quotes: "John Patterson out-nigguhed me. And boys, I'm not going to be out-nigguhed again" (Frady 1968, p. 127).

At the time Wallace had only a few months left to use his legitimate public forum, as his term as circuit judge was due to expire in January 1959. He did not waste any time. Several petitions had been filed asking for the Barbour County voting records—presumably there were some questions as to the appropriate registration of Negroes. The Civil Rights Commission was demanding to see them, and in December Wallace himself impounded the records, saying that he would not turn them over to the commission, but would instead hold them for the grand jury. Maintaining that his action was legal, he refused to turn them over even when subpoenaed to do so, threatening to jail any agent who came to get them (Jones 1966, p. 22). A series of cat and mouse legal proceedings between Wallace and the federal courts took place, and Wallace then entrusted the voting records to grand juries in Barbour and Bullock Counties. There was a contempt trial, and surprisingly, Wallace was found not guilty.

The court, Judge Frank M. Johnson, found that

> George C. Wallace ... for some reason judicially unknown to this court attempted to give the impression that he was defying this court's order by turning said [voting] records over to hastily summoned grand juries in Barbour and Bullock Counties, Alabama. However, this court finds that said action did not constitute defiance or disobedience, since Wallace, from all appearances, continued to maintain control of said records in each of said counties. This court further finds that George C. Wallace, through devious methods, assisted said [commission] agents in obtaining the records in these

two counties.... The court further finds that, even though it was accomplished through means of subterfuge, George C. Wallace did comply with the
order of this court. As to why the devious means were used, this court will not
now judicially determine.... If these devious means were for political
purposes, then this court refuses to allow its authority and dignity to be
bent or swayed by such politically generated whirlwinds. (Dorman 1976,
pp. 23, 24)

Wallace, furious that his show of defiance had been shown to be a fraud
(Dorman 1976, p. 25), maintained that he had indeed been in contempt of
the order, and said that a constitutional question had been at stake and that
he hoped to take the issue to a higher court (Jones 1966, p. 30).

The next four years were spent in limbo. Jones (1966, p. 36), in an official
biography, says that Wallace spent the time productively, traveling all over
the state meeting people and making speeches. Frady (1968, p. 130)
describes Wallace during this hiatus as "haggard and dingy and sour,
grabbing people by the coatsleeve and talking to them with the fierce,
blank-eyed, inexhaustible urgency of a street-corner evangelist." Although
he had set up a law practice with his brother, he handled few cases, living
mostly off of a few friends and marking time until the next gubernatorial
contest.

His next official campaign began with a frontal attack on Judge Frank
Johnson's 1959 court decision. Wallace insisted that despite what Johnson
had indicated, he, Wallace, had indeed defied the government rather than
cooperated with the Civil Rights Commission. He even called Johnson "an
integrating, carpet-bagging, scalawagging, race-mixing, bald-faced liar"
(Jones 1966, p. 37). No, Wallace was not about to be "out-nigguhed" again.
Evidently the climate was right, too. " 'By 1962,' says one Wallace aide,
'folks understood the Supreme Court Decision of 1954 would put colored
kids in their schools. They didn't really understand that in 1958. Patterson
just educated them for us' " (Frady 1968, p. 133).

Wallace's style had also changed from that of his first campaign. He
dropped his big words and spoke in the vernacular of the people, refining
his manner by trying out things on the crowd. His aides watched for
reactions and told him what was working, what was getting people excited.
Wallace worked hard, and when he had perfected something he stuck to it
with almost ritualistic consistency (Frady 1968, pp. 133-134). The style that
he evolved guaranteed attention:

> He stood flatfooted on the back of the truck. He hollered into the
> microphone about the outside evils encroaching on these good peoples'
> everyday lives, and when he got that bait planted real good and solid, he'd
> jerk the old fishing pole. "First thing you know, the federal courts'll be telling
> you who you can invite over for Sunday dinner and who you can't," he

allowed. They whistled and clapped. They liked that. They'd punch each other in the sides with their elbows and nod and grin. "Ol' George'll tell 'em," they said. He would rock forward on his toes and back on his heels. "The federal government up in Washington is breathin' down our backs, and we got to fight 'em off! You elect me yo' governor and I'll fight 'em!" And they knew he would. (Greenhaw 1976, p. 122)

Folsom lost in the first primary and threw his support to Sen. Ryan de Graffenried, but Wallace, with his flaming campaign promise to stand in any schoolhouse door rather than let it be integrated, captured the imagination of the people and won the runoff by 71,608 votes.

In his inaugural speech in January 1963, Wallace dared the federal government to try him:

> Let us rise to the call of freedom-loving blood that is in us and send our answer to the tyranny that clanks its chains upon the South. In the name of the greatest people that have ever trod this earth, I draw the line in the dust and toss the gauntlet before the feet of tyranny ... and I say ... segregation now ... segregation tomorrow ... segregation forever. (Wallace 1963b)

Events weren't very long in emerging. In April, demonstrations began in Birmingham, led by Martin Luther King, Jr. Bull Conner, head of Birmingham's police and later Alabama's representative to the Democratic National Committee, held down the trouble for a time, but the demonstrators persisted, and Wallace sent state troopers into that city. The action had its effect; the demonstrations subsided almost immediately. At this point, Wallace stepped into the spotlight.

The Stand in the Schoolhouse Door

Although Wallace had been in the news before, it was the "stand in the schoolhouse door" which marked the beginning of his national notoriety. When it became evident that a major effort would be made to desegregate the University of Alabama in June 1963, Wallace made preparations. The event had been preceded by a visit from Attorney General Robert Kennedy in April. This visit was recorded on tape and is reported in Frady (1968, pp. 151-169). Wallace tried to provoke the attorney general into threatening to use federal troops if he did not comply with court orders, but his provocation did not succeed.

President Kennedy had met with Wallace in Alabama in May at the thirtieth anniversary of the Tennessee Valley Authority. Jones (1966, p. 83) reports, however, that there was no talk about the impending integration attempt. A week later, a federal judge ruled that Vivian Malone and Jimmy Hood, both Negroes, must be admitted to the University. In response,

Wallace issued a statement that he would represent the people of Alabama by being present at the University to bar the attempt at enrollment personally.

The federal court in turn issued a summons stating that Wallace had no right to "obstruct or prevent the execution of the lawful orders of a court of the United States" (Jones 1966, p. 85), but Jones is not specific on where or when or if the papers were ever actually served. On June 2, Wallace appeared on "Meet The Press," where he succeeded in evading the questions of the panel, not giving them any definite information except to say that he would "stand in the door." When asked why he planned to do this, Wallace replied: "I think it is a dramatic way to impress upon the American people this omnipotent march of centralized government ..." ("Meet The Press" 1963).

With the publicity mechanisms at work, Wallace returned to Alabama and began preparations. A doorway at the University of Alabama at Tuscaloosa was selected, and a large circle drawn around it and painted white. The circle was pronounced a "restraining line," to keep the press back. Jones remarked afterwards that no one "seemed to realize that it was there so all would have an equal chance to see the confrontation" (Jones 1966, p. 96).

Newspapers throughout the state were issued pleas from Wallace asking the people to stay away from the University on June 11; he reiterated his promise to represent them. He also took the action of alerting certain National Guard units for possible duty and ordering approximately 500 guardsmen to the campus. His announced purpose in doing this was to prevent "possible violence." Two days before the scheduled confrontation, Wallace appeared on statewide television urging people to remain at home, away from the campus.

With the stage set, the audience (both Alabama and the nation) primed, and the press alert and ready, the drama began. (See Dorman 1976, pp. 128-132). When the assistant U.S. Attorney General, Nicholas J. Katzenbach, and the two students arrived, Wallace took his place in the doorway. Around his neck was a microphone connected to a public address system (Sitton 1963b); the white circle dramatized his stance. Katzenbach, leaving the two students in the car, walked up to Wallace. When he arrived at the appropriate spot, Wallace "solemnly threw up his hand, halting Katzenbach" (Frady 1968, p. 170). Katzenbach began by introducing himself, saying that he had a "cease and desist" order from President Kennedy (Jones 1966, p. 98) and asked that Wallace not interfere with the enrollment. Wallace interrupted him: "I have a statement to read," he said, and then proceeded to read a document approximately five minutes in length. It was his proclamation, which in formal legalistic words claimed the constitutional right of the people of Alabama to operate their public schools as they wished, and tried to label the exercise taking place as one which raised "basic and fundamental constitutional questions." In it Wallace also took credit for the lack of violence at the scene.

After Wallace had finished reading, Katzenbach tried to persuade him to move from the doorway but "Wallace stared straight ahead at ramrod attention, and spoke not a word" (Jones 1966, p. 100). Katzenbach then returned to the waiting car, drove the students to their dormitories, and had lunch with them (Sitton 1963b). Almost immediately after the initial confrontation, President Kennedy federalized the Alabama National Guard. Meanwhile, Wallace waited for four hours in the auditorium behind the already famous doorway.

The second confrontation took place when the General of the Alabama Guard, now federalized, met Wallace at the door, and informed him (sadly, Jones says) that he must step aside under orders from the president. Wallace read a short statement pledging to fight federal interference and to continue working for constitutional government (Jones 1966, p. 101) and left the doorway. Shortly thereafter, the two students registered without incident.

In the aftermath, Wallace portrayed himself as successfully defying a court order for the purpose of testing constitutional questions; he considered that

> Kennedy was in violation of the Constitution when he dispatched troops to the University when they were not requested by the appropriate state authorities. There could be no excuse of disorder or violence because it was peaceful and tranquil. It was an imposition of military dictatorship. (Jones 1966, p. 104)

Letters poured in from every state. Some even contained contributions for his cause—he collected $4,000 in little over two months (*New York Times* 1963b). An aide was put to work cataloging the names and addresses of those who had sent positive messages. Not only was money being received, Wallace was also getting invitations to speak to groups all over the United States. He accepted as many as he could, venturing mostly to colleges. Starting in October, he spoke at Harvard, Dartmouth, Brown, Duke, Colorado State, UCLA, the University of Oregon, and many other places.

Chapter Four

The 1964 Presidential Primaries:
Breaking in on the National Scene

At first there had been talk that Wallace and Mississippi Governor Ross Barnett would lead a "free elector" movement, in which unpledged electors would be on the 1964 presidential primary ticket in some southern states. If their slates were elected, then Wallace and Barnett would be in a position to bargain at the convention. They could trade off votes for promises to slow down, or perhaps even stop the move toward integration (Wicker 1963; *New York Times* 1963b; Sitton 1963b). But during Wallace's college tours the idea began to emerge that Wallace personally might run in some primaries; he even announced that he was considering several contests. Evidently the general response to his speeches was positive enough to make him somewhat confident.

Bill Jones, his press secretary, took advantage of every opportunity to get as much publicity for Wallace as possible (Jones 1966, p. 108); in addition to the speeches in each town, Wallace was scheduled for radio, television, and newspaper interviews. He also scheduled a press conference whenever he would arrive some place. In the meantime, Jones had been writing down and categorizing all of the questions Wallace was asked, and the candidate spent time perfecting his answers (Jones 1966, p. 128). Wallace also did "homework" on each area he visited (Jones 1966, p. 126) so that he would know something about the problems and the politics of the area. His sources were the local police and citizens (Jones 1966, p. 278). With this information he was able to personalize his issues; he told residents of each area what the Civil Rights Bill was going to do to them in particular (Jones 1966, p. 132). His messages hit home.

27

When there was criticism about Wallace's spending Alabama taxpayers' money for his forays out of state, he freely admitted it, saying that the people didn't mind because he was representing the majority opinion in Alabama and educating outsiders about the realities in Alabama. In addition, he said that he was looking for new industry for the state and was giving the remunerations from his speaking engagements to the Alabama state treasury (Jones 1966, p. 129).

Several versions of the story exist about how Wallace arrived at the decision to enter the primaries. Frady says that a Montgomery newspaper editor had suggested to Wallace that he enter some of the primaries (Frady 1968, p. 174), and Frady and Jones both tell of a mystery man who approached Wallace about the Wisconsin primary (Frady 1968, p. 174f; Jones 1966, p. 171f), driving from Oshkosh to Madison where Wallace was speaking at the University of Wisconsin to deliver an outline of the Wisconsin primary qualifications and to explain how it could be done. It was only a brief meeting, but Wallace's imagination was kindled: he knew from his mail that there was some support for his views in the North.

Robert Kendall, a former Alabama Senator and a participant in the 1964 Wallace campaign, tells a different story about how the Wisconsin entry was initiated (Kendall 1974). He said that when Wallace was speaking at the university, among those present in the audience was Dolores Herbstreith from Oshkosh. A devout conservative, Mrs. Herbstreith was excited by Wallace's speech and contacted his office with her plan for Wallace to enter the primary. The governor sent his banking director, Bob Checkler, up to Wisconsin to check out the situation. It looked promising and on March 6, Wallace announced that he would be a candidate.

The Wisconsin Primary made a cross-over vote possible—despite party registration, one could vote for any candidate. Wallace took advantage of this, announcing that "he would welcome the votes of anyone—Democrats, Republicans, and members of the John Birch Society" (*New York Times* 1964t). His stated mission was to be a rallying point for those who were against the civil rights legislation pending in Congress.

Mrs. Herbstreith became the Wisconsin campaign director. Her husband, Lloyd, was an advertising man who had "conducted a campaign for the 'Liberty Amendment' to abolish the Federal income tax" (Wehrwein 1964j), an issue position which is definitely right wing (Bell 1963, p. 27). Kendall said that Mrs. Herbstreith literally ran the operation from her kitchen table; she found the delegates and scheduled all of Wallace's appearances.

Reaction to Wallace's entry into the Wisconsin campaign wasn't long in coming. The clergy first denounced his candidacy and urged their parishioners not to vote for him (Sitton 1964g). Wallace responded by offering to meet with them; most refused (Jones 1966, p. 177). He was also attacked by Governor Reynolds. In turn, Wallace ignored Reynolds, concentrating solely on his own issues.

There were other responses. The southern author, William Bradford Huie, noted for his stand against human injustice, journeyed from Alabama to Wisconsin and announced that sixteen of Wallace's Wisconsin delegates were members of the John Birch Society. Upon his return Huie and his wife were harrassed for several nights by carloads of youths (*New York Times* 1964o). The Wisconsin AFL-CIO sent out bulletins trying to dissuade their members from supporting Wallace (Jones 1966, p. 185). An investigative report of Wallace's political manipulations as governor was published in *The New York Times* (*New York Times* 1964g). President Johnson sent a telegram praising Governor Reynolds (*New York Times* 1964p) and dispatched Attorney General Robert Kennedy and Postmaster General Gronouski (who was originally from Madison) to let Wisconsinites know that Washington supported Reynolds wholeheartedly.

Wallace's opposition attacked him mainly on the race issue; it was gently conceded that all Americans were prejudiced, but there was a call for people to rise above these prejudices so that problems could be solved quietly and intelligently through the adoption of the Civil Rights Bill (Jones 1966, p. 197). Wallace meanwhile maintained that he was not a racist (*New York Times* 1964s) and continued to focus solely on the issue of states' rights. He contended further that "any votes I get would be significant because I wasn't supposed to [get] any" (Wehrwein 1964i).

Wallace's campaign entourage "consisted of a handful of country boys and a half dozen tough-looking state troopers" (Greenhaw 1976, p. 20). It was a limited campaign, both in time and place. Kendall reports that Wallace stayed in metropolitan centers expanding his exposure to the people through the medium of television. During the author's interview with Kendall, Pete Mathews, an Alabama state legislator at the time, was also present and the two of them laughed uproariously at the memory of that campaign. Kendall said that Wallace would get into a car not having any idea where the hell he was going, except that it was someplace that Mrs. Herbstreith had scheduled. Wallace generally relied on one basic speech (confirmed during interviews with Billy Joe Camp, Wallace's press secretary, and Milo Howard, director of the Archives and History Department, State of Alabama, 1974), adlibbing when necessary. When the car stopped, Wallace would get out and speak to whomever was present. He'd stand before the crowd feeling them out and in doing so, determine what they wanted to hear. Then Wallace would give it to them.

Wallace's tack in Wisconsin was not to argue for segregation but to take the position that each state should do what it wanted to do on racial issues and not to submit to being told by the federal government that they had to do it in a particular way. His chief objective was the defeat of the Civil Rights Bill, and he raised the specter of communism to drive home his objectives:

> We are faced with the astounding spectacle, for the first time in a civilized nation, of high officials calling for the passage of a so-called civil rights bill for fear of threat of mob violence ... This bill takes a long step toward transferring private property to public domain under a central government ... Under any name, it will create a dictatorship the like of which we or our fathers have not witnessed. It will bring about the ultimate in tyranny. It will make government master and God over man ... I believe that people have the wisdom, the sense of justice and the decency to govern their own local affairs ... There are those who would amalgamate us into a unit of the one, subservient to a powerful central government, with laws designed to equalize us into the common denominator necessary for a slave people ... If victory for freedom is impossible, then surrender to communism is inevitable and we can begin fitting the yokes of slavery to the necks of our children even now as the riots and mobs lap at the streets of these United States. (Wallace 1964d)

Wallace seemed to think that a substantial primary vote for him in the North would cause senators to reconsider their positions on the Civil Rights Bill. He didn't appear to entertain any possibility of winning, and said that he had "no illusions about becoming President" (*New York Times* 1964u).

April 7 was a surprise for everyone. Wallace did far better than either he or the Reynolds forces expected. Altogether he got 266,136 votes: 33.7 percent of the Democratic vote and 24.4 percent of the total vote (*New York Times* 1964k). The tally for Wallace in Wisconsin was interpreted as a backlash against civil rights (Mazo 1974b).

Two things about the Wisconsin primary are worth special notice. The first is that Wallace, by ignoring his opposition, made them even more angry. The resulting "overkill" on the opposition's part drew more attention to him than he would have gotten otherwise and engendered a certain public sympathy for his carefully cultivated image as a man who continues to press for those causes in which he believes despite the forces against him. The audacity displayed in doing battle against the president and the United States government was a repeat performance of Wallace's "stand" in the schoolhouse door.

A second thing that the Wallace people quickly picked up on is that if politics are personalized, efforts are much more effective. For instance, a chance remark by the candidate to someone who brought up the question of the effects of segregation in Alabama—"before you criticize us in the South, take a look at your Indian reservations"—resulted in his getting all of the Indian votes cast in Menominee County (the result is reported by Wehrwein 1964h. The reporter states that there was no apparent reason for the vote, but an earlier story had reported Wallace's quote). Second, the appearance before a predominately Polish and Eastern European ethnic background audience on Milwaukee's south side and a couple of Wallace quotes from that appearance also illustrate how personal Wallace's delivery was: "The audience, including many who have relatives behind the Iron Curtain, cheered loudly when Wallace said the Communist *Daily Worker* had called him 'America's No. 1 criminal and I am glad I have their opposition'" (Fox, 1964). He also received a standing ovation by concluding his speech with the promise that

> ... a vote for this little governor will let the people in Washington know that we want them to leave our house, schools, jobs, businesses and farms alone and let us run them without any help from Washington. (Fox 1964)

This effort among ethnic groups paid off heavily in votes (Wehrwein 1964h).

In Wisconsin, the Wallace group had had a naive start. No one, including the candidate, knew quite how to handle the pacing of or the reactions to the campaign. There were many startling incidents and Wallace and his staff responded intuitively, in some areas relying heavily on the police for information and advice. They had started with a poorly financed campaign and an unsophisticated staff, and they learned as they went along (Jones 1966, ch. 8).

Indiana

Wallace had already announced in January that he would run in the Indiana and the Maryland primaries (*New York Times* 1964u). People there seemed likely to be receptive; the mail received after the stand in the schoolhouse door had been notably heavy from both states (*New York Times* 1963b). Wallace had also tested the waters in Maryland the previous September, at which time

> Maryland political observers said Mr. Wallace was here ... to check political attitudes because he had been urged to enter the state's Democratic primary in an effort to win the state delegation's convention from President Kennedy. (*New York Times* 1963a)

After the surprisingly good showing in Wisconsin, the Wallace people were eagerly anticipating the Indiana campaign (Kendall 1974). But running in Indiana brought a host of problems. Initially there was some question about whether or not Wallace's petition for ballot positioning was legitimate, but the Indiana secretary of state went ahead and certified him as a candidate (*New York Times* 1964r).

The Wallace camp intended to conduct a "stump" campaign in Indiana, a strategy which consists of making a speech in every town with a population of 5,000 and over. Almost immediately they ran into the very tightly organized political influence of Gov. Matthew Welsh, who had decided to run as a stand-in for Johnson. Hastily, they changed their strategy: they would proceed as they had in Wisconsin, with "sponsored" appearances. Such appearances, Jones says, made it easier to "semi-control the audience and, more importantly, put us in a better position to deal with the pickets, who might not be nonviolent as they advertise themselves to be" (Jones 1966, p. 216). But the sponsored appearances proved to be a bad idea, too. "In more than one instance Welsh pressured civic groups either to stop an invitation from being issued to the Governor or to withdraw one already issued" (Jones 1966, p. 231).

Once Wallace began campaigning, he followed the same course as in Wisconsin. He pushed a "return to constitutional government in this country" (Sitton 1964d), arguing for states' rights and against the Civil Rights Bill. Welsh attacked Wallace constantly (Wehrwein 1964e), even to the point of calling Alabama "a police state" (*New York Times* 1964j). Wallace remained quiet in turn but challenged Welsh to a television debate on the Civil Rights Bill. Welsh refused (Sitton 1964e) but he did appear on television with Dr. James McBride Dabbs, president of the Southern Regional Council, in an attempt to explain Wallace. Dabbs portrayed Wallace as "one of the slickest salesmen the South has ever produced" and said that his style was "simple, uncomplicated, and suave," but that he was essentially a resister, standing "firm against everything" (Wehrwein 1964d). Wallace responded by calling his opponents "little pinkos and left-wingers" (Wehrwein 1964c).

As the campaign proceeded, anti-Wallace activity was stepped up. Full-scale newspaper and television propaganda was launched against him. Throughout Indiana the clergy cautioned their congregations against voting for him; he was jeered at an appearance at Notre Dame (*New York Times* 1964i). Welsh blasted Wallace and said that his "beliefs were responsible for the deaths of innocent children in the bombing of a Sunday School class" (*Indianapolis Star* 1964). Those who held state patronage jobs were warned that those jobs could be jeopardized if the party was weakened (*New York Times* 1964i), and Welsh received the loud endorsement of the state AFL-CIO (Jones 1966, p. 238).

The big guns were rolled out. President Johnson, accompanied by the two Indiana senators, Birch Bayh and Vance Hartke, flew into Indiana in a show of support for Welsh (Jones 1966, p. 248), and Sen. Edward Kennedy was persuaded to speak at a dinner in Indiana in Welsh's behalf (Wehrwein 1964f).

Wallace in the meantime had begun to use some of his own tactics. He cited the endorsement of Alabama labor leaders, and began "playing on the fears of union members that the pending civil rights bill would destroy their seniority rights" (Wehrwein 1964e). Although he spoke only of the constitutional question, he evidently was getting his message across. The *New York Times* (Wehrwein 1964f) reported that "Governor Wallace argues his case in terms of states' rights, but the Hoosiers who drop by the headquarters are thinking in racial terms."

The candidate also tried to appeal to Republicans to jump party lines and vote in the Democratic primary, a phenomenon that was said to have been effective in the Wisconsin vote. But Welsh was not to be outdone: although there was no penalty on the books for crossing one's party lines, it was announced that crossovers would be permitted only if voters "are prepared to sign when challenged an affidavit promising to vote the same way next fall." It was also strongly suggested that a vote for Wallace would be a direct slap at President Johnson.

When all the votes were in, it was apparent that Welsh had out-maneuvered Wallace in the Indiana primary and had definitely succeeded in holding back some of the potential Wallace votes. Altogether, Wallace got 170,146 votes: 29.8 percent of the Democratic total and 17.6 percent of the total votes (Wehrwein 1964a). He carried Lake and Porter Counties in the northwest corner of the state, around Gary. The fact that Welsh did less well than was hoped was attributed to a heavily resented two percent sales tax increase which had recently been imposed by the Indiana legislature (Sitton 1964d; *New York Times* 1964i; Jones 1966, p. 238; Harris 1964). The key factors in the Wallace vote were said to be "fear of neighborhood integration and 'white backlash'—resentment of Negro militancy on civil rights" (Wehrwein 1964a).

Wallace had won three delegates. However, Indiana Democratic headquarters quickly announced that rule changes for the election of state delegates were forthcoming (Wehrwein 1964a). Shortly afterwards the state Democratic committee adopted a resolution that delegates be elected "at large rather than by district," explaining that the change was "motivated largely by their inability to get three Lake County delegates to pay $500 each for the expenses of going to the national convention" (*New York Times* 1964f). Thus Wallace lost his three delegates.

In the meantime, a slate of unpledged electors back in Alabama had overwhelmingly defeated by a margin of five-to-one a slate pledged to back the Democratic Party's nominee. These unpledged electors essentially belonged to Wallace (Wehrwein 1964b). The rumor was that they would "vote for President Johnson provided that Attorney General Robert Kennedy is not his running mate" (Herbers 1964b).

Maryland

Politicians in Maryland had been preparing for Wallace ever since Wisconsin. The *New York Times* reported that Wallace's announcement that he would run in Maryland had come as a "shock to the Democratic organization in Maryland, which had expected to deliver the voters to Johnson without a fight" (Franklin 1964o). Evidently Wallace's appearance in Maryland the previous September, although thought to have political implications, had not been taken seriously. The Maryland party decided that Senator Brewster, not Governor Tawes, would be Wallace's foil.

As time passed, Maryland officials began to realize that an unusual number of people were coming in to register; many of them admitted openly that they were planning to support Wallace (*New York Times* 1964m). In preparation, Senator Brewster began to amass his own traveling show. President Johnson and ten well-known and popular U. S. Senators were solicited to support his efforts in the primary (Franklin 1964n).

Meanwhile, Wallace's showing in Wisconsin had brought in more money. A Southern Committee to Help Elect the Next President of the United States was organized, its main purpose being to raise campaign funds for Wallace (*New York Times* 1964l). With more money in the coffer he began to take his candidacy more seriously, and planned a ten-day, $100,000 television campaign to be telecast over Washington, Baltimore, and Salisbury stations (Franklin 1964m).

The Maryland clergy started to attack. The Protestant Episcopal Bishop of Maryland said that the campaign's base of bitter racial hatred was reminiscent of Nazism (*New York Times* 1964h). But Wallace had testified in Washington in late April in support of the "prayer amendment" to the Constitution, and his testimony had fortuitously been publicized along with Bishop Fulton J. Sheen's (Jones 1966, p. 260).

Brewster's campaign against Wallace had started out blandly, but the Indiana result quickly changed that. Johnson appeared in Maryland and spoke in Brewster's behalf, and Brewster himself began to launch vitriolic attacks on Wallace whom he called "a professional liar, a bigot and an aspiring dictator and a certain enemy of the Constitution of the United States" (Franklin 1974l).

Wallace and his staff were forced to move from a hotel in Baltimore because the manager refused to allow the use of rooms for news conferences. Jones reports that they had decided in Wisconsin that small rooms were best for press conferences; the security problem was not as great and the campaign organization felt that mobs outside of the rooms, whether they were supporters or pickets, gave them a more favorable press (Jones 1966, p. 188). But the *New York Times* reported that Wallace forces had begun to pack rooms in advance with supporters who disrupted the conferences by booing reporters' questions and cheering Wallace's answers. This was more than the hotel could stand; the Wallace organization was asked to leave. Wallace used the incident to his advantage, saying in his speeches that under the pending Civil Rights Bill the manager couldn't have asked them to leave because the Wallace group could have claimed discrimination. "In such a case," he continued, "they couldn't act in the best interests of their own business without some federal bureaucrat in Washington telling them to go to jail" (Franklin 1964k).

The same article reports one of Wallace's new techniques used in the two earlier campaigns as well (Jones 1966, p. 287). Wallace had Alabamians of various ethnic backgrounds appear with him on stage as visual evidence that he had wide appeal to all groups. In a similar fashion, when Brewster charged that Wallace didn't have the backing of any member of the Alabama congressional delegation, Wallace simply imported all eight Alabama representatives to stand with him at an appearance in College Park. They were accompanied by four Alabama ministers and Wallace's "U.N. Squad" (an assortment of Alabamians of various ethnic backgrounds) (Franklin 1964i).

Labor forces in Maryland also conducted a massive campaign to present Wallace as antilabor. David J. McDonald, president of the United Steelworkers of America, alarmed by Wallace's showing in Hammond and Gary, Indiana (Jones 1966, p. 273), made an appearance in Maryland and sent a message to all local union officials throughout the United States (reprinted in *Steel Labor* 1964, p. 2) that propaganda was being spread about the pending civil rights legislation. It was incorrect, said McDonald, that the bill would harm jobs, strip laborers of seniority rights, or cause them to be laid off in favor of employing quotas of Negroes. Members of the union were urged to write their senators immediately requesting support and cloture for the bill.

In combating this effort by labor officials to take away his support, Wallace used advertisements to show that he had labor support in Alabama; he exhibited seventy-foot long petitions from union members (Jones 1966, p. 274) and flew numerous Alabama labor officials to Maryland to prove it (Jones 1966, p. 287).

The candidate made only ten public speeches in Maryland, the rest of the effort was in television, radio, and newspaper advertising (Jones 1966, p. 263). Yet his impact was immense and his campaign gained a great deal of additional publicity from events following a speech in Cambridge, on Maryland's Eastern Shore.

Cambridge had been the heart of civil rights activity in Maryland for over a year. The Wallace forces were aware of the trouble there and were very cautious about making an appearance in Cambridge. They seemed to be concerned about the safety of the candidate but were also very much aware that the Eastern Shore represented a potentially fertile area of support (Jones 1966, p. 279). Jones reports:

> I reminded the staff that the top issue in the Wallace campaign was the Civil Rights Bill then pending in the Senate. The issue could be drawn clearly in Cambridge, and with Wallace in the Eastern Shore city there would be no mistaking his position by anyone. Further, I suggested that the Eastern Shore apparently was going to be a major source of strength for the Governor and by going there, we, in effect endorsed the stand they were taking—which was similar to the position Alabamians assume. Even if he did not say so pointedly, the people there would know that Wallace was with them.

With the assurance of the state police and the state commander of the National Guard in Cambridge, the entourage decided that the political rewards were potentially greater than the risks. Jones reports that Wallace was nervous about the decision; it almost backfired. There was a race riot after his speech, but it didn't start until he had already left Cambridge (Franklin 1964j). There were repercussions but the only people who seemed upset at the events were those who were already anti-Wallace.

As before in the Wisconsin and Indiana campaigns, there were reports that various extremist groups were working for Wallace. Wallace deftly brushed aside the matter by refusing to repudiate anyone who wished to help him. "I cannot be responsible for everything that someone does who supports me," he remarked (Franklin 1964h).

Brewster had been caught by a shortage of campaign funds (Franklin 1964g) but got last minute help. The Democrats evidently considered the vote in the blue-collar districts of east and south Baltimore most crucial because the night before the primary, Brewster, David McDonald, Governor Tawes, and Sens. Inouye and Edward Kennedy stumped these areas, known to be heavily populated by union members. In a series of street-corner rallies enhanced by the flow of free beer, the speakers urged everyone to bring all of their friends, relatives, and neighbors to the polls to vote against Wallace (Franklin 1964f). But the next day Wallace got this vote and also succeeded in carrying fifteen out of twenty-three Maryland counties, ending up with 212,068 votes, or 42.7 percent of the total vote cast (Franklin 1964e). Wallace had almost won the Maryland primary; in fact there are some claims that he did win it.

Maryland had originally operated under the county unit rule, in which the popular vote winner in a county gets all of that county's units. The previous year a federal court had ruled that the unit system was unconstitutional in statewide elections but failed to mention the presidential preference primary. Most legal experts said that the ruling had been intended to cover the presidential primary as well, and a hearing was hastily scheduled (Franklin 1964g). At the hearing, the county unit rule in presidential primaries was quickly voided (*New York Times* 1964o).

Jones maintains that Wallace led up until 8:00 p.m., at which time there was an abrupt change. He says that the Wallace organization was fully aware that there was no possibility that the Maryland Democratic party would allow a Wallace victory, no matter how close he came, and he lists two additional handicaps—not enough poll watchers and a large Negro bloc vote in Baltimore (Jones 1966, pp. 303-305).

The immediate reaction from the Senate, where the Civil Rights Bill was pending, was that "the Wallace vote was very largely a protest against the civil rights movement, if not the bill itself," but the general feeling was that the support exhibited for Wallace would have no impact on the passage of the bill (Kenworthy 1964c).

A close analysis of the Maryland vote indicated that liberals and those who voted for the passage of the Civil Rights Bill in the House of Representatives also ran strongly in those same counties in which Wallace was strong. The results demonstrated that the voters were apparently "more against Negro militancy than against the civil rights bill" (Franklin 1964d).

While these primaries were being waged, Wallace had also gotten some write-in votes: 3,761 in Illinois, 565 in Massachusetts, 1,067 in Nebraska, 491 in New Jersey, 1,365 in Oregon, and 12,104 in Pennsylvania (Runyon 1971, p. 17). His success appeared much greater than he had expected.

The Passage of the Civil Rights Bill

On July 2, 1964, President Johnson signed the Civil Rights Bill into law. This legislation culminated that which President Kennedy had introduced to Congress just eight days after Wallace's "stand in the schoolhouse door." It was almost as if, by some odd twist, Wallace was directly responsible for the relatively swift passage of that very legislation that he was fighting. The congressional action in turn gave Wallace even more material for his protests. He could now represent himself to his supporters as one who *knew* the direction in which the federal government was heading; after all, he had predicted it. Further, it gave him an even bigger threat against which he could fight.

The Civil Rights Bill may have been an idea whose time had come. Violence, particularly in Alabama and Mississippi, had aroused public sympathy for the bill. But the fact remained that Wallace, with relatively little organization and little sophistication about national politics, had managed to engender a total protest vote of 672,984 in all three primaries (Runyon 1971, p. 17), all of which were in the North, and support for his position was a certainty within the South.

Although Washington chose to ignore Wallace's rustlings on the political scene, the Republican party did not. Lodge had won the New Hampshire Republican primary on March 11 with an impressive write-in victory. Although Goldwater had come in second, Harris Poll results released on the very day of the Wisconsin primary showed that Goldwater was considered one of the weakest Republican candidates when paired with Johnson (only Rockefeller had made a worse showing). Against Johnson's sixty-six percent, Goldwater would only be able to muster a poor twenty-six percent (Ingalls 1964). According to the poll, Lodge had a better chance; thirty-three percent to Johnson's fifty-two percent. The *New York Times* reported that one aftermath of the Wallace vote in Wisconsin was that it "revived interest in Senator Goldwater, the Republican contender who is most attractive to anti-integrationists" (*New York Times* 1964n).

One week after the passage of the Civil Rights Bill, Goldwater won the Illinois primary, and it was noted that Wallace had gotten almost equal numbers of Democratic and Republican write-in votes (Wehrwein 1964g). In the next three primaries the Goldwater showing was relatively poor. The *Times* reports him as remarking on May 1 that Wallace would do well in the primaries because "the people in the North and West, while they are eager for the Negro to have all his rights . . . don't want their property rights tampered with." Goldwater also "repeated his opposition to the proposed civil legislation, especially the public accommodations and fair employment provisions" (Sitton 1964c). The next day Goldwater won the Texas Republican primary. Three days later he won in Indiana, and a week after that added Nebraska to his victories.

The Wallace vote had been carefully noted. While there had been some cross-over voting in both Wisconsin and Indiana, it was evident that most of the defection to Wallace in the three primaries had come from ranks within the Democratic party.

Withdrawing from the 1964 Campaign

Wallace, in the meantime, despite slight snubs from the governors of neighboring Georgia and South Carolina, announced that he would run for president in November as an "Alabama Democrat" in as many as thirty states. Further, he predicted that he could win as many as seventy electoral votes and thereby "prevent the election of either President Johnson or the Republican nominee, and leave the choice to the House of Representatives" (Mazo 1964a). But when Wallace actually began to investigate the rules on ballot positioning, he ran into severe problems; each state had different rules. Some filing dates had already passed, in other states petitions with a great many signatures were required.

At the end of June, Goldwater won the California primary. He also voted against the Civil Rights Bill. Conservatives began to press for his nomination. A rightist group called the National Conservative Council announced that if Goldwater didn't get the Republican presidential nomination, they were going to run Wallace as a third party candidate in at least twenty-nine states (Turner 1964).

While the polls never showed Goldwater doing well compared to the other Republican candidates, an examination of public opinion measured by letter writing shows that in this medium he clearly out-distanced other candidates; it also showed that he was potentially very strong against Johnson (Converse, Clausen and Miller 1965, p. 334). While these authors also note that ultraconservatives are usually known for their high frequency of letter writing as political activity, it is possible that public opinion measured in this way had some bearing on the final decision as to who would be the Republican candidate most likely to offer Johnson a challenge.

Given this and the Wallace showings in the North, as well as his probable strength in the South (shown by Gallup Polls released May 13, 1964 and July 13, 1964 to be eighteen to twenty percent, equaling Goldwater's nationwide twenty percent against Johnson only in the July 13 poll), it seemed likely that a Goldwater candidacy could cut inroads into normally Democratic strongholds where people were incensed by the Civil Rights Bill. Further, Converse, Clausen and Miller (1965, p. 327) relate that

> Goldwater felt, to begin with, that he could hold on to essentially the same states that Nixon had won in 1960. This meant a clean sweep of the populous states of the Pacific Coast, most of the Mountain and Plains states, and a scattering east of the Mississippi.

This rationale, despite the displeasure of the Republican majority with the idea of Goldwater as a candidate, must have made the choice seem possibly productive. The only problem was Wallace.

Goldwater began to plan for getting rid of Wallace and gaining his supporters. Appearing in the South, he suggested that "it would not be wise for either political party to promise new action in civil rights until the Civil Rights Act of 1964 had been thoroughly tested." He also said that Wallace was a "capable man who had lots of wisdom," but suggested that he withdraw from his presidential campaign since continuing it would only "add more chaos to what he thinks is happening" (Mohr 1964). Wallace brushed aside Goldwater's suggestion. Although there were rumors that Goldwater officials were meeting with Wallace staff members and a photograph appeared in *Life Magazine* showing James D. Martin, the Alabama Republican leader, conferring with Senator Goldwater on the roof of the Mark Hopkins Hotel in San Francisco (Sitton 1964b), Wallace would say only that "the leaders of both parties have been very concerned about this [Wallace] movement."

Wallace was evidently looking for some concessions. He had spoken in Little Rock, Ark., calling for a "coalition government" that would give him the power to review the "appointment of such key cabinet officials as the Attorney General" as well as the "selection of Justices of the United States Supreme Court." He also insisted that no Negro civil rights leaders be allowed in the White House and that Communists be put in jail (Franklin 1964c). Martin was apparently the go-between, for he was quoted by the *Birmingham News* as saying that

> Senator Goldwater told me he thought the South was entitled to a voice in major appointments and that the South would be consulted, along with other sections of the country on the appointment of the United States Attorney General, of Supreme Court Justices and so on.

Martin also said that "I have a feeling he [Wallace] is influencing Goldwater's thinking and that Senator Goldwater is influencing Governor Wallace's thinking" (Sitton 1964b).

Goldwater was nominated by the Republicans on July 15. Almost immediately Wallace's support began to crumble. A number of former Wallace backers, including Lester Maddox of Georgia and Mississippi Governor Ross Barnett, endorsed Goldwater (Sitton 1964b). More to the point, the wellspring of his campaign funds suddenly dried up:

> This money—particularly large contributions from wealthy right-wing sources—is now believed to be in the hands of Goldwater supporters, who apparently believe the Senator can form a satisfactory conservative coalition of his own by winning the election without Mr. Wallace's help. (Franklin 1964c)

It was felt that if Wallace continued his efforts, Goldwater's chances against Johnson would suffer greatly (*New York Times* 1964e). William E. Miller, Goldwater's running mate, told James Martin that "your Governor Wallace is the key to Goldwater's election in November" (*New York Times* 1964e).

And so, in an appearance on "Face the Nation" on July 19, Wallace withdrew his bid for the presidency. In withdrawing Wallace proclaimed that he "was the instrument" through which "the high councils of both major political parties" had been conservatized. He "denied that he or his staff had had any communication or made any deal with the Goldwater forces," and "declined explicitly to endorse Mr. Goldwater" ("Face the Nation" 1964). Goldwater's comment upon hearing about Wallace's withdrawal was that it was a "surprise" to him. "'I never gave this Wallace thing much thought,' the Senator said" (*New York Times* 1964e).

The Problem of Wallace's Electors

The decision to withdraw left Wallace in trouble at home. It was understood that the slate of unpledged electors that had been elected in Alabama belonged to Wallace, but he released them from supporting him almost immediately. In doing so, however, he insisted that they vote as a unit at the convention. "This," he said, "would enable the delegation 'to be unanimous in whatever approach we take, or rather, you take.'" But there were many objections, and a vote was not taken on this suggestion (*New York Times* 1964d). Wallace evidently wanted the delegation to remain under instructions from him (Kenworthy 1964b).

There was also the rumor that some of the electors wanted to withdraw, but that Wallace wouldn't let them. Many wanted to support Goldwater, but the same legislation that had left them "unpledged" also bound them to vote for a Democrat. This presented a quandary. One thing was sure; Wallace didn't want them to be bound to vote for President Johnson.

There were few ways to assure this, but Wallace began by making a quick trip to appear before the National Democratic Platform committee. As the members sat in "dazed disbelief," Wallace upbraided the prevailing Democratic leadership, saying that it had "consciously and deliberately advocated, sponsored, and sold an alien philosophy of government." He "warned of an 'uprising' by the South against the Democrats. He said he would lead a third-party movement after the election if his views did not find expression in the established parties." Partly out of fear that the delegation would balk along with Wallace, the committee formally challenged the Alabama delegation, and "Governor Wallace, talking with reporters outside the platform hearing room, indicated that he did not care whether the Alabama delegation was seated or not. He said he was 'not here to beg'" (*New York Times* 1964c). He then flew back to Montgomery.

It was a curious gesture. Wallace had not presented any material for insertion into the platform, but he had succeeded in assuring that the Alabama delegation would be challenged. His actions and words suggest that he wanted a confrontation to materialize. What it was to be didn't really matter; the strategy was most probably to present the delegation as somehow being unfairly victimized by the party. If the Credentials Committee had refused to seat them and there had been a floor fight, that would have served the purpose. As it so happened, the Credentials Committee immediately suggested that the Alabama delegates be required to sign a pledge to support the party's nominees; most refused (Kenworthy 1964a). This was a desirable outcome from the Alabamiams' point of view. The delegation contended that they had been singled out for something that, if required of them, should have been required of all delegates. It did appear publicly as if they were being coerced by the party. Any confrontation would have done the trick—magnified the issue and given the Alabama delegation exactly the publicity that Wallace seemed to want.

The Democratic Convention

The party seemed to want to avoid direct confrontation. The delegation was not pressured about the loyalty oath, and the first two days of the convention the Alabama delegates pushed past the sergeant-at-arms and took their seats. Nothing happened. Unbeknownst to the convention at large, President Johnson had ordered the floor leadership to avoid any minority reports on platform pronouncements or delegates' credentials. It was said that he did not want any party divisions exposed and was trying to prevent disorderly scenes on the floor that would be prime targets for television cameras (*New York Times* 1964b).

On the third day in a private meeting, the party demanded that each member of the Alabama delegation sign the loyalty oath. Most of them left the convention immediately, but nine delegates chose to remain. That evening, Eugene "Bull" Conner, the Alabama National Democratic Committeeman (and one of those who had refused to sign), pushed past the guards, tried to take his seat and grabbed for the microphone. However, other pledged Alabama delegates prevented him and one of them, securing the microphone, yielded immediately to Texas. Representing Texas, John Connally placed Johnson in nomination (Sitton 1964a). The confrontation had been averted.

The Question of a Third Party

After the convention, Wallace issued this perfunctory statement:

> We resent the fact that our state, with its unbroken record of support of Democrats, was required to sign the oath, while other states which have never

been able to support the ticket were not required to sign. (*New York Times* 1964b)

Wallace's motives in these incidents are not definitely known, but it seems most likely that he wanted assurance that the Alabama delegation would be freed from the obligation of supporting the national party. There was speculation that

> ... the Wallace forces had intended all along to force the national party's hand and thus to clear the way for the Governor to support Sen. Barry Goldwater ... or to initiate another third party movement. (Sitton 1964a).

Whatever his rationale, the plan had failed. Wallace's machinations had been effectively ignored and thereby defused by the Democrats.

It is unlikely that a third-party move was even being considered. As Bob Kendall told the author (Kendall 1974), Goldwater "got" the issue in 1964; the feeling conveyed was that he had taken it from Wallace. Thus, with no issue distinctly his own, no organization beyond that of his immediate staff (Rogin, p. 38), and no strong financial support (all of his supporters were now on Goldwater's bandwagon), there were few possibilities left open for Wallace.

Wallace's bargaining power with the Democrats had been more on the level of trouble making, rather than power wielding. He lost that power when the Democrats had not played the game the way Wallace had defined it. Whereas the Republicans had initially been more responsive to Wallace, they had openly repudiated the need for his support after Goldwater's nomination was secured and Wallace had publicly dropped out of the race. This series of lessons had shaped all of Wallace's subsequent political decisions.

Wallace could give only minimal support to one party or another, as he had been snubbed by both. Evidently the fact that he had run well in three northern Democratic primaries had given him some hope that he could eventually make inroads in the Democratic party and kept him from openly supporting Goldwater. In addition, as one of his aides put it: "Mr. Wallace is not in a position to join the Republican party, even if he wanted to ... He differs from local Republicans in that on economic issues he is liberal" (Herbers 1964a). The Democrats, meanwhile, were silent.

The overwhelming sentiment in the South was for Goldwater. Although Goldwater had Wallace's "issue" and reflected many of his positions, Wallace was in a dilemma. If he openly threw his support to Goldwater many of his Democratic cronies, people he had to protect in order to protect himself, could conceivably be eliminated by a Republican sweep of Alabama. And there was still the problem of the slate of unpledged electors. They were forbidden by law to vote for a Republican, and being Wallace's former ace-in-the-hole, they could not very well support Johnson and remain faithful to Wallace. He tried to get them to resign and make way for a separate group pledged to support Johnson; that way a clear-cut confrontation between Johnson and Goldwater electors could take place, and Wallace would not be held responsible for the outcome. But the electors refused to resign (*New York Times* 1964a), and on the ballot in November there was a national Republican slate and an unpledged Alabama Democratic slate; Johnson and the national Democratic party were not on the ticket.

Chester, Hodgson, and Page (1969, p. 657) document a report that in September 1964, Wallace was considering turning Republican. The reason they say that he didn't is because Strom Thurmond "beat him to it." One of Wallace's friends said that "Wallace thought that one was enough."[1]

Publicly, Wallace supported neither national party. Before the election he made several out-of-state speeches billed as nonpolitical belated "thank you's" to persons who had voted for him in Wisconsin, Indiana, and Maryland (Franklin 1964b). He maintained that these anti-civil rights speeches were not for the purpose of helping Goldwater (Franklin 1964a) but to express his own positions. And while verbally giving his support to local Democrats in Alabama, Wallace did not campaign for them. He was trying to ride the fence.

On November 3, the Republican slate in Alabama defeated the unpledged Democrats by a margin of three to one. Even the local Democratic candidates went down in the Republican sweep, and Wallace was held responsible for the "shambles" which had been made of the state Democratic party.

Note

1. This report, although not noted in any other source, is given added validity in that Joe Azbell, Wallace's public relations expert, recommended the book (Chester, Hodgson, and Page 1969) to the author as a good source of information about the 1968 campaign. It is not particularly flattering to Wallace, Azbell said, "but it is essentially correct" (Azbell 1974).

Chapter Five

Wallace Support in 1964:
Building a Constituency

In 1964, Lou Harris polled preprimary Indiana and predicted a thirty percent Wallace vote among Democrats. The actual total was almost identical—29.8 percent—and the majority of voters queried revealed that in voting for Wallace they were actually voting against Governor Welsh, in protest of Welsh's fiscal policies. Only one-third of the Wallace voters said that they had cast their votes for him primarily because he was against civil rights (Harris 1964).

These results are interesting and they illuminate the Indiana primary, but they give us little information about who the 1964 Wallace voters actually were and what they actually thought. A Gallup Poll (AIPO 694) conducted nationwide from June 25 through June 30, 1964 provides additional data.[1]

This poll was used to separate respondents into three candidate supporter groups, using the question: "If Barry Goldwater were the Republican candidate and Lyndon Johnson were the Democratic candidate and Gov. George Wallace of Alabama were the candidate of a third party, which would you like to see win?" Those who were unwilling to commit themselves to a candidate were eliminated from the sample, which resulted in a net 3346 persons interviewed. Of these, 76.7 percent (2565) supported Johnson, 16.4 percent (551) were for Goldwater, and 6.9 percent (230) supported Wallace.

Demographics

Who are those who support Wallace in 1964 and how do they compare with the supporters of Johnson and Goldwater? A review of demographic characteristics, shown in Table 5.1, shows some interesting differences.

45

TABLE 5.1
Selected Demographic Characteristics*

	Johnson	Goldwater	Wallace
Race			
White	80.7	97.3	99.1
Black	18.6	2.0	0.9
Sex			
Male	45.6	58.4	50.4
Female	54.4	41.6	49.6
Age			
21-24	7.7	6.0	5.7
25-44	39.5	31.5	37.4
45-59	26.4	27.9	30.9
60 and over	26.4	34.6	26.1
Region			
Northeast	32.1	23.8	7.4
Midwest	31.1	26.5	9.2
South	20.8	30.3	74.7
Far West	16.0	19.4	8.7
Size of Place			
Under 2500	26.7	40.6	43.5
2500-9999	7.9	5.8	8.5
10,000-49,999	7.4	9.5	9.1
50,000-249,999	12.9	13.8	18.7
250,000+	45.1	30.3	19.9
Party Affiliation			
Republican	21.6	75.0	32.3
Democrat	70.5	15.4	52.7
Independent	7.9	9.7	15.0

*Percentages add vertically by columns to 100 percent, except for rounding errors.

As might be expected, practically no blacks support either Goldwater or Wallace. By contrast, 18.6 percent of the Johnson support is black. Sex also differentiates 1964 supporters. Goldwater supporters are predominately male and Johnson supporters predominately female; Wallace supporters are almost evenly split between males and females.

Age distribution for the candidate groups are relatively similar, but there is a great difference in modal ages. Goldwater supporters appear much older than Johnson supporters; the modal age of Johnson supporters is a low forty-two years of age; for Wallace it is forty-five; and for Goldwater it is a much higher fifty-nine years of age.

Another contrast emerges with place of residence. Supporters of the three candidates live in very different locales. Fully three-quarters of all Wallace supporters in 1964 are from the South, as compared with thirty percent of the Goldwater supporters. Most of the Johnson support, by contrast, is among residents who live in the Northeast and the Midwest.

There is also a difference in the size of the places where they live. A rural category, including the classifications farm, open country/nonfarm, and place with a population under 2500 accounts for 26.7 percent of the Johnson support, 40.6 percent of the Goldwater support and 43.5 percent of the Wallace preference. The largest proportions of Johnson supporters (45.1%) live in cites with populations of 250,000 and over. In comparison, 30.3 percent of Goldwater supporters and 19.9 percent of Wallace supporters live in cities of that size.

Party affiliations also serve to demarcate the Wallace support. Party loyalty plays a part in mainstream politics: not surprisingly, most supporters of Johnson are Democrats and most supporters of Goldwater are Republicans, but the party affiliations of Wallace supporters do not follow expectations. Wallace ran as a Democrat in 1964 and slightly over half of his supporters identify themselves as Democrats. The remainder of his support is approximately one-third Republicans and fifteen percent Independents, almost twice as large a proportion of Independents as those found among supporters of Johnson or Goldwater.

Attitudes

What kinds of attitudes do Wallace supporters have which set them apart from supporters of other candidates? First of all, they are more likely to be disapproving of how Johnson is handling the presidency than are supporters of either Johnson or Goldwater. Over half of them (54.6%) say that they are dissatisfied with Johnson as president as compared with 45.5 percent of the Goldwater supporters. By contrast, 87.4 percent of the Johnson supporters approve of his presidency.

As might be expected, Wallace supporters' disapproval of Johnson is directly related to their anti-civil rights posture. Fully 91.7 percent of Wallace supporters who disapprove of the way Johnson is running the government are also against civil rights.

In fact, attitudes toward civil rights (see Table 5.2) are a major factor distinguishing Wallace supporters from supporters of other candidates; 85.8 percent of Wallace supporters say that they are against civil rights compared with 51.6 percent of Goldwater supporters and 15.1 percent of Johnson supporters.

TABLE 5.2
Position on Civil Rights

	Johnson	Goldwater	Wallace
In Favor	84.9	48.4	14.2
Against	15.1	51.6	85.8
	100.0%	100.0%	100.0%

One might suspect that most of the Wallace supporters who are against civil rights are also from the South. While living in the South does relate to position on civil rights for both Johnson and Goldwater supporters, it has little to do with Wallace supporters' attitudes, for Wallace supporters in 1964 are racist no matter where they live. Holding region constant, we find that Wallace supporters who are against civil rights are evenly distributed in all regions, except for the Far West.

Far West	45.0%
Midwest	89.5%
South	89.7%
Northeast	94.1%

Political party membership, however, does serve to specify position on civil rights; 70.6 percent of the Wallace supporters who say they are Republicans are against civil rights, compared to 90.7 percent of the Democrats and 100 percent of the Independent Wallace supporters.

When asked the most important problem facing this country today, each supporter group most often mentions civil rights. Given the fact that the Civil Rights Act was being debated in Congress at the time of the survey, it is not surprising to find this response given by so many; 41.6 percent of Goldwater supporters, 48.0 percent of Johnson supporters and 51.3 percent of Wallace supporters mention it as their major concern. No other issue is mentioned nearly so often.

Among both Wallace supporters and Goldwater supporters, the next most often mentioned problem is communism, or Communist infiltration.

Both candidates mentioned this issue in their campaigns, and 11.7 percent of the Wallace supporters and 10.7 percent of the Goldwater supporters think it the most important problem. A comparable 7.1 percent of Johnson supporters are also concerned with communism. The Johnson supporters tend, however, to be slightly more concerned with problems of peace and war (8.4%) and Vietnam (7.9%).

The third most frequently mentioned problem by Wallace supporters is fiscal: the high cost of living, inflation, high prices, and taxes (8.3%). This area does not appear to be of any great concern to either Johnson or Goldwater supporters.

Other attitudes which serve to distinguish Wallace supporters from others or show similarities to them include the matter of ideology. Table 5.3 shows answers to the question, "Suppose there were only two parties, liberal and conservative, which would you be more likely to prefer?"

Goldwater supporters consider themselves conservatives in higher proportions (66.2%) than do supporters of other candidates. Wallace supporters are somewhat less likely to feel allegiance to conservatism, but the majority of them (54.0%) also give that response. Fully one-third of the Wallace supporters answer "no opinion" when questioned about whether they would align themselves with a liberal or a conservative party, and most Johnson supporters (44.4%) identify themselves as liberal.

TABLE 5.3
Respondent's Definition of His/Her Own Ideology

	Johnson	Goldwater	Wallace
Liberal	44.4	14.3	11.7
Conservative	26.4	66.2	54.0
No Opinion	29.2	19.4	34.3
	100.0%	100.0%	100.0%

There is a relationship between party affiliation and ideological self-perception. As expected, if one considers himself a liberal, he is more likely to be a Democrat than a Republican; conversely, if one considers himself a conservative, he is more likely to be a Republican. An exception is noted among Wallace supporters, however; if they consider themselves conservatives, they are as likely to be Democrats as Republicans. And those Wallace supporters who have no opinion about their ideological stance are those who are also more likely to declare themselves Independents.

By contrast, Wallace supporters' perception of ideology seems to have little meaning when examined in relation to their racial attitudes. Among those who call themselves liberals, ninety-two percent of the Wallace supporters are against civil rights; among those labeling themselves conservatives, eighty-three percent are against civil rights.

Authoritarian Personality

While there are no specific F (Authoritarianism) Scale items on this schedule, one could argue that a focus on communism or Communist infiltration represents a preoccupation with dominance-submission and a concern with strength and toughness. Those people so concerned are likely to be authoritarian. The data show that mention of the threat of communism as the "most serious problem" is similar in all of the candidate support groups and does not serve to differentiate one group from another; 11.7 percent of the Wallace supporters, 10.7 percent of the Goldwater supporters and 7.1 percent of the Johnson supporters give this reply.

Thus, while there is some evidence of authoritarianism among the general populace, it is not any more prevalent in one group than in another.

Marginal Voter Theory

Those who call themselves Independents are almost always considered marginal voters (McEvoy 1971, p. 124). While labeling oneself an Independent does suggest that one considers oneself outside of the mainstream of American politics, it is not a clear indication of marginality, as most people continue to vote within the framework of the two "legitimate" parties. Moreover, proportions of Independent voters have been increasing over the last few electoral periods, and now constitute over one-third of the electorate (Flanigan and Zingale 1979, p. 54). One-third of the electorate is not marginal, particularly when there are more Independents than there are Republicans.

A more fruitful way of exploring marginality is to consider the question of participation, rather than that of nominal affiliation. Actual voting history is one index of political participation. The percentages of the 1964 candidate supporter groups who did not vote in 1960 include 12.9 percent of the Goldwater supporters, 23.5 percent of the Johnson supporters, and 34.3 percent of the Wallace supporters.[2] It should be noted here that this sample includes voters as well as nonvoters and differs from later samples used in this study in that respect. It may very well be that many nonvoters are Wallace supporters, but we are not concerned with nonvoters in this study, only with those who are in a position to affect the outcomes of an election. Thus, the fact that a larger percentage of Wallace supporters did not vote in 1960 is interesting but not conclusive.

Another factor which has relevance for marginal voting theory is voter registration. Registration statistics show no significant differences among the groups: in fact, slightly more Wallace supporters are registered to vote (80.4%) than are those in the Johnson (73.9%) and Goldwater (79.3%) groups.

Additional evidence of marginality might come from a "no" or "don't know" answer to the question, "Do you plan to vote in the election for president in November, 1964?" Here again, there are no significant differences among the supporter groups. An identical number (89.6%) of both Wallace and Johnson supporters say they are planning to vote. Further, a slightly higher 92.5 percent of the Goldwater supporters are also planning to vote.

Since nonparticipation in other types of activities is also used to denote marginality, whether or not one is a labor union member adds useful information. Johnson supporters or members of their families are much more likely to belong to labor unions than are Goldwater or Wallace supporters, but Wallace supporters' proportionate membership is not very different from the Goldwater supporters. Johnson supporters include 29.8 percent who are either members of a labor union or have someone in their family who is a member of a union, followed by 19.1 percent of the Wallace supporters and 18.1 percent of the Goldwater supporters.

At best there is only mixed support for the theory that Wallace supporters are more likely to be politically marginal than are supporters of other candidates. While they voted in less proportions in 1960 than did supporters of other candidates, they are registered to vote and plan to do so in November 1964 in percentages which do not differ from those of other candidates' supporters.

Status Theories

Status politics has been the most frequently discussed explanation of Wallace support. Analysis of status politics as a theoretical question procedes here from two vantage points: whether Wallace supporters differ from Johnson and Goldwater supporters in terms of the status they have and in terms of the status anxiety they feel in regard to the rising status of blacks.

A number of variables are used to create a measure of socioeconomic status (see Appendix for full explanation and Table 5.4 for all status measures). The first combination, ascribed status, combines scores on race and religion. It is apparent from these figures that Wallace supporters are not lacking in ascribed status. In fact, more of the Wallace supporters are both white and Protestant (83.5%) than are supporters for either Goldwater (81.7%) or Johnson (48.2%).

The second component of socioeconomic status, achieved status, is calculated from education and income. On the education measure, Wallace supporters are less likely to have been in college than are those in other candidate groups. Over 55 percent of the Wallace supporters as compared to 46.8 percent of the Johnson supporters and 40.3 percent of the Goldwater supporters have a high school education only.

Income is coded into rough thirds. In the group which has the highest income, Goldwater supporters are overrepresented with 41.7 percent and Wallace supporters are underrepresented with 23.8 percent. The tendency of Wallace supporters to be low on both income and education variables has implications for the measure of achieved status as calculated. Half (50.7%) of all Wallace supporters in 1964 have low achieved status. Less than one-fourth of the Wallace supporters are in the upper two achieved status levels, while the comparable statistic for both the Goldwater and Johnson supporters demonstrate that over one-third are at that level.

Ascribed and achieved status are combined to form a measure of socioeconomic status (SES).[3] The top SES category, high, means that one is white, Protestant, in the upper third of income distribution, and has some college education.

Wallace supporters in 1964 fall somewhere between Goldwater and Johnson supporters on this composite measure of socioeconomic status.[4] When the figures for low and working SES are combined, 50.4 percent of Goldwater supporters, 58.7 percent of Wallace supporters and 70.6 percent of Johnson supporters constitute the two lower classes. Thus Wallace supporters are more similar to Goldwater supporters than they are to Johnson supporters on socioeconomic status. They do not differ, therefore, from supporters of other candidates on objectively judged status characteristics.

Status theory is also concerned with subjective status anxiety. Questions on this schedule allow a check on whether those with relatively high status feel threatened relative to the rising status of blacks. Looking at those who are against civil rights by the number of ascribed characteristics which they possess (Table 5.5) we find that there are no supporters of any candidate who have no ascribed statuses and are also against civil rights. Also noticeable is that having one or both ascribed status characteristics makes virtually no difference among Wallace supporters. By contrast, having both characteristics increases the likelihood of being against civil rights for Goldwater and Johnson supporters. Goldwater supporters with both ascribed statuses are almost twice as likely to be against civil rights as are

TABLE 5.4
Selected Status Characteristics*

	Johnson	Goldwater	Wallace
Ascribed Status			
None	2.8	0.7	0.0
One	49.0	17.6	16.5
Both	48.2	81.7	83.5
Education			
Grade school	34.9	34.1	36.5
High school	46.8	40.3	55.7
College	18.2	25.6	7.8
Income Distribution			
Lowest third	36.7	36.2	39.6
Middle third	32.2	22.1	36.6
Highest third	31.1	41.7	23.8
Achieved Status			
Low	43.3	39.1	50.7
Working	23.2	22.6	26.4
Middle	24.3	18.2	19.8
High	9.1	20.0	3.1
Socioeconomic Status			
Low	36.9	13.4	13.0
Working	33.7	37.0	45.7
Middle	24.6	32.3	38.3
High	4.8	17.2	3.0

*Percentages add vertically by columns to 100 per-
cent, except for rounding errors.

those with only one status, and for Johnson supporters the likelihood is 3.6 times as much. Thus, while there is no indication of status anxiety among Wallace supporters, there does appear to be some indication of that condition among supporters of both Johnson and Goldwater.

Looking only at those against civil rights by SES, shown in Table 5.6 below, we find that although Wallace supporters are clearly more anti-integration than supporters of other candidates at all levels, the differences among them by SES level is relatively small. The biggest change noted is between low- and working-class Goldwater supporters. Among all candidate groups the change most noticeable is between low- and working-class SES; the higher three classes are somewhat consistent. This seems to indicate that anticipated status deprivation is not particularly important for any group of supporters who already possess some status. The observation is especially so for Wallace supporters. Racism may be operative, but it does not seem connected to fears of status deprivation.

Reviewing these findings, it appears that status theories are not useful in explaining Wallace support in 1964. On the objective measures of status, Wallace supporters are solidly within the middle and not at all different from supporters for other candidates. Nor does status anxiety relative to attitudes toward blacks seem important in distinguishing Wallace supporters from others. There is more evidence that such anxiety may be present and operative among Goldwater and Johnson supporters, but not among Wallace supporters. Wallace supporters' racism is there regardless of status level and does not appear to have anything to do with status anxiety.

The Power Theory

One way of defining political powerlessness is the "individual's feeling that he cannot [himself] affect the actions of the government" (Finifter 1970). This would seem especially important relative to political decisions which determine the conditions under which one lives; such feelings are the opposite of what is generally referred to as feelings of political efficacy.

While this particular poll does not ask questions which would specifically reveal these feelings of powerlessness, there are some queries which bare skepticism about the effectiveness of the political system.

The most obvious form of skepticism in 1964 is not to list oneself as a member of either party. It has already been mentioned (Table 5.1) that a higher proportion of Wallace supporters describe themselves as Independents than do supporters of the other two candidates. The party system as it exists is definitely of questionable value to such persons.

TABLE 5.5
Proportions Against Civil Rights by Number of
Ascribed Social Characteristics*

	Johnson	Goldwater	Wallace
None	0.0	0.0	0.0
One	7.1	31.6	81.1
Both	25.4	56.1	86.8
n =	(337)	(240)	(181)
gamma:	.657	.501	.210

*The proportions of those for civil rights in each category are the differences between 100 percent and the percentages noted here in each cell.

TABLE 5.6
Proportions Against Civil Rights by Percentage in Each SES Group*

	Johnson	Goldwater	Wallace
Low	6.8	19.0	76.6
Working	19.4	63.6	91.3
Middle	24.0	50.6	81.5
High	12.8	61.0	100.0
n =	(336)	(240)	(178)
gamma:	.366	.194	-.017

*The proportions of those for civil rights in each category are the differences between 100 percent and the percentages noted here in each cell.

Further, respondents are asked which party can (1) better solve the most important problem facing this country today and (2) increase respect for the United States throughout the world. Answering either question by citing one party or the other demonstrates belief in the effectiveness of the party system; any other answer indicates some skepticism. The data show that more Wallace supporters than Goldwater or Johnson supporters respond "no difference" or "the same" in answer to these questions. Further, most of the Wallace supporters who give these answers are Independents.

This combination of labeling oneself as an Independent and seeing no difference between the existing parties' abilities to handle either area would seem to indicate that those particular respondents view the existing party system as virtually ineffective. Under our original definition such persons can definitely be said to be exhibiting a sense of powerlessness, and not of marginality as others have argued.

Another question also gives some evidence of Wallace voters' expression of powerlessness in relation to the party system. Responses of disapproval to the following question are indicative:

> As you know, the Supreme Court has ruled that the number of representa-
> tives in state legislatures should be in proportion to the population. In most
> states, this means reducing the number of representatives from the rural areas
> and increasing the number from the cities. Do you approve or disapprove of
> this ruling?

This percentage of those disapproving of reapportionment by candidate supporter group is as follows: Johnson 28.3 percent; Goldwater 39.2 percent; and Wallace by a majority of 57.8 percent.

Further exploration of this attitude reveals that, as might be expected, city size is a factor: rural residents (inhabitants of places with populations under 2500) are more likely to disapprove of reapportionment than are residents of cities of 500,000 and over in population.

While it is evident that the residents of smaller places are more likely to disagree than those residing in larger places who have less to lose from reapportionment, proportionately more Wallace supporters (85.2%) from rural places are against such a change than are those in the other candidate groups. One might suspect further that attitudes toward civil rights specify attitudes toward reapportionment. This proves to be so for both Johnson and Goldwater supporters but not for Wallace supporters.

Holding attitudes toward civil rights constant, we find that among those who are against reapportionment, attitudes toward civil rights distribute as shown in Table 5.7.

TABLE 5.7
Proportions Against Reapportionment by Attitudes on Civil Rights*

	Johnson	Goldwater	Wallace
In Favor of Civil Rights	29.5	35.4	66.7
Against	58.0	65.1	65.5
n =	(613)	(181)	(124)
gamma:	.536	.562	-.027

*The proportions of those for reapportionment in each candidate support group are the differences between 100 percent and the percentages noted here in each cell.

It is reasonable to argue that being against reapportionment is related to the fear of a loss of power, evinced by the prevalence of the attitude among those who would be most affected. While this attitude is more prevalent among Wallace supporters than among the other candidate support groups, it does not seem to be related to their attitudes on civil rights. They are racist regardless of their attitudes toward reapportionment.

Summary

In the 1964 campaign, racial politics overrides almost every other factor in distinguishing Wallace supporters from both Johnson and Goldwater supporters. Of the four major theories advanced to explain preference for Wallace, only the power theory has any credence.

The presence of the authoritarian personality is difficult to ascertain from the content of the questionnaire. It is clear, however, that attitudes which might be indicative of such a personality are evenly distributed among all candidate groups. Support for the marginal voter theory is evident only when nonvoting in 1960 is examined, but the nature of the sample raises questions about that conclusion. An examination of proportions registered to vote or planning to vote in 1964 is a more definite way of ascertaining marginality, and given the data, the theory of marginal voting seems to have little explanatory value in explaining Wallace support.

Tests of status theory demonstrate that Wallace supporters have as much status as do supporters of the two other candidates. There is some evidence that status anxiety may be operative among otherwise secure (at least in ascribed attributes) supporters of Johnson and Goldwater when attitudes toward civil rights are examined, but there is no evidence that the same anxiety is present among Wallace supporters. Further, an examination of a cross-tabulation of the two components of SES, achieved and ascribed (permitting the examination of discrepancy), in relation to attitudes toward civil rights, shows that persons with both ascribed statuses and low achieved status are more likely than others to be against civil rights. This is true of each of the groups, however, and does not serve to distinguish among them. Thus all data point to the conclusion that the status theory is of little use in explaining the 1964 Wallace support.

The power theory shows some explanatory possibilities. Wallace supporters reflect powerlessness in showing a great deal of skepticism about the political system—in listing themselves as Independents in greater proportions than other groups and in saying that no one party is better than the other in solving problems or in gaining respect for the United States. Being against reapportionment can also be understood as indicating a fear of losing power; Wallace supporters have this attitude in greater proportions than do others.

Both racial politics and feelings of powerlessness are important components in the 1964 Wallace support. By using more extensive data sets we will be able to demonstrate in successive chapters exactly how these two attitudes are related in explaining most of the public support for the presidential bids of George Wallace.

Notes

1. The Michigan Survey Research Center's 1964 Election Study has no questions concerning voting for Wallace in a 1964 primary (understandable, as he ran in only three state primaries), or expressing a liking for him as a political personality (not understandable, as the very fact of Wallace's candidacy should have been enough to make him of interest).
2. Goldwater supporters voted overwhelmingly for Nixon in 1960. Johnson supporters voted in great proportions for Kennedy. Wallace supporters' votes are evenly distributed between the candidates.
3. While the distribution of occupational status deserves some attention, the classification used by this Gallup Poll differs too much from that used by the Michigan Survey Research Center to allow comparison of the 1964 data with that of later years. It also does not allow the incorporation of a prestige factor of this type into a socioeconomic status designation. Thus SES is figured from a

straight calculation of race and religion and education and income as explained in the Methods Appendix. For reference, the distribution of work status as described in the 1964 data is as shown below:

Distribution of Work Status

	Johnson	Goldwater	Wallace
Not in labor force	20.5	21.8	13.8
Farmers	7.2	11.6	15.6
Blue collar	44.3	29.9	45.9
White collar	17.9	25.9	18.7
Professional	10.0	10.9	5.8
	100.0%	100.0%	100.0%

4. This particular calculation of socioeconomic status places a great deal of emphasis on ascribed status characteristics. Although it is the standard way of calculating socioeconomic status, in the latter half of the twentieth century achieved status might well be the more important component in people's judgments of themselves and others. At the very least it does seem important to reconsider the components of socioeconomic status.

Chapter Six

Analysis of 1964 Speeches:
"George C. Wallace for President"

Wallace's central focus in the 1964 campaign speeches is to express a strong opposition to changes in segregation laws and mores being required by the federal government in its legislative and judicial actions. Almost everything that Wallace says can be interpreted as an attempt to reinstitutionalize white supremacy, but his efforts are generally undercover and appear under the guise of an intellectual argument as to what should be the proper form of decision making as described in the Constitution of the United States (Wallace 1963a). The question, as he puts it, is one of states' rights versus the power of the federal government.

In the most specific statement of the time, made at the occasion of the stand in the schoolhouse door, Wallace begins by referring to the tenth amendment: "... the powers not delegated to the United States by the Constitution, nor prohibited by it to the states, are reserved to the states respectively, or to the people," and he says specifically that among the powers reserved to the states is the operation of the public schools and colleges. Since only Congress makes the law and

> ... there has been no legislative action by Congress justifying this intrusion [this occurred before the enactment of the Civil Rights Act of 1964], the action of the government results solely from force, or threat of force, undignified by any reasonable application of the principle of law, reason, and justice. (Wallace 1963a)

Wallace says further that such action is an attempt to subordinate the rights of self-determination by individuals and states to the wishes of the federal

61

government, and that "there can be no submission to the theory that the Central Government is anything but a servant of the people" (Wallace 1963a).

In focusing on states' rights versus the power of the federal government, Wallace warns that "power has passed from the people to the government" (Wallace 1964a); in such situations "the state becomes sovereign, the citizen becomes subject" (Wallace 1964c). The only alternatives possible are "between democracy and dictatorship" (Wallace 1964b).

Such words are designed to instill fear and alarm into listeners, as well as to capitalize upon feelings of powerlessness. Wallace builds his constituency by so educating his listeners, warning of dangers which face them as a result of the actions of the federal government. Decisions which were once the province of the people are no longer; social interchange is legislated, not chosen. People are left bereft of will, essentially powerless in the face of governmental actions.

Until Wallace emerged as a spokesman, people were concerned about governmental moves toward equality, but had only vague anger and no conceptual structure with which to explain the changes. Wallace's explanations made sense to those who were watching the events of the beginning of the civil rights movement over their television sets. He shaped their understanding of these events in a way that made sense to them, and it all began in June, 1963, when he burst into the national consciousness with his "Stand in the Schoolhouse Door."

Wallace was fully aware of the national attention he would attract by blocking the entry of two black students to the University of Alabama. The proclamation given on that occasion was clearly designed for attention getting. It would be his first prime time television appearance.

From the "Stand in the Schoolhouse Door," Wallace alerts the public to the dangers of government enforcement of integration laws:

> The unwelcomed, unwanted, unwarranted and force-induced intrusion upon the campus of the University of Alabama today of the might of the Central Government offers frightful example of the oppression of the rights, privileges and sovereignty of this State by officers of the Federal Government. This intrusion results solely from force, of threat of force, undignified by any reasonable application of the principle of law, reason and justice. It is important that the people of this State and nation understand that this action is in violation of rights reserved to the State by the Constitution of the United States and the Constitution of the State of Alabama.

The issue is one of state's rights, he argues, and the particular rights and privileges which are threatened are local control over schools:

> I claim today for all the people of the State of Alabama those rights reserved to them under the Constitution of the United States. Among those powers so

reserved and claimed is the right of state authority in the operation of the public schools, colleges, and universities.

Wallace stresses that he is not blocking the doorway out of mere defiance—the Constitution is at stake. He carefully educates the listening public:

> My action does not constitute disobedience to legislative and constitutional provisions. It is not defiance—for defiance sake, but for the purpose of raising basic and fundamental constitutional questions. My action is a call for strict adherence to the Constitution of the United States as it was written.

He sets himself forth as the people's champion—he is their symbol, their voice of protest.

> I stand before you today in place of thousands of other Alabamians whose presence would have confronted you had I been derelict and neglected to fulfill the responsibilities of my office. It is the right of every citizen, however humble he may be, through his chosen officials of representative government to stand courageously against whatever he believes to be the exercise of power beyond the Constitutional rights conferred upon our Federal Government. It is this right which I assert for the people of Alabama by my presence here today.

In closing, Wallace thunders his disapproval: "I . . . hereby denounce and forbid this illegal and unwarranted action by the Central Government."

Four hours later he stepped out of the doorway and the University of Alabama was integrated. It appears that Wallace never intended to halt the integration of the university, but he was intensely interested in how his action would be perceived. With Wallace, defiance masquerades as power; it is legitimated by his calling upon history, God, and the Constitution for justification.

This pose becomes more apparent in the 1964 "Campaign Speech." Wallace used this basic speech at every appearance (Howard 1974; Camp 1974), modifying it only to take account of and use local examples.

He opens with a rousing challenge to patriotic Americans. Their proud and noble heritage is at stake, and it will take all of the strength and courage which they can muster to remain steadfast in the face of coming adversity:

> Patriotic Americans have a great duty before them. It is a duty that will require patience, persistence and courage. We must have patience to continually point to the truth. We must exercise that patience even in the most violent storm of recriminations against us by those who seek through centralized authority to vanquish freedom in the name of freedom; to destroy human rights and dignity in the name of civil rights; to inspire hatred and chaos in the name of love and peace. Our efforts will require character,

> individualism, and vitality. It will require that we exercise the heritage bequeathed to us by those who stood firm against adversity, fought their way across this country, and established a strong, virile United States.

Wallace sketches a situation in which traditional values have been turned upside down. Those who believe in the basic precepts on which the country was founded are finding themselves suddenly at odds with those who are supposed to be their representatives. They, the faithful and upstanding citizens of the United States, are being unjustly accused of hatred. Although Wallace never mentions civil rights, it is clear to the audience that he is talking about government's promotion of civil rights for blacks:

> We have witnessed a scheme to create national chaos in recent months. Much has been written and said about the "hate" that is purportedly prevalent in our society. Much has been written and said regarding the "haters." Invariably those who are identified as the purveyors of "hate" are: Those who believe in the rights of the individual states. Those who believe in fiscal responsibility. Those who object to amendment of the Constitution of the United States without regard to the basic precepts of the Founding Fathers. Those who stand firm for the retention of the checks and balances system of government. Those who object to a socialist ideology under which a few men in the executive and judicial branches of our government make decisions and laws without regard to our elected representatives who reflect the decisions of the people.

The culprit in all this is the Supreme Court:

> We find these men [Supreme Court] reaching outside the realm of legal precedent, ignoring the basic precepts as established by the Founding Fathers.

Constitutional government is at stake, and the people have everything to lose:

> This gathering of absolute power by men, into a central body of government, was greatly feared by the Founding Fathers of this country. With rights and power divided among separate State governments, close to and answerable to the citizens of each state, no single group could hope to gain control over the people. But with the rights and powers of the states destroyed, with power centralized into one seat of control, tyranny—benevolent or otherwise—is assured over the people.

The situation is beyond comprehension. American leaders are gutless, and the candidate is outraged:

> We are faced with the astounding spectacle for the first time in a civilized nation, of high officials calling for the passage of a so-called civil rights bill for fear of threat of mob violence.

The Court is evil; the government is becoming master rather than remaining servant. What is being ignored is the people's ability to make their own wise decisions. Wallace stresses the rationale of states' rights:

> I believe that people have the wisdom, the sense of justice and the decency to govern their own local affairs. I believe the people of each state must live with their specific conditions, must raise their families and develop their children under particular conditions peculiar to that State.... And I have faith in the wisdom of the people of each State to make decisions in the best interest of all.... I do not have faith that a central government operating at the caprice of a few powerful men is capable of those decisions—nor do I consider them as keepers of the wisdom of the people.

Although race is never mentioned specifically, it is the central core of Wallace's whole campaign. Here, as is typical in his speeches, only one paragraph hints at the real subject, and even then Wallace speaks in parables:

> We have always been a united of many divergences, for this has been our freedom, this has been our secret of dynamics, our will to creativeness. From these fountain heads of differences have come the diversities of free men before the open forum of honest controversy and rich contribution from which decisions are arrived at that speak the will and the wisdom of free and diverse people. But now there are those who would amalgamate us into a unit of the one, subservient to powerful central government, with laws designed to equalize us into the common denominator necessary for a slave people.

The senseless changes in the priorities of the federal government can only be explained if the government itself has succumbed to communism. The speech ends on a chilling note:

> If victory for freedom is impossible, then surrender to communism is inevitable and we can begin fitting the yokes of slavery to the necks of our children even now as the riots and mobs lap at the streets of these United States.

One can imagine the response accounted this speech. Jones speaks of cheering crowds and standing ovations (1966, pp. 193, 198, 207). For sure, it attracted attention—the opposition came out in droves, even to point of overkill.

These two speeches are representative of the issues as well as the style of the 1964 campaign. They demonstrate not only Wallace's arguments and appeal, but also show how he develops and plays on feelings of powerlessness. The situation is one in which the federal government, supposed to function as the servant of the people, is instead becoming their master, entering areas of their lives which were once in the realm of personal decision, usurping their freedom, telling them what to do.

There are no appeals to marginal men. These words are addressed to people who consider themselves mainstream, in harmony with the ideals of the founding fathers, in agreement with the Constitution. It is they who are the essence of Americanism. Likewise, there is no question of loss of status. Throughout these speeches, being a white is a fact of life that is relatively secure in its meaning. Integration would not mean a loss of status. It would mean a loss of choices, of opportunities, of jurisdiction. The issue is one of power.

Chapter Seven

1968: The Third Party

Between November 1964 and September 1965, Wallace reinstated himself as the indisputable head of Alabama politics. Although there is no specific information about how he went about rebuilding the wreckage of the Democratic party after the 1964 elections, he probably used Alabama fiscal spending selectively to reingratiate himself (Frady 1968). The *Times* reported in the spring of 1964 that Wallace was in the process of building a political machine in Alabama.

> Mr. Wallace has used every resource of his office, including awarding and withholding contracts, to build his political faction and cut off support of the national Democratic party. Office holders who opposed the governor's plan ... have found themselves opposed for reelection by Wallace men. *(New York Times* 1964q)

The awarding of contracts was the likely method through which Wallace was able both to placate his friends and to fill his campaign chest. Patronage was distributed around two industries, the asphalt supply business and the liquor industry. Both types of businesses had begun to reap huge successes when Wallace entered office. He had kept his original campaign promises of building more and better roads and subsuming the liquor business under state control. This had saved the taxpayers thousands of dollars and both patronage systems masqueraded as reforms (Chester, Hodgson and Page 1969, pp. 273-75; Brill 1975).

George Wallace's brother Gerald was perhaps involved in both businesses (Brill 1975; *New York Times* 1970j). There is another connection that has not been explored. The *Times* mentions in 1964 (Sitton 1964b) that the H.L. Hunt interests owned a refinery in Tuscaloosa, Alabama, which sold asphalt to highway contractors. Although Hunt was a Wallace supporter in 1964 (until Goldwater became a candidate), there is no evidence that he donated very much to Wallace in direct financial contributions. After the 1968 campaign, however, Seymore Trammell, Wallace's financial director as well as his campaign manager in 1964 and 1968, was found guilty of having accepted bribes for the awarding of such highway contracts and spent fourteen months in prison (*New York Times* 1972k). There are also stories that Gerald Wallace was suspected of selling asphalt to the state at an inflationary price and reaping the profits from such activities (Waldron 1972b).

The other part of the patronage system, the state liquor industry, came under Wallace's control when he, in keeping with his professed aversion to liquor and the social problems it caused, placed all liquor stores under the auspices of a state system. Although Wallace advertised how much he had saved for the people in doing so, the state of Alabama had begun to make enormous profits from the selling of liquor. Chester, Hodgson, and Page (1969, p. 274) note that for a few months favorite national brands disappeared from the shelves. During this period, the sole suppliers of liquor to Alabama were two unknown firms in Baltimore, Md., the state that Wallace had almost carried in 1964. With Gerald Wallace's connections with both industries, and Seymore Trammell's definite involvement in one of them, it is a reasonable assumption that monies from alcoholic beverage as well as asphalt sales eventually passed into the campaign chest (*cf.* Greenhaw 1976, p. 222; Dorman 1976, chap. 5). A great many native Alabamians were profiting from the mutual benefits (see Dorman 1976 for a full account of these and other activities).

On the political side, Wallace could now convince his fellow Democrats that he was "the only one" who could effectively crush the Republican threat to Alabama politics which had become apparent with the election of five Republicans to the House in 1964 in the Goldwater rush (see Franklin 1965). It was apparent that Wallace once again was reasonably secure in Alabama politics.

In the meantime, Wallace's image as champion of the people of Alabama had never flagged. A *New York Times* article (Franklin 1965) mentions that in September 1965 he was at the "peak of his popularity." The Alabama Freedom March from Selma to Montgomery (March 21–25; see Greenhaw 1976) had helped to reinforce the way Wallace presented himself to his public. Jones' (1966) account of the incidents surrounding the march present Wallace's reaction to the "harassment" as one of patience and responsibility despite the countering irresponsibility displayed by the civil disobedience of Martin Luther King and his followers. The feeling conveyed by Jones is one of pride that so little violence occurred given the enormity of the provocations. This attitude was also reflected by Azbell (1974c) when he mentioned that in view of what was going on during the "shooting gallery period" in Alabama, especially along the "Gaza Strip of the United States" (the road between Selma and Montgomery), it was quite remarkable that so few people were hurt. To illustrate his point, Azbell compared the local statistics with others from riots in northern cities which occurred later that year.

The *Times* article (Franklin 1965) also reports that Wallace had developed a new pose: that of "a statesman leading a reluctant Southland into an age of 'social revolution' emerging in Alabama." It is a curiously managed image, however. Wallace clearly accepts the continuing fact of racial prejudice but keeps it under control by making himself the gladiator against the perpetrator of the changes, the federal government. He appears to resist and yet moves forward at the same time:

> The Governor's agressive, seemingly unyielding hostility to the Federal Government and the civil rights revolution is expected to keep Alabama's Ku Klux Klan and other anti-Negro radicals in check as the South slowly moves toward an adjustment to the new social order. (Franklin 1965)

Wallace's immediate problem between 1964 and 1968 was to insure himself a political base from which to run again in 1968. Alabama law did not permit the governor to succeed himself, and there were rumors that he would run for Sparkman's seat in the Senate (Franklin 1965). Although being a senator would have been a respectable and much more usual place from which to conduct a presidential campaign, Wallace evidently decided against pursuing a senatorial race.

There are several possible reasons for this. Wallace's projected constituency was probably a strong consideration. Wallace had been representing himself for the past three years as governor of all of the people of Alabama as well as a spokesman for the South. His primary forays in 1964 had shown him that he also had some support outside of the South. If he had run and won the Democratic senatorial race, that projected constituency would have diminished considerably. For a Democratic senator from Alabama could not have easily presented himself as the representative of the numbers and kinds of people for whom Wallace had begun to portray himself as the champion.

Further, the year and a half in Congress before the 1968 election would not give Wallace enough time to make much of an impression as senator. Taking a lesser political position was unacceptable; it would have meant the end of his political base. And leaving political office was out of the question.

A second possible reason for Wallace's deciding not to run is that the resources available to him as senator would have been considerably less than those available to him as governor. In the 1964 campaign Wallace had freely used state personnel as advisors, workers, and bodyguards, and state finances as well as state property to conduct his campaign. It was also evident that he did not yet have people other than Alabamians who would work for his campaign without recompense; almost all 1964 campaign workers had been imported from Alabama. As a senator, Wallace would be able to provide for less political favors than as governor. Thus the governorship was a much stronger position from which to build patronage and responsive, dedicated followers.

There was only one thing to do: try to change the succession law and run again for governor. Appearing on public television Wallace asked the people of the state to let him know whether or not they wanted him to run for a second term (Herbers 1965). Shortly thereafter his office announced that the result of the mail was overwhelmingly in favor of a second term. Armed with the "will of the people," Wallace promptly called a special session of the state legislature to consider the question of succession. Frady gives a vivid description of the orchestration of that effort. Wallace opened the joint session of the legislature with a television address, insisting that "the issue is the right of the Alabama people to vote to amend or not to amend their own constitution. It is a precious right. . . . Let the people speak!" (Frady 1968, pp. 180-87).

The bill passed the House in a mere twenty seconds, but ran into trouble in the Senate. There were several senators who felt strong-arm tactics were being used, and they engaged in a filibuster.

Wallace meanwhile threatened the senators who were being troublesome. He stopped road construction in a few counties, and in desperation even threatened to withhold funds from a junior college in one senator's district. As an added measure he tried to get the state supreme court to alter the number of votes needed to override a filibuster. When that failed, he turned to his public, concentrating on those counties which the opposing senators represented. In public speeches he held those individual senators up to ridicule in front of their constituents, but stopped suddenly when he saw that the technique was beginning to backfire into resentment. When the issue finally came to a vote, Wallace lost the succession issue by three votes (*New York Times* 1965).

The Election of Governor Lurleen Wallace

Shortly after the amendment failed, Wallace persuaded his wife, Lurleen, to run for the office of governor. Although she had recently had an operation for cancer and was still in fragile condition, she agreed. Frady

(1967, 1968) gives the best account of that campaign. Wallace was routinely introduced by Lurleen's short, toneless, uninteresting campaign speech, basically a pledge to continue four more years of George Wallace's leadership. This was followed by a long and dynamic Wallace campaign speech met with loud whistles, cheers, and applause (See also Jenkins 1966).

The campaign was a success. Lurleen Wallace won the Democratic primary over nine other candidates (Roberts 1966) and handily defeated her Goldwater-endorsed Republican opponent in November with sixty-five percent of the vote. In doing so, she helped Wallace pay off his old campaign debt; the Republicans lost all of the seats in the House which they had gained in 1964 (Reed 1966a). Further, all fourteen of the senators who had successfully opposed the earlier succession bill either lost their elections or had previously dropped out of their contests. In one stroke all of the opposition to the Wallace camp was eliminated.

Lurleen Wallace's election further entrenched Wallace's hold over the state. The original intent of the succession law had been to assure that one governor would not be able to control the various state boards and commissions (Reed 1966a). The positions on these boards and commissions had staggered terms. Thus if one person served two consecutive terms as governor, he would theoretically be able to stock the boards with his supporters, thereby assuring the continuation of his policies and minimizing his opposition. With Mrs. Wallace's election, Wallace was in a position to assure such loyalty. The relationship between the new governor and her number one advisor was that she "served as head of state while he acted as prime minister; she attended to the ceremonial functions, leaving him that much freer for his maneuverings" (Frady 1968, p. 200).

The Third-Party Candidacy

As early as July 1966, Wallace had been saying that he might run in 1968 as a third-party candidate (Broder 1966). In September (Reed 1966b) he said that he had no illusions that either of the two major parties might nominate him (Wallace 1974) and provided a simple formula which showed how he might win. Running as a third-party candidate, he could win all the electoral votes of a state simply by getting a plurality of the popular vote. Given enough states, he could conceivably win the presidency.

As soon as his wife took office as governor of Alabama, Wallace began to step up his candidacy for president. A few scattered Wallace-for-President headquarters opened in various states. Evidently the decision was made early not to run in the primaries, but to try instead to get on the ballot for the general election in some states (Weaver 1967c). This strategy had formidable implications, for while running in primaries is both expensive and time-consuming, achieving ballot position is even more so. Each state has its own rules for getting on the ballot; deadlines differ, as does the number of signatures required for a petition, ranging from 300 in Colorado and North Dakota, to 433,000 in Ohio (Chester, Hodgson and Page 1969, p. 284) and the amounts of time in which these signatures must be gathered vary tremendously from state to state. Simply getting correct information from the various state election boards is a difficult task.

The first state selected was California, ostensibly because it had the earliest deadline for qualifying a third party. It is not certain whether Wallace yet planned to run on a third-party ticket in every state. The California effort has all of the earmarks of an experiment, and as an experiment, it was one of the most difficult possible. In order to qualify as a third party in California, one percent of the number of people who voted for governor in the last election (66,059 in this case) had to register under the aegis of that party. Thus it was not the relatively simple matter of petition-signing; the number of people required actually had to go through the procedure of changing their registration affiliations from Democratic or Republican to that of the new party (Hill 1967). The Wallace people had decided to go for California partly because it was tough. "We knew if we could get on the ballot in California we could get on it almost anywhere," said one of Wallace's campaigners (quoted in Chester, Hodgson and Page 1969, p. 287).

A close look at the activity in California gives some idea of how the Wallace campaign for ballot positioning was waged in almost every state. The first contacts were gathered from the list of well-wishers which had been meticulously maintained since 1963. The "list" now had a total over 1.5 million names, those who had donated one dollar or more to the Wallace effort. Periodically they were asked for more in a direct mail campaign operated by Trammell (Franklin 1967a). Presumably others had written or called Wallace campaign headquarters in Montgomery and had expressed an interest in the candidate's running in California, and still other contacts had been made when Wallace had made speeches in the state. As 1968 approached, Wallace held private conferences with local supporters at almost every speaking stop. These meetings proposed and accomplished the organization of various fund-raising operations (Weaver 1967a), as well as expanded the list of contacts and possible workers. In June 1967, an American Independent Party headquarters was officially opened in California and was headed by William K. Shearer (Hill 1967), a local citizen and a writer of Citizens Council publications.

The California drive initially ran into some resistance. Many voters were reluctant to change their registrations; some seemed to hope that the

Republicans might nominate someone conservative. Wallace countered this with the argument that if the Republicans should nominate a liberal— it was assumed that the Democrats would do so—then the people would be left without a choice unless Wallace were on the ballot. Workers began to assure prospective party members that they could change their registration back to that of a major party the next year, and that registering with the American Independent Party (AIP) would not obligate them forever, but just permit Wallace to get on the ballot (Roberts 1967b, p. 40).

In November it became apparent that the California drive was in trouble. The Wallace campaign was still 50,000 short of the number of registered party members needed (Roberts 1967b). A massive offensive was immediately mounted in Alabama (Franklin 1967a). All of the key people from Montgomery went to California to throw their energies into the campaign.

During the month of December, Wallace held numerous rallies. All followed a prescribed format—a lively country music band would hold the crowd's attention while tens of registrars who had been bused to each rally enrolled voters for the new party. The candidate was deliberately late in arriving so as to allow enough time for the registration process (Wicker 1967). Other workers were able to get new adherents by knocking on doors and canvassing in shopping center parking lots and on city street corners. By the time of the deadline, Wallace's AIP had more than enough party members. The accomplishment of this nearly impossible feat so buoyed Wallace's spirits (Hill 1968) that the day after the qualifying date in California he announced that he expected to be on the ballot everywhere. He had, he said, set up headquarters in every state.

Most of the other ballot positioning efforts were accomplished relatively easily when compared to the difficulty in California. Only in Ohio did the effort demand more energy, as over 400,000 petition signatures had to be gathered. After the signatures were secured and filed, the secretary of state announced that they were void; the petitions had been filed too late. The Wallace people immediately initiated a suit to get on the ballot (*New York Times* 1968g), but a three-judge federal court refused to order Wallace's name placed on the ballot. They maintained that the AIP had the appearance of a fictional party organized from the top down, in contrast to a real party, which would have risen from the bottom up in search of a leader (Franklin 1968g). The fight was taken to the Supreme Court, which found the Ohio decision unconstitutional (Graham 1968), and Wallace's name was placed on the ballot.

After much effort, Wallace made ballot position in all fifty states, by any standards a remarkable achievement. Altogether, the Wallace campaign claimed they had collected a total of 2,717,338 signatures across the country (Chester, Hodgson and Page 1969, p. 285).

Wallace ran in 1968 as the candidate of the American Independent Party (it was called by six different names, including the Conservative Party in Kansas and the Courage Party in New York, because of different state statutes concerning the naming of such parties). But the AIP was not an integrated, functioning party; it existed only as a vehicle for Wallace's candidacy. He issued a platform only when it appeared that he had to for the sake of legitimacy (Reed 1968b), and he named an official vice-presidential candidate only when it became apparent that several states would not be able to list him on their ballots unless he had a running mate. As a Wallace aide said, "We didn't wind up with a national party.... we wound up with 50 state parties" (Rugaber 1968a).

This fragmentation was a natural consequence of the way that the Wallace people ran things. While each state had its own nominal head, Alabamians were essentially directing the campaign, and they maintained tight control.

The Wallace Campaign: An Alabama Organization

The Wallace campaign had the air of a small, personally-run business. The largest number of employees they ever had was 325 in 1968 (Dauphin 1974). Major personnel were trusted cronies, and almost everyone was a native Alabamian. In 1968 as in 1964, Seymore Trammell was the national campaign chairman and Cecil Jackson the national campaign director. Ed Ewing and Bill Jones were the national campaign coordinators (Chester, Hodgson and Page 1969, p. 659).

In every state, even if a group had spontaneously decided that they wanted Wallace represented on their state's ballot, the people from Montgomery came in to advise. Most of the footwork was done by five young lawyers, each of whom was in charge of twelve or thirteen states (Lamott 1968). The executive staff could be mobilized at a moment's notice, as could a cadre of Alabama students who were sent to help in states where drives were lagging (Fenton 1968a).

Many of the Wallace campaign workers were on the Alabama state payroll (Franklin 1968i). A few of these were removed from the state's rolls when Wallace announced his presidential candidacy, but most remained Alabama employees, and with Wallace's wife as governor, this fact was not mentioned. After Lurleen Wallace died in May 1968, Governor Brewer, her successor, continued the practice without complaint. When questioned in September 1968, Wallace admitted that seven Alabama state troopers who worked for Wallace full-time and three Wallace airplane pilots were still on the state payroll (Reed 1968f). He said that he would repay the state for their services, but it was October before anyone really tried to stop him. At that time Alabama State Representative Bryce Graham filed suit asking for an injunction forbidding Wallace's use of state money, property, or employees in his campaign (*New York Times* 1968b).

Wallace's choice of personnel is illuminating. Both Charles Snider and Michael Griffin, senior people on Wallace's 1972 and 1976 campaign staffs, started their careers in the 1968 campaign. Griffin was a college student in 1968, and presumably part of the Wallace student cadres. In 1972 and 1976 he was in charge of ballot positioning (Griffin 1974, 1978). Snider's history is also revealing. He told the author that he had been an Air Force pilot in the late 1950s and had become a contractor in Alabama after he got out of the service. One night in 1968 his telephone rang and the person calling asked, "Charlie, do you still know how to fly a plane?" Snider answered, "Yeah, sure," and the man said, "Well, get down here to the airport right away. The pilot has the flu and the governor has to be in Wisconsin first thing in the morning." Snider got out of bed, flew the Wallace entourage around for several weeks and had been with the Wallace campaign ever since (Snider 1974). By 1972 he had become the campaign manager for the Wallace forces; he also held that position in the 1976 campaign.

The personalities of the personnel in the Wallace organization are also notable. While very pleasant, they are relatively colorless personalities (with the exception of Joe Azbell, who only functions behind the scenes, and Mickey Griffin, who came into his own in the 1976 campaign), and they were apparently selected for these qualities. Mark Bablin, the New York-New Jersey-Pennsylvania Coordinator for the 1976 Wallace campaign, said in an interview (Bablin 1975), "I just had to get rid of the New Jersey chairman; he had too many ideas of his own. He wanted to take over." Bablin went on to explain that they had to be very careful about the kinds of people they put into leadership positions. "Wallace doesn't like anyone to outshine him; he wants to be the only star." Bablin also said that he was closely supervised by Montgomery. While he made some decisions, such as where to concentrate his efforts, he stayed in close touch by telephone and met often with Alton Dauphin, Wallace's brother-in-law, the campaign's finance director. (Bablin subsequently got into trouble with the Wallace campaign.)

This choice of personnel assured Wallace's remaining in the top spot. It also had another consequence; there was no mechanism for succession. If Wallace had died, there would simply have been no replacement (a point drastically demonstrated by Schmitz's AIP candidacy in 1972). No one was groomed for the job or even allowed to approach it; anyone who showed any such desire was fired.

The staff was carefully chosen and closely controlled. Further, only trusted Alabamians could occupy strategic positions. Outsiders were allowed in only when absolutely essential, and then used solely as figureheads.

Local coordinators had no power in the Wallace organization; they were charged with little responsibility (Lamott 1968). They ran their operations out of storefronts centered in small towns or the suburbs. Many centers were also located in white residential working-class neighborhoods (Borders 1968). These people had to buy their campaign materials through Wallace headquarters, and the monies from sales and contributions received were forwarded directly to Montgomery (Chester, Hodgson and Page 1969, p. 664). Money to accomplish ballot positioning was then parceled out to the various state organizations according to strategic decisions made by the Alabamians.

There was another aspect to the control radiating from Montgomery. The American Independent Party attracted many varieties of people who were essentially political dissidents. Wallace and his stance seemed to be a rallying point for many of the right-wing groups these people represented, and the formation of the new party brought these groups out of obscurity. Their members joined, contributed and worked for the AIP, and Wallace welcomed their help (*New York Times* 1967a). Azbell (1974a) said that Wallace and his staff thought that these people were "kooks" and tried to keep them in line without offending them or letting it be known to the general public that they were there. This was not easy, for noticeable among the key persons in local headquarters were a former member of the American Nazi Party (*New York Times* 1967b), members of the John Birch Society (Weaver 1967) and the Ku Klux Klan (Franklin 1967b). The evidence was that Wallace had been a friend of these and other right-wing groups for some time (Greenhaw 1976, pp. 150-163; Dorman 1976, pp. 80-92). However, any open acknowledgment would have been politically unwise. Wallace's stated public position was that he would accept the support of everybody who believed what he believed; he didn't care what their other affiliations were.

Sometimes this policy created awkward situations. The press and the Anti-Defamation League were watching Wallace very closely. There was one incident in which an ABC cameraman happened to be shooting when Robert Shelton, the Imperial Wizard of the United Klans of America, shook Wallace's hand in a receiving line at a fund-raising dinner. The film was immediately seized and destroyed by one of Wallace's bodyguards (Adams 1968). There were also fights among various factions in California, Texas, and South Carolina, but Wallace was able to temper these by giving his "official" sanction to one group rather than to another.

Although he could not control those who wanted to support him,

Wallace could keep them from being noticeably and officially affiliated with him by the simple declaration that he would be the only AIP candidate. Since the Alabamian controlled the money and the manpower, he was also able to make certain that no one else was allowed to run on his ticket at the local and state levels, in all except one state—Oklahoma— where he had to make a compromise in order to get on the ballot.[1] Thus, Wallace was able to keep his image relatively straight and not hamper himself with the responsibility for anyone else.

As in every campaign, finances were of crucial importance. For the 1968 effort Trammell had come up with the idea of using pledge cards. Essentially, a supporter would pledge an amount which he wanted to contribute and be billed for it monthly (Rugaber 1967). Delinquent accounts would be pressed to pay up. By February 1968 there were over 21,500 subscribers to the pledge system (Franklin 1968i). Those who did not have much money could give their time to fund raising. The idea was to spend ten to fourteen hours a week getting pledges totaling $100 (Rugaber 1968c), or one could decide to try for an average contribution of ten dollars from a minimum of eighty-five families (Fenton 1968b).

When Wallace was on the campaign circuit, he would spend lunches and afternoons meeting privately with wealthy citizens (Rugaber 1968c), but this did not prove very productive. Twenty-five-dollar-a-plate dinners were much more successful. They were held at 6:00 p.m. every evening (occasionally there were $100-a-plate dinners; there was even one $1000-a-plate affair). The dinners were usually followed by a rally, in which fund raising was built into their very structure (Chester, Hodgson and Page 1969, p. 667). Wallace girls passed yellow plastic buckets regularly; continuous pitches were made about the need for money, and campaign items and souvenirs were sold rather than given away. All of these ideas worked well. From February 1968 to October 1968, the official financial statement showed the total income had amounted to at least 6.2 million dollars (Shanahan 1968). And with total expenditures running at 5.8 million dollars, the campaign could be termed a financial money-maker.

On the Road

There were the usual campaign expenses. Most of the expenditures for publicity went toward producing videotapes for television (Franklin 1968k). But Wallace was able to generate his own publicity mechanisms largely for free. Twenty-five to thirty advance men—businessmen and lawyers from Alabama—were in various cities at all times (Reed 1968h). Their tasks were to publicize upcoming visits by the candidate and to work to get out the crowds. When the candidate arrived, there were televised airport news conferences (Frankel 1968c) which provided a maximum of self-promotion and necessitated a minimum of paid advertising. Wallace also made use of television talk shows, appearances with disc jockeys, and spots on dial-a-question radio shows (Roberts 1967c). He was also continually invited to speak before business and professional clubs (Roberts 1967a). Wallace was very much in demand, often as a curiosity. And he exploited that curiosity to the fullest, gaining extensive publicity for himself.

The rallies were very carefully orchestrated. In 1964, when Wallace had depended mainly on the entertainment provided by country music bands and the power of his own oratory, he had still had quite an effect. Pete Mathews, a former Alabama state representative who accompanied Wallace on many of his 1964 excursions, said that he would sometimes get frightened watching a crowd respond to Wallace. For the candidate could draw them into a "frenzy that seemed about to break into a riot at any moment" (Mathews 1974).

By 1968, Wallace had developed that technique to perfection. Essential to his performance was the presence of hecklers. An account of the baiting of them is revealing in this description:

> As usual, Mr. Wallace used the disruption effectively. By skillful manipula-
> tion of the hecklers, he roused his own supporters in the auditorium,
> estimated at 5,000 persons, from a state of moderate interest to one of real
> enthusiasm. Then he taunted the hecklers and, when he had urged them into a
> near-frenzy of noise, jumping and fist-shaking, he invited the television
> cameramen to record them. . . . Hecklers have become so important to Mr.
> Wallace's set performance that, when too few appear or when they make too
> little noise to be disruptive, he frequently interrupts his speech and eggs them
> on. (Reed 1968d)

At times the audience and the hecklers were turned on each other. Wallace's technique was to "drive it along to build up the tension, until violence became all but inevitable" (Chester, Hodgson and Page 1969, p. 756). He would hold the violence just below eruption with his use of humor (Reed 1968g). It was very skillfully done, and a rally was a very involving experience for those present. It was essentially an emotional release, and it gave people the illusion of having participated in something very important. At the same time, Wallace managed to come across as a brave man. (See Crass 1976, ch. 1 for an account of Wallace's Madison Square Garden appearance.)

By 1968, Wallace had also perfected a stance which further endeared him to his followers: he seemed to know their deepest concerns. While this quality has always seemed mystical to many of those who have known him

(Frady 1968; Howard 1974; Pirtle 1974; Azbell 1978), it is actually the result of conscious experimentation coupled with his skillful use of available sources of information. Kendall (1974) said that Wallace "has a special knack of adjusting to the feel of a crowd as he is speaking. He modifies his speeches according to the reaction he senses." Mathews's comment was that "George is able to convince people that they believe what he believes" (Mathews 1974).

What Wallace presents as his beliefs before any particular audience is geared to what he knows about them. In 1964 local policemen served as a main source of information about people and problems in a particular community. Both Wallace and the workers who briefed him spent a great deal of time gathering this kind of intelligence. When a speech was delivered, Wallace knew exactly whom he was talking to and what they were worried about. It is not surprising that so many people felt that there was a mystical connection between audience and speaker, and that he inspired such devotion. Wallace made them feel visible and important; they knew he was their champion, and that he would tell the government in Washington that they didn't like the way they were being treated.

Throwing the Election into the House

Wallace had only one goal in 1968—to get on the ballot as a presidential candidate. The real target would be the campaign of 1972 (Chester, Hodgson and Page 1969, p. 657; Reed 1968a; Franklin 1968b). Thus the strategy for 1968 seems to have been to broaden his exposure so that both he and his positions would be well known to the voters by the time of the next campaign. But in late August and September it began to look as though there might be a possibility of victory (Chester, Hodgson and Page 1968, p. 651). Wallace's support on the Gallup Poll was at twenty-one percent, and his advisors claimed that he would win seventeen southern and border states plus Ohio, which would give him an electoral vote count only sixty-seven short of the 270 needed to win (Reed 1968f).

The possibility of being a spoiler does not seem to have occurred to Wallace at first. In February 1968, Wallace mentioned publicly for the first time that he might be able to deny both candidates a majority in the electoral college (Franklin 1968j). This would not be for the purpose of winning, but to force them to bargain with him. He envisioned some concessions, and was not interested in being consulted about the Supreme Court. Others, newsmen and politicians, discussed the possibility of the election being thrown into the House; Wallace mentions only that he expected to get concessions before that would happen (Chester, Hodgson and Page 1969, pp. 657-658). In order to assure having bargaining power to make good his threat to ask for concessions should the opportunity arise, he "obtained notarized affidavits from all of his electors in every state that they will vote for him or for the candidate for president for whom he may direct them to cast their vote" (Franklin 1968b).

While throwing the election into the House does not seem to have been his real intent, it is evident that Wallace delighted in the havoc created by the possibility. Both major parties were very upset at what a sizeable third party vote might mean. Several well-meaning persons—Professor Orfield and Congressmen Goodell and Udall (Weaver 1968, *New York Times* 1968a)—came up with ideas that might have provided an acceptable solution in that eventuality.

Chester, Hodgson and Page note (1969, p. 656) that

> ... these improvised stop-Wallace schemes were based on two premises: first that Wallace was a uniquely wicked fellow and his doctrines so intolerable that he deserved to be singled out for a unique exclusion from the constitutional/political process; and second, that the fundamental law of the Constitution is that the will of a majority, even of a plurality must triumph— so that where, through an oversight, a conflict might appear between the letter of the Constitution and this fundamental law, the Constitution must give way.

But there is evidence that such proposals would have played right into Wallace's hands. As Tom Wicker (1968) pointed out:

> ... those who fear George Wallace the most should fight this plan the hardest, for he is a veritable artist of defiance, a virtuoso of defeat, who has found his greatest strength in picturing himself as the little man run down in the schoolhouse door, the "average American" ignored by the "pseudo-intellectuals" controlling the major parties. Any such plan aimed at Wallace, or even based on his presence in the race, will prove to be his meat and potatoes. By the time he gets through picturing himself as the down-trodden victim of the political establishment—which is in bad enough odor with all too many voters—he may well add millions to his total next November.

Playing Politics with Major Party Candidates

In 1968, Lyndon Johnson was serving his last year in office. In an early attempt to attract Wallace voters, he had sent Vice President Humphrey in May 1967 to visit Lester Maddox, then governor of Georgia. Humphrey had posed arm in arm with Maddox and assured all that there was plenty of room in the Democratic party for a great variety of views, including Maddox's segregationist views (Weaver 1967b). Sometime later, after the 1968 campaign was in full swing, Republican presidential candidate Richard Nixon's southern campaign director, Bo Callaway, suggested that

Wallace become a Republican. Nelson Rockefeller demanded immediately that Nixon repudiate the statement (Apple 1968). In answer, Nixon quietly said that Mr. Callaway had been misinterpreted (Semple 1968d). "What he was trying to say," said Nixon, "was that people who want a change in the United States should not waste their vote on a third party." Mr. Callaway, he assured, was "urging them that if they were against the politics of the present administration, and wanted a change, to support the party that offers change."

Both major party candidates were caught in a dilemma. The American Independent Party was a serious threat. Each candidate needed the Wallace vote to win, but neither wanted to appeal directly to what they thought was the basis of that vote: racial hatred. Manifest appeals were politically too dangerous. Each accused the other of trying to get the Wallace vote while courting it himself.

Democratic presidential candidate Hubert Humphrey would lose the most if he went after the Wallace vote overtly; any attempt to do so would cast aspersions on his liberal civil rights record (Chester, Hodgson and Page 1968, p. 553). So Humphrey simply suggested that Nixon and Wallace were collaborating to take votes away from him and generally stayed away from the South.

Nixon's response was much more calculated. His political strategy was apparent in his courting of the South. He first named Strom Thurmond as an advisor (Chester, Hodgson and Page 1969, p. 447), assuring him that he would take his interests to heart. Thurmond worked very hard, and Nixon appeared to consult with him on many things and to take his advice on how to approach the southern delegations. Accounts of a meeting with delegates at the convention (Chester, Hodgson and Page 1969, pp. 462-63; Herbers 1968) show that Nixon very skillfully led the southerners to think that he shared many of their positions, but had been forced by considerations of expediency (to help the Republicans beat the Democrats) to endorse certain stands to which he had been personally opposed—open housing legislation, for instance. He also convinced them that he shared their positions on the courts and on busing.

Unabashedly, Wallace claimed that he had influenced the selection of Spiro Agnew as Nixon's running mate (Franklin 1968h). He was not alone in thinking this; *New York Times* columnist James Reston mused aloud that it seemed that Agnew might have been chosen to cover the Wallace dissident elements (Reston 1968). Larry O'Brien, the Democratic National Chairman, said that Agnew had apparently been charged with the task of showing Wallace supporters that they could feel comfortable with the Nixon-Agnew ticket (Phelps 1968).

In the meantime Nixon was speaking about the "forgotten American"

(Semple 1968c). Humphrey retorted that Nixon and Wallace were in competition against him. They were trying to exploit fear aroused by the issue of human rights. He angrily accused Nixon of joining forces with the most reactionary elements in American society (Frankel 1968b). In turn, Wallace said that Nixon was trying to cut into his movement and reminded his followers that Nixon had been involved in Little Rock (Franklin 1968f).

Nixon then reported that he had received information about a collusion between Humphrey and Wallace designed to deny him votes. This was interpreted by the press as a move to counteract the suggestion from Humphrey that Nixon had been appealing to racist instincts (Semple 1968b).

In general, Nixon tried to appear as if he were ignoring Wallace (Bigart 1968). He did not want to grant him any legitimacy, and he refused to debate Wallace and Humphrey on television (Semple 1968a). Agnew, for his part, urged Wallace supporters to vote Republican and make their votes count (Franklin 1968d). The idea seems to have been to point out the absurdity of the idea of an effectual third party, so the "wasted vote" was mentioned many times (Chester, Hodgson and Page 1969, p. 626).

There was some evidence of at least one "dirty trick." AP and UPI reported that they had received a counterfeit press release. It was printed on the Democratic National Committee letterhead and announced that Humphrey and Wallace would "meet on law and order" (*New York Times* 1968e).

Another of Nixon's strategies was to chip away slowly at Wallace without criticizing him directly. Nixon apparently did not want to denounce Wallace outright for fear of alienating Wallace's supporters. He carefully said that Wallace had some good ideas, but that he did not have the kind of experience that Nixon had had, experience really necessary for a president, particularly in the field of foreign affairs (Kenworthy 1968).

Wallace had also realized that foreign policy was a weak spot. He began to mention ideas much more frequently in his speeches (Reed 1968e) and eventually set forth a series of foreign policy statements in a speech to the National Press Club (Reed 1968c).

In attempts to promote the legitimacy of his third party, Wallace issued a platform (Reed 1968b) and began the process of choosing a vice-presidential candidate to replace Marvin Griffin, the former governor of Georgia who had been a stand-in to meet some ballot positioning requirements. His first choice was said to have been John Connally (Chester, Hodgson and Page 1969, p. 694), but Connally was not interested. Wallace needed someone who would give the ticket a broader appeal, and said that he wanted a man with the qualities of J. Edgar Hoover (Reed 1968f). Chester, Hodgson, and Page (1969) say that Wallace actually wanted Hoover, but got no response. The subsequent choice was Happy Chandler, the former governor of Kentucky, but the AIP people from Kentucky thought that Chandler was too liberal on the race issue and resigned in protest at the last minute (Chester, Hodgson and Page 1969, p. 697). Trammell was charged with the responsibility of settling matters and visited Chandler to cancel the arrangement. Chandler was given a vague excuse, and Wallace finally announced his choice a few weeks later; it was Curtis Le May.

From the moment of the announcement it was apparent that deciding on the former Air Force chief of staff had been a mistake (Rugaber 1968b). Wallace had expected Le May to let him do the talking, but it didn't happen that way. Le May dropped a bomb when he said that he would not hesitate to use nuclear weapons if the situation called for it, and the press exploded. There is the reported picture of Wallace anxiously tugging at his vice-presidential candidate's sleeve at the press conference of the announcement, trying his best to get him to stop talking (Franklin 1968c). But Le May would not stop, and his elaborations on his original remarks made things even worse. It was an issue made for the competition.

Both Humphrey and Nixon immediately seized at Le May's remarks (Franklin 1968e). Humphrey tried to associate Wallace and Le May with the spectre of nuclear war (*New York Times* 1968d). Not long after that, Wallace sent Le May on a fact-finding mission to Vietnam (Waldron 1968), presumably to get him out of the country and away from the candidate, but it was to no avail. Wallace's hold on the polls had begun to slip. Chester, Hodgson, and Page (1969, p. 702) say only that with the Le May press conference Wallace's fortunes began to dwindle. They do not impute causality, but point out that the coincidental anti-Wallace campaign waged by the unions also came to full flower around that time (1969, p. 707-709).

The leadership of the unions had been greatly disturbed by the rank-and-file support for Wallace. Numerous polls taken in automobile plants and other union shops had shown Wallace the winner; a few unions had even endorsed him outright. In response, union leadership had taken action by waging an all-out informational campaign to enlighten the workers (Loftus 1968; *New York Times* 1968c). Materials were distributed comparing the plight of the working man in Alabama with that of the working man in the North (Reed 1968h). "Missionaries" were used; they organized rallies and used anti-Wallace radio appeals (*New York Times* 1968f). Anti-Wallace rallies were even held in some cities (Schanberg 1968), and Walter Reuther denounced Wallace as a police-state candidate (Flint 1968).

When it was all over, the election had been amazingly close. Nixon had won by a very narrow margin, and Wallace had come close to denying victory to either candidate. He received a total of 9,291,807 votes, 13.3

percent of the total cast, and carried five states (Arkansas, Louisiana, Mississippi, Alabama, Georgia) with forty-five electoral votes (Frankel 1968a). Wallace claimed that he had gotten what he had been after. Nixon had been forced to the right (Frankel 1968a), and Wallace said that he was responsible.

Note

1. The American Party ticket in the Oklahoma presidential primary of August 27, 1968, had the following candidates: President, George Wallace; Vice-President, Marvin Griffin; United States Senators, George Washington and Landis B. Hiniker (Scammon 1970, p. 319).

Chapter Eight

Wallace Support in 1968:
From Southern to National Politics

Because 1968 is the only general election in which Wallace actually ran on the presidential ticket, it allows the most thorough look at voting data on Wallace.

As candidate of the American Independent Party, George Wallace strikes an alternative note to regular party politics. His political positions are sometimes conservative, sometimes liberal. Where Wallace differs most from the others, Republican Nixon and Democrat Humphrey, is in his racial myopia and his vehement criticism of the growing power of the federal government in its moves toward integration.

As expected we will find that Wallace voters mirror their candidate on the issues. The picture which emerges, however, is one in which Wallace voters are shown as not very different from the voters for other candidates on measures used traditionally to explain voting behavior. In fact, they are solidly in the middle between voters for the other candidates on most of the measures which would be expected to show differences.

In this chapter we will look at factors mentioned in the literature as important in voting, at attitudes which might be expected to show differences, and at the theories of the marginal voter and the authoritarian personality. The data also allow for complete and thorough testing of the theories of status politics as well as a systematic look at the politics of powerlessness. It is this latter group of theories which most distinguishes Wallace voters from other voters.

Complete data is available for 1027 voters in the Michigan Survey Research Center's 1968 American National Election Study: 47.7 percent

(490) voted for Nixon; 41.0 percent (421) voted for Humphrey; and 11.3 percent (116) voted for Wallace.

In the first part of the chapter we will examine demographic variables which distinguish Wallace voters from other voters, as well as those which lay important misconceptions to rest (see Table 8.1).

Demographics

As was found in 1964, in 1968 practically no blacks support Wallace. Few blacks support Nixon, either. Humphrey's black support, by contrast, constitutes twenty percent of his total vote.

Wallace voters are also distinguished from others by the presence of proportionately more males (57.9%) among their ranks. This figure is not only different from those in the other groups (+14.2% from the nearest group), but it is also distinct from the distribution of sex in the general population.

Age distribution, by contrast, differs little among the candidate groups. An examination of the data quickly deflates the contention that young people voted disproportionately for Wallace (Lipset and Raab 1970, p. 367), for ages 21–24 constitute almost equal percentages (ranging between 5.3% and 6.1%) in each voter group.

Party affiliation differs from 1964. Far more people in each voter group now declare themselves Independents. (This declaration does not represent affiliation with the American Independent Party, but the historical designation of oneself as Independent). Independents make up 40.4 percent of Wallace voters, compared to 32.5 percent of Nixon voters and 17.5 percent of those who voted for Humphrey. As expected, a majority (50.8%) of Nixon voters say that they are Republicans, and a much larger majority (78.0%) of Humphrey voters declare themselves Democrats. The proportions of Democrats (46.5%) and Independents (40.4%) among Wallace voters are similar, and 13.3 percent of Wallace supporters call themselves Republicans.

Region is also a factor which distinguishes Wallace voters from others in 1968. More than half of the Wallace vote (twice the proportion in the other two groups) comes from the South, and one-quarter of it is from the Midwest. Approximately one-third of both Nixon and Humphrey voters are from the Midwest.

Viewing region from yet another perspective, McEvoy (1971) and Lipset and Raab (1970) mention the importance of having been brought up in the South as a factor in Wallace voting outside of the South. A comparison of those whose childhood residences were in the South and who have since moved out of that region show that while those who have left the South constitute a greater proportion of the Wallace vote (45.4%) than those from other regions, a similar proportion of Humphrey voters (46.4%) have the same history.

The question, "In what type of locality were you raised?", reflective of size of place, shows some distinctions. Wallace voters are more likely to have come from farm or rural backgrounds than other voters—42.9 percent as compared to 30.9 percent of the Nixon voters and 23.4 percent of those who voted for Humphrey. Looking at those who presently live on farms, slightly larger proportions of Wallace voters are either farmers or live on farms than those in the other two groups, but the differences by percentage are not significant.

Another measure of type of place where one lives involves a calculation of the distance from the place where one was interviewed (not necessarily the voter's residence, but usually close to it) to the central city of the nearest SMSA (census designation for Standard Metropolitan Statistical Area). The data show that Wallace voters tend to live further from major population centers than do other voters. Those who live at least one hundred miles from the central city of the nearest SMSA make up 41.2 percent of the Wallace voters, 22.1 percent of those who voted for Nixon and 17.2 percent of Humphrey voters. Thus it appears that spatial isolation as well as farm or rural background continue to play a part in voting and attitudinal patterns, as both Campbell, et al. (1960) and Stouffer (1963) have suggested.

To summarize, sex, party affiliation, and region of residence all serve to distinguish Wallace voters from others. Wallace voters also grew up in more rural localities and presently live in more isolated places than do voters for other candidates in 1968.

Attitudes

In this next section we will examine various attitudes, aside from those which fit into the specific theories of interest, that serve to distinguish Wallace voters from other voters in the 1968 election. Such comparisons not only enable us to see exactly how conservative these voters are in relation to others but also provide an opportunity to check the degree of agreement with their candidates' various positions. We will start with general attitudes and move toward attitudes which reflect foreign and domestic policy positions.

Religion

Statistics which indicate the nature of religious feelings provide interesting and valuable insight into the differences among voter groups. Wallace

TABLE 8.1
Selected Demographic Characteristics*

	Nixon	Humphrey	Wallace
Race			
White	98.4	79.3	99.1
Black	0.6	20.0	0.0
Other	1.0	0.7	0.9
Sex			
Male	43.7	41.9	57.9
Female	56.3	58.1	42.1
Age			
21-24	6.1	5.7	5.3
25-44	37.1	44.2	43.9
45-59	32.3	27.7	35.0
60 and over	24.6	22.4	15.8
Party Affiliation			
Republican	50.8	4.5	13.1
Democratic	16.7	78.0	46.5
Independent	32.5	17.5	40.4
Region			
Northeast	25.3	28.1	9.6
Midwest	33.7	31.9	25.5
South	22.0	26.0	56.1
Far West	19.0	14.0	8.8
Region of Childhood of			
Those Who Moved Out			
Northeast	24.7	20.3	18.2
Midwest	45.2	31.9	27.4
South	23.3	46.4	45.4
Far West	6.8	1.4	9.0
Type of Place Where			
Voter Grew Up			
Farm, rural	30.9	23.4	42.9
Small town	27.9	30.9	25.9
Small city	16.2	17.0	9.8
Large city	23.6	27.5	19.6
Mixed type	0.4	0.7	0.9
Suburb	1.0	0.5	0.9

Table 8.1 (Continued)

	Nixon	Humphrey	Wallace
Distance From Place of Interview to Central City of Nearest SMSA			
Lives in SMSA	43.3	52.6	31.6
15-24.9 miles	2.0	2.6	0.0
25-49.9 miles	5.5	6.4	7.9
50-99.9 miles	27.1	20.7	19.3
100-199.9 miles	18.2	14.8	33.3
200-399.9 miles	3.9	2.9	7.9

*Percentages add vertically by columns to 100 percent, except for rounding errors.

voters are less likely to be frequent churchgoers than are those in other groups; 57.6 percent of them say that they seldom or never attend church, as compared to 40.1 percent of the Nixon voters and 38.5 percent of Humphrey voters.

When it comes to fundamentalist religious beliefs, however, a majority of both Wallace (60.9%) and Humphrey voters (54.1%) say that they believe that everything in the Bible is true. Nixon voters are a bit more skeptical: less than half (47.8%) of them believe that everything in the Bible is true. Holding region constant, we find that Humphrey and Wallace voters who express the most fundamentalist belief are disproportionately from the South.

Religious beliefs, however, are generally strong throughout the United States. Looking again at feelings about the Bible, we can surmise that the following percentages of each voting group indicate a belief in God (tallying the answer "the Bible is God's word and everything in it is true" and the answer "the Bible was inspired by God but written by man"): Humphrey 91.6 percent, Nixon 94.3 percent, and Wallace 97.3 percent. Thus, it is not surprising to also see high proportions in each voter group who think that prayer should be allowed in the public schools; fully 89.0 percent of Wallace voters, 80.5 percent of Humphrey voters and 80.4 percent of Nixon voters take this stance.

The fact remains that Wallace voters' religious attitudes do not differ remarkably from the religious attitudes of the voters. They do, however, attend church less often.

Economics

The role of economics in voting decisions is also of interest (Sindler 1963, p. 175; Campbell, et al. 1964). When asked, "How is your family getting along financially compared to a year ago?" there are no differences among the voter groups in percentages answering better, the same, or worse. Both Humphrey and Wallace voters demonstrate more of a general concern for the country's future economic security than do Nixon voters, however. Although it is not the view of the majority, Wallace voters (37.7%) tend to demonstrate slightly more pessimism about future national financial affairs than do Humphrey voters (29.9%) or Nixon voters (14.2%), saying that they see bad times ahead for business conditions in this country. Although not a large factor, negative evaluations of future business conditions seems to be a persistent stand among Wallace voters regardless of their own objective financial situations.

Ideology

Looking at factors which fit into traditional liberal/conservative categories gives us some insight into what could be termed the political ideology of Wallace voters. Although there is no self-identification question about one's own politics on this schedule, scales measuring attitudes toward liberals and conservatives reveal some information. On an attitude scale, respondents are asked to rate their feelings about specific persons or groups of persons on a scale from zero to one hundred (fifty represents neutral; numbers below that indicate progressively cooler feelings and numbers above progressively warmer). Mean scores by voter group give an indication of how voters feel.

Comparing mean scores on the scale measuring sentiment toward liberals and conservatives, Humphrey voters show the least difference in their mean scores and Nixon voters show the most difference; as might be expected, Nixon voters have warmer feelings for conservatives (59.87) than they do for liberals (47.33), while Humphrey voters feel warmer about liberals (54.42) and somewhat neutral about conservatives (51.92). Wallace voters show dislike for liberals (42.45), but are relatively neutral about conservatives (52.77). It is clear from this that Wallace voters do not particularly identify with conservatives, at least not to the extent that Nixon voters do.

What about attitudes which would confirm these ideological positions? In general, Wallace voters' views are somewhat surprising. On attitude scores for big business, the mean of Wallace voters' answers (55.55) does not differ very much from that of Humphrey voters (55.53). Nixon voters are more positive toward big business, with a mean score of 59.80. On feelings for labor unions, Wallace voters are neutral (50.24) and more like Nixon voters (48.14) than Humphrey voters (56.84).

Other attitudes also give clues to ideological position (see Table 8.2). While the query, "Should the federal government help people get doctors and hospital care at low cost?" does not approach the question of socialized medicine, the answers do show that Wallace voters are proportionately more liberal in this area than are Nixon voters (48.2% to 35.1% saying yes), but less so than Humphrey voters (67.6% saying yes).

Answers to the question, "Should the federal government see to it that every person has a job and a good standard of living?" show the majority in all three groups registering disagreement. Wallace voters tend to be slightly more liberal than Nixon voters (27.2% to 19.8% saying yes), but less so than Humphrey voters (41.5% saying yes). Obviously, the Protestant Ethic still flourishes in the United States.

On domestic issues it appears that Wallace voters are more liberal than Nixon voters and more conservative than Humphrey voters. On some measures they are closer to one or the other group, but they never leave the middle.

Foreign Policy

Questions dealing with foreign policy (see Table 8.3) present a different perspective. In answering "Should the United States give aid to other countries?" a larger proportion of Wallace voters (43.4% as compared to 26.9% of the Nixon voters and 23.1% of the Humphrey voters) reflect the most conservative position. The presence of this type of sentiment among Wallace voters is further confirmed when we note that 31.7 percent agree with the statement, "This country would be better off if we just stayed home and didn't concern ourselves with problems in other parts of the world." Comparable figures for Nixon and Humphrey voters are 21.4 percent and 16.8 percent respectively. Thus Wallace voters are more likely to reflect the isolationist attitude than are other voters, although this position is not represented in the majority of any of the groups.

Wallace voters are also slightly more likely to take a hard line with Communists, although the majority of each group want some sort of settlement to take place. A large proportion of all three groups have a firm objection to admitting Communist China to the United Nations, Wallace voters being slightly more adamant than the others; 67.2 percent of them say that Communist China should not be admitted to the United Nations, compared to 60.7 percent of Nixon voters and 50.8 percent of Humphrey voters.

On the question of Vietnam, a major issue in the 1968 campaign, Wallace

TABLE 8.2
Selected Domestic Policy Issues

	Nixon	Humphrey	Wallace
"Should the government in Washington see to it that every person has a job and a good standard of living?"			
Don't know, no interest	8.6	9.1	8.7
Government should assure	19.8	41.5	27.2
Both checked	13.1	11.2	13.2
Each person should get ahead on his own	58.5	38.2	50.9
	100.0%	100.0%	100.0%

voters reflect the somewhat contradictory positions of the candidate. A majority (64.2%) feel that we should have stayed out of Vietnam, more so than Nixon voters (61.7%) or Humphrey voters (55.2%). But when it comes to the question, "Which of the following do you think we should do now in Vietnam?" Wallace voters, despite feeling that the United States should have stayed out of Vietnam, want now to take a stronger stand, even if it means invading North Vietnam. A majority of 67.1 percent feel that a stronger stance is necessary. Only a minority of Nixon voters (40.5%) share this more adamant position, and less than one-fifth of Humphrey voters (28.1%) concur.

The attitudes of the voters on this last question are generally in agreement with the attitudes of their candidates. When all foreign policy questions are taken into consideration, we find that Wallace voters tend to have more conservative attitudes than do other voters on practically every issue on foreign policy.

Other Issues in 1968

Moving from foreign policy towards other specific issues of the 1968 campaign, we find a lot of animosity for Vietnam war protestors in all voter groups, but especially among Wallace voters. Means on the attitude scale for Vietnam war protestors run a low of 14.72 among Wallace voters, and are only slightly more positive for Nixon voters (24.09) and Humphrey voters (27.54).

The issue of law and order, also important in 1968, includes two facets. One covers the activities of war protestors. Another is urban unrest, which, in many people's minds, is connected to the civil rights movement. Both the civil rights movement and antiwar protestors used many of the same

TABLE 8.3
Selected Foreign Policy Issues*

	Nixon	Humphrey	Wallace
"Should the United States give aid to other countries?"			
Don't know, no interest	9.3	8.6	7.1
Yes, give aid	42.0	49.0	26.5
Both checked	21.8	19.3	23.0
Each country should make own way	26.9	23.1	43.4
"Do you think we did the right thing in getting into the fighting in Vietnam, or should we have stayed out?"			
Did right thing	36.6	43.1	31.5
Both checked	1.7	1.7	4.3
Stayed out	61.7	55.2	64.2
"What do you think we should do now in Vietnam?"			
Pull out	20.0	21.9	13.8
Stay, try to end	39.5	50.0	19.1
Stronger stand	40.5	28.1	67.1

*Percentages add vertically by columns to 100 percent, except for rounding errors.

tactics, and while questions about such tactics do not distinguish among those who use them, they undoubtedly reflect attitudes toward law and order. As such, they serve to distinguish Wallace voters from others (see Table 8.4).

In response to the question "Do you approve of taking part in protest marches, provided they are permitted by local authorities?" larger proportions of Wallace voters disapprove than do those who voted for other candidates (71.2% compared to 54.0% of Nixon voters and 45.3% of Humphrey voters). A question dealing with civil disobedience, "refusing to obey a law which one feels is unjust rather than obey," also shows higher proportions of Wallace voters disapproving. There is not much difference, however, between the proportions of Nixon voters (64.0%) and Wallace voters (67.3%) who disapprove. And only slightly fewer Humphrey voters (59.3%) disapprove of the idea of civil disobedience.

Sit-ins, mass meetings, and demonstrations as a means of stopping the government seem to engender the most disapproval. Again, Wallace voters are proportionately more adamant when asked about this tactic (83.5% disapprove). Also disapproving are 77.5 percent of Nixon voters and 67.7 percent of Humphrey voters.

In each of the questions involving tactics, Wallace voters constitute the largest percentage of those disapproving, followed by Nixon voters. Humphrey voters are more lenient than the other two groups, but all voters are most adamant about sit-ins or mass demonstrations. For Wallace voters, civil disobedience (refusing to obey a law which one feels is unjust) is less important than is taking part in protest marches. The reverse is true for the other two groups.

Racial Attitudes

As in 1964, racial politics continues to play a part in Wallace's 1968 campaign, even though the issue is generally not verbalized. The clearest evidence of its continued importance is found in a comparison of the racial attitudes of Wallace voters with those of other voters (see Table 8.5).

In answer to the question "What about you? Are you in favor of desegregation, strict segregation, or something in between?" Wallace voters clearly differ from others: 37.5 percent of them say that they are in favor of strict segregation and 49.1 percent say that they prefer something "in between." Moreover, only 13.4 percent of the Wallace voters opt for desegregation, compared to 36.2 percent of Nixon voters and 52.9 percent of Humphrey voters.

Answers to other questions also demonstrate the distinctively different racial politics of Wallace voters. The question was asked: "Which of these statements would you agree with: (a) White people have the right to keep

TABLE 8.4
Selected Attitudes Toward Law and Order*

	Nixon	Humphrey	Wallace
"Do you approve of taking part in protest marches provided they are permitted by local authorities?"			
Approve	16.1	28.0	6.7
Depends	29.9	26.7	22.1
Disapprove	54.0	45.3	71.2
"How do you feel about refusing to obey a law which one feels is unjust if one feels so strongly that he is willing to go to jail, rather than obey?"			
Approve	11.0	18.8	12.9
Depends	25.0	21.9	19.8
Disapprove	64.0	59.3	67.3
"Suppose all other methods have failed and one decides to stop the government with sit-ins, mass meetings, demonstrations?"			
Approve	5.1	10.3	4.8
Depends	17.4	22.0	11.7
Disapprove	77.5	67.7	83.5

*Percentages add vertically by columns to 100 percent, except for rounding errors.

TABLE 8.5
Selected Racial Attitudes

	Nixon	Humphrey	Wallace
Racial Politics*			
Desegregation	36.2	52.9	13.4
In between	53.0	38.0	49.1
Segregation	10.8	9.1	37.5
Views on Neighborhood Integration*			
Keep out	22.5	13.3	46.1
Live anywhere	77.5	86.7	53.9
Judgment of Rate at Which Civil Rights Leaders Have Pushed*			
Too fast	68.6	51.1	90.0
About right	26.9	37.0	10.0
Too slow	4.5	11.9	0.0
Those Who Think Speed of Civil Rights Movement Is Too Fast by Attitude on Race**			
Integration	50.0	35.1	78.6
In between	77.3	65.1	90.4
Segregation	85.7	83.3	92.9
n =	(277)	(177)	(80)
gamma:	-.512	-.525	-.328
Judgment of Most Actions Taken by Blacks to Get the Things They Want*			
Most violent	77.5	62.3	90.5
Both checked	4.0	5.9	0.0
Most peaceful	18.5	31.8	9.5

Table 8.5 (Continued)

	Nixon	Humphrey	Wallace
View Whether Federal Government Should Assure Equality*			
No	19.8	10.0	48.2
Yes	14.9	35.5	5.3
Inconsistent	65.3	54.5	46.5

*Percentages add vertically by columns to 100 percent, except for rounding errors.

**Listed in each cell are the proportions of those in each category of the independent variable (position on integration/segregation) who are found in the category of the dependent variable (perception of the speed of the civil rights movement as too fast). Those in other categories of the dependent variable (viewing the speed of the civil rights movement as too slow or just right) total 100 percent when added to each cell. Compare figures down.

Negroes out of their neighborhoods if they want to, and (b) Negroes have a right to live wherever they can afford to, just like anybody else." The responses are: 46.1 percent of the Wallace voters say "keep out," compared to 22.5 percent of Nixon voters and 13.3 percent of Humphrey voters. Although the majority in each voting group appears more lenient than strict on all questions, Wallace voters continually register a much larger proportion with the most vehement position than do the other groups.

Another realm of racial politics which separates Wallace voters from others is their perceptions about the civil rights movement. Wallace voters are more likely to think that civil rights leaders have pushed too fast (90.0% than are Nixon voters (68.6%) or Humphrey voters (51.1%). In all cases, those who think changes in race relations are occurring too fast are more likely to be for segregation, but among Wallace voters this tendency is less marked than for the other two groups. Although most voters think that the civil rights movement has been violent rather than peaceful, Wallace voters

(90.5%) are more often likely to have this perception than are voters for Nixon (77.5%) or Humphrey (62.3%).

Wallace voters also differ from others in their view of the appropriate role of the federal government vis-a-vis race relations. Three questions on the schedule deal with this:

1. Should the federal government make sure that Negroes have the right to go to any hotel or restaurant they can afford, just like anybody else?
2. Should the federal government make sure that Negroes are getting fair treatment in jobs?
3. Should the federal government make sure that white and Negro children are allowed to go to the same schools?

Combining the answers to these questions, we find that 48.2 percent of Wallace voters consistently say "no" to all three questions, maintaining firmly that the federal government should stay out of such matters. Only 19.8 percent of Nixon voters and 10.0 percent of Humphrey voters have a similar pattern of responses.

It is apparent from this data that racial politics is an important factor in Wallace voting in 1968. These voters consistently show more racist attitudes than do other voters, and firmly believe that the federal government should play no role in assuring equal rights to blacks.

Authoritarian Personality

In testing the four theories being considered as possible explanations for Wallace voting, we will first consider the theory of the authoritarian personality.

The 1968 election study, like other studies used in this book, offers little opportunity to adequately examine the theory of the authoritarian personality. Several questions, however, deal with "toughness" and are construed to be indicative of the presence of authoritarianism (see Table 8.6). The first is in reference to incidents between police and demonstrators at the 1968 Democratic convention in Chicago. Wallace voters definitely have the "tougher" attitude. In answering the question "Do you think the police used too much force, the right amount of force, or not enough force with the demonstrators?" 49.5 percent of them reply "not enough force," compared to 30.1 percent of the Nixon voters and 23.9 percent of the Humphrey voters.

Two other questions ask the respondent to rate his preferred solution to specific problems on a seven-point scale.[1] The first question asks about urban unrest and rioting. The lenient end of the scale refers to solving problems of poverty and unemployment; the tougher end suggests the use of all available force. A majority (52.4%) of Wallace voters support the use of all available force. Most Nixon and Humphrey voters refuse to commit themselves to one position or the other, and remain somewhere in the middle on the question. A large percent (43.8%) of Humphrey voters, however, take the more lenient position, saying that they prefer solving problems of poverty and unemployment.

The second measure is a self-rating on the Vietnam action. The lenient end of the scale calls for an immediate withdrawal; the tougher end for a complete military victory. Once again a majority of Wallace voters opt for the more authoritarian solution: 60.0 percent are for a complete victory, compared to 28.6 percent of Nixon voters and 21.2 percent of Humphrey voters.

While none of these questions relate directly to Adorno's F Scale, they are still concerned with power and toughness and give unequivocable evidence of an authoritarian mentality. On such measures, Wallace voters' responses differ markedly from those of other voters. They repeatedly state that the government should "get tough" in solving problems, and are unquestionably more authoritarian-minded than are voters for other candidates.

Marginal Voter Theory

Several aspects of the marginal voter theory can be tested here (see Table 8.7). The first involves frequency of voting. Answers to the question, "For whom did you vote in 1964?" reveal the following percentages not voting in 1964: 11.9 percent of Wallace voters, 6.7 percent of Nixon voters, and 5.4 percent of Humphrey voters.[2] Although a larger proportion of Wallace voters did not vote in 1964, this number is not significantly different from the others to merit the conclusion that Wallace voters are politically marginal. In the complete sample, the portion of nonvoters in 1968 who were also nonvoters in 1964 is 42.5 percent, giving some indication of a true measure of nonparticipation. Wallace voters do not begin to approach that level of marginality.

Other statistics also serve to support the contention that Wallace voters are not very different from other groups in their nonvoting. A Kendall correlation coefficient generated to compare the number of presidential elections one was eligible to vote in with the number actually voted in shows these results by voter group: Nixon .7739, Humphrey .6977, and Wallace .6430.

Another aspect of marginal voting theory deals with party membership, or the lack of it. The distribution of declared membership among voting groups shows that there are more Independents among Wallace voters (40.4%) than among any other voting groups, but not substantially more than the proportion of Independents among Nixon voters (32.5%).

TABLE 8.6
Authoritarian Measures

	Nixon	Humphrey	Wallace
Views on Actions of Chicago Police Toward Demonstrators at 1968 Democratic Convention*			
Too much force	20.3	33:9	7.3
Right amount	49.6	42.2	43.2
Not enough force	30.1	23.9	49.5
Solutions to Problems of Urban Unrest and Rioting**			
Solve problems	23.0	43.8	8.9
Use force	17.7	10.3	52.4
Solutions to Vietnam**			
Immediate with- drawal	18.6	25.3	12.0
Complete victory	28.6	21.2	60.0

*Percentages add vertically by columns to 100 percent, except for rounding errors.

**The addition of those who are relatively neutral brings each column total to 100 percent.

Consistency of membership is also enlightening. Nixon voters are more likely to have changed parties than other voters (33.8%), while Wallace voters are as consistent in their party membership as are others.[3] Wallace voters who have never changed parties total 71.1 percent compared to 80.0 percent of Humphrey voters and 66.2 percent of Nixon voters.

Another aspect of marginality is the respondent's perception of which party would be the most likely to do what the respondent wants on a most important program just mentioned. Wallace voters are more likely to answer "no difference" (46.9%) than are other voters and prefer to put their trust in Republicans rather than in Wallace, their own candidate, but the implications of this are not clear. When it comes to the Democratic party, however, Wallace voters are clearly negative.

TABLE 8.7
Marginal Voter Measures*

	Nixon	Humphrey	Wallace
Voting in 1964			
Johnson	39.9	91.4	45.7
Goldwater	53.4	3.2	42.4
Didn't vote	6.7	5.4	11.9
Party Membership**			
Democrats	16.7	78.0	46.5
Independents	32.5	17.5	40.4
Republicans	50.8	4.5	13.1
Change of Party			
Yes	33.8	20.0	28.9
No	66.2	80.0	71.1
Party Which Would Be Most Effective in Doing What Respondent Wants			
Democrats	3.9	51.7	8.2
No difference	32.8	38.5	46.9
Republicans	62.2	9.0	32.7
Wallace	1.1	0.8	12.2

*Percentages add vertically by columns to 100 percent, except for rounding errors.

**Independent Democrats and Independent Republicans are both classified as Independents in this table and in all other calculations.

Another check as to whether people feel marginal is an investigation of their campaign activities. Wallace voters are slightly less likely than others to belong to a political club or to give money to a political party. They are also less likely to work for a party or a candidate. On each of these measures, however, they are not different from the others by any more than five percentage points, insignificant in statistical terms. In other ways, Wallace voters are more active than others; they are more likely to wear a campaign button, to put a bumper sticker on their cars, and to try to convince someone to vote for a particular candidate. They are also more likely than are other voters to say that they are very interested in the campaign and to mention that they follow public affairs most of the time.

Before the election, Wallace voters' general interest in politics and public affairs are rated by the interviewer as "very high" more frequently than the level of interest shown by voters for other candidates. In addition, the amount of information which Wallace voters appear to have about politics and public affairs is similar to that of Humphrey voters; slightly larger proportions of Nixon voters are rated higher on this measure. After the election, however, both the level of interest and of information drops for all voter groups.

Another aspect of marginality is measured by membership in groups or clubs. Although Wallace voters are less likely to belong to political clubs than are other voters, they are slightly more likely than other voters to belong to labor unions (or have someone else in their household who belongs).

In general, there is little evidence that Wallace voters are marginal either as voters or as participants. On all measures they are remarkably similar to everyone else, except for the fact that they are more often Independent voters and more cynical than others on the effectiveness of political parties. We will show, however, that this is not evidence of marginality as the concept is defined here, but the manifestation of extreme feelings of political powerlessness.

Status Theories

The 1968 American National Election Study offers many more possibilities for an examination of status theories than do the studies available for 1964, 1972, and 1976. We will first look at the standard measure of SES used throughout this study and then explore other concepts which formulate status politics.

Socioeconomic Status

Ascribed status is calculated (See Appendix for explanation and Table 8.8 for all status measures) by adding values assigned to the variables of religion and of race.[4] First, looking at each component separately, we find that religion is distributed very similarly among Nixon and Wallace voters. Slightly over three-quarters of both of these groups are Protestant. Only 14.9 percent of Wallace voters are Catholic, compared to 18.1 percent of Nixon voters and almost one-third of Humphrey voters (31.3%). As shown earlier (Table 8.11), almost all Nixon voters (98.4%) and Wallace voters

(99.1%) are white; twenty percent of Humphrey voters are black. On both of the components of ascribed status, Humphrey voters are markedly different and Nixon and Wallace voters are markedly the same.

Combining the two variables yields a measure of ascribed status on which Nixon and Wallace voters are also very similar (79.0% of Nixon voters and 79.8% of Wallace voters have both ascribed statuses). Humphrey voters are recognizably different—only 39.5 percent have both ascribed statuses.

The second exercise in determining SES score is to calculate achieved status from the variables of education and income. The distribution of education shows Wallace voters to be somewhat less well-educated than other voters. Only 17.5 percent of them have some college, compared to 26.4 percent of Humphrey voters and 39.1 percent of Nixon voters. Income, herein divided into equal thirds, shows no essential difference among the three voting groups.[5] Nixon voters are slightly more likely to be overrepresented among the highest group and underrepresented among the lowest income group.

Codes for income and education, when combined into a measure of achieved status, show lower achieved status among Wallace voters. The two extremes on the measure of achieved status show the most difference— 39.3 percent of Wallace voters, 33.7 percent of Humphrey voters, and 24.9 percent of Nixon voters have low achieved status. The figures for high achieved status are 9.8 percent, 15.3 percent and 21.8 percent, respectively.

When ascribed and achieved status are combined into a measure of socioeconomic status, these percentages of each group are in the categories of middle and high SES: Nixon 58.5 percent, Wallace 44.7 percent, and Humphrey 26.2 percent. To summarize briefly, Wallace voters are solidly in the middle when it comes to socioeconomic status, and they are closer to Nixon voters on this measure than they are to Humphrey voters.[6]

The wealth of data available in the 1968 American National Election Study makes other comparisons possible which also confirm this observation. A calculation of the mean of the Duncan SES score for the head of household's main occupation for every respondent (here ranging from a low of 02 to a high of 94) yields further documentation. The mean for Nixon voters is 47.37, for Wallace voters 40.19, and for Humphrey voters 39.62. These calculations also support the contention that Wallace voters' socioeconomic statuses do not differ perceptibly from those of other voters when viewed on objective measures.

Status Mobility

Such data also permits, for the first time, a thorough examination of the question of mobility (see Table 8.9). A crosstabulation of the Duncan SES

TABLE 8.8
Selected Status Characteristics*

	Nixon	Humphrey	Wallace
Religion			
Protestant	79.8	58.6	79.8
Catholic	18.1	31.3	14.9
Jewish	0.5	6.6	0.9
Other	0.3	0.7	1.8
None	1.3	2.8	2.6
Race			
White	98.4	79.3	99.1
Black	0.6	20.0	0.0
Other	1.0	0.7	0.9
Ascribed Status			
None	1.0	1.9	0.9
One	20.0	58.6	19.3
Both	79.0	39.5	79.8
Education			
Grade school	12.2	22.4	24.6
High school	48.7	51.2	57.9
College	39.1	26.4	17.5
Income Distribution			
Lowest third	28.6	31.7	33.9
Middle third	33.2	32.4	33.9
Highest third	38.2	35.9	32.3
Achieved Status			
Low	24.9	33.7	39.3
Working	27.3	25.6	22.3
Middle	26.0	25.4	28.6
High	21.8	15.3	9.8
Socioeconomic Status			
Low	11.7	36.7	8.8
Working	29.9	37.1	46.5
Middle	41.4	21.7	38.6
High	17.0	4.5	6.1

*Percentages add vertically by columns to 100 percent except for rounding errors.

scores of the occupation of the father of the respondent by the same measure for the occupation of the head of the household yields interesting statistics on mobility. Depending on the distance between the two scores (see Appendix), the respondent is classified as being at one of five levels of mobility, ranging from very upwardly mobile to stable to very downwardly mobile.

Combining the percentages shown in Table 8.9, we find slightly larger proportions of upwardly mobile persons among Wallace voters (60.6%) when compared to Nixon voters (56.9%) and Humphrey voters (55.0%). All groups are remarkably similar; in fact, Nixon and Humphrey voters have identical percentages (20.9%) which can be classified as downwardly mobile, compared to 15.0 percent of Wallace voters.

Two other measures move toward a more subjective definition of mobility. The first is a crosstabulation of the answer to the question: "In what social class was your family when you were growing up?" With the objective measure of SES calculated earlier, it yields a measure of gain or loss of status. If the status of the family of origin is said to be higher than our objective measure of the respondent's present SES, a loss is designated; if that of the family of origin is lower than the determination of the present status, a gain is registered. Identical designations render a judgment of same. (This crosstabulation is found in Table 8.9.)

This measure of mobility shows most gain among Nixon voters (42.2%). Wallace voters are in the middle with 37.2 percent, followed by Humphrey voters with the lowest proportion of the upwardly mobile (17.9%). Humphrey voters tend to be much more downwardly mobile than those in the other two groups. A majority of them (51.3%) have lost status.

Another measure of mobility is based on two subjective judgments and involves a crosstabulation of the question, "In what social class was your family when you were growing up?" with the query "In what social class do you think others would put you?" Answers give some indication of subjective status security. On this measure all three voter groups have practically the same distributions: most feel they have the same status as did their parents. A slightly larger proportion of Wallace voters (28.1%) feel they have gained status; 24.8 percent of Humphrey voters and 23.5 percent of Nixon voters also feel that they have gained status.

To summarize, questions of mobility, whether they rely on a researcher's judgment or are based on the person's perception of his own mobility, do not distinguish Wallace voters from other voters in any way. Wallace voters are just as likely to be upwardly mobile as are others, and are far less likely to be downwardly mobile than are Humphrey voters. Thus theories of mobility are not useful in explaining the 1968 Wallace support.

TABLE 8.9
Measures of Mobility*

	Nixon	Humphrey	Wallace
Respondent's Mobility Relative to Father's Status			
Very upwardly mobile	15.6	9.8	19.0
Upwardly mobile	41.3	45.2	41.6
Same as father	22.2	24.1	24.4
Downwardly mobile	19.3	19.7	11.8
Very downwardly mobile	1.6	1.2	3.2
Respondent's Mobility Based on Self-Judgment of Family of Origin's Status and Objective Calculation of SES			
Loss	23.9	51.3	15.5
Same	33.9	30.8	47.3
Gain	42.2	17.9	37.2
Respondent's Mobility Based on Self-Judgment of Family of Origin's Status and Self-Judgment of Present Status			
Those who feel they have:			
Lost status	3.8	3.8	3.1
Same as parents	72.7	71.4	68.8
Gained status	23.5	24.8	28.1

*Percentages add vertically by columns to 100 percent, except for rounding errors.

Status Anxiety

Another aspect of status theory, not yet discussed, is status anxiety. Status anxiety is seldom a discernable part of the consciousness of the individual; it is almost always a matter of inference by the researcher. It is thought present if some sort of incongruity is found either among status components or between ascribed and achieved statuses.

The data shows no such incongruency among Wallace voter. Kendall correlation coefficients generated on education and income show Wallace voters as the most status consistent of the three groups; readings are Wallace .4432, Humphrey .3441, and Nixon .3272. Further, a crosstabulation of achieved and ascribed statuses shows that of those who have both ascribed statuses, the following percentages in each group have either middle or high achieved status: Nixon 38.3 percent, Wallace 25.9 percent, and Humphrey 15.8 percent. Wallace voters are solidly in the middle.

Some measures of status anxiety do try to deal with subjective perceptions (see Table 8.10), but here again, it is more often the researcher's assumption rather than the respondent's assertion that such anxiety is present. For instance, some researchers think that identification of oneself as working class is a measure of status anxiety. While a greater proportion of Wallace voters feel that they are members of the working class (63.6%) than do Humphrey voters (54.5%) or Nixon voters (43.5%), such identification does not inherently reveal any status insecurity. Status anxiety might show up in answers to the question, "How close do you feel to that class to which you have said that you belong?" When this question is crosstabulated with self-identification of class, in each case Wallace voters are more likely than not to say that they feel close to their respective subjective social class. Thus Wallace voters are secure in their class identifications and do not feel alienated.

Another perspective on status anxiety results from looking at the correspondence between ones self-identified social class and the social class in which one thinks others might place him or her. If they match, we can assume that the respondent feels relatively secure, without such status anxiety. If, however, there is a discrepancy, we can assume some kind of status anxiety, although the social meaning of it would differ depending on whether the respondent's self-identified social class is higher or lower than that in which he or she thinks others might place him or her. The data show that the two kinds of discrepancies combined result in these proportions likely having some kind of status anxiety: Nixon 7.1 percent, Wallace 7.3 percent, and Humphrey 11.7 percent. Again, Wallace voters are no different when compared to others, and seem subjectively secure in the status with which they identify relative to what they think others perceive them to be.

TABLE 8.10
Measures of Status Anxiety

	Nixon	Humphrey	Wallace
Subjective Social Class*			
Lower	0.0	0.2	0.0
Working	43.5	54.5	63.6
Middle	56.5	45.3	36.4
Upper	0.0	0.0	0.0
Respondents in Each Subjective Social Class Who Say They Feel Close to Class**			
Working	62.6	66.8	63.2
Middle	54.5	49.4	59.0
Respondents' Perceptions of Social Class Relative to Where They Think Others Place Them*			
Others place them lower	0.4	1.8	0.0
Others place them same	92.9	88.3	92.7
Others place them higher	6.7	9.9	7.3

*Percentages add vertically by columns to 100 percent, except for rounding errors.

**Adding those who do not feel close to their respective classes brings the total in each cell to 100 percent. Compare figures across.

A comparison of subjective status (one's self definition of his/her status) with the objective measure of socioeconomic status which we calculated earlier shows that the following percentages of each voter group perceive themselves to be the status that we have judged them to be: Wallace 51.0 percent, Nixon 38.7 percent, and Humphrey 26.1 percent. Thus it would seem that Wallace voters are realistic about their relative status positions and are as secure as are those in other voter groups.

In summary, Wallace voters are no different from Nixon voters on practically any measure of status. They are securely in the middle on both objective and subjective measures of status, and have as much upward mobility as any other group. Further, status anxiety is practically nonexistent among them. The result is clear: theories of status politics are useless in explaining any aspect of Wallace voting in 1968.

Status and Race

One last question to be considered in regard to status is: Do status variables relate in any way to position on race? (See Table 8.11) A crosstabulation of position on integration by SES shows that among both Nixon and Wallace voters, the working class is more likely to have the more vehement racial sentiment, while among Humphrey voters, the middle class is more likely to have that attitude. Gammas, however, demonstrate that SES is more important in explaining position on race for both Humphrey and Nixon voters than it is for Wallace voters. The gamma for Wallace voters is only –.069, almost negligible.

Another possible status relation may be determined by looking at subjective social class relative to attitudes on racial politics. This factor appears to be stronger than objective social class in determining attitudes on race, at least for Nixon and Wallace voters. In each case, those who think of themselves as working class are more likely to be for segregation, while those who identify themselves as middle class are more likely to be for integration. Gammas reveal the strength of the relationship between the variables and demonstrate the importance of subjective social class definition for Wallace voters (–.299). Thus, among all status variables, only subjective social class seems to play a role in Wallace voters' racial politics.

The Power Theory

Of all the theories considered in this study, the power theory has the most relevance in explaining the Wallace vote. Here we will examine variables that deal with respondents' views of political power; without exception, all differentiate Wallace voters from the others.

This issue is particularly apparent during the 1968 campaign. Throughout, Wallace constantly draws attention to the growing power of the

TABLE 8.11
Status and Racial Attitudes

	Nixon	Humphrey	Wallace
Respondents for Seg-regation by SES*			
Low	7.1	8.2	20.0
Working	16.4	7.3	45.3
Middle	10.2	14.9	34.9
High	4.9	5.3	16.7
n =	(51)	(37)	(42)
gamma:	-.137	.193	-.069
Subjective Social Class by Attitudes on Race**			
Working Class			
Integration	34.3	53.7	40.0
In between	45.8	53.3	65.4
Segregation	56.0	66.7	70.7
n =	(140)	(150)	(53)
Middle Class			
Integration	65.7	46.3	60.0
In between	54.2	46.1	34.6
Segregation	44.0	33.3	29.3
n =	(196)	(87)	(43)
gamma:	-.256	-.083	-.299

*Adding those who say they are "for integration" or "for something in between" brings the total in each cell to 100 percent. Compare figures down.

**Proportions of those in each category of the dependent variable (attitude on race) add to 100 percent except for those Humphrey voters who des-ignate themselves as "in between." A few of the Humphrey voters who consider themselves lower class are for "something in between" and consti-tute the missing .6 percent in the tabulation.

federal government. It is one of his primary issues, and the data show that Nixon voters are equally concerned. When asked "Is the federal government getting too powerful?" 77.9 percent of the Wallace voters and 70.9 percent of Nixon voters respond "yes"; only 35.3 percent of Humphrey voters share the same sentiment. When it comes to specific attitudes toward the government, however, Nixon voters tend to be less critical than Wallace voters, who are markedly more negative on every measure (see Table 8.12). For instance, when asked whether the government is run by a few big interests looking out for themselves or for the benefit of the people, Wallace voters overwhelmingly (70.3%) reply "big interests." Less than half of the Nixon (43.2%) and Humphrey voters (34.6%) feel that way.

A majority (51.4%) of Wallace voters say that they don't know whether those who are running the government are smart and know what they are doing. Only a third of the Nixon (36.2%) and Humphrey voters (33.8%) agree with them.

Wallace voters again lead other voter groups when asked how many people in government are dishonest; 49.1 percent of them reply "quite a lot," followed by 24.9 percent of Nixon voters, and 19.3 percent of Humphrey voters.

Wallace voters also have least faith in national government, whereas Nixon and Humphrey voters are more likely to say that they have least faith in local government. One of the reasons why Wallace voters might tend to trust the federal government less is advanced by the candidate himself during the 1968 campaign; people are angry because they think that the federal government has too much control over local education. Indeed, Wallace voters feel that this is true much more often than other voters (81.3% compared to 53.9% for Nixon supporters and 26.3% for Humphrey voters). In fact, when those who say that the federal government has too much control over local education are crosstabulated with those who say that the federal government is getting too powerful, the following percentages agree with both positions: Wallace 67.6 percent, Nixon 47.4 percent, and Humphrey 21.3 percent.

The general opinion reflected by a majority of both Wallace voters (72.8%) and Nixon voters (62.9%) is that education is most appropriately the province of state and local government, exactly what their candidates advocate. In contrast, only one-third of Humphrey voters feel this way (36.0%).

Operationalizing Powerlessness

Five measures were created in order to test the power theory. Two are most appropriately considered measures of anomie and three are measures of powerlessness. They are further dichotomized as being on a personal

TABLE 8.12
Selected Attitudes Toward the Federal Government*

	Nixon	Humphrey	Wallace
"Is the government run by a few big interests looking out for themselves or for the benefit of the people?"			
For all	56.8	65.4	29.7
Few big interests	43.2	34.6	70.3
"Are those running the government smart and know what they're doing?"			
Know	63.7	66.2	48.6
Don't know	36.3	33.8	51.4
"How many people in government are dishonest?"			
Hardly any	19.0	23.6	9.6
Not many	56.1	57.1	41.3
Quite a lot	24.9	19.3	49.1
"Does the federal government have too much control over education?"			
Too much	53.9	26.3	81.3
About right	32.6	43.0	13.7
Too little	13.5	30.7	5.0
"What about the amount of control which state governments have over local education?"			
Too much	23.2	15.1	21.9
About right	49.5	50.2	31.5
Too little	27.3	34.7	46.6
"Should education be handled by national, state or local government?"			
Don't know, no interest	14.2	16.9	13.2
National	18.8	42.1	11.4
Both checked	4.1	5.0	2.6
State and local	62.9	36.0	72.8

*Percentages add vertically by columns to 100 percent, except for rounding errors.

level and on a political level, or in relation to one's self and in relation to the polity. This division follows Aberbach's (1969) lead, with the exception that he uses the terms "trust"and "efficacy" while we have chosen to define them precisely as "anomie" and "power." The five measures being used are termed personal anomie, personal power, political anomie, political power, and power in relation to political institutions.

The measures of anomie used relate to what is generally referred to in the literature as "normlessness" (Seeman 1959). Theoretically, individuals believe that there are certain standard ways to do things, a system of culturally defined means to prescribed ends that are considered desirable. Anomie results when a person begins to perceive that means as prescribed are not being followed; the resulting incomprehensibility and feelings of despair (for the desirability of the ends is never questioned) are usually referred to as anomie. The distinction used here is between personal and political anomie, relating to interaction with other individuals in the first instance, and to expectations about the workings of government in the second.

Seeman (1959) distinguishes what has been defined as anomie (what he calls "normlessness" from powerlessness by describing the latter as "the expectancy or probability held by the individual that his own behavior cannot determine the occurence of the outcomes, or reinforcements, he seeks" (Seeman 1959, p. 784). This definition is the one used to identify powerlessness in this study; again a distinction is made between the personal and the political as described above.

In calculating the five measures, a simple additive technique is used (see Appendix) and the responses are divided into levels of high, medium, and low.

Personal anomie is discerned from answers to the following questions:

1. Generally speaking, would you say that most people can be trusted or that you can't be too careful in dealing with people?
2. Would you say that most of the time people try to be helpful or that they are mostly just looking out for themselves?
3. Do you think most people would try to take advantage of you if they got the chance or would they try to be fair?

These are the same questions that Aberbach (1969) uses from the 1964 Election Study in determining his measure of interpersonal trust. Rosenberg's (1956) "Misanthropy Scale" and the "Trust" and "Faith in People" scales of Robinson and Shaver (1969) use questions that are phrased similarly.

A measure of political anomie is created from these questions:

1. Do you think that people in the government waste a lot of the money we pay in taxes, waste some of it, or don't waste very much of it?

2. How much of the time do you think you can trust the government in Washington to do what is right: just about always, most of the time, or only some of the time?
3. Would you say the government is pretty much run by a few big interests looking out for themselves or that it is run for the benefit of all of the people?
4. Do you feel that almost all of the people running the government are smart people who usually know what they are doing, or do you think that a lot of them don't seem to know what they are doing?
5. Do you think that quite a few of the people running the government are a little crooked, not very many are, or do you think hardly any of them are crooked at all?

This measure of political anomie uses questions that have been used to describe political trust by Aberbach (1969) and Miller, Brown, and Raine (1973). Both studies employ questions from the Survey Research Center's National Election Studies.

Personal powerlessness as a measure has its beginnings in Rotter's (1966) I-E Scale and also incorporates Seeman's (1959) definition of powerlessness on an individual level. Aberbach (1969) has also used the same questions as a measure of personal efficacy:

1. Do you think it's better to plan your life a good way ahead, or would you say life is too much a matter of luck to plan ahead very far?
2. When you do make plans ahead do you usually get to carry out things the way you expected, or do things usually come up to make you change your plans?
3. Have you usually felt pretty sure your life would work out the way you want it to, or have there been times when you haven't been sure about it?
4. Some people feel they can run their lives pretty much the way they want to; others feel the problems of life are sometimes too big for them. Which one are you most like?

Political powerlessness is measured by two different scales. The first has its origin in Campbell, Gurin, and Miller (1954, pp. 187-194), *The Voter Decides*. Sokol (1967) makes use of some of the questions in studying McCarthyism, and Aberbach also uses them as a scale of political efficacy (1969). There are only two possible answers to each question, agree or disagree:

1. People like me don't have any say about what the government does.
2. Voting is the only way that people like me can have any say about how the government runs things.
3. Sometimes politics and government seem so complicated that a person like me can't really understand what is going on.
4. I don't think public officials care much about what people like me think.

The second measure of political powerlessness is created by the author and is a product of the available data. While there are many individual questions that can be used to investigate whether or not one feels powerless, it seems advisable to create another composite scale. The questions above which measure political powerlessness do so only in a general way. The 1968 Election Study schedule has several questions that permit one to investigate powerlessness in relation to governmental institutions that have been created to facilitate representation, or more specifically, to foster a sense of power to the individual through participation. These governmental structures are either real entities or institutionalized procedures. The measure designed to investigate feelings of power in relation to these embodiments of government is labeled institutional power.

The first component is a measure of faith in political parties and results from an additive combination of three questions:

1. How much do you feel that political parties help to make the government pay attention to what the people think: a good deal, some, or not much?
2. Do you think that the parties pretty much keep their promises or do they usually do what they want after the election is over?
3. Parties are only interested in people's votes and not in their opinions. (Agree or disagree)

While it could be argued that some of these questions measure anomie rather than powerlessness, we maintain that taken together they result in a measure of how effective one thinks he can be in relation to the existing party structure, ostensibly a power measure rather than a normative description.

The second component of the measure of power in relation to institutions is a view of effectiveness relative to congressional action. This component evolves from a cross-tabulation of two questions:

1. Generally speaking, those we elect to Congress in Washington lose touch with the people pretty quickly. (Agree or disagree)
2. How much attention do you think most Congressmen pay to the people who elect them when they decide what to do in Congress: a good deal, some, or not much?

The third component is a single question: And how much do you feel that having elections makes the government pay attention to what the people think: a good deal, some, or not much? While elections are an institutionalized ritual rather than a recognizable structure, they are still very much a part of the way one is supposed to get his political needs met, as much of an avenue as using the instruments of political parties and congressional representatives.

The final component of the measure of power in relation to institutions is a measure of one's influence on the activities of the federal government. This deduction, as the second component above, is based on a cross tabulation of two questions:

1. Over the years, how much attention do you feel the government pays to what people think when it decides what to do: a great deal, some, or not much?
2. People like me don't have any say about what the government does. (Agree or disagree)

While the second question is a part of the first definition of political powerlessness, it is treated differently and is dependent on the preceding questions for its value. Thus it has only minimal effect on the ultimate value of power in relation to institutions; it is unlikely that the two measures overlap in any meaningful way. The sense of power in relation to institutions is then created by adding together the values of faith in political parties, faith in Congress, efficacy in relation to elections, and power in relation to governmental actions. The final score is arbitrarily divided into low, average, and high designations.

We will examine each of these measures in turn relative to certain demographic preconditions, and summarize our findings at the end of the section (see Table 8.13).

The Politics of Powerlessness

Personal anomie is distributed among voter groups as shown in Table 8.13. A score of low reflects low anomie, corresponding to a high level of trust in people; a score of high anomie is the value that specifically relates to the power thesis. While Wallace voters do have greater proportions (40.8%) in the category of high personal anomie and thereby exhibit less trust for other people and more personal alienation, they differ by only a few percentage points from Humphrey voters (35.3%). More evident is the smaller proportion of Nixon voters (23.0%) who exhibit this factor.

Looking at personal power next, we are most interested in the category low, reflecting a sense of personal powerlessness. Larger proportions of Humphrey voters have readings of low (32.3%) than do Wallace (25.8%) or Nixon (19.5%) voters. Thus Wallace voters are as secure as other voters in their feelings of personal power.

The political variables begin to show some differences. The first, degree of political anomie (shown in Table 8.13) is especially discerning of Wallace voters. They are a full 24 percentage points above the nearest group, with 61.1 percent registering high political anomie. Nixon and Humphrey voters are somewhat alike; 37.0 percent and 29.3 percent respectively show high political anomie.

On the first definition of political power, a much higher proportion of

Wallace voters (52.4%) have a sense of low political power than do Humphrey voters (37.9%) or Nixon voters (32.0%). While this is not as strong a factor as political anomie, it still serves to differentiate Wallace voters from others.

The second measure of political power measures power felt in relation to institutions. On this measure Wallace voters again have a higher proportion (33.9%) with a low reading, about twice as much as the almost identical percentages of Humphrey and Nixon voters who have readings of 16.4 percent and 15.4 percent respectively. Thus institutional powerlessness is a stronger factor than the other definition of political powerlessness, but not as strong as political anomie for distinguishing Wallace voters.

On this list of power variables, four of the five distinguish Wallace voters from other voters. In order of increasing importance they are: personal anomie, political powerlessness, powerlessness in relation to institutions, and political anomie. In each case, it is the negative value of the variable that is highest among Wallace voters. The remaining variable, personal powerlessness, shows Wallace voters in the middle; Humphrey voters' scores are proportionately higher.

Power Variables and Their Associations with Other Variables— Comparison of Voter Groups

One might think that the same factors would be associated with the presence of any one of these variables among all voting groups. In examining this assumption, we will look briefly at the results of a multivariate analysis of other factors with each of the power variables.

Status variables account for the presence of high personal anomie among all voters; such feelings are associated with lower socioeconomic status as well as lower subjective status. Both of these measures are stronger factors in explaining the presence of high personal anomie among Humphrey and Nixon voters than among Wallace voters.

A sense of personal powerlessness is related to lower levels of education, income, SES, and subjective SES among all voting groups, but the importance of each differs widely. For Humphrey voters SES is the strongest factor; income is the most important among Wallace voters; and education is the primary factor among Nixon voters.

The preconditions of low political power represent the largest number of variables common to all voting groups. Political powerlessness is connected to being black (for Nixon and Humphrey only; there are no black Wallace voters), being older, being Democratic, having a lower income and less education, and having a lower subjective socioeconomic status. In addition, lower SES is also important, but more so for Nixon and Humphrey voters than for Wallace voters. Of this list, lower subjective SES

TABLE 8.13
Measures of Personal and Political Anomie and Powerlessness*

	Nixon	Humphrey	Wallace
Personal Anomie			
Low	55.0	44.0	35.9
Average	22.0	20.7	23.3
High	23.0	35.3	40.8
Personal Power			
Low	19.5	32.3	25.8
Average	22.5	21.4	25.8
High	58.0	46.3	48.4
Political Anomie			
Low	16.2	23.1	6.5
Average	46.8	47.6	32.4
High	37.0	29.3	61.1
Political Power			
Low	32.0	37.9	52.4
Average	19.0	21.7	21.0
High	49.0	40.4	26.6
Power in Relation to Institutions			
Low	15.4	16.4	33.9
Average	41.2	43.8	50.8
High	43.4	39.8	15.3

*Percentages add vertically by columns to 100 percent, except for rounding errors.

is the most important precondition of low political power for both Wallace and Nixon voters (more important for the latter), and less education is the most important factor among voters for Humphrey.

Low institutional power is related to subjective SES in all three voter groups, but less so for Wallace voters than for the others. No other variables are shared by all three groups. Nixon and Humphrey voters show relationships between lower levels of education, income and SES and a sense of institutional powerlessness. These two groups also give an indication that those who classify themselves as Independents and yet vote for the main party candidates also feel institutional powerlessness. High political anomie has no similar preconditions among the different voting groups.

Power Variables and Racial Attitudes

How do the power variables relate to racial attitudes? (See Table 8.14). Throughout this discussion we will use the statistic gamma as a measure of the strength and the direction of the relationship between the variables involved. Looking first at personal anomie, we find that a reading of high is related to a more adamant opinion on race only for Nixon voters (.208). It is of little consequence for Humphrey (−.029) and Wallace voters (.112) on their attitudes toward segregation. On one's evaluation of the speed of the civil rights movement, however, high personal anomie has some consequence for Wallace voters. The higher the sense of personal anomie among Wallace voters, the more likely one is to perceive the rate of the civil rights movement as too fast. The gamma for Wallace voters is a high −.322, while the figures for Humphrey and Nixon voters are a low −.079 and −.077 respectively. Looking at sense of personal power, we find that those with low personal power are more likely to be for segregation, except for Humphrey voters (.105), where the opposite relationship holds. The relationship is more marked for Wallace voters (−.358) than for Nixon voters (−.167). Sense of personal power is not relevant to perception of the speed of the civil rights movement in any of the voting groups.

Looking next at those with a high degree of political anomie, we find similar patterns among Nixon (.154) and Wallace (.248) voters—the higher the degree of political anomie, the more likely one is to be for segregation. The correlation is negligible for Humphrey voters (.050). There is a similar (and stronger) pattern among those with a high sense of political anomie in regard to the perception of the speed of the civil rights movement. Gammas are: for Wallace −.313, for Nixon −.282, and for Humphrey −.153.

In all three voter groups, those with a low sense of political power exhibit a more adamant view on racial politics. The relationship is stronger among both Wallace (−.370) and Nixon (−.325) voters than among Humphrey voters (−.139). A low sense of political power is also related to seeing the rate of the civil rights movement as too fast, particularly for Wallace voters. Gammas demonstrate that the relationship between the two variables is quite strong for Wallace voters (.421). It is not as strong for either Nixon (.121) or Humphrey voters (.022).

The other measure of political power, power vis-a-vis institutions, is even stronger than the previous definition of power in determining racial attitudes and particularly singles out the Wallace voter as different from the other two groups of voters. Both Wallace (–.397) and Nixon (–.168) voters with low institutional power are more likely to be for segregation. Humphrey voters (–.019) present no clear pattern.

Looking at those with a low sense of power vis-a-vis institutions, Nixon (.257) and Wallace (.831) voters are more likely to perceive the rate of the civil rights movement as too fast. There is no consistent direction among Humphrey voters (.065). The gammas for this relationship are the most revealing; for Wallace voters they demonstrate that this relationship is the single most important factor that we have yet discovered about the power variables in relation to racial attitudes.

On practically every measure of racial politics which we have examined, Wallace voters stand in the forefront reflecting antiblack attitudes. We find (see Table 8.5) that Wallace voters are more likely to be for segregation (26.7%). They believe that whites should be able to keep Negroes out of their neighborhoods if they want to (23.6%), and a larger proportion of them perceive the civil rights movement as being too fast (21.4%). They are more like others in thinking that the actions of blacks have been violent (13.0%). While this attitude does not necessarily reflect racial bias, it is clearly evident from these data that discriminatory racial politics is one of the most important distinguishing aspects of the Wallace vote.

Status variables are not particularly useful in understanding racial politics in 1968. Objective SES is not important in relation to Wallace voters' views on race, and has different effects for Humphrey voters, who are more likely to be for segregation if they have a high SES, and for Nixon voters, who if they have the same high SES, are more likely to favor integration. Subjective SES is important for both Wallace and Nixon voters—the higher the subjective SES, the more likely one is to be for integration, while it is not a factor among Humphrey voters. Thus, relative to Wallace voters, the only status measure applicable to racist attitudes shows up among those who subjectively feel that they are working class; they are more likely to be for segregation (gamma = –.299).

The power variables are statistically more important in understanding the adamant racial position of Wallace supporters. Reviewing the ways in which they are related to the general attitude on race, we find that, except for the measure of high personal anomie, Wallace voters have the strongest gammas measuring the strength of the relationship between degree of political power and a corresponding position on race. In order of ascending importance (for Wallace voters only):

- Political anomie .248. The higher the sense of political anomie, the more likely one is for segregation.
- Personal power –.358. The lower the sense of personal power, the more likely one is for segregation.

- Political power −.370. The lower the sense of political power, the more likely one is for segregation.
- Institutional power −.397. The lower the sense of institutional power, the more likely one is for segregation.

Political power is the only variable listed above in which another group of voters even approaches the strength of the relationship with racial attitudes shown for Wallace voters.[7]

The other attitude to which the power variables are strongly related is perception of the speed of the civil rights movement. Personal power is not important here, but the other four variables are: again Wallace voters show the strongest gammas. In order of importance, the variables are as follows:

- Political anomie −.313. The higher the sense of political anomie, the more likely one is to perceive the speed of the civil rights movement as too fast.
- Personal anomie −.322. The higher the sense of personal anomie, the more likely one is to perceive the speed of the civil rights movement as too fast.
- Political power .421. The lower the sense of political power, the more likely one is to perceive the speed of the civil rights movement as too fast.
- Institutional power .832. The lower the sense of institutional power, the more likely one is to perceive the speed of the civil rights movement as too fast.

On all of these variables as well, only the political anomie gamma for Wallace voters is near the gamma for another voting group.[8]

Summary

In this chapter we have been able to test the four original theories as well as to glean some additional information about the voting groups in 1968. There is some evidence that Wallace voters are more authoritarian than other voters, but the right kinds of questions are not available for determining whether or not they exhibit the authoritarian personality per se. Wallace voters, however, definitely focus on the use of force as a problem-solving and control mechanism in both domestic and international situations.

The findings on marginal voter theories suggest that this explanation is not very important to the question of Wallace support. Status theories also provide no clues to understanding Wallace voters; in all tests, the Wallace voter is solidly in the middle between Nixon and Humphrey voters, and cannot be said to be different in regard to the concept of marginal voters or questions of status.

Of the four theories, the power theory is the most promising. Four of the five power variables distinguish Wallace voters from others. A check to see if status factors are related to the three most important power variables

TABLE 8.14
Position on Race by Degree of Power*

	Nixon	Humphrey	Wallace
Respondents with High Personal Anomie by Attitudes on Race			
Desegregation	17.9	36.8	53.3
In between	23.3	32.1	31.9
Segregation	40.4	37.8	47.5
n =	(101)	(133)	(42)
gamma:	.208	-.029	.112
Respondents with High Personal Anomie by Perceptions of Speed of Civil Rights Movement			
Too fast	23.7	32.5	43.2
About right	18.5	39.2	18.2
Too slow	38.1	37.2	0.0
n =	(100)	(134)	(40)
gamma:	-.077	-.079	-.322
Respondents with Low Personal Power by Attitudes on Race			
Desegregation	16.8	35.4	7.7
In between	17.1	29.5	17.8
Segregation	37.8	24.2	44.1
n =	(78)	(114)	(24)
gamma:	-.167	.105	-.358
Respondents with High Political Anomie by Attitudes on Race			
Desegregation	33.8	27.8	53.3
In between	37.6	31.4	54.9
Segregation	50.0	26.5	70.7
n =	(153)	(96)	(65)
gamma:	.154	.050	.248
Respondents With High Political Anomie by Perceptions of Speed of Civil Rights Movement			
Too fast	42.4	35.3	63.4
About right	25.5	23.8	45.5
Too slow	23.8	20.5	0.0
n =	(149)	(98)	(64)
gamma:	-.282	-.153	-.313

Table 8.14 (Continued)

	Nixon	Humphrey	Wallace
Respondents with Low Political Power by Attitudes on Race			
Desegregation	25.8	35.0	28.6
In between	30.6	40.0	45.8
Segregation	60.0	44.4	66.7
n =	(141)	(145)	(54)
gamma:	-.325	-.139	-.370
Respondents with Low Political Power by Perceptions of Speed of Civil Rights Movement			
Too fast	34.2	41.1	54.4
About right	25.2	33.3	36.4
Too slow	28.6	40.5	0.0
n =	(138)	(147)	(53)
gamma:	.121	.022	.421
Respondents with Low Institutional Power by Attitudes on Race			
Desegregation	12.4	14.3	15.4
In between	12.9	21.9	30.8
Segregation	36.0	5.3	52.6
n =	(40)	(41)	(20)
gamma:	-.168	-.019	-.397
Respondents with Low Institutional Power by Perceptions of Speed of Civil Rights Movement			
Too fast	19.7	19.1	36.5
About right	7.8	12.2	0.0
Too slow	7.1	19.2	0.0
n =	(42)	(42)	(19)
gamma:	.257	.065	.831

*Each column adds to 100 percent when those in the other categories of the independent variable are added. Compare figures down.

shows that they do not explain either the presence of political anomie or of institutional power. They are, however, somewhat useful in explaining level of political power for all three voting groups.

In regard to position on racial issues, subjective perception of status plays some part in being for segregation, but the more important factors which go along with this attitude are the power variables.

In general, the picture of the Wallace voter that emerges from the 1968 Election Study is of one who is indistinguishable from others in most of his demographic characteristics. While more conservative on foreign policy issues than others, he is like other voters on most domestic issues—except for views on racial politics and perceptions of the power of the federal government. Where he differs most, however, is on measures of political anomie and of political power.

The sense of powerlessness which the Wallace voter expresses seems to arise from feelings that he cannot get what he wants from the federal government. These feelings are coupled with the sentiment that government is not functioning as it should according to his expectations or desires. For the Wallace voter, the behavior of government is somehow both incomprehensible and inappropriate—thus the high political anomie scores and the attitudes that government is getting too powerful. This powerlessness seems directly related to issues of education, especially integration. It does not appear to be the result of racial prejudice itself; radical attitudes among Wallace voters do not vary in response to actual situations in which a neighborhood, school, or workplace is integrated. Rather, powerlessness seems to result from the idea that the federal government would force integration. Whether or not a particular locality wants such does not matter to the Wallace voter; it is the idea that the federal government would actually force it that is particularly abhorrent.

At the same time, the Wallace voter does not necessarily disapprove of someone refusing to obey a law which he considered unjust. He also, despite expressing the sentiment that we should have stayed out of Vietnam, feels that since we have found ourselves there, we should try for complete military victory.

The Wallace voter believes the government should work to suit him. When it doesn't, this realization heightens his sense of powerlessness. The Wallace voter feels powerless and anomic, especially in view of the feeling that the government seems to be helping someone else—in this case, blacks. The Wallace voter believes in the forceful use of governmental power to solve problems that bother him—Vietnam, urban unrest. But the same voter resists the use of that government power when it is applied against what is regarded as his or her own interests. That these interests represent a problem for another group of American citizens is beyond the Wallace voter's comprehension. It is perceived as an illegitimate act, an interference with the voter's own rightful domain. Thus the voter mirrors the candidate.

Notes

1. Here answers three, four, and five will be considered relatively neutral; answers one and two will be classified as more lenient, and six and seven as more authoritarian. For contrast, only the latter two categories are compared.
2. It is interesting to note where the Wallace vote came from. Before the 1968 election, pollsters said that the Wallace vote was more likely to come from Republicans than Democrats. Our figures do not support that contention; almost equal proportions of Wallace voters had voted for the candidate of both parties in 1964. More interesting is the relatively large proportion of 1964 Johnson voters who voted for Nixon in 1968, as well as the proportions of nonvoters in 1968 who had voted for Johnson in 1964.
3. A relatively large percentage of the Wallace voters switched parties only recently:

Date of Switch	Nixon	Humphrey	Wallace
1961–1964	30.8	20.2	50.0
After last election	18.2	8.6	23.3
% of total changers	49.0%	28.8%	73.3%

As other tabulations suggest, switching might have been given impetus by anti-administration or anti-civil rights attitudes; the dates at least coincide with the rise of these feelings in the public consciousness.
4. Olsen and Tully (1972) use the distinction of nativity in their ascribed status measure. As that variable is not available in the other two studies, we will not include it here in the calculations. It was a question, however, on this schedule, and the tabulations are interesting. In answer to the question "Were both your parents born in this country?" respondents answer as follows (does not include blacks):

	Nixon	Humphrey	Wallace
Yes	82.9	70.9	93.5
One of them	9.1	9.9	1.9
Neither	8.0	19.2	4.6
	100.0%	100.0%	100.0%

A much higher proportion of Humphrey voters have foreign-born parents, while Wallace voters are the group most likely to have native-born parents. This is not enough evidence to classify Wallace voters as "Old American," however; it only means that they are not first generation Americans. The data base did not include a question on which country one's family had originally come from (although that information is available in the 1968 Election Study); this knowledge plus the unavailable information on how long one's family has been in the United States would be necessary in order to really determine whether or not "Old Americans" were more prevalent among Wallace voters than among other voters.

The nativity factor, along with another variable, head of household's method of employment, discredits Martin Trow's (1957) findings in "Right Wing Radicalism and Political Intolerance." The distribution of type of employment is:

	Nixon	Humphrey	Wallace
Self-employed	23.2	21.0	19.0
Work for someone else	76.8	79.0	80.0
Both self and someone else	0.0	0.0	1.0
	100.0%	100.0%	100.0%

5. Income is estimated family income for the year. For purposes of standardization and comparison with both earlier and later measures of the same variable, we have controlled for change in buying power and the resulting effect of status by dividing income into rough thirds. In 1968, the division is as follows:

Lowest third	$0 – 5999	552 cases
Middle third	$6000 – 9999	474 cases
Highest third	$10,000 and up	481 cases

6. While it is evident that the high ascribed scores for the Wallace voters overcome the deficit of low achieved scores in being recalculated into an SES score, we will follow standard practice and hold this to be valid. Status theorists, however, should reexamine the basis on which they assign relative status. It is quite possible, especially in light of the changes of the last fifteen years, that heretofore unquestioned religious and racial status discriminations are no longer accurate.

7. Nixon voters have a gamma of −.325 summarizing the strength of the relationship between political power and segregationist attitudes.

8. Nixon voters have a gamma of −.282 summarizing the strength of the relationship between political anomie and perception of the speed of the civil rights movement.

Chapter Nine

Analysis of 1968 Speeches: "Stand Up for America"

The 1968 campaign took place during an intense and violent period, a time of unprecedented domestic and foreign crisis. The civil rights movement and black rebellion were in full force; the antiwar movement was gaining momentum, and the assassinations of two major political figures, civil rights leader Rev. Martin Luther King, Jr. in April 1968 and presidential candidate Sen. Robert F. Kennedy in June 1968, left the American people stunned. The dynamics of protest coupled with the violence of the Chicago police toward protestors at the Democratic convention and the accompanying scenario at the Republican convention in Miami Beach left many angry and confused. Taking advantage of the situation, Wallace capitalized on anger and despair, bringing the American political system even closer to the edge of collapse. As candidate of the American Independent Party, he almost succeeded in his goal of throwing the election into the House of Representatives. (See Chester, Hodgson and Page 1969 for a most vivid account of the 1968 Presidential Campaign.)

The platform of the American Independent Party brilliantly illustrates the tenor of Wallace's candidacy. Reflecting his speeches, it voices his positions and stands as a revealing document of self-righteous rhetoric, citing problem after problem, offering little in the way of solid and workable solutions. The following passages from that platform resound with indignant eloquence and show Wallace's talent for picking up on and giving vivid expression to the anger and despair of those around him:

> Our citizens are deeply concerned over the domestic plight of this nation. Its cities are in decay and turmoil; its local schools and other institutions stand stripped of their rightful authority; law enforcement agencies and officers are

127

hampered by arbitrary and unreasonable restrictions imposed by a beguiled judiciary; crime runs rampant through the nation; our farmers exist only through unrealistic government subsidies; welfare rolls and costs soar to astronomical heights; our great American institutions of learning are in chaos; living costs rise ever higher as do taxes; interest rates are reaching new heights; disciples of dissent and disorder are rewarded for their disruptive actions at the expense of our law-abiding, God fearing, hard working citizenry. America is alarmed that these conditions have come to exist and that our national leadership takes no corrective action. (Porter and Johnson 1969, pp. 2, 3)

While the American Independent Party platform gives expression to the general malaise of the time, Wallace's speeches and interviews focus on his continuing interest in civil rights. As in 1964, the idea of strict constitutionalism rings out loud and clear, as does the idea of states' rights, but Wallace does not waste his time arguing the relative merits of the tenth and the fourteenth amendments. Instead he takes a more aggressive stance, maintaining that the federal government and the judiciary are now merged into an omnipotent and evil central government (Wallace 1968, p. 17), which he labels socialist, rather than Communist or liberal as before.[1] In its commitment to civil rights, this "central government" rides shotgun over the people, threatening the free enterprise system and disregarding the sanctity of private property. Ranting that the civil rights bill is little more than malicious duplicity, Wallace contends that the people have been sold a bill of goods. The upshot of it all is that they have lost their freedom; they are powerless:

And you know, what do you hear from liberals in Tennessee and the country? "We believe in free choice," they say. "Let every man choose." Well, we had a school system in Alabama that allowed people to choose to go to any school they want to go to regardless of their race or color. You had that in Tennessee. The courts recently have stricken it down because they filed a court suit in which they said not enough people have chosen to go to school from *this* side of Los Angeles to *this* side of Los Angeles, and not enough people from this side of Memphis have chosen to go to school on this side of Memphis. And we said, "Well, they could choose if they so desired. What are we gonna do about that?" And the Justice Department says "That's *your* problem." And the federal court wrote a decision that's now been affirmed by the Fifth Circuit Court of Appeals and also the Supreme Court of our country that says that "you can *choose* if you choose *properly*, but if you don't choose right, *we gonna choose for you*." They want you to choose if you choose correctly, but they look down their noses at Alabamians and Tennesseans and the working man in California. And I want to say that one of the first things we're going to do when we get into the White House, and we're going to do it within the law, we're going to turn back to you these domestic institutions. (Armstrong 1970, p.185)

Besides taking away the rights of the average American, Wallace maintains that the Civil Rights Act has another dangerous consequence: it encourages lawlessness. While the other candidates in the presidential race agree that law and order is a central concern, they do not agree with Wallace about the causes of disorder. Wallace holds the federal government directly responsible for rioting and civil disobedience (House 1969, pp. 67, 120), saying that the federal courts in their desire to secure the passage of the Civil Rights Bill have set an example which had led to the defiance of law by those who support civil rights. This breakdown of the courts, he further contends, has not strengthened race relations, but has instead led to their deterioration.

Wallace is particularly intolerant of civil disobedience, the "breaking of laws," and those who do not follow the "American way of dissent," which he defines as picketing and voting (House 1969, p. 34). In his view those who are doing the rioting and demonstrating are a small group of revolutionaries, anarchists, and Communists (House 1969, p. 67), and the reason for their existence and the cause of their dissension is permissiveness on the part of the federal government.

Wallace's hard line on law and order is well illustrated in the following quotes. Note also his disclaimer of racist interests, common in the 1968 speeches:

> Well, it's a sad day in the country when you can't talk about law and order unless they want to call you a racist. I tell you that's not true and I resent it and they gonna have to pay attention because all people in this country, in the great majority, the Supreme Court of our country has made it almost impossible to convict a criminal. And if you walk out of this building tonite, and someone knocks you in the head, the person who knocked you in the head will be out of jail if you don't watch out. (Armstrong 1970, pp. 188, 189)

> President Johnson wanted a crime commission report to tell him why they were burning cities down. Well, I could have told him why they were burning them down like you could, "because you let them burn them down, that's the reason they burn them down!" (House 1969, p. 29)

> You elect me the president, and I go to California or I come to Tennessee, and if a group of anarchists lay down in front of my automobile, it's gonna be the last one they ever gonna want to lay down in front of! (Armstrong 1970, p. 190)

> A good crease in the skull would stop some of this lawlessness. (House 1969, p. 68)

The question of Vietnam, the other main issue in the 1968 campaign, is one which Wallace seems to avoid addressing directly. Instead, he utilizes the symbol of having chosen former U.S. Air Force Chief of Staff Gen. Curtis LeMay as his running mate to indicate a strong stance, and when unavoidably confronted on the issue, chooses his words carefully, avoiding the critical question of whether or not we should be in Vietnam. At most Wallace speaks of maintaining our commitments; clearly he prefers railing out against the lawlessness of protestors to answering the question:

> There are many fine people in our country who conscientiously believe that we should not be in Vietnam. They love this country and feel that our being there is a mistake but they are not against our being there because they love some other system. They are against it because they think it's not in our interest. But we are in Vietnam and today 400,000-odd young men and women are there committed between life and death against Communist aggression, and just because the theoreticians say there formally is no war we still have the right of freedom of speech which we do, and the right of dissent . . . [but] anyone who raises money and clothes and blood for the Vietcong, and college professors, as some have recently done, who stand and tell student bodies that they long for a victory of the Vietcong Communists over the American imperialist troops in the name of academic freedom, I say to you that is not academic freedom, that's treason. (Wallace 1968, p. 156)

Wallace seems to feel uncomfortable when discussing foreign policy as well as when he finds himself in a position where thoughtful suggestions are more in order than fiery criticism. When confronted, he talks a hard line. In Vietnam our allies must support us; if they refuse, we simply cut off our aid to them. Solutions to dilemmas in foreign policy are easily arrived at if we act tough, use intelligent planning, and negotiate from a position of strength (Wallace 1968, p.158). It is all that simple.

When cornered, Wallace skillfully turns the confrontation back onto safe ground, declaring that the domestic needs of the American people are much more important than are foreign policy needs (House 1969, p. 90).

> To those who say we don't know anything about foreign policy, let me ask you this: What do the Republicans or the Democrats know about it? We've had four wars in the last fifty years. We've spent $122 billion of our money. We've got less friends than we had when we started. We could have built an interstate highway system better than the one we have now with that $122 billion. We could have raised every pension under Social Security for the elderly. We could have solved the problems of the cities. But we gave most of our money away. (House 1969, p. 46)

In Wallace's view, the real problem in America is that there has been a breakdown in old-fashioned democracy, and he holds the Civil Rights Act responsible. While he admits to the existence of the racial problems which the Civil Rights Act has been designed to alleviate (Wallace 1968, p. 50),

Wallace does not see deliberate discrimination as the cause of those problems. Solutions lie therefore not in government decree but in education (Wallace 1968, p. 49) and the free enterprise system:

> It is the free enterprise system which enables all men, regardless of their station in life, to rise to the top—to mold success or failure—to make for themselves what they will with the only limitation being their own courage and industry. (House 1969, p. 50)

> The free enterprise system has solved more poverty problems than all government projects combined and when government tries to solve all of these problems with some decree and some theory, it just doesn't work. We've got to let this free enterprise system do it. (House 1969, p. 50)

Another facet of the breakdown in old-fashioned democracy is that there is little choice in the American political arena. Republicans and the Democrats are pretty much the same, and what's more is that they are both trying to get on Wallace's bandwagon:

> I used to say that there wasn't a dime's worth of difference in what the national Republicans and the national Democrats were saying. Now there's not a dime's worth of difference in what they are saying and what I've been saying all along. (House 1969, p. 84)

Wallace suggests that the American Independent Party represents a real alternative.

> What is so sacred about the two-party system in this country? We've got a one-party system. We've got a Tweedledee and Tweedledum system. We've got a me-too system. And so we need a second party and, really, we are the second party. (House 1969, p. 120)

Carefully referring to his efforts of the last four years as the Alabama Movement, Wallace seeks to transform his personal concerns and the issues of the 1968 campaign into a national movement. What is interesting is that he makes little reference to the American Independent Party, preferring instead to mobilize action around the "struggle against federal tyranny," a reflection of his own particular brand of defiance. His rhetoric rings out loud and clear, but there is little here of substance, only a call to arms. As in 1964, the 1968 campaign is ultimately little more than Wallace's exploitation of the fear, anger, and despair around him:

> We have now reached the points in our nation's history where this great Alabama Movement has become the national movement to which people from Maine to California are looking in hope that we shall continue. We are

reaching the turning point in our struggle against federal tyranny. They are scared of The Alabama Movement. They are scared of the fire of patriotic faith that Alabamians have begun and which is now sweeping, day by day, hour by hour, across the United States. We shall continue until the debris is swept clean from our streets and our constitution is secure and bright and promising for our children. (House 1969, p. 9)

Note

1. The general absence of the term "communism" (as well as the issue of communism) in the 1968 campaign is curious, particularly as it reappears in the 1972 campaign. This can possibly be attributed to the fact that Wallace in 1968, as a third-party candidate, had the support of a variety of obviously right-wing dissidents, wanted and needed that support, and yet did not want to call attention to it. Had he mentioned the issue of communism to any great extent in this campaign, it would have most likely been seized as proof that he was indeed right-wing himself and aligned with the causes of the Birchers and the Ku Klux Klan, who were his supporters despite his disavowals.

Chapter Ten

1972: Going After the Democratic Nomination

Wallace as private citizen lent his energies to a variety of causes before he began to concentrate on reestablishing his power base in Alabama to permit yet another try for the presidency. He campaigned for an AIP congressional candidate in Tennessee (*New York Times* 1969g) and spoke at an American Party Convention. Homage was paid elsewhere by his presence and speeches. He was seen at such right-wing fetes as the John Birch Society annual dinner (Charlton 1970), the Citizens Council of America leadership conference (Wooten 1969d), and Billy James Hargis' Christian Crusade (Janson 1969).

Wallace's consuming concern between 1968 and 1972 was the federally ordered desegregation of public schools. The federal government at the time was proceeding with desegregation plans. In September 1969, as the new school year approached, Wallace urged parents to ignore court orders on school assignments and to enter their children in the schools of their choice. As a private citizen and with the help of his campaign staff, he drafted a resolution for the Alabama state legislature calling for the public's support of parents who chose to defy school desegregation orders. The resolution was quickly passed (Wooten 1969b), but those schools which had been ordered to desegregate opened without incident (Wooten 1969c). The governors of southern states, while upset about the proceeding of federal integration plans, offered only mild protests and no overt defiance (Wooten 1969a).

Wallace offset these activities with a fact-finding tour to Vietnam. He returned professing the conviction that the situation called for a military solution and urged Nixon to act on the situation in Southeast Asia and on a variety of domestic problems (*New York Times* 1969b).

He then turned again to the local issue, calling a meeting in Birmingham of parents concerned over school desegregation. Fifteen thousand attended. Before his audience Wallace urged southern governors to defy court orders calling for school desegregation. His actions were interpreted as a sure sign that he was planning to run for governor and would subsequently run again for president in 1972 (Wooten 1970g). His Vietnam trip and the following incident also seem to indicate this.

The My Lai Massacre and the trial of Lieutenant William L. Calley was an issue made to order for Wallace. From Wallace's perspective, it was a perfect example of the little man being victimized by the federal government (Apple 1971d). He went to Columbus, Georgia to meet with Calley and came away criticizing the handling of the case by the news media (*New York Times* 1970k). It was most likely a move for publicity because six days later Wallace announced that he would enter the Alabama gubernatorial race and run against incumbent Brewer in the Democratic primary (Wooten 1970f).

It was essential that Wallace win the gubernatorial race in order to be able to run again for president in 1972. No one had expected him not to run. Brewer, long before Wallace announced his candidacy, had been saying that Alabama needed a full-time governor, intimating that someone running for the presidency would not have the proper amount of interest in the state (*New York Times* 1970l). Wallace, when he finally announced (Wooten 1970f), retorted that if he were elected governor, he might not have to run for president. His election, he assured, would pressure Nixon to fulfill his campaign promises of returning school decision-making responsibility to local control. He also warned that Nixon strategists were likely to put money into Brewer's campaign in an effort to defeat him. Subsequent Watergate disclosures showed that he was right: a total of $400,000 was actually invested for this purpose (Hersh 1973a; Rosenbaum 1973, Naughton 1973). What the money bought, however, is not clear.

The preprimary contest was low key. "I never seen one like this before," remarked one Alabamian (Wooten 1970d). Brewer refrained from criticizing his opponent and insisted that Wallace should be president, not governor (Wooten 1970e). The two men had the same issues; they were careful not to attack each other.

Nixon began almost immediately to react publicly to Wallace's announced candidacy. He reaffirmed his commitment to the concept of neighborhood schools and said he was against forced busing in an attempt to undermine Wallace's contention that he had no intention of fulfilling his campaign promises (Reed 1970). When the Senate rejected Nixon's southern candidate Harold Carsdale's nomination to the Supreme Court, he lost his temper. He called those senators who had voted against Carsdale hypocrites and said that they were prejudiced against Southerners (Frankel 1970). This remark was seen by seasoned observers as an attempt by Nixon to represent himself as an able defender of the South, thereby preempting some support from Wallace, the object being to defeat Wallace.

Other tactics were used. The news that George Wallace's brother Gerald was being investigated by the Internal Revenue Service was leaked to Jack Anderson, who noted the fact in his column three weeks before the gubernatorial primary (*New York Times* 1970j). Later revelations suggested that some high level White House staff members were probably responsible for the leak (Shanahan 1974) and that it had most likely been a deliberate attempt to cut into Wallace's vote.

As the primary approached, a large number of IRS agents were seen around Alabama. They seemed to be concentrating their inquiries not only on Gerald Wallace, but on other prominent Wallace supporters as well. In addition, Vice President Agnew and Postmaster General Blount, an Alabama native, endorsed Brewer.

As the pressure began to build, Wallace abandoned gentlemanly tactics (Apple 1970d). He insisted that twenty-five federal registrars had been brought into the state to register black voters. He contended that the blacks would then vote in a bloc for Brewer, against Wallace. His advertising maintained:

> If out-of-state forces and in-state bloc voters defeat Wallace, we all lose! Our voice is gone, our fight is over. George Wallace stood up for you again and again. He needs your help now. Don't turn your back on him. (Apple 1970e)

Brewer's publicity was more relaxed: "We want a governor who is for something, not against everything" (Apple 1970e).

Wallace, in growing desperation, began to turn more and more often to his surefire tactic of appealing to racial hatred (Apple 1970d). Doctored photographs appeared showing Governor Brewer with prize fighter Muhammed Ali and Black Muslim chief Elijah Muhammed, but the Wallace staff insisted that they were not responsible for the pictures.

Brewer did not strike back; he quietly promised a "look to the future, not to the past," and it worked. When the primary votes were counted, Brewer had edged ahead of Wallace by 5,908 votes (*New York Times* 1970i). He had gotten substantial black support as well. The third runner-up refused to endorse either Brewer or Wallace (*New York Times* 1970h), and the runoff was scheduled for June 2. It called for an all-out effort by the Wallace forces if their candidate was going to win. They tried many things.

Wallace's brother Jack paid for a twenty-four page campaign brochure enclosed in the monthly magazine of the Ku Klux Klan (*New York Times*

1970g). And when student unrest developed at the University of Alabama approximately two-and-a-half weeks after the Kent State incident, Governor Brewer sent state troopers onto the campus. The students felt that Brewer had done it just to show that he could be as tough on law and order as could Wallace (Wooten 1970c).

Astute observers noted that almost 30,000 new voters were registered in the period between the primary and the runoff. "Most signed up in areas of Wallace strength, and most were transported to the registration offices in cars festooned with Wallace stickers" (Apple 1970c).

Wallace, referring to the large black vote which Brewer had gotten in the primary as the bloc vote, inferred that Brewer must have made some secret promises to get that vote. Brewer contended that he got no such bloc vote, or else he would have won the election (Wooten 1970b).

Wallace was endorsed by Robert Shelton, the Imperial Wizard of the Ku Klux Klan (Apple 1970b), and in the last few nights before the run-off, many people found bumper stickers mysteriously appearing on their cars, contending "I'm for Brewer and the Blacks" (Apple 1970c). There were also last-minute rumors that Mrs. Brewer was an alcoholic, and the Brewer's two daughters were pregnant by blacks (Apple 1970a).

Wallace's efforts paid off. He won by a margin of 33,881 votes (*New York Times* 1970f), a showing of 51.56 percent. In the first flush of victory he challenged Nixon to fulfill his campaign promises to the South or answer to the wrath of Wallace's Alabama movement (Wooten 1970a).

In turn, Nixon evidently decided that he could not out-do Wallace on his own ground, for his aides immediately vowed more integration for the South in the fall than had been accomplished in any previous year (Herbers 1970). They apparently did begin moving in that direction, for Sen. Strom Thurmond angrily accused Nixon of going back on his word and dropping his southern strategy. Nixon replied that he had no southern strategy, only a one-nation strategy, and was moving ahead on desegregation (*New York Times* 1970e).

All of this led Tom Wicker to observe astutely that

> the Wallace party is one of the most important political forces in America—not because it holds any office or has any real authority. It is because through the 1968 campaign, in the years since, perhaps prospectively for 1972, it wields profound influence on Mr. Nixon and his associates, their attitudes and their programs. With all due respect to these men, most of whom are by no means segregationists, the Wallace pressure on their right flank has constantly limited their vision and insidiously undermined their political confidence. (Wicker 1970)

Wallace had conducted a very ugly run-off campaign; he had been desperate, and did not want to leave anything to chance. After Brewer was defeated, the Alabama Republicans decided not to run anyone against the sure winner in the November gubernatorial contest. His major opponent was a black dentist, Dr. John Cashin, chosen by the predominantly black National Democratic Party of Alabama as their candidate. In addition to Cashin in the governor's slot, this party also ran a slate of 169 candidates in the general election (*New York Times* 1970c).

Wallace campaigned vigorously, although few thought that Cashin would provide any real competition. Wallace's sole object seemed to be a large margin of victory. That, he seemed to hope, would erase from memory the fact that he had only narrowly defeated Brewer.

In the election, Wallace reclaimed the governorship with a landslide victory: 208,981 votes (*New York Times* 1970a). Elected along with him were two black state legislators and four black county sheriffs, bringing the total of elected black officials in Alabama to 105, making the state second only to Michigan with 110 (Rosenbaum 1970).

In September, between the primary and the general election, Wallace had tried once again to urge parents to defy federal court orders assigning their children to desegregated schools (*New York Times* 1970b). As before, there were no incidents. His inaugural speech in January 1971 (Reed 1971) was the first indication of a shift in his attitude—a reporter present said that he had detected a "quiet appeal for black friendship."

The recent election had demonstrated that black political power in Alabama had grown tremendously. A black voter registration of just over 300,000, about one-fifth of Alabama's total number of voters, and 105 elected officials (*New York Times* 1970d) was a reality that would be suicidal to ignore. Further, Wallace had not been able to stir up the whites enough to get them to defy the federal government on anything except the issue of busing. The writing was on the wall. Wallace's focus on the issue of desegregation became increasingly obscured. As the 1972 campaign approached, he dropped his overt stance, and his position on the basic issue of segregation could no longer be so easily identified. This refocusing seemed to be the result of a very pragmatic appraisal of conditions around him and of popular sentiment.

As the new school year approached, Wallace began to ready his new issue—busing. He announced that he would not permit any additional busing, and said that he would hire an additional 200 state troopers to insure tranquility (*New York Times* 1971h). In August he telegrammed Nixon, demanding that he back up his antibusing statements (*New York Times* 1971g). Without hesitation, Wallace stepped right into the busing quagmire in Alabama. Disregarding court orders, he began to rezone school districts and quotas according to his own plans. Next he ordered the school boards to disregard busing orders (*New York Times* 1971g; *New York Times* 1971f). He then quickly announced that he was only assisting "Mr. Nixon in his anti-busing campaign" (Wooten 1971f).

The heat was on. Federal Judge Pointer, newly appointed by Nixon, ruled that Wallace's orders were of no consequence and told school board members to ignore them. Rather than confront Wallace directly, the judge said that the governor's orders were merely an exercise of his right to free speech (Wooten 1971e). Wallace tried to force the issue, saying that the federal government had to take him to court to halt his antibusing orders. He would agree to abide by the decision of the court. Reporter James T. Wooten commented that either way, Wallace would get what he wanted:

> The logic in the Wallace camp is that, should the President and Attorney Gen. John N. Mitchell bring the weight of the Federal Government to bear on the Governor, he will, as he always has, stridently agree to abide by the law. This would add just one more point to his now familiar sermon on the demise of state's rights and the pervasively demonic powers of Washington bureaucrats. On the other hand, if no one moves against him, and his anti-busing orders to local school boards are allowed to stand, Mr. Wallace will have, in effect, successfully countermanded the Federal Court's directions and substantially improved his image as a courageous champion of those millions of Americans who share his lack of faith in the Federal motive. (Wooten 1971b)

The White House responded by telling government officials to use busing only as a last resort in the desegregation of schools. Wallace in the meantime ordered the reopening of some all-black schools which had been closed by the government previously. Shortly afterwards, Nixon asked the Supreme Court to delay the court-ordered integration of a Corpus Christi, Texas school district (Wooten 1971c). But it was not enough for Wallace, who insisted that he would issue additional orders in a challenge to the president "to prove that he means what he says about busing" (*New York Times* 1971e). To a Citizens Council convention he carefully delineated his position:

> Governor Wallace said that his present position of advising Alabama parents to defy federal orders on busing was not based on opposition to school integration as such but on opposition to Federal officials trying to control the education of children. (Waldron 1971b)

Wallace had the Alabama legislature pass a law allowing parents to disregard court-ordered desegregation plans if they objected to busing their children (Wooten 1971a; *New York Times* 1971d). He even got the approval of the Alabama Senate Finance Committee to withhold state funds allocated for busing (*New York Times* 1971c).

Increasingly, however, he found himself on tenuous ground. Two of the school boards that he had ordered to disregard busing plans refused to listen to him and obeyed the court instead (Wooten 1971a), and an integrated parents' group in Mobile quietly put into effect a mass busing plan which they had worked out in a series of meetings over the summer. No incidents were reported (Waldron 1971a).

The fact that many parents weren't willing to defy government orders didn't bother Wallace. His view was that whatever their actual response, people were angry and upset about busing. He had found an issue for his 1972 campaign.

The 1972 Presidential Campaign: The Primaries

Wallace entered the 1972 presidential campaign with a newly constituted executive staff. There had been a shakeup in early 1970, and Trammell, Jackson, Jones and Ewing had resigned. Bablin told the author that he had heard it had something to do with the mismanagement of money (Bablin 1975). Another report suggests that the four "objected to Gerald Wallace's usurping what they considered to be their power in the campaign" (Waldron 1972b; This is corroborated by Dorman 1976, pp. 74-5).

Tom Turnipseed, one of the regional coordinators from the 1968 campaign, was appointed director, but lost his post before long (Apple 1971a). Turnipseed evidently remained with the campaign in some capacity, because he was identified in a Strachan-to-Haldeman memo dated February 16, 1972 as being the White House contact man inside the Wallace campaign (Crewdson 1974). He was replaced as director by Charles Snider, the former Wallace campaign pilot. Alton Dauphin, Wallace's brother-in-law, became the assistant director in charge of finances. They were joined by Joe Azbell who was responsible for publicity and speechwriting.

The men formed a loose team, usually working in solitary efforts without consulting each other. Azbell said that this arrangement worked well because they had very well-defined areas of responsibility (Azbell 1974b). Each brought his own special expertise, and slowly they began to shape things according to their own ideas of how a campaign should be run.

During this time the *George C. Wallace Newsletter* came into existence, supported by a paid subscription list of 40,000 (Bigart 1969). In time it became *The Wallace Stand*, a slick-paper publication with a circulation of over 300,000 (Wooten 1971g). Copy was written solely by Azbell after consultation with Wallace. In preparation for the 1972 campaign, *The Wallace Stand* was printed in a variety of editions—large type for the elderly, a labor edition for workers, and in several foreign languages— Chinese, Polish, Yiddish, German, and Spanish. This gave Wallace a readymade claim that his appeal extended to all ethnic groups and was used to counter accusations of prejudice (Azbell 1974b) .

Azbell also came up with a new gimmick, the Appreciation Dinner. This was a variation on the theme of the $25-a-plate dinner. If a Wallace supporter wanted to fly to a Wallace Appreciation Dinner in another city, the campaign was more than happy to oblige him. For the price of an air ticket and a dinner ticket, the supporters would be flown by chartered jet to the festivities. The profits went into the campaign coffers. Occasionally, the Wallace people would give a very generous contributor a free plane ride on the campaign trail (Azbell 1974a). The opportunity to join the entourage proved a successful encouragement to those who could be induced to give more.

At Azbell's suggestion, the campaign began to combine their polling and funding operations. The Wallace people were distrustful of national polls, and had only seldom used polling organizations to sample an area of interest. Then Azbell hit upon combining the two procedures (Azbell 1974a, 1974b, 1974c).

The Wallace polls, after announcing that "Governor Wallace wants your opinion," asked such attitudinal questions as "What do you consider the most important issues facing our nation at this time?" as well as the respondent's estimate of Wallace support in the respondent's area. The questionnaire could be filled out in less than five minutes, but many of those who replied wrote letters to Governor Wallace on the back.

Besides bringing in contributions and recruiting possible workers as well as identifying geographical pockets of Wallace supporters, the questionnaires served another important function—they alerted Wallace and his staff as to what the current issues were as well as what the upcoming ones would be.

They also used the polls to give them an idea of what the people from a particular town or area were angry about—what their "devils" were. Thus when Wallace visited that community he could easily ignite a crowd by playing on their deepest concerns.

In 1972 the staff decided to get their candidate before as many people as possible. Television and radio appearances were more frequently used than ever before. They also continued the practice of selling all of their campaign publicity materials.

Money was probably still flowing in from the patronage systems. But "patronage" does not adequately describe the following fund-raising technique. It was revealed during the campaign by *The Montgomery Advertiser* that businessmen with state contracts had been invited to a dinner for Wallace and had each been advised to bring $1,500 as a donation. Fifty-seven of the one hundred invited actually came and complied, and an unidentified state official said that the state finance office had been telling contractors "how much to donate to Wallace's presidential campaign before they receive a state contract" (*New York Times* 1972v).

The campaign staff continued to experiment with ways of getting money and ways of presenting their candidate to the people. Just one week before Wallace was shot, they hit upon a new technique—shopping center rallies. Wallace had complained that airports were not satisfactory locations for rallies; they were too far from cities. "You ought to bring the candidate where the people are," he had remarked, and the new idea had seemed to be a good one (Franklin 1972).

The Florida primary was the first real combat scheduled for the 1972 election. Every Democrat who had any aspirations for the presidency entered the contest. Before it started, most commentators had thought that Wallace would run again as a third party candidate.

The American Independent Party in 1972

The machinery of the American Independent Party was still there, although there is some evidence that what was left was not altogether friendly toward Wallace. He had exerted such control in 1968 that there was no cohesive structure linking the fifty state organizations. Shortly after the 1968 election, William K. Shearer, who had originally been head of the Wallace efforts in California and later ousted, called for a meeting of AIP representatives (*New York Times* 1968a). The expressed purpose was to insure a continuing national organization and to preserve ballot qualifications.

In May 1969, a meeting of former AIP workers finally took place. One hundred and sixty delegates from thirty-eight states were present. They named themselves the American Party and elected T. Coleman Andrews, the former Virginia AIP chairman as their national chairman (*New York Times* 1969f). Wallace gave the new party his blessing and called it "the official arm of his southern-based third party movement." He said that if he did run again for president, it would be under the banner of the American Party (*New York Times* 1969e).

At the same time, Wallace said that he intended to remain an Alabama Democrat (*New York Times* 1969d). This was a reference to the fact that he had run and won electors as the presidential candidate on the Democratic ticket in Alabama in the 1968 election, after having successfully blocked the national Democratic ticket from being on the ballot in that election. He was very proud of having won the state's presidential votes as a nominal Democrat. It gave him more legitimacy.

When the American Party held its convention in the summer of 1969 Wallace was a key speaker. At the convention, T. Coleman Andrews announced that he was going to run for governor of Virginia on the American Party ticket. But Wallace cautioned the party against running too many local candidates: "It is better to have no candidate at all, many times, than one who can't be elected," he said (*New York Times* 1969c).

Apparently there was a split among Wallace's former supporters, because in December 1969 there was yet another meeting, this one called by William K. Shearer. It was attended by representatives from twenty-seven states and was listed as the National Committee of Autonomous State Parties, At the gathering, Shearer criticized T. Coleman Andrews and the American Party, and suggested that Wallace sever his Democratic ties. He was also angry about Wallace's relationship to his supporters: "The point is," he said, "our people want a political party, but it shouldn't belong to George Wallace; it should belong to the membership" (*New York Times* 1969a).

Sometime in 1971, Wallace sent word to Nixon that he would draw off many Democratic votes if he ran as a third-party candidate in 1972. The implication was "that he wanted to conclude a tacit alliance with Mr. Nixon." The White House replied that it wanted to see a Republican-Democratic contest with Wallace not running (Apple 1971c).

As the 1972 election approached, Richard B. McKay, one of Lieutenant William Calley's lawyers, announced that he would seek the presidential nomination of the AIP. McKay stated that he was entering the race in order to make the AIP a viable national party not solely dependent on Wallace (*New York Times* 1971a). Rumblings of mutiny from Wallace's 1968 political creation continued to be heard. Wallace refused to commit himself to an AIP candidacy, but he didn't say no, either. Snider maintained some time later that "up until three weeks before the Florida primary, all of our efforts had been geared toward a third-party campaign" (*New York Times* 1974o). It seems likely, however, that the certain decision to run as a Democrat in all possible primaries was made only after Wallace's showing in the Florida primary, and not before.

Wallace had commissioned polls to check his chances in Florida before he even entered the primary (Apple 1972k). He was not at all sure of his strength as a Democrat. In the meanwhile, his staff was quietly checking ballot positioning requirements in all of the states.

"It started," his friends said, "almost as a whim. He would enter a Democratic primary or two, partly to practice for a third-party candidacy in the fall" (Apple 1972h). The second run as a Democrat likely resulted from his showing in the first. The decision to continue was tenuous; it most likely became more firm as it became more and more apparent that Wallace had a great deal of support among the voting populace whatever his political declaration might be, but both options were kept open. The third party possibility provided security. Wallace could fall back on it if he needed to. It could also be used as a weapon to threaten the leadership of both major parties.

The Reaction of the Democratic Party to Wallace's Candidacy

The Democrats wanted no part of Wallace. In anticipation of his candidacy, the Florida State Democratic Party considered passing a measure that would permit any candidate winning delegates in the Florida primary to be stripped of that support if he later ran on a third-party ticket in another state (*New York Times* 1971b).

Although Wallace had announced as a Democratic primary candidate, Larry O'Brien, the Democratic National Chairman, sought repeatedly to discredit him (Apple 1972j). O'Brien called a Wallace third-party candidacy essential to the Nixon-Mitchell campaign strategy, and the Democratic party even issued a statement that they had denied hotel convention space to the Wallace campaign and their delegates. The justification was that Wallace wasn't considered a legitimate member of the party (*New York Times* 1972bb). After some consideration, O'Brien telegrammed Wallace and said that he would be granted space only if he proved his loyalty to the party by swearing to support the 1972 Democratic nominee (*New York Times* 1972aa). Pressure came from somewhere, however, because afterwards, Wallace was awarded the necessary space without having to submit to the loyalty oath (*New York Times* 1972z).

Wallace gained positions on several Democratic primary ballots soon after declaring his candidacy in the Florida primary. But throughout the primary campaigns he was never really taken seriously as a Democratic contender, a rather curious thing considering his showings, but an impression which Wallace took great pleasure in fostering (Apple 1972d). He constantly baited his fellow contenders with the threat of a possible third-party candidacy if he didn't get what he wanted, or if he wasn't treated with respect by the national party (Waldron 1972d; *New York Times* 1972y).

The Florida Primary

The Democratic run in Florida started with a plethora of candidates—eleven to be exact. Busing was a prime topic in the state. Governor Askew was a strong proponent of busing, but much of the citizenry was against it. An antibusing referendum was to appear on the ballot, and it was feared that many people who felt strongly about racial issues and might not otherwise come would be drawn to the polls. These people, it was felt, were certain to vote for Wallace (Nordheimer 1972f):

> Appearing before record-breaking crowds not only in the Florida panhandle, which has been called an extension of Alabama, but also in the metropolitan

areas of Miami, Tampa, and Jacksonville, he tore into busing with his old vitality. He termed Nixon a "double-dealer, a two-timer, and a man who tells folks one thing and does another." He put the busing decision on Nixon's back. He said Nixon was only another part of the government in Washington which was run by "bureaucrats, hypocrites, and uninterested politicians". . . . When he put his finger directly on the issue, he complained, "This senseless business of trifling with the health and safety of your child, regardless of his color, by busing him across state lines and city lines and into kingdom come, has got to go! He said the entire business was "social scheming" imposed by "anthropologists, zoologists, and sociologists." With the applause breaking up his sentences, he became wound up. His delivery was fast, as powerful and enunciated as ever. He was sending them his message, saying that busing was "the most atrocious, callous, cruel, asinine thing you can do for little children" and that the national politicians were the "pluperfect hypocrities who live over in Maryland or Virginia, and they've got their children in a private school," and told those same politicians that "tomorrow the chickens are coming home to roost. They gonna be sorry they bused your little children and had something to do with it. (Greenhaw 1976, pp. 39, 40)

As it became apparent that Wallace was reaching a lot of people with his antibusing message, the other candidates began to reevaluate their own positions on busing. Sen. Henry Jackson was one of the first to capitulate. He introduced an antibusing constitutional amendment in the Senate. R. W. Apple, Jr. commented that Jackson's move seemed desperate, a vain effort "to sell himself as a respectable alternative to Wallace" (Apple 1972i). Wallace then began to use his advantage to the hilt. Maintaining that he had never been a racist, he successfully tied the busing issue to the idea that the federal government was impinging on what should be people's basic rights.

In response, Governor Askew bought television time, not to combat Wallace directly, but to try to assuage the widespread antibusing sentiment (Nordheimer 1973e). John Lindsay railed the U.S. Senate for even considering the two antibusing amendments which had been placed before it, saying that it had bowed to Wallace in doing so (Waldron 1972g), and Muskie supporters bought a full-page ad in the *Miami Herald* which featured a picture of Wallace along with the caption, "If You Wouldn't Give Him the Presidency, Don't Give Him Our Primary" (Waldron 1972e). In the meantime, labor unions in Florida were distributing anti-Wallace literature (Waldron 1972f).

Ultimately, in a field of eleven candidates, Wallace got forty-two percent of the vote and seventy-five of the state's eighty-one delegates (Waldron 1972c).

His positions had been accurately chosen. He steered between the Scylla and Charybdis of busing and desegregation without getting caught up in either, and captured the sentiments of the populace at large, who were overwhelmingly in favor of integration and yet opposed to busing. Even stronger was the sentiment for allowing prayer in public schools, also one of Wallace's favorite issues.[1]

The press and the professional politicians focused on the fact that Humphrey had come in second in the primary and publicly ignored Wallace's victory; many felt that the large number of contestants and heavy support for Wallace as a non-Democrat made the first place win meaningless as a test of Democratic strength (Waldron 1972c). Muskie, however, could not contain himself, and angrily called Wallace a demagogue (Ayres 1972), saying that the Wallace vote had disclosed "the worst instincts of which human beings are capable" (Wicker 1972c).

Other politicians were not so ready to attack the winner. It would not pay to alienate voters who seemed to be attracted to Wallace's appeals. Vice President Agnew carefully criticized Muskie's attack on Wallace, saying that he had heard nothing radical from Wallace during the campaign. Agnew said further that Wallace had evidently struck a chord with the voters (Ayres 1972). Three days after the Florida primary ended, President Nixon called for a halt to forced busing. Lindsay, outraged, saw Nixon's act as a "'cave in' to the segregationist views" of George Wallace (Hunter 1972). Democrat Hubert Humphrey, meanwhile, praised Nixon's decision to stop the busing. But when his advisors strongly objected, Humphrey changed his position the next day. The decision was, he said, "deceptive" and "insensitive to the laws and Constitution of this nation"(Apple 1972g). Meanwhile, Wallace's showing had persuaded a number of politicians that busing was the prime issue. Immediately, almost all of them began to use it.

Wallace, in another political move, announced that Norman F. Jones, a black political columnist for several Florida newspapers, was to be chairman of the newly formed National Black Citizens Committee for Wallace (*New York Times* 1972w). Despite this seeming show of broader perspective, the candidate did not hesitate to attack his opponent Terry Sanford on the last night of the North Carolina primary. Sanford had a liberal position on integrated schools, and Wallace did not agree with his stance (Charlton 1972).

The Other Primaries

The Wisconsin contest was next. Wallace apparently thought that his chances were slim, for he campaigned only nine days, making eleven appearances in all (Wooten 1972m). He also chose not to rely heavily on the busing issue. "They don't have the problem here," he had said, and concentrated on tax reform and inflation instead (Kneeland 1972d). Evidently, the other candidates were watching Wallace and followed suit, because Wallace complained that he had given them the issue and that they were using it heavily (Nordheimer 1972d). He had again judged the mood of the voters correctly, as a Yankelovich survey conducted at the time showed that economic issues accounted for both McGovern's victory and Wallace's second place (Rosenthal 1972c).

In spite of an all-out anti-Wallace campaign by labor leaders (Kneeland 1972c) and Wallace's half-hearted effort, he got twenty-two percent of the vote, second only to McGovern with thirty percent (Kneeland 1972b). Wallace seemed genuinely surprised, and responded by stepping up his campaign, announcing a hectic thirty-two day schedule (Wooten 1972m). McGovern, meanwhile, was emerging in the eyes of the Democrats as a major contender, despite his previous poor showings. Many of the Wallace voters had indicated that McGovern was their second choice (Rosenthal 1972c), and McGovern himself said that he had tried to listen very closely to the anger and frustration of Wallace voters. He stated tactfully that Wallace didn't have the answers, but that he was successful in articulating the frustrations of his followers (Apple 1972f). Thus, McGovern was being increasingly seen as possibly providing a legitimate appeal to Wallace voters as well as to mainstream Democrats (Wicker 1972a).

Wallace began to have troubles among his political peers as his popularity among the voters increased. He was often snubbed by the other candidates as well as by the Democratic party. One obvious oversight by the party during the Michigan campaign was in not inviting him to the annual Jefferson-Jackson Day Dinner in Detroit along with all of the other major Democratic candidates. The justification for his exclusion was that Wallace had refused to pledge unconditional support for the eventual Democratic nominee, but Wallace managed a coup. He set up his own rival rally a few miles away for the same time and drew five times the number of people that the official function drew—10,000 (in comparison with the 2,500 who attended the Jefferson-Jackson Day Dinner). Four thousand heard him speak and then filed out and were replaced by another 4,000. A crowd of 2,000 who were unable to get in were left outside (Wooten 1972l). Six years later the Wallace staff in Montgomery were still talking about the coup (Azbell 1978; Griffin 1978). In additional efforts to discourage Wallace support, Michigan Democrats spent $10,000 on anti-Wallace television and radio commercials, an unusual move, since Wallace was running in their own party's primary (Flint 1972b).

Meanwhile, all of the other candidates were seeking to identify themselves with the issues that Wallace had "brought to the fore: tax reform, the remoteness of government, urban disorder and decay, and an overwhelming sense of frustration" (Apple 1972e).

Toward the end of April, as the Democratic primary approached in

Alabama, ads began appearing in the local newspapers demanding, "Come Home, Governor." The text accompanying the ads suggested that if Wallace was interested in national politics, he should resign and let someone else take care of Alabama's problems. The Wallace staff was certain that the national Democratic Party had planted the ads (Nordheimer 1972c). At the same time there was growing criticism about Wallace's record in Alabama, as well as criticism of his brother Gerald's activities and the behavior of his aides. In reply Wallace "made a special appeal to Alabamians not to embarrass him in Tuesday's primary by failing to give him a majority of delegates to the Democratic National Convention" (Waldron 1972b). His state didn't let him down; he got control of thirty-seven Alabama delegates (Nordheimer 1972b).

More serious problems were beginning to develop, problems that had first became apparent in the Wisconsin primary. The results of that primary began to draw attention to one of the handicaps that eventually kept Wallace out of the serious running in 1972—the delegate election procedure. In Wisconsin a candidate had to carry a district in order to get that district's delegates, and Wallace, although he had gotten twenty-two percent of the popular vote, did not carry any of the nine congressional districts. Thus, he got no delegates. In contrast, Humphrey, who was third with twenty-one percent of the vote, carried two districts and got thirteen delegates (Kneeland 1972b), and McGovern had netted fifty-four delegates.

The same kind of thing happened in two other primaries, Pennsylvania and Indiana. Wallace had not expected to do well in Pennsylvania and had held only one rally there (Janson 1972a). He had also fielded only four delegates (Janson 1972b). When he came in second, he was ecstatic. "Pennsylvania is the most phenomenal victory of my entire career," he beamed, and seemed to begin to think that he might actually win the nomination (Wooten 1972k). Although he had twenty-one percent of the vote, only two of his delegates were elected. Humphrey, first with thirty-five percent of the vote, got fifty-seven delegates; McGovern, also with twenty-one percent, got thirty-seven delegates and Muskie, fourth with twenty percent, got twenty-nine delegates. The Wallace people had not been prepared, but their candidate didn't seem to be worried. The popular vote totals were of much more interest to him than the lack of delegates. Wallace's rationale told him that "when no one wins on the first, second, third, or fourth ballots, they'll ask who can draw the popular vote" (Janson 1972b).

Indiana was much the same. Humphrey came in first in that primary with forty-seven percent of the vote, and Wallace was a strong second with forty-one percent (King 1972b); however, the delegate totals each won were even further apart—fifty-four for Humphrey and twenty-one for Wallace (King 1972a).

There were some states in which Wallace did win a large number of delegates, and in those states he had a very different problem, a threat of mutiny. In the Tennessee primary, Wallace had gotten sixty-eight percent of the vote but many of those who were running for delegate positions (to be decided at district conventions in May and June) said that they would refuse to vote for him. Despite the fact that the law required them to vote for the winner of the popular primary on the first two ballots at the convention, there was no certainty that they would do so (Kovach 1972).

Maryland was also giving Wallace trouble. Maryland statutes required that delegates vote for the candidate who received thirty-five percent of Maryland's primary vote on the first ballot and on the second. If delegates refused to follow the law, there was nothing that could be done. In speculation, the attorney general of Maryland "ruled that the law would be unenforceable since it would be violated in Miami Beach, an area over which he lacks jurisdiction" (Delaney 1972). North Carolina Democrats threatened to do the same kind of thing (Apple 1972d), and Michigan seemed to be involved in yet another plan, an attempt to minimize the backing that Wallace had won (Rugaher 1972). Wallace retorted that he might consider a third-party run (Apple 1972d).

The Assassination Attempt and its Aftermath

Suddenly, on May 15, 1972, the Republican and Democratic parties' difficulties with Wallace were over. The candidate was shot while campaigning at a shopping center rally in Maryland, and was permanently paralyzed from the waist down. The day after he was shot, he won both the Maryland and the Michigan primaries. It was generally contended that the shooting did not affect the results of either primary (Rosenthal 1972b; 1972a). At the time he was shot, Wallace was ahead in total number of popular votes. Tallies through May 16 are as follows (Scammon 1973):

Wallace	3,354,360
Humphrey	2,647,676
McGovern	2,202,840
Total Vote	11,724,795

Electoral vote tabulations gave a different picture. Through May 16 they ran (Apple 1972c):

McGovern	409.35
Wallace	323
Humphrey	291.35

The Wallace organization, in concentrating on getting the popular vote, had neglected to concentrate on the crucial delegate election procedures.

"We didn't know the rules the way the McGovern people did," said campaign manager Charles Snider (Greenhaw 1976, p. 75).

After Wallace was shot, there was not much chance for him to gain more electoral votes; only six primaries remained. He had not entered either California or Ohio, where he might have had a chance to pick up a substantial number of delegates (Apple 1972d). James T. Wooten (1972i) commented:

> In the short run, on the primary level, there is among those who have worked for the governor and with him a nagging suspicion that there can be little campaign without his actual presence and participation. He was the campaign—all of it. His feisty, fiery oratory and his magic presence in the halls and arenas around the country were the most powerful ingredients in the grasp he held on the thousands of supporters whose discontent was answered by his own.

Some attempts were made to pick up more votes (Rugaber 1972). The staff used videotapes (Wooten 1972j) and a number of men were asked to speak in Wallace's behalf. Wallace headquarters put $25,000 into a television blitz the last two weeks of primary campaigning (Apple 1972b). And George Wallace, Jr. barnstormed California and New Mexico (Kneeland 1972a; Waldron 1972a). All of these efforts yielded an additional 401,064 votes (Scammon 1972, p. 19) and fifty-four delegates, bringing the totals to 3,755,424 popular votes and 377 delegates (Apple 1972a).

Wallace's shooting gained him some immediate respectability. He was visited in the hospital by President Richard Nixon, Vice President Spiro Agnew, Democratic presidential candidate Edmund Muskie, Sen. Edward Kennedy, Congresswoman Shirley Chisholm, Sen. Hubert Humphrey, Democratic presidential candidate George McGovern, and Ethel Kennedy, among others. McGovern urged Wallace delegates to vote for their candidate on the convention's first ballot. He also encouraged them to file a minority report, and said that he would try to make sure that their proposals reached the floor. The McGovern supporters would of course vote against the Wallace proposals, but at least they would be heard (Naughton 1972c). This was viewed by the press as an attempt by McGovern to get the Wallace votes.

The Wallace people were, in the meanwhile, working hard to keep options open for their candidate. Mickey Griffin announced that Wallace could be an independent candidate in all but five states; the third parties, he said, already had the "required spots on ballots of twenty states" and were at work on twenty-five more. However, the reporter present noted that there was actually very little talk of a third party run in campaign headquarters. "Instead, there is a feverish bustle of plans for the convention and an unabashed optimism that when the final gavel falls in Miami Beach, the governor will be the nominee" (Wooten 1972h).

Because of the assassination attempt, most delegations seemed willing to give Wallace the support he had won. The Michigan delegates pledged to vote for him through two ballots (Flint 1972a). There were even a few individual state efforts to get Wallace on the ballot. Wisconsin Citizens for Wallace filed incorporation papers (*New York Times* 1972t), and the Courage Party in New York State started a petition drive to get Wallace on the ballot for the general election. (*New York Times* 1972s).

Wallace representatives were placed on the Democratic Platform Committee (Herbers 1972d), but their positions on issues were repeatedly defeated. They finally threatened to take them directly to the convention (Herbers 1973c), and filed minority reports that

> oppose busing for desegregation, call for a constitutional amendment permitting prayer in schools, support the rights of citizens to bear arms, defend capital punishment, oppose "bureaucratic price controls," and soften the section of the platform that calls for immediate withdrawal of American troops from Vietnam. (Herbers 1972b)

Meanwhile Wallace, although hospitalized, met regularly with his staff, who in turn met with Wallace delegates on the platform and credentials committees. He orchestrated all of their moves, most of which were focused on trying to promote platform changes. Snider insisted to the questioning press that Wallace was not thinking of a third-party move. "The governor decided to be a Democrat, he is participating in good faith in the convention." Others also felt sure of that

> there are many . . . who are persuaded that the governor is quite elated with the surface respectability he seems to have achieved with the Democratic Party and the outward changes in attitude of many of its leaders. (Wooten 1972g)

The facts were that Wallace held the key to a large number of delegates as well as to a very large constituency, and despite the fact that he obviously could not win the nomination, he could still make trouble. As time went on, observers detected

> a subtle but visible shift in the psychological premises of those who are working for him during the convention. Where once they held stubbornly to the fragile dream of his eventual nomination, they now speak optimistically of his role as a "man of influence" in the convention deliberations. (Wooten 1972f)

During this time, McGovern forces stayed in close contact with Wallace's staff, as did the Nixon strategists.

McGovern's associates assured that the Wallace delegates were heard. They joined the regular Alabama delegation in standing against the challenge from the predominately black National Democratic party of Alabama, and the Alabama delegation in turn supported the McGovern forces in their attempt to combat the disintegration of McGovern support in the California delegation (Wooten 1972e). McGovern appealed to the convention that Wallace be given a polite reception when he appeared to speak before them (Frankel 1972b); he wanted Wallace's platform planks defeated, but felt "that graceful opposition might keep Mr. Wallace within the party" (Naughton 1972a).

In July, Wallace spoke to the convention, delivering his speech from a wheelchair. He said that he would stay within the party because he wanted to help it "become what it used to be—the party of the average working man." The speech was generally well-received, although ten delegations sat silently through the speech and the applause afterwards (Wooten 1972e). His platform proposals were put before the convention also, but it was a mere formality. They were voted on by voice vote, not by a roll call procedure, and the voting took place late at night at a time when most Americans were asleep (Herbers 1972a). All proposals were rejected by an overwhelming majority.

The Wallace people felt that they had been tricked. Although they were acknowledged in a friendly manner and given a forum, they were very angry at what they perceived to be only superficial respect. When they arrived at the convention, they found themselves up against a myriad of rules which they didn't understand. No one gave them any help in learning what the proper procedures were for doing things either; they couldn't even get their delegates into caucuses. When they complained to someone on the rules committee, that person answered that there was really no discrimination going on. Democratic officials insisted that things were just like a ball game: "Our team is here and other teams are here and everybody gets his turn at bat. It's all very fair." Snider lost his temper and replied that it was the first ballgame he had ever been in where the umpire got up to bat (Snider 1974).

Although they were shut out of a great many operations, the Wallace people began to lay the groundwork for 1976 at the convention. They made sure that Wallace would have representatives on both the Democratic National Committee as well as the executive committee. "At the very least," said Snider, "we'll know what the rules are in 1976" (Snider 1974).

The Republicans were more solicitous. Snider said that the Republican Platform Committee contacted their people and wanted to know the kinds of issues that might appeal to the Wallace constituency. The Republicans wanted to include them in their platform so that they could get that vote

(Snider 1974). Nixon "then asked Postmaster General Blount to deliver a copy of the Republican platform to Wallace for his perusal" (*New York Times* 1972n). The finished platform contained positions much closer to Wallace's own than did the Democratic platform (*New York Times* 1972m). Nixon people made overtures to Snider, who revealed that he had been offered a post as head of an "Independents for President Nixon Movement . . . coupled with a promise of a sub-Cabinet post in the Nixon administration" (Vecsey 1972b). Snider turned it down.

At this point, the Wallace campaign found itself $250,000 in debt. Snider was still saying that Wallace might run as a third-party candidate, but Wallace insisted that he had no such plans. Many saw Snider's motivation as an effort to once again bring in funds (Wooten 1972d). Campaign contributions had dried up immediately after Wallace was shot (Franklin 1973).

The American Party

Shortly afterwards, an official from the Texas American party announced that the party would try to draft Wallace as its presidential candidate, even though he had said he was not interested in running (*New York Times* 1972q). Wallace was listed as the keynote speaker at the upcoming American Party Convention, but an aide insisted that he would not attend the convention because of his physical condition as well as his decision to remain within the Democratic Party (*New York Times* 1972p).

Among the rank-and-file Wallace workers, however, the understanding fostered by campaign headquarters was that Wallace was going to make the American Party run (Bablin 1975). Some of the former Wallace delegates to the Democratic convention made plans to attend the American Party convention in Louisville, Kentucky, but the signs back at headquarters did not seem to indicate that Wallace would continue to be a candidate. His staff had been cut from over one hundred persons to around eight (Wooten 1972c).

In Louisville, a statement from Wallace was distributed to the 2,000 American Party delegates (*New York Times* 1972o); it said that he was bowing out of a draft for health reasons. The delegates, however, did not believe the statement and demanded that Wallace be nominated. Even when he pleaded with them via a telephone hookup, some of them refused to believe that it was really Wallace who had made the phone call (Bablin 1975). They did, however, come to an agreement. John J. Schmitz, an ultraconservative California Republican congressman, would be their presidential candidate.

Schmitz was an avowed Bircher, and Mark Bablin told the author that his impression at the American Party convention had been that most of the delegates were members of the John Birch Society (Bablin 1975). The platform adopted echoed Wallace's positions (Vecsey 1972c), but Schmitz said that he also "favored more bombing in Vietnam and abolition of the federal income tax and . . . opposed sex education in public schools" (Vecsey 1972b).

Richard B. McKay, who had announced his candidacy some months earlier, was shut out by the convention in favor of Schmitz. He angrily charged the convention leaders with running "a police state" (Vecsey 1972c). Others placed in nomination for the presidential slot were Lieut. William Calley and Lester Maddox (Vecsey 1972b). The vice-presidential candidate selected was Tom Anderson, a publisher of farm magazines (Vecsey 1972a).

Schmitz ran an unusual campaign, maintaining that most public events could be explained in terms of a conspiracy (Vecsey 1972a). He went on to say that the shooting of Wallace was the result of a Communist conspiracy, and brought his source of information to the press to testify. The press, however, could get no confirmation of this (Wooten 1972b). Schmitz also turned up in front of a Manhattan abortion clinic and joined protestors. "There's murder going on in there," he said (*New York Times* 1972m). He also contended that Kissinger was the true president of the United States and that Kissinger was "dedicated to creating a one-world socialist system" (*New York Times* 1972j).

The effort did seem to be, as American party official Del Myers put it, "a distillation of the John Birch Society, the Christian Crusade and the Minutemen" (Lesher 1972). Most Wallace supporters could not identify with them (Lesher 1972; Bablin 1975; Azbell 1974a). Of those voters who felt very positive about Wallace in 1972, only 2.4 percent actually voted for Schimtz; the Wallace appeal simply did not translate into an interest in Schmitz. As Mickey Griffin put it, "When we left the American party, we left an empty bag. It was a good vehicle while it lasted, but when Wallace left, he took the voters with him" (Griffin 1974). Schmitz and Anderson were on the ballot in thirty-three states (Frankel 1972a), and Schmitz got a total of 1,095,266 votes (*New York Times* 1973h).

In a meeting in December, the American party elected their vice-presidential candidate, Tom Anderson, as the chairman of the party. His opponent for the position was William Shearer of California. John Schmitz, the former presidential candidate, had not been interested in seeking the chairmanship (*New York Times* 1972d). At the meeting, both Anderson and the previous chairman, T. Coleman Andrews, announced the party's divorce from George Wallace. Anderson said that if Wallace "decided to seek the presidency in 1976, he would have to find a vehicle other than the American Party" (*New York Times* 1972c).

The New Respect

By September, it became apparent that Wallace was being treated with special consideration by other politicans. The chairman of the Southern Governor's Conference, Gov. John C. West of South Carolina, resigned his position as vice-chairman so that it could be bestowed on Wallace. The gesture made Wallace eligible for chairman the next year. Named as the second man was a black Republican governor from the Virgin Islands. These events were viewed by the press as an indication that Wallace had become fully respectable to his fellow southern governors. Further, since a black man had been selected as his coworker, it was felt that Wallace's new political moderation was finally being recognized (Reed 1972).

Another courting of Wallace's favor was shown by Sen. Edward Kennedy's visit to Wallace in Montgomery. Kennedy said that he hoped that Wallace would consider supporting McGovern, as "Wallace's support would be meaningful to any candidate." There was no response, however, from Wallace (*New York Times* 1972k).

Around this time Wallace's former finance officer and campaign aide, Seymore Trammell, was convicted of evading income taxes for bribes and kickbacks taken while he was in office. It was said that "'goods and services' were provided to him personally by contractors in return for doing business with the state" (*New York Times* 1972l). Wallace, however, was not directly implicated in any of this.

In October, Wallace began to make a few nonspeaking appearances on behalf of local Democratic candidates. He said he wanted to prevent a Republican sweep in Alabama (*New York Times* 1972i).

Wallace finally made a public statement that he would not endorse either national candidate. The next day Agnew dropped by to visit and Wallace said afterwards to reporters that he might decide to support one of the candidates publicly (Wooten 1972a). In the end Wallace never gave his support to either candidate. The reason he gave was that he was "interested for the moment only in his own recovery and [did] not have the time or energy for partisan politics" (Nordheimer 1972a).

Nixon, as expected, won the presidential election in a landslide. It was noted, however, that the crucial factor had been the fact that Wallace did not run:

> In state after state, Mr. Nixon's margin was remarkably close to the combined total won by him and the third-party candidate, George C.

Wallace, in 1968. Had Mr. Wallace not been eliminated from contention this year by a crippling bullet, the 1972 contest would have been much closer. (Frankel 1972a)

Wallace placed the blame for the Democratic defeat on the party's rejection of his platform planks. He also said that he intended to play a major role in reshaping the recovery of the Democratic party. And Snider said, "If he's going to run again, it's going to be as a Democrat. There will be no more third-party effort" (*New York Times* 1972h).

Part of the reason that Wallace was not interested in a third-party candidacy, according to Azbell (1974), was because of the sheer cost of a third-party campaign versus a major party run. The 1968 campaign had cost at least nine million dollars (Apple 1971b) in constrast to two million in 1972 (Azbell 1974c).

McGovern said later that Nixon's election had been assured when Wallace decided not to run as an independent candidate and refused to throw his support to McGovern. Continuing, McGovern intimated that he could not have compromised in good conscience on the kinds of issues which would have brought him Wallace's support. Wallace had not wanted to shift on the things that he was concerned about. McGovern also thought that if it had been a three-way race, then he, McGovern, would have won. "What we have now," he said, "is a country presided over by a president who has married the Republican Party to the Wallace people, and they'll make a strenuous skillful effort to preserve that coalition" (*New York Times* 1972g).

Wallace dedicated his initial efforts after the election to bringing changes to the Democratic party. He said that if the party wanted to win in 1976, it would have "to be reconstituted to reflect the attitudes of his constituents" (*New York Times* 1972f). Toward that end, Wallace headquarters opened a temporary office in Washington for the purpose of trying to influence the makeup of the Democratic National Committee (*New York Times* 1972e). He sent the committee a letter urging them to "listen to the people" and "unite on common ground to avoid another presidential defeat in 1976" (*New York Times* 1972b). With Wallace's support, the chairmanship of the Democratic National Committee went to Robert Strauss. Strauss, aware that he owed his election to the help of Wallace, among others, paid his respect to the governor in a visit to Montgomery. He was friendly but noncommital toward Wallace. Strauss "said his motive was to 'seek unity among the real leadership of the Democratic party,' adding, 'Governor Wallace certainly fits into that group. He represents a large and important constituency'" (*New York Times* 1972a).

The Wallace group was somewhat successful in their attempt to penetrate the membership of the Democratic National Committee. The

National Committee, a group of 300 persons, allowed 3 representatives from the Wallace faction; the executive committee of the Democratic National Committee, with a membership of twenty-five, authorized one Wallace representative, Mickey Griffin (Griffin 1974). Griffin was perturbed that Wallace representation on these respective committees was not proportionately reflective of Wallace support in the larger population. Snider, however, saw it differently (Snider 1974). He contended that the number of people on a committee doesn't really make any difference; even one representative would assure them never again having the disadvantages of 1972. The Wallace people would be in on the rule-making; they would not be shut out of finding out how things operate.

There was also the feeling among the staff, best expressed by Alton Dauphin (1974), that both Strauss and the Democratic party were impressed by Wallace because he controlled such a large constituency. Dauphin said that the press was also aware of this fact and was depicting Wallace much more fairly than they had been in the past. Wallace said that he had never changed, that his political philosophy had always been the same. The feeling was that the country had come to him (Wallace 1974). "I'm finally being understood," he said.

Note

1. The three straw ballots on the ballot yielded these results:

> Do you favor an amendment to the U.S. Constitution that would prohibit forced busing and guarantee the right of each student to attend the appropriate public school nearest his home?
>
> | | |
> |---|---|
> | Yes | 74.0% |
> | No | 26.0% |
>
> Do you favor providing an equal opportunity for quality education for all children regardless of race, creed, color, or place or residence and oppose a return to a dual system of public schools?
>
> | | |
> |---|---|
> | Yes | 78.9% |
> | No | 21.1% |
>
> Do you favor an amendment to the U.S. Constitution to allow prayer in the public schools?
>
> | | |
> |---|---|
> | Yes | 79.6% |
> | No | 20.4% |
>
> (Source: *Laws of Florida*, ch. 72-3, p. 115; Tabulation of Official Votes Cast, Presidential Preference Primary Election; March 14, 1972. Compiled by Richard Stone, Secretary of State.)

Chapter Eleven

Wallace Support in 1972: The Florida Primary

The most complete study of the Wallace vote in 1972 is a survey of voters in the Florida primary, conducted by Philip Meyer of Knight Newspapers on the actual day of the primary, March 14, 1972, two months before Wallace was shot.[1] Every twelfth voter was asked to fill out a questionnaire as he left the polling booth. The end result is a sample of 1246 respondents.[2] While the findings of this study cannot be used to generalize to what might have been true of Wallace voting in the United State in 1972, they do provide some important information.

In examining this data, we will look at the balloting for Wallace in relation to the vote for all other Democrats and the vote for all Republicans. To use the candidates actually chosen as party nominees as the bases of comparison with the vote for Wallace would not make sense, as Richard Nixon received approximately eighty-seven percent of the discernible Republican votes cast in the Florida primary in comparison with George McGovern's seven percent of the Democratic vote. Altogether, fourteen candidates are represented in the sample.

Demographics

Despite Wallace's attempts to represent himself in 1972 as a moderate on the racial issue and his public announcement that he would consider chosing a black as his running mate ("Meet The Press" 1971), he does not receive a single black vote among those in this study. The Republicans are also overwhelmingly rejected by blacks; only one percent of all Republican votes are cast by blacks. In contrast, 15.9 percent of the votes for other Democrats represent black votes (see Table 11.1).

As in previous campaigns, Wallace voters are more often men than women; 58.4 percent of the Wallace voters in the primary are men, compared with 51.0 percent among the Republicans and 48.7 percent among the other Democrats.

Although much has been written about younger voters being attracted to Wallace (Lipset and Raab 1970; McEvoy 1971), the youth vote in this primary is no different for Wallace than it is for the other candidates. The presence of a slightly higher proportion of those ages 25-44 among Wallace voters (11.5% more than among Republicans and a less significant 5.3% more than other Democrats) is interesting. Persons this age would presumably be parents with children in school and thus be very concerned about busing; they may be attracted to Wallace because of that. Another notable difference is the proportion of Republicans over the age of sixty; there are about twice as many Republicans as there are Democrats of the same age (33.6% to 17.7%).

In terms of place of birth, Wallace voters are more likely to have been born in the South than are voters for other candidates. For instance, 77.6 percent of the Wallace voters, 54.5 percent of the voters for other Democrats, and 39.4 percent of the Republicans were born in either Florida or in another Southern state.

Attitudes

While there have been many who have thought that the basis of the Wallace attraction was the issues, these supporters do not admit to that. One of the questions asked: "Thinking about the candidate whom you actually voted for, tell us what you like about him." While most voters in every group gave no answer, among those who did, a slightly larger proportion of Wallace voters is likely to say that they voted for their candidate because of his personal qualities, and among Wallace voters alone, almost twice (31.5% to 18.9%) as many say they voted for Wallace for his personal qualities rather than his stand on the issues (see Table 11.2).

Even though Wallace emphasizes economic issues in the 1972 campaign, voters for him in Florida seem less concerned with these kinds of issues than are other Democrats. Republicans are even less concerned. This is shown by the answers to two questions on the schedule.

The first, whether one agrees or disagrees with the statement, "The government's wage-price controls are solving our economic problems," finds a majority (70.3%) of Wallace voters and voters for other Democrats (74.9%) disagreeing with the statement. Republican voters, on the other hand, are different; 50.2 percent of them agree that wage-price controls are working, perhaps reflecting their belief in and approval of the policies of the Republican president.

TABLE 11.1
Selected Demographic Characteristics*

	Wallace	Other Democrats	Republicans
Race			
White	100.0	84.1	99.0
Black	0.0	15.9	1.0
Sex			
Male	58.4	48.7	51.0
Female	41.6	51.3	49.0
Age			
18-24	8.9	13.9	10.2
25-44	42.7	37.4	31.2
45-59	30.4	31.0	25.0
60 and over	17.9	17.7	33.6
Place of Birth			
Florida	39.9	28.7	11.9
Other South	37.7	25.8	27.5
North	20.2	41.3	55.3
Outside U.S.	2.2	4.2	5.3

*Percentages add vertically by columns to 100 percent except for rounding errors.

On the next statement the alliance changes. When asked whether "there are plenty of good jobs available in this part of the state for people who want to work," large majorities of both Wallace supporters (72.8%) and of Republican voters (71.7%) agree. A small majority of other Democrats (55.7%) also agrees with the statement. The difference between the two sets of Democrats is probably accounted for by the fact that many voters for other Democrats are in a lower income range than are Wallace voters. In addition, many are black. Such people may simply be more likely to feel that the optimism of the statement is untrue for them. Given the fact that in Florida Wallace voters and Republicans have similar demographic characteristics (see Table 11.1 and Table 11.6), it is not surprising that they share many of the same opinions on the issues.

Another area addressed on this schedule has not been explored in any of the previous campaigns. It provides some very interesting data on generalized fear. When asked to respond to the statement, "the crime situation is so bad, I'm afraid to walk around my neighborhood at night," the following percentages in each voter group agree: Wallace 52.5 percent, other Democrats 42.7 percent, and Republicans 38.9 percent. Further investigation shows that while the fear of crime is related to attitudes on racial issues, it affects all parties equally, and Wallace voters are significantly more bothered than others. While there is no way of checking their answers relative to the objective reality of the situations in their neighborhoods, it is abundantly clear that they differ from others on this measure.

Racial Politics

Although most Wallace voters maintain that they voted for him because of personal qualities and not because of issues (Table 11.2), the general consensus is that busing is at the heart of his support (Waldron 1972). In fact, the busing issue is central to the Florida primary (Wooten 1972). This is underscored by the fact that there was an antibusing referendum present on the ballot, despite several attempts before the election to get it off. Some think that the referendum brought many more voters to the polls than usual, particularly the kinds of people who voted for Wallace (Nordheimer 1972). In actuality, however, the busing issue is not a clear-cut matter of segregationists expressing their views; it is much more complex. The contradictory tallies of two related questions appearing on the ballot demonstrate how complicated the matter really is.

The first asks: "Do you favor an amendment to the U.S. Constitution that would prohibit forced busing and guarantee the right of each student to attend the appropriate public school nearest his home?" (Florida 1972). As expected, this question garnered an overwhelming yes vote against busing, 1,127,631 to 396,778. The second question, however, yields unexpected results. Voters were asked, "Do you favor providing an equal opportunity for quality education for all children regardless of race, creed, color, or place of residence and oppose a return to a dual system of public schools?" Surprisingly, 1,095,879 persons voted yes (for integration) to 293,775 no's, registering approval for integration by a margin of 802,104. We therefore conclude that antibusing sentiment in the 1972 Florida primary is not motivated primarily by antiblack feelings. Thus, any information about Wallace voters' feelings on the issues of busing and segregation deserves particular scrutiny.

Two questions on this study deal with busing. The first asks agreement or disagreement with the statement: "If busing is the only way to achieve school integration, then we ought to go along with it." The results show that a very large majority, 85.1 percent, of the Wallace voters disagree with

TABLE 11.2
Position on Selected Issues*

	Wallace	Other Democrats	Republicans
"Why did you vote for your candidate?"			
No answer	46.0	44.6	43.8
Issues	18.9	22.1	24.5
Personal qualities	31.5	29.8	23.9
Best of bad lot	3.6	3.5	7.8
"The government's wage-price controls are solving our economic problems."			
Agree	29.7	25.1	50.2
Disagree	70.3	74.9	49.8
"There are plenty of good jobs available in this part of the state for people who want to work."			
Agree	72.8	55.7	71.7
Disagree	27.2	44.3	28.3
"The crime situation is so bad, I'm afraid to walk around my neighborhood at night."			
Agree	52.2	42.7	38.9
Disagree	47.8	57.3	61.1

*Percentages add vertically by columns to 100 percent, except for rounding errors.

the statement, followed by 74.4 percent of the Republicans and 43.7 percent of the voters for other Democrats (see Table 11.3).

The second question is phrased: "If the courts require busing to integrate schools, we might as well close the public schools." In response, the voters appear less adamant than on the previous question. 62.1 percent of the Wallace voters agree, compared to far less Republicans (43.3%) and voters for other Democrats (27.2%).

Given their responses to each of the questions, it is clear that Wallace voters are more unyielding about the question of busing than are other voters.

The difference in the percentages above indicate that the two statements do not mean the same thing to those who answered them. While it is difficult to determine exactly what they did mean to each person, a cross-tabulation of the questions yields some interesting results and suggests a typology of resistance to changes in schools related to the issue of race. Let us review the statements again:

1. If the courts require busing to integrate schools, we might as well close the public schools.
2. If busing is the only way to achieve school intergration, then we ought to go along with it.

As the idea of busing is present in both statements, we can assume that the other elements in each statement account for most of the variation.

The first statement suggests the possibility of closing schools, and provokes less negative response than does the second, perhaps because of the seriousness of that very suggestion. Closing the schools would be a very drastic measure, indeed. The idea of the public schools is of particular

TABLE 11.3
Attitudes Toward Busing and Integration*

	Wallace	Other Democrats	Republicans
"If busing is the only way to achieve school integration, then we ought to go along with it."			
Agree	14.9	56.3	25.6
Disagree	85.1	43.7	74.4
"If courts require busing to integrate schools, we might as well close the public schools."			
Agree	62.1	27.2	43.3
Disagree	37.9	72.8	56.7

*Percentages add vertically by columns to 100 percent, except for rounding errors.

importance in American society, and however one might feel about courts requiring busing to integrate schools, few people would want to close the schools rather than allow busing and integration.

In the second statement, school integration is most likely the factor generating the stronger response. Conversely, dislike of busing may be strong, but if integration is important, one will be willing to put up with the inconvenience of busing.

Cross-tabulating these questions yields a two-by-two table which further illuminates and separates the attitudes elicited in these responses. Three categories emerge from the cross-tabulation (see Figure 11.1):

1. Those who would rather close schools than allow busing and who disagree that busing is necessary to achieve integration (cell 3). These voters are so adamant against busing that we can only suspect that they are motivated by racial considerations.
2. Those who are against closing the schools but who are angry at busing (cell 4). They represent the middle category.
3. Those who are clearly for integration (cell 2).

FIGURE 11.1
Crosstabulation of Questions on Busing with Explanation of Significance of Each Cell*

| | | Close Schools Before Allowing Busing | |
		AGREE	DISAGREE
Busing Necessary to Achieve Integration	AGREE	Cell #1 Contradictory, ambivalent; illogical as a response; not many expected here.	Cell #2 For integration.
	DISAGREE	Cell #3 Adamant: no integration, no busing.	Cell #4 Against closing schools but angry at busing; integration viewed as less dangerous than in Cell #3; reflects some acceptance of idea.

*Qustions on Busing:

1. If the courts require busing to integrate schools, we might as well close the public schools.

2. If busing is the only way to achieve school integration, then we ought to go along with it.

The fourth cell (cell 1) represents answers that are contradictory; voters in this cell will be ignored in the analysis.

As might be expected, the majority of Wallace voters (57.3%) fall within category one (Cell 3), segregation diehards. They are ahead of the nearest voting group (Republicans at 36%) by more than twenty percentage points, a substantial margin. Further, only 19.2 percent of the voters for other Democrats can be typified as having these sentiments.

Republicans, on the other hand, are more likely to fall within the middle category, number 2 (Cell 4), against closing the schools but angry at busing. Their 37.1 percent is followed by 28.1 percent of Wallace voters and 24.9 percent of the voters for other Democrats.

Almost half of the voters for other Democrats (48.4%) fall into the third category (Cell 2), for integration. One-fifth of the Republicans (20.6%) also share that sentiment. Few (10.2%) Wallace voters can be described as integrationists.

These findings are in keeping with earlier ones from the 1964 and 1968 campaigns, and serve to demonstrate the continuing importance of racial politics in the 1972 Wallace campaign.

Authoritarian Personality

There are no questions on this schedule which clearly delineate the presence of a classic authoritarian personality. One question which more

TABLE 11.4
Proportions in Each Cell of Figure 11.1 by Voter Groups

Categories	Wallace	Other Democrats	Republicans
Adamant segregationists (cell #3)	57.3	19.2	36.0
Middle: angry at busing, against closing schools (cell #4)	28.1	24.9	37.1
Integrationists (cell #2)	10.2	48.4	20.6
Contradictory (cell #1)	4.4	7.5	6.3
	100.0%	100.0%	100.0%
n =	(342)	(510)	(272)

rightly delineates an attitude on foreign policy than an authoritarian orientation tests agreement with the statement, "The U.S. government should be moving faster to get out of Vietnam." Results show Wallace voters in the middle between the other two groups. Reflecting the changing times, a majority of all groups agree, with other Democrats leading at 86.7 percent. 75.6 percent of Wallace voters and 68.9 percent of Republicans also favor a fast exit from Vietnam.

TABLE 11.5
Attitude Toward Withdrawing from Vietnam

	Wallace	Other Democrats	Republicans
"The U. S. Government should be moving faster to get out of Vietnam."			
Agree	75.6	86.7	68.9
Disagree	24.4	13.3	31.1
	100.0%	100.0%	100.0%

Marginal Voter Theory

Marginal voters are essentially nonvoters, those who do not participate in any meaningful way in American political life.

When voters in the Florida primary are asked about their voting for presidential candidates in the general election of 1968, voters for other Democrats are twice as likely to say that they did not vote in 1968 than are Wallace voters.[3] Also in 1968, 14.7 percent of the voters for other Democrats did not vote, followed by 8.2 percent of the Republicans and 7.0 percent of Wallace voters. While the differences between these groups are not significant, there is little support for the theory that Wallace voters are more marginal to the political system than are others.

Status Theories

Status components available in this study are race, religion, education, and income, of enough variety to produce measures of ascribed and achieved statuses as well as a measure of SES (socioeconomic status) comparable to those in other studies.

Race was reviewed earlier (see Table 11.1). That Wallace captures almost none of the black vote in Florida is no surprise, despite his trying to tone down the racial issue and promote his appeal to blacks (Wooten 1972: *New York Times* 1972w).

Religion is distributed as shown in Table 11.6. The similarity of Republican and Wallace voters is the most outstanding feature of the findings—75.7 percent of Wallace voters and 71.9 percent of the Republicans are Protestant. As before, Catholics are most often among voters for other Democrats (23.6%); the same is also true of Jews (8.1%).

When race and religion are combined in a measure of ascribed status (described in Appendix), Wallace voters more often have all status characteristics (here white and Protestant) than do others; 75.5 percent of them have both characteristics, compared to 70.9 percent of the Republicans and 41.8 percent of the voters for other Democrats.

The distributions of achieved status characteristics, education and income, are also similar to those observed in earlier campaigns. As before, Wallace voters are much more likely to have less education than are voters for other candidates. The majority of them have not gone beyond high school (only 38.8% have some college education). Percents for the majorities of those voters for other candidates with college educations run 57.1 percent for other Democrats and 61.6 percent for Republicans respectively.

Tabulations on income show that Wallace voters are slightly more likely to be in the middle third of income[4] than are other voters, but otherwise there are essentially no differences in income among the voter groups. There is even less difference among those who are making $10,000 and up (the middle and highest thirds in income combined): Wallace 58.0%; other Democrats 57.9%; Republicans 53.8%. It should be noted that the Republican figure here is different from the income levels observed for Republicans in the two national campaigns. This may be due to the fact that fully one-third of the Republican vote cast in the Florida primary is by persons age sixty and over (see Table 11.1); the lower income most likely reflects the lower income of the retired.

Before creating a measure of achieved status we tested the congruence of education and income, using a Kendall's tau (see Appendix). The remitting coefficients, all significant at the .001 level, are Wallace .296; other Democrats .210; and Republicans .210. While the level of congruence is not high, the coefficients demonstrate that Wallace voters' achieved status characteristics are no more incongruent than those of other voters.

The measure of achieved status is then created from the same variables. Results show that Wallace voters are more likely than their counterparts to have low achieved status; 62.4 percent of them are at low or working class achieved status levels compared to 54.5 percent of the Republicans and 52.1 percent of the voters for other Democrats. In general, we find that the distribution for other Democrats and for Republicans is more evenly distributed than it is for Wallace voters.

A measure of SES is created following the calculations of Olsen and Tully (1972) used in the other data chapters (see Appendix for a full explanation). What emerges is a picture in which Wallace voters are solidly in the middle on SES, sandwiched between the two other candidate groups. Those in the upper two levels of middle and high SES include 51.2 percent of the Republicans, 50.8 percent of the Wallace voters, and 34.0 percent of the voters for other Democrats.

All of these calculations negate the hypotheses that Wallace voters are status inconsistent, lower class, or drastically different on status measures from other voters. While most of the similarity of SES scores is due to higher ascribed status among Wallace voters compensating for a lack of achieved status (mostly due to a pervasive lack of education), the traditional sociological measure of SES still places a great deal of emphasis on ascribed statuses. Given the changing times, the issue of whether whites and Protestants are really more socially prominent than other ethnics or religions should definitely be reconsidered.

One of the questions on this schedule has been used by Pettigrew, Riley, and Vanneman (1972) to measure relative status deprivation. Agreement with "In spite of what some people say, the condition of the average man is getting worse, not better" is assumed to reflect a condition of relative deprivation. In their research, Pettigrew, Riley, and Vanneman are particularly interested in exploring feelings of deprivation in relation to blacks and maintain that this measure is an even more potent predictor of Wallace voting than is racial prejudice. Earlier, however, Leo Srole had used the same sentiment to describe personal anomie (Srole 1956), thus what the statement actually identifies is open to question.

A majority of Wallace voters—55.2 percent, say that the condition of the average man is getting worse, compared to 46.9 percent among voters for other Democrats and 38.2 percent of voters for Republicans.

The real question, beyond whether or not this is a matter of status politics or power politics, is whether or not this attitude is related to racial politics. When the categories of Figure 11.1 are used to specify the question, we find that sentiment on the condition of the average man has little to do with specific racial sentiments. Among integrationists, 60 percent believe that the condition of the average man is getting worse, compared with 56.7 percent of the segregationists and 47.3 percent of those who are angry at busing but against closing the schools. Thus relative deprivation has little to do with racial attitudes among Wallace voters in the 1972 Florida primary. While it is more prevalent among Wallace voters than among others, it does not provide a useful index to their racial attitudes.

TABLE 11.6
Selected Status Characteristics*

	Wallace	Other Democrats	Republicans
Religion			
No answer	10.1	15.6	8.8
Protestant	75.7	52.7	71.9
Catholic	13.7	23.6	18.0
Jewish	0.5	8.1	1.3
Ascribed Status			
None	7.0	10.9	3.3
One	17.5	47.3	25.8
Both	75.5	41.8	70.9
Education			
Grade school	4.3	4.1	2.8
High school	56.9	38.8	36.1
College	38.8	57.1	61.6
Income			
Lowest third	42.0	42.1	46.2
Middle third	35.1	30.9	26.5
Highest third	22.9	27.0	27.3
Achieved Status			
Low	32.6	22.3	21.9
Working	29.8	29.8	32.5
Middle	23.6	27.7	24.5
High	14.0	20.2	21.1
SES			
Low	15.5	34.2	17.4
Working	33.7	31.8	31.4
Middle	39.8	24.8	37.1
High	11.0	9.2	14.1

*Percentages add vertically by column to 100 percent, except for rounding errors.

TABLE 11.7
Measures of Status Deprivation

	Wallace	Other Democrats	Republicans
"In spite of what some people say, the condition of the average man is getting worse, not better."			
Agree	55.2	46.9	38.2
Disagree	44.8	53.1	61.8
	100.0%	100.0%	100.0%

Percentages of Wallace Voters in Each Cell of Figure 1.1 Agreeing With the Statement, "The condition of the average man is getting worse."*

Category	Cell	Percent
Adamant segregationists	3	56.7
Middle: angry at busing, against closing schools	4	47.3
Integrationists	2	60.0

*Adding those who disagree with the statement brings the total in each cell to 100 percent.

Does SES qualify attitude on race? An examination of the distribution of SES for those in cell three (the more adamant attitude) and cell two (the more lenient attitude) in comparison with the original SES distributions shows that while the variable socioeconomic status does specify attitudes on race, it is not in the direction expected. Those who have the least to lose in actual status terms, the working and lower classes, are more likely to have adamant attitudes than those in other classes. Conversely, those in middle and high status categories are more likely to favor integration than the original distributions would predict. Thus status politics does little to explain racial bias by Wallace voters, nor does it play a big part in the 1972 Florida primary.

The Power Theory

Although there are no questions on the 1972 Florida primary study that would indicate powerlessness as we have defined it, one question does serve to pinpoint a dimension of political anomie (Finifter 1970). It reads: "The federal government is pretty much run by a few big interests looking out for themselves." Miller, Brown, and Raine (1973) use this question with slightly different words as a part of their political trust scale, as does Aberbach (1969).

The results show that Wallace voters have the highest proportions agreeing with the statement (66.2%) closely followed by voters for other Democrats (63.7%). A slight majority of Republicans disagree with the statement (see Table 11.8). The difference here may be due to the fact that at this time the "federal government" is Republican, and the scandal of Watergate is as yet unknown. Republicans undoubtedly would be more likely to trust their own party, especially while it is in power.

Looking at the distribution of those who agree with this question in each cell position of Figure 11.1, we find that other voters are more likely to demonstrate a relationship between political anomie and racism than are Wallace voters, whose racial politics seem all pervasive.

As the question of powerlessness is not adequately addressed in the Meyer study of the 1972 Florida primary, we cannot draw any conclusion here about this particular theory.

Summary

In these data, there is little support for the marginal voter theory, as is evidenced by the fact that there were fewer nonvoters in the 1968 election among Wallace voters than among the other two groups in the 1972 primary. The question of whether status factors are prevalent among Wallace voters is also not supported by the data. While Wallace voters are generally less well-educated than other voters, they have the same levels of income and higher ascribed status relative to other voters. This might suggest the possibility that education and income are discrepant among Wallace voters, but a Kendall's tau correlation of the two factors shows no basis for this supposition. Wallace voters are as status consistent on these two variables as are other voters. Thus we find no evidence of the importance of status factors in this election.

Unfortunately, it is impossible to test the theories of the authoritarian personality or of powerlessness with the data available. The authoritarian personality may be indicated by the presence of a strong antiblack bias, but as Adorno (1950) chose to keep the E and F scales separate, we will also view ethnocentricity as differing from the authoritarian personality.

TABLE 11.8
Measure of Political Anomie

	Wallace	Other Democrats	Republicans
"The federal govern-ment is pretty much run by a few big in-terests looking out for themselves."			
Agree	66.2	63.7	45.5
Disagree	33.8	36.3	54.5
	100.0%	100.0%	100.0%

There are also no variables which are clearly representative of powerlessness per se; the variables which are similar tend to be more representative of political anomie, economic concerns, and generalized fear. On two of these three measures Wallace voters differ from other voters. What particularly distinguishes them is a greater fear of walking in the streets at night (epsilon of +9.5 from the nearest group) and a higher percentage of those agreeing with the statement that the condition of the average man is getting worse (epsilon of +10.3 from the nearest group). While a larger proportion of Wallace voters also agree with the statement that the federal government is run by a few big interests looking out for themselves, this is a statement of political anomie rather than of political powerlessness.

In reviewing the questions it is evident that Wallace voters are far ahead of others in the frequency with which they give racially charged responses. This immediately brings into question the candidate's affirmation that he is no longer racist in outlook or in policy.

The issue remains one of power. Wallace's appeals constantly point out that blacks are getting rights at the expense of whites; thus protests against integration are actually protests against powerlessness.

Notes

1. The 1972 American National Election Study offers little in the way of data on Wallace voting because Wallace was shot before the general election took place. A question on the schedule asks about primary voting, but only thirty-one persons reply that they voted for George Wallace in a primary, too small a sample for comparison purposes.

   Another way of analyzing the 1972 election is to examine the vote for John Schmitz as a stand-in for Wallace on the American Independent Party ticket. But there is little to indicate that the sentiment for Wallace transfers into voting for Schmitz. Data from the 1972 American National Election Study shows that

those registering pro-Wallace sensibilities give only 2.4 percent of their vote to Schmitz. The majority of the pro-Wallace vote goes to Nixon (78.5 percent); McGovern picks up 19.1 percent. Thus the voting for Schmitz is useless for understanding Wallace sentiment.
2. These data are gathered under the direction of Philip Meyer of the Washington Bureau of Knight Newspapers and made available for analysis by the Michigan Inter-University Consortium for Political Research. In the sampling, every twelfth voter was stopped as he left the polling booth and asked to fill out a questionnaire. The sample is reasonably representative. The official total that Wallace received in the primary was thirty percent of the vote cast (combining both Democratic and Republic votes). A similar tally of the sample shows that Wallace received thirty-one percent of the sample's votes.
3. The observation for whom the groups in the Florida primary had voted in the 1968 general election is also of interest.

1972 Primary Vote in Relation to 1968 General Election Vote

	Wallace	Other Democrats	Republicans
1968 Vote			
Nixon	41.2	28.8	82.1
Humphrey	4.8	50.9	4.5
Wallace	47.0	5,6	5.2
Didn't vote	7.0	14.7	8.2
	100.0%	100.0%	100.0%

The Republicans are the most consistent voters, followed by the Other Democrats. The largest group of Wallace voters in 1972 are repeaters, but Wallace also gained from those who had voted for Nixon in 1968; fully 41.2 percent of his 1972 vote came from them. Very few of those who voted for Wallace in 1972 had voted for Humphrey in 1968. Among the votes lost by Wallace in 1972 from those who had been Wallace voters in 1968, almost equal percentages went to Other Democrats and Republicans.
4. Here, the thirds are as follows:

lowest third	$0-9999	466 cases
middle third	$10,000-14,999	337 cases
highest third	$15,000 and over	278 cases

While this tends to skew income toward the lower end of the scale, it affects all groups equally. This distribution is less specific than the distributions of income noted for 1964 and 1968, primarily because income was strictly coded into four codes.

Chapter Twelve

Analysis of 1972 Speeches:
"Send Them a Message"

After a fling in 1968 as the American Independent party candidate, Wallace in 1972 aimed for respectability and legitimacy as a mainstream candidate in the Democratic party. He toned down his rhetoric, expanded his repertoire of issues, and aimed at creating a broader constituency. He began to act like the other candidates and pursued the center, hoping to convince most that he had left his old ways behind.

Despite this new, more respectable image, Wallace had no trouble keeping his old supporters; through the sensible, smooth and confidently spoken words they spotted his old positions and were assured that he had not left them behind.

Although Wallace had declared himself a Democrat, the threat of a third party lay thick in the air around him. If "they" didn't pay any attention to him, he warned, he'd show them. And he almost did. At the time he was shot, George Wallace was the leading Democratic contender in the popular vote tally. He had gotten 1.5 million more votes than any other Democrat in the first fourteen primaries (Ayres, 1974b). Five of these primaries he had won; he came in second in five others.

What was the source of his appeal? The 1972 campaign speeches, more than do those of any other campaign, show his use of the politics of powerlessness.

The 1972 campaign is particularly interesting because while it appears more open and broader-based than the two earlier runs, an analysis of the speeches shows that little has changed. Wallace addresses issues more completely than in the past, but his positions remain in the realm of complaints rather than the expression of problems and the exploration of their possible solutions. Under the guise of populism as a device designed to broaden appeal, the 1972 campaign is a very deliberate and narrowly focused attempt to foster and manipulate powerlessness. Once this powerlessness is established, Wallace is able to address a wider audience, but his appeals are the same as they have been and his moves toward the center are firmly rooted in racism:

> I have always maintained that the average man is capable of running his own country and commanding his elected servants. I believe our people do have a good heart and good sense and that there is nothing wrong with America but there is something wrong with leadership that refuses to listen to average citizens and counsel with them on their real needs and real problems. (*The Wallace Stand* 1972a)

While intonations of "the people" and "people power" resound throughout the speeches, and while some argue that this emphasis is indeed populism (Mueller 1972; Reich 1974), Wallace does little more than praise the people's wisdom. At the same time he presses relentlessly his contention that while the government is refusing to "listen to average citizens" (who can be understood to be whites), it is being very responsive to blacks at the expense of those whites (literally—with their tax dollars), and the whites are powerless to do anything about it, particularly in the face of a government which kowtows to minority violence and its attendant demands:

> ... the average citizen feels that he has been ignored, that the leadership of the Democratic Party and the Republican Party have paid attention to the exotic and those who made the most noise, they have given their money away in foreign aid, they have given it away to welfare loafers, and they have skyrocketed administrative costs of government to the point that they have broken his back financially, and ... the average man says that "I am through with that." ("Meet the Press" 1972b)

The appeal masquerades as mourning for a loss of freedom in the face of an omnipotent and unresponsive government, a huge bureaucracy which "overwhelms and isolates the people" (Wallace 1972a). The call to arms is a powerful and emotional one in which Wallace asks others to join him in standing steadfast against the trends and to move to reclaim the lost freedoms:

> Together we must press on toward a more productive and more responsive government designed to meet the needs of the people we serve—all of whom must feel that they have a voice in their destiny and fate. This can only be accomplished in an atmosphere of freedom from unwarranted, unwise and unwanted intrusion and oppression by the federal government—a man must

be free and unfettered by federal encroachments in this employment—his home—his community—his domestic institutions, including his schools and in his associations with his fellow man. (Wallace 1971b)

All of this—the inherent wisdom of the people and their loss of power in the face of an uncaring and omnipotent government—is made to order for the issue of the year: busing, particularly in the way that Wallace explains the issue, as a matter of freedom of choice. His arguments sound like common sense:

> Why not just have the school systems under a freedom of choice plan, as was accepted some time ago by the courts, and let people make the choice of the school they want to attend, or let the parents choose for them. Then we would have nondiscrimination, a most democratic method of school attendance. That is what I would do. Then I would not worry about whether we had so many of one group in a particular school. I would only then be concerned about quality education for every child, black and white. ("Meet the Press" 1972b)

> If the pseudointellectuals think it is good to bus little children backwards and forwards in Michigan and Wisconsin and Alabama, the average man doesn't, and there are more of them than there are the pseudos. I frankly think we must have a rollback. So, have the schools open under freedom of choice, with no discrimination because of race, and then, you have your neighborhood schools, and in my judgement everyone ought to be satisfied. ("Meet the Press" 1972b)

But in stressing that trying to meet a quota system of a certain percentage of blacks and whites in a single school by busing is undemocratic and unwise, Wallace is actually trying to keep the schools segregated.

He knows his constituency well enough to rest assured that the strongest safeguard to segregation would be a "return to local control." He knows that control of neighborhood schools, or whatever it is called, would result in gross discrimination without recourse and the protection of those who do not live in that neighborhood but want "freedom of choice." Neighborhood definitions can be arbitrary, and when school board jurisdiction lines are drawn by the white power structure, neighborhoods remain segregated despite civil action.

Little has changed, despite Wallace's protestations that he is a believer in the policy of nondiscrimination (*Sunday Bulletin* 1972). In a rather strange way, Wallace's attempt to explain his segregationist past gives insight into his present pose. When asked if he was misquoted when he said, "Segregation now, tomorrow, and forever," Wallace answered:

> In the context of the times, that's what we had in our part of the country, that had been accepted as lawful by the Supreme Court, that was practiced by law,

and even practiced by some who claimed otherwise. We Southern people tried not be hypocritical about it. But you must consider that an overwhelming majority of the people in our part of the country don't consider that as racist. You have to consider what emanates from a man's heart. If it emanates because he thinks it's in the best interest of everybody, even though he's mistaken, then his heart's right. (*Sunday Bulletin* 1972)

Economic issues also play a big part in the 1972 campaign, and are second only to the issue of busing. As part of the campaign to broaden his appeal, Wallace's prime concern here is with the tax burden of the "average citizen" (*The Wallace Stand* 1971c). Referring to the average citizen as the middle class, he simply appoints himself their champion and thereby incorporates them into his constituency. The middle class, Wallace contends (1971b), is footing the bill for welfare loafers, multimillion dollar corporations, and wealthy individuals who use tax loopholes:

> Middle America is caught in a tax squeeze between those who throw bombs in the streets and engage in disruptive and destructive protest while refusing to work and the silk stocking crowd with their privately controlled tax-free foundations on the other hand. I say it is past time to put an end to these illegal activities and let every citizen pay his share of taxes. (Wallace 1971a)

The solution, he suggests, is to tax some of these tax-free foundations, particularly the ones which are promoting civil disruption with their funding and contributing to the defense funds of criminals:

> Private foundations and religious organizations spend large sums of money to encourage revolutions and riots in our streets; promote discord and destructive sit-ins in our schools and colleges; support subversive activities in this nation; and contribute to the defense fund of avowed Communists who are under indictment for murder and other felonies. They should no longer enjoy their exempt status from paying federal income taxes. If these organizations and institutions are forced to pay their proportionate share of the staggering income tax burden that now rests upon the average American, it will bring about a reduction in the amount of taxes that the white collar and blue collar workers, the businessmen, and the farmers are now forced to pay. (Wallace 1971a)

Another problem Wallace identifies is the government's budget priorities. One of Wallace's prime targets is able-bodied welfare loafers. He scorns "liberal giveaway programs," maintaining that they encourage people to not work. Instead, he urges more social security for the elderly, stating emphatically that this is not freeloading, but an earned benefit by the elderly, quite unlike the lot of welfare recipients (*The Wallace Stand* 1972b).

Another area of governmental misspending is in foreign aid. Aid is given to some countries who do not respect the United States. Wallace urges that we reassess the quality of support that foreign nations give the United States and suggests that we cut off aid to any country critical of United States policy. He contends (*The Wallace Stand* 1972b) that the money spent for foreign aid is critically needed to solve domestic problems within the United States:

> All of this money we have given away overseas—the government has brought about inflation. The Democrats sometimes blame big business, and the Republicans sometimes blame labor, as has been in the past, but the blame for inflation is on the Government of the United States. They have brought about inflation running these multibillion-dollar deficits, putting this money into circulation that devalues the dollar in a man's wallet and in his bank account, giving this money overseas by the billions and billions of dollars, and the day of reckoning is here. I think that what they ought to do is cut down on federal spending, and one way you can start cutting is HEW. All these bureaucrats that go around and draw up these busing decrees. Let them go into industry. ("Meet the Press" 1971)

Wallace emphasizes that welfare spending, foreign aid funding, and tax loopholes are responsible for inflation and the economic crisis (*The Wallace Stand* 1972b). He urges cutbacks in each area and suggests that a constructive, free enterprise approach would curtail inflation (Wallace 1972a).

Law and order is still a hot issue even though riots are no longer as frequent as in 1968. In touting the issue Wallace concentrates on "common criminals," and complains about lenient courts that make it almost impossible to convict those criminals ("Meet the Press" 1972a). The common man, Wallace thunders, is losing his own rights to the rights of these common criminals (*The Wallace Stand* 1972b).

> More than half of the cities are so infested with crime that citizens cannot walk the streets unmolested at night. Law-abiding citizens are imprisoned behind the locked doors of their homes because criminals, who should be locked up, are in the streets. We must attack crime of every type from the street molester to the organized criminal. Our cities must be removed from the problem charts. People in our cities must have security in opportunity, law and order, and a decent way of life. (Wallace 1972a)

Problems of this kind exist, Wallace claims, because of the continuing permissiveness of the federal government (*The Wallace Stand* 1972b). He blames the "permissive attitude of [the] executive and judiciary at national levels for setting [a] tone of moral decay" (*The Wallace Stand* 1972), and says that "criminal lawlessness can only be controlled by a strong action that protects the law-abiding citizen" (Wallace 1972a). He warns that "unless law and order is restored in this country and people can walk on the streets safely, there may come a time in which civil rights will have to be abrogated ("Meet the Press" 1972b).

Wallace stresses that his supporters are "law abiding," (Wallace 1972a), and asserts that tolerance for those who are lawless is neither logical nor reasonable. "The mob destroying a bank, school or business is not the American way of change" (Wallace 1971b).

> The place to get desired change is within the law and not by destruction of the system. The street is not a proper place to change America, but the ballot box through people power. This is the method and the forum. Every American can participate in government by voicing his or her thoughts within the law at every level of government. (Wallace 1972a)

The other issue in the campaign is Vietnam. In 1969, Wallace acknowledges the antiwar movement, but disagrees with the idea of simply pulling out:

> One reason the public has been disenchanted with the war is that we have been there so long. We couldn't negotiate it to conclusion and they didn't bring it to a military conclusion, so they said, "What are we doing there, we are not going to continue to expend lives and money for a no-winnable war." When you say escalation, you are going to have to escalate to get out, so I'd rather escalate to win than to escalate to get out. ("Meet the Press" 1969)

Later on Wallace accepts the idea of leaving Vietnam, but calls for a commitment to never again send American troops anywhere to fight in a no-win war (*The Wallace Stand* 1972b). During the campaign Wallace

> calls U.S. Vietnam involvement a mistake benefiting the Communists, [and] suggests [that the] American will to win, continued bombing of the North, and strong action against North Vietnamese regulars in Laos and Cambodia might have won the war. (*The Wallace Stand* 1972b)

There is an implication throughout the speeches that the Vietnam War was not won because the military was not allowed to follow their own judgement; they were held back by politicians. From this it is clear that Wallace considers military men the "experts" on war, and politicians only supplementary. It is also apparent that he considers strength the main deterrent to war and any problems of disrespect among allies. Military strength and a show of determination are the only possible defenses against the threat of communism, which is everywhere a possibility:

> Only a nation with strength and courage will survive in the deadly game with the Communist adversaries who threaten the safety and security of all free nations. (Wallace 1972a)

As reasonable and peace-loving men, we should always be willing to stop making war and start making peace. But we should be aware that the key to enslavement is "peace at any price." We must pursue every avenue to peace as men of goodwill, strength, and courage but we should never grovel to the enemy in weakness. (Wallace 1972a)

To the Wallace mind, a strong united front is the only way to solve problems—both domestic and foreign. In the interest of this, anything except strong American patriotism is suspect.

Although Wallace presents a more detailed analysis of problems in 1972 than in the 1968 campaign, he is still the loud complainer, here saying that people have been overlooked and forgotten. While he reflects on problems that concern everyone, such as busing, taxes, inflation, law and order, and foreign policy, this can be understood not in terms of abiding concerns, but as an attempt to broaden his appeal. For he is not interested in either the problems or their solutions; no real remedies are offered. People are asked to stand steadfast in the hope that government will come to its senses mainly as a result of Wallace's attempts to call federal oversights to the attention of all. His solution is as empty as is his protest. The real Wallace hides powerless behind the symbol of his raised fist.

Chapter Thirteen

1976: The Last Hurrah

Wallace spent the first few months after the "accident," as he called it (Wallace 1974), recuperating. It was a very difficult period. He spent more than 140 days in hospitals, and underwent surgery more than a dozen times (Wooten 1974). When he was able, he began to systematically engage in acts and activities which would demonstrate to the American people that although the body was paralyzed, the mind was fit, and the stamina that a president might need was still there.

Public excursions were often followed by periods of seclusion. Wallace attended Nixon's inauguration in January, 1973, and afterwards returned to the hospital for six weeks. As soon as he was released, he "plunged into a schedule of public appearances that seemed designed to silence his critics" (Nordheimer 1973). He continually stressed that he was still politically viable (King 1973) and worked carefully on his appearances in public.

He had a "standing box" devised (*New York Times* 1973a), a podium with straps and braces designed to support his hips and legs (Nordheimer 1973), and inaugurated its use at the Spirit of America Festival on July 4, 1973, in Decatur, Alabama (Klein 1974), an event at which he shared the platform with Sen. Ted Kennedy (Apple 1973). Kennedy spoke first, and

> when the applause died, the master of ceremonies said, "We will now ask Governor Wallace to, uh, stand at the podium." To *stand* at the podium? There was a barely audible gasp from the crowd. Wallace was wheeled in from behind, grabbed the metal frame and appeared to rise toward the microphones. He rose jerkily, straining to maintain his balance. The place went berserk. People were crying, snapping shaky Instamatics, praying aloud. Oral Roberts couldn't have done it any better—George Wallace was standing. At that point, Ted Kennedy could have crawled under the stage completely unnoticed. (Klein 1974)

As late as 1974, the Wallace staff was still determined to give Wallace the appearance of walking, thinking that it might be essential to a viable candidacy (Griffin 1974). As the 1976 campaign neared, however, this strategy was quietly abandoned. The staff decided to go with the wheelchair.

To the political onlookers, Ted Kennedy's appearance with George Wallace at the Decatur, Alabama festivities was momentous. The purpose of the event had been to honor Wallace with an award, and the presence of both Kennedy and Democratic National Committee Chairman Robert Strauss on the same platform with their old adversary signaled a new day. Some were incensed; Ralph Abernathy of the Southern Christian Leadership Conference denounced Kennedy and warned that it would cost him black votes. The visit to Alabama, Abernathy said, was "the height of political opportunism" (Farrell 1973). *New York Times* columnist William Safire also thought the event significant: "Not only did it mark the beginning of a serious effort to reconstruct the old Democratic coalition but it happily meant the ending—at least for a long time—of the steady injection of vitriol into the body politic." Mused Safire: "We may have passed the peak of us-against-them politics" (Safire 1973).

In his speech on that occasion Kennedy had portrayed himself and Wallace as "fellow warriors," and listed a number of issues on which they agreed, including "the power which has been absorbed by bureaucracies ignorant of [people's] needs" (Apple 1973). Such verbiage fit Wallace's contentions perfectly. For some time he had been maintaining that the Democratic party was moving toward his philosophy (King 1973), and after Kennedy's visit he commented that "political leaders who have been ultraliberal see now that the center is the place to get" (*New York Times* 1973d).

Whether or not that was true, the hierarchy of the Democratic party certainly appeared to be paying a lot of attention to Wallace. His staff was constantly in touch with Democratic National Chairman Strauss, and Wallace representatives were "intimately involved in the counterreformation of party rules" (Lydon 1974c). The candidate himself was a member of the party's policy advisory committee (King 1973), and spoke as a representative of the party at a Democratic delegation selection conference in Atlanta (*New York Times* 1973e). In general, the party was primed to treat Wallace gingerly—and as a Democrat in good standing (Lydon 1974c).

The Watergate Hearings

Around this same time, the Watergate hearings were taking place. Apparently, CREEP (the Committee to Re-Elect the President) had tried desperately to keep Wallace from winning the Alabama governorship in 1970. In testimony before the House Judiciary Committee, Haldeman revealed that the group had funneled $400,000 to Wallace's opponent in that race "in an unsuccessful effort to prevent George C. Wallace from winning the governorship and using it as a base for a third-party presidential campaign" (Naughton 1973).

Further testimony revealed other such gestures by CREEP. In 1971, McGruder paid a California state Republican official $10,000 to purge voter names from the state's American Independent party rolls (Reed 1973; *New York Times* 1973e). It was also rumored that the American Nazi party had been involved in trying to get the AIP dropped from ballot position as well (Roberts 1973). CREEP's thinking was that a third-party Wallace candidacy might throw the election into the House of Representatives (*New York Times* 1973c), and the group was merely trying to enhance Nixon's chances by cutting off Wallace's third-party escape route (*New York Times* 1973e).

Throughout the 1972 campaign, the Nixon interests had distributed anti-Wallace publicity implicating other Democrats (Reed 1973). One choice "dirty trick" was Donald Segretti's distribution of cards at Wallace rallies which read, "If you liked Hitler, you'll love Wallace." The flip side contained an appeal for Muskie (*New York Times* 1973f).

Other Watergate testimony revealed that the key White House contact within the Wallace staff had been none other than a former (although short-lived) campaign manager (Crewdson 1974). In addition, the IRS had passed on tax information about the Wallace campaign to the White House staff. And it was most likely someone on the White House staff who had leaked information to the press during the 1972 campaign that the IRS was auditing the returns of Wallace's brother Gerald.

As a result of these and other Watergate disclosures, Wallace began to wonder aloud about his shooting. He had read his assailant's (Arthur Bremer) diary and mused publicly that "a busboy doesn't have the money to go around the country buying guns, riding around in limousines, flying planes, traveling to Canada." He suggested that his assassination attempt might have been a conspiracy, but declined to speculate on who might have been behind it (Klein 1974). Others were also so concerned. Martha Mitchell told David Frost that Wallace knew of a White House link to his attempted assassination. Wallace hastily denied it (*New York Times* 1974f), but Daniel Ellsberg "called for an investigation into the possibility that the White House 'plumbers' engineered the shooting of Gov. George C. Wallace" (*New York Times* 1973b).

On all such issues Wallace kept silent. He refused to discuss Watergate, Nixon, or the disclosures. In the meantime, however, the disclosures were having an effect on the public. Wallace's fan mail grew to more than 4000 letters a day, and in a few short months his contributions "increased fivefold." During this period, campaign manager Charles Snider confided to a reporter that "people are sending in $18,000 to $20,000 a day" (Reed 1973).

Preparation for the 1976 Campaign

In the summer of 1973, Wallace had hired a professional fund raiser, Richard A. Viguerie of Falls Church, Virginia. Viguerie had taken the list of Wallace supporters started a decade earlier and merged it with his own list of 2,500,000 conservative names (many from a list of Goldwater contributors in 1964). Viguerie then prospected "to selected magazine lists ... to buyers of Hank Williams records, to firemen and policemen around the country, and to a variety of political lists" (Lydon 1975d). In October 1973 campaign debts were listed at $72,000. In a mailing sent out by Viguerie at the time, Wallace explained to potential donors that after he was shot, his funds had "dried up overnight" (Franklin 1973).

Viguerie's technique was to ask people to give a specific amount, an amount that had been gleaned from the list of computerized records as the largest donation they had ever given "to any previous political cause" (Albright 1974). It worked. By the end of November, the Wallace campaign debt was down to $50,000 (Ayres 1973a), and three months later he had $103,751 on hand (Ripley 1974). Altogether, Viguerie sent out around four million fund raising letters in 1973. These letters grossed $1,410,033, and of that amount, 53 percent went to Viguerie for expenses (Albright 1974).

In addition to working on his finances, Wallace was working on his image. He started by trying to change the public's perception of him as a racist. To that end, he began to appear in public with blacks and insisted that he had never been a racist (Ayres 1973a). He even crowned a black homecoming queen at the University of Alabama. Belying tradition, however, Wallace did not kiss her (Ayres 1973b). "The people of Alabama aren't ready for that," he commented (Range 1974).

Despite the lag in social customs, it was apparent that Alabama had indeed changed. The extension of the franchise to the state's twenty-six percent black population had made a vast difference in Wallace's electoral constituency (Ayres 1973b), and as Wallace had to win the gubernatorial race in 1974 before he could even think about running for president in 1976, black voters were a big consideration.

In his eight years as governor, Wallace had appointed seven blacks and 1549 whites to various boards and commissions (Range 1974). There was much to be done. Amid a flourish of publicity, he began systematically to name blacks to a variety of state positions (Ayres 1973a). These efforts were not lost on black voters. Observers began to comment that the politics of Alabama and the New South were "more concerned with pragmatism than with racism" (Ayres 1973b), and a group of southern black mayors gave Wallace a standing ovation (Ayres 1973b). In his public utterances, Wallace reiterated that he had "never been against any citizen realizing the American dream." He explained further: "My position has been against central government meddling in local affairs" (Ayres 1973b).

Another type of groundwork being laid in preparation for the 1976 campaign was the matter of the Democratic party's delegate selection procedures. The rules were being changed, and as the Wallace forces had been seriously hurt in 1972 by their ignorance of the rules (they had not been able to translate voter strength into delegate strength), they were not about to take chances in 1976 (Wicker 1974b; Griffin 1978). From the beginning, the Wallace camp made sure that they had representatives on every important subcommittee of the Democratic National Committee. As Wallace staffer Mickey Griffin tells it:

> We started out running [in] the primaries in 1972, and we didn't even know what the Democratic National Committee was. De Carlo and I went to Miami ... and they thought we were from outer space. That was the first contact the Wallace campaign ever had with the structure of the national committee—because we'd been running as a third party ... but you were talking about a whole different game where numbers meant a lot. When we first went up there in '72, I became buddies with Strauss .... We got hooked up with him and realized right off the bat that Strauss was going to be elected chairman of the DNC .... I told De Carlo, this was gonna be our ticket, and I went up there and I finagled a commitment out of Strauss for representation on the committee if he were elected. We convinced Strauss that we had three votes on the Democratic National Committee ... and Strauss won by one and a half votes, and I used to hang that over him all the time .... [He wouldn't] have been sitting there if it wasn't for me .... He knew he had to take somebody after he'd been elected, so he figured hell, I might as well take Griffin, 'cause he's just a punk, and I can handle him if necessary ... I worked into this position hoping it would happen and it did .... That gave me a ticket and a key to anything in the Democratic party that I wanted. (Griffin 1978)

In an attempt to get delegate totals to more nearly reflect popular voter strength, the Mikulski commission of the Democratic party planned to do away with unit rule convention delegations and winner-take-all primaries (Ayres 1973a; Ayres 1974b). The intent was to have delegates apportioned according to the percent of votes they received in a primary; but a candidate had to get at least fifteen percent of the primary vote before the candidate could share in the delegates (Ayres 1974a). In states which had precinct caucuses, a candidate had to win at least fifteen percent before the candidate could send delegates to the national convention. Tom Wicker saw these developments as most positive for Wallace, as Wallace's strength, more than any other candidate, lay in his popularity. Mickey Griffin saw it this way, too, and went about assuring Wallace input into the new rules:

> I went back and talked to all these people who had gone [to] . . . the drafting committee conferences and all, which is the most important [thing]. Anything in a political flow that ends up in a commission, you'd better start your research at the drafting committee, because that's where all the axing and twisting and all that [takes place], so we figured that out real quick, too, that this was where it was happening. In fact I got Drayton put on the damn thing. . . . Drayton and I were the only two people in the United States other than staff members of the DNC involved in this area that attended every one of the conferences . . . that the Mikulski commission ever had. We knew more about it than anyone else involved. We were learning to adapt our structure and our candidate to their rules . . . the key was that we knew what our candidate was good at . . . . We knew that we wanted primaries—proportional primaries or direct primaries. The Daley organization, and the groups inside the Democratic committee that got screwed in '72, like organized labor . . . wanted to make sure from there on out they could protect their delegates, and so that was going hand in glove [with us]. We would threaten to vote against it or hold a press conference against something if they didn't pass it, or we would act like we wanted something else so that they would cut this out and put something else in. I mean it was beautiful; Drayton was doing a great job; he was playing possum like crazy. And they thought he was the dumbest son-of-a-bitch they had ever seen. And when the rules came out, we were in hog heaven. We were at the corner of Got-It-Made Avenue and What's Happening Now Street. (Griffin 1978)

In February 1974 the Wallace organization began to hold regional conferences to analyze the delegate selection rules in various states (Lydon 1974b). Griffin said that the purpose of the meetings was to convert "popular strength into delegate strength" (Lydon 1974b). Teams of attorneys (*New York Times* 1974o) and strategists made sure that they thoroughly understood the wording as well as the implications of each state's set of rules. Wherever necessary, they developed plans to modify those rules to make them more advantageous for Wallace (Griffin 1978). Later they would use political pressure to work for changes in states where conditions were unfavorable (*New York Times* 1974o).

In the meantime, Wallace said publicly that he was unsure about whether he would run for the presidency in 1976. "It may be there won't be any necessity for that," he stated. "The message has already been carried" (Lydon 1974c). Whenever he spoke, however, he focused on national issues, and talked about tax reform in particular.

In early January, the Wallace campaign announced that the Wallace forces would participate in the Democratic mini-convention in December.

Not only would they participate, campaign manager Charles Snider said, they would elect pro-Wallace delegates to that convention from every state (*New York Times* 1974o).

The trek southward of Democratic party regulars and other distinguished political figures continued. Many made the pilgrimages in attempts to capitalize on Wallace's support (Shannon 1974). Henry Jackson paid a visit in early 1974, and shortly afterwards George Meany met privately with Wallace (*New York Times* 1974m). In 1972 Meany had withheld support from George McGovern, keeping the AFL-CIO neutral. In discussing his meeting with Wallace, Meany said that they were "in the same ball park" on the issues of taxes, pensions and social security. Reporters saw their meeting as highly significant, and viewed it as an effort by the AFL-CIO to "regain its influence within the Democratic Party." Other AFL-CIO officials explained Meany's visit by observing that "Governor Wallace might well hold the balance of power in the party now" (Shabecoff 1974).

Even President Nixon got into the act. Amid heavy Watergate reverberations, Nixon announced that he was going to Huntsville, Alabama for Honor America Day. The White House said that the celebration fit the president's schedule, and explained that "he's been looking for some time for such a celebration" (Ayres 1974g).

Despite the general uneasiness throughout the country, Nixon found the crowd at Huntsville friendly. In his speech, he assailed the "distorted view that America is sick" and criticized the national news organizations. For his part, Wallace told Nixon that he was "among friends" (Herbers 1974).

Another visitor to Alabama during this time was Mrs. Rosa Parks, the black woman who had started the Montgomery bus boycott in the fifties. Mrs. Parks had since moved to Detroit, and on a trip back to Alabama, went by the governor's office. Presumably, she had been summoned; afterwards, Mrs. Parks reported that during the visit she was tricked into being photographed with Wallace (Reed 1974).

The 1974 Gubernatorial Race

Wallace had started a busy schedule of appearances in late 1973 in anticipation of the 1974 gubernatorial contest. He traveled with his specially designed lectern and "stood up" to make his speeches (*New York Times* 1973a). In February he formally announced his candidacy for the governorship. In the announcement, he insisted he had no specific plans for the 1976 presidential campaign. "But as Governor of Alabama," he said "I'm sure I'll be in a position to make certain that the people I spoke for in

1972 will be represented in the councils of both major parties in 1976"
(Reed 1974).

Nobody thought Wallace had any competition. As Kohn put it:

> This fellow—what's his name? Bremer?—he made a martyr out of Wallace.
> So it really doesn't matter about scandal or race or what people think about it
> one way or the other. They're just not going to turn a man in a wheelchair out
> of office .... Neither Jesus Christ nor Robert E. Lee could beat that man
> now. (Wooten 1974)

But Wallace was thinking beyond Alabama. He knew that if he could
"impress national politicians with his ability to draw votes all across the
political spectrum—a prerequisite for running for national office" (Ayres
1974f), he would have it made, and he kept going after black support. In
doing so, he ignored references to his segregationist past and "boasted of
providing educational and employment opportunities for all Alabamians,
black and white" (Ayres 1974e).

Black support wasn't long in coming. Johnny Ford, the black mayor of
Tuskegee, Alabama, endorsed Wallace for reelection, saying that Wallace
had given aid to Tuskegee, and had "demonstrated his willingness to 'help
all the people, particularly those who really need it'" (*New York Times*
1974l). Two black organizations, the Southern Democratic Conference of
Birmingham and the Voters League of Ozark, also came out in support of
Wallace (Ayres 1974f). In addition, he was backed by William M. Branch, a
black probate judge from Greene County, and even got the endorsement of
a black newspaper, *The Birmingham Times,* which reported that he had
"softened" on the race issue (*New York Times* 1974j).

Black leaders outside of Alabama were particularly disturbed by the new
show of support. Several, including Julian Bond and Hosea Williams,
visited Alabama and urged blacks there not to support Wallace. But the
reality was that Wallace had tight control over state and federal funds, and
blacks in political positions had to play politics with the governor to get
their hands on the money. As Mayor Ford explained it, "Our citizens have
come to realize that voting for people is one way of insuring that their
community will get at least its fair share of resources" (Ayres 1974f).

Despite the fact that he had four opponents, Wallace won the
Democratic gubernatorial primary easily. He got sixty-four percent of the
vote. The final tally was 495,733, twenty to twenty-five percent of which
was estimated to be black votes (Jenkins 1974). In claiming victory, he told
a cheering crowd "that he would serve as the Governor of both 'whites and
blacks' and would help all 'achieve the American dream'" (Ayres 1974d).

The large black vote which Wallace had received in the primary attracted
national attention. In response, black civil rights leader Charles Evers

offered his opinion that "Wallace had changed to the degree that he could support him as a Vice-Presidential candidate." Wallace represented the thinking of at least one-third of the country, Evers maintained, and "that's what we're trying to bring together, the poor whites and blacks, and George Wallace represents the same folks I do—those who have been left out" (*New York Times* 1974i).

Other black leaders immediately denounced Evers' endorsement. Six black mayors, including Maynard Jackson of Atlanta, swore that they would not share a ticket with Wallace in 1976. Manhattan Borough President Percy Sutton summed up their sentiment best: "If Jesus Christ were nominated President and Governor Wallace Vice-President, I'd vote against Jesus Christ" (Range 1974).

Wallace's victory in the primary and the prospect of insignificant Republican opposition in November left him in a very strong position. He had gained the support of blacks and made increasing inroads into the votes of blue collar and other unionized workers. The Alabama Labor Council had also endorsed him. In fact, his only dilemma was whether or not he could continue to make progress toward the "regular Democratic vote without losing the support of his own fanatical following" (*New York Times* 1974j).

Tom Wicker remarked on the political significance of the Alabama primary results:

> Together with Edward Kennedy's visit to Alabama to honor him, his high standing in most Democratic polls, and public sympathy for his having been left an invalid—some invalid!—by a would-be assassin, the Alabama primary has gone a long way to give Mr. Wallace the political respectability he never quite had before. That is a major national political development and one that will make an even more formidable Democratic or third-party presidential contender for 1976. (Wicker 1974a)

As one Democratic party strategist put it "Wallace is the hinge of the whole question. We can't win a presidential election without getting back his voters" (*Newsweek* 1974).

Meanwhile, delegate selection to the mini-convention was taking place, but Wallace did not do well in the local caucuses. He was shut out in South Carolina as well as in Tennessee. He also made an effort in Texas, but met with failure there as well (Lydon 1974a). In July he finally abandoned the idea of going to the mini-convention with large numbers of delegates. He planned instead, he said, to set forth his platform before the convention.

This announcement made onlookers uneasy. If Wallace's proposals were rejected by the party, he might well decide to run as a third-party candidate. Wallace strategist Joe Azbell tried to waylay the anxiety. Wallace, he assured, "plans to stay in the Democratic party, to work to bring the party back into the middle" (*New York Times* 1974h). Azbell's words did little to calm party regulars.

On August 9, 1974, Richard M. Nixon resigned as president of the United States. Later, Nixon told David Frost that it was Wallace who had prompted his decision. In the last few days before the resignation, Nixon had called Wallace and asked him to talk to Rep. Walter Flowers, an Alabama Democrat who was a member of the House Judiciary Committee. Nixon wanted Wallace to try to persuade Flowers to oppose impeachment. Mr. Wallace, reported Nixon, "seemed not to understand why I was calling." He said, "I don't believe that there is anything I can do to be helpful." And when pressed further, Wallace allegedly responded, "If I were to call, it might be misinterpreted" (Frost 1978).

A couple of months later Wallace began twittering the Democrats again, warning that "he might bolt the Democratic party and run as an independent candidate if the party does not heed his call, and move toward the right" (Ayres 1974b). To make matters worse, he sent out a mailing to find out how many people might back him if he ran on a third-party presidential ticket (*New York Times* 1974e).

Among party regulars the debate over whether or not they would support Wallace continued. Jackson said that he would run with Wallace on the Democratic ticket (Cadell 1974), but Ted Kennedy declared that if Wallace was on that ticket, he would not back the party (*New York Times* 1974d).

As the Alabama gubernatorial campaign continued to roll toward its expected conclusion, attorney Morris Dees filed a lawsuit in federal court accusing Wallace of discriminating against blacks in making political appointments. Dees charged that Wallace made appointments only when "required for receipt of federal funds" (*New York Times* 1974g), and a former director of the Alabama Department of Public Safety testified that Wallace had repeatedly told him not to hire blacks for positions as state troopers (Ayres 1974c).

In spite of these disclosures and the accompanying publicity, Wallace won an unprecedented third term. His Republican opponent, State Sen. Elvin McCary, gave him only token opposition (*New York Times* 1974c).

There is some debate about exactly how much black support Wallace actually got in the 1974 gubernatorial election. The black-dominated National Democratic Party had told its followers to stay away from the polls. While fifty-two percent of the registered black voters turned out statewide, Wallace got less than ten percent of their vote; they voted primarily for black candidates (Range 1974).

Wallace followed his reelection with a speech at the Progressive Baptist

Mission and Education Convention. It was delivered at the Dexter Avenue Baptist Church, Martin Luther King's ministry in the sixties. There Wallace reiterated what was rapidly becoming a familiar refrain: "As far as I was concerned, there was never a race question; it was a question of big government" (*New York Times* 1974b).

At the inauguration Wallace projected a moderate image in contrast to that which accompanied his "segregation now ... segregation forever" speech at the first inaugural in 1963. The "new" Wallace listened reverently while a black choir sang and he emphasized "all the people, both black and white" in his inaugural speech (Ayres 1975i).

Meanwhile the rumors of a third party were becoming more elaborate. The newest idea was "the possibility of Reagan and Wallace joining in a third-party coalition" (Reston 1974b; Reston 1974a). Wallace refused to comment, but continued to use the possibility of a third party to bait the Democrats. "I've got the biggest constituency in the party," he told an interviewer, "but if the Democrats have a boss-controlled convention and a platform like 1972, then I might just do something else" (Kraft 1974).

A week later the Wallace staff announced that their candidate would run in almost every Democratic primary (*New York Times* 1974a). Other Democrats were making plans, too; apparently a number of Southerners were thinking about taking on Wallace in the Southern primaries (Kraft 1974).

December arrived and, as expected, Wallace showed up at the Democratic mini-convention. The half-term convention had been scheduled, one party regular said, to mend bad feelings left over from the 1972 convention and to "get Daley and Jesse Jackson back under the same roof, and on waving terms, with McGovern and Wallace" (Wills 1975). At the convention, "Wallace did not go to the floor, but held court in his hotel room. People came to see him .... Daley called up. Delegates clogged the approaches to his suite. And Sen. Robert Byrd of West Virginia, the keynote speaker, came to consult very visibly with Wallace on the party's future" (Wills 1975). In many ways the Wallace campaign considered their appearance at the mini-convention a success. Griffin observed that "no party organization is treating George Wallace any longer like an outsider." But Griffin had no illusions: "We've got what they want," he said, "and that's people" (Lydon 1974b).

The Issue of Delegate Selection

The next hurdle was a big one—the party's newly written delegate selection rules were complicated. First, crossover voting, a source of Wallace support in Wisconsin in particular, would be eliminated; primaries were for Democrats only. Second, there would be no winner-take-all primaries; no longer would a candidate getting a majority of votes win every delegate.

The only possibilities were a presidential preference primary in which delegates would be divided proportionately among those candidates winning over fifteen percent of the vote, and a direct delegate election convention system. The latter was a system in which voters in each congressional district elected delegates to a statewide convention. Final decisions on whom to support were then made at the convention. New York and Illinois already had this system. In direct delegate elections there was no proportional requirement, and a number of states immediately saw the "loophole." California quickly changed its laws, and the word was that other states would soon follow suit.

The best situation for Wallace was a winner-take-all primary, or some other contest in which popularity with voters could be directly translated into delegate strength. Under the new rules, however, these primaries were all but eliminated. Under the new system the feeling was that Wallace might do reasonably well in proportional primaries, but would do considerably less well in direct delegate elections. The Wallace campaign did not seem particularly worried. They said that problems with the direct delegate convention system could be overcome by focusing their efforts on selected congressional districts (Apple 1975i).

There was some talk of winner-take-all races in congressional districts, a system which would mean even more trouble for Wallace. In races of this kind, Wallace's name-recognition advantage would be considerably diminished (*Newsweek* 1975). An additional rumor was that some states were thinking about abandoning the primaries altogether.

The Wallace campaign had been working on delegate selection problems for some time. They were fully aware of the difficulties that their candidate would have with every different type of primary, and were engaged in a systematic effort to ascertain more favorable arrangements. The Wallace strategists, accompanied occasionally by the candidate, visited many state legislatures and Democratic committees to make concerted pitches for changing the election laws to provide for presidential preference primaries. The speech used on these occasions was a rousing one, permeated with Wallace's pseudopopulist phrases:

> The McGovern-Fraser reforms were conceived to broaden participation in our Party, but they served to limit it. Groups of political activists and highly paid political operatives used these rules to perpetuate their selfish motives under the guise of participatory democracy. The average citizen was once again the victim. The result of shortchanging the people was the worst political defeat in the history of the Democratic party. From the ashes of this defeat, the Democratic party is faced with the challenge and the opportunity

to rebuild itself. The strength of its rebuilding effort is in the people. If the rebuilding job is done properly, the people will feel their strength in the party. Only with such a program will the quality and character of the Democratic party be elevated in the minds of the people to a position that the people believe that the goals of the Party are good. The best way in which to build such trust is to guarantee the people that their wishes will be truly reflected in the selection of national convention delegates. (Wallace 1975)

In a challenge to North Carolina legislators debating changes in their delegate selection procedures, Wallace said, "The Democratic party talks about 'participatory democracy,' and now we have a move on to remove the little man—the textile worker, the farmer—from the process" (Ayres 1975g). Wallace "called for primaries in every state and argued that conventions were 'undemocratic' because they were subject to power-brokering instead of the will of the people" (Ayres 1975g).

The Democratic party responded to Wallace's charges immediately. Marc A. Siegal, executive director of the Democratic National Committee, said that while modifications in the primaries' rules were being considered, "there was no party effort to limit the influence of the public" (Ayres 1975g).

Wallace retorted that the moves were indeed limiting "the will of the people." In fact, he contended, the changes most affected states in which he had done well in 1972—North Carolina, Tennessee, Michigan, Maryland, and Wisconsin (Ayres 1975g). He maintained that "the Democratic Party's hierarchy was so afraid that he might run again for the Presidency that [additional] efforts were being made in several states to stack delegate-selection procedures against him" (Ayres 1975g).

In this interchange a reporter saw the dynamic of Wallace politics again: "Whatever the outcome of the Senate vote [in North Carolina], Mr. Wallace seems sure to gain, coming off either as a giant killer or as the bullied defender of the little man" (Ayres 1975g).

As usual, the Wallace forces got what they wanted. As Griffin explained it:

> We forced, through Wallace outside agitating and us working to stoke the fire at the national level, to get kind of a hue and cry to eliminate the precinct caucuses and switch them with proportional primaries where the people could speak .... There were about ten or twelve states that switched from caucus methods to primaries, and about ten of them out of the twelve were our good states. (Griffin 1978)

Third Party Talk

In February 1975 Sen. Jesse Helms of North Carolina called a meeting of conservatives to consider a third party. Reagan was a guest speaker at the meeting (Apple 1975g), and one month later the Committee on Conservative Alternatives was established (*New York Times* 1975t). Gallup Polls of the time indicate that a third party might be a good bet: equal numbers of voters (24%) in both major parties said that they would be likely to support a conservative third party in 1976. (*New York Times* 1975a).

Although Reagan had denied that he was interested in running on a third-party ticket with Wallace (*New York Times* 1975t), and Wallace had said he would stay within the Democratic party unless the party was "unfair to his supporters in the election of convention delegates" (Lydon 1975i), the clamor for a third party continued.

William Loeb, publisher of the Manchester, New Hampshire *Union Leader* wrote that "George Wallace and a new party are the best prospects for rescuing this nation," (Lydon 1975g) and the Indiana American Independent Party announced that "it would circulate petitions to put Reagan and Wallace on the 1976 primary ballot" in Indiana (*New York Times* 1975r).

In early February, Henry Jackson announced his candidacy, and using Wallace-type phraseology vowed aid to "little people" (Apple 1975h). Former governor of North Carolina Terry Sanford also let it be known that he was running for president, but was careful to say he would support Wallace if Wallace were the Democratic nominee (Lynn 1975c). Former Gov. Jimmy Carter of Georgia, on the other hand, in New York City to present himself as an alternative to Wallace, said that George Wallace's being on the Democratic ticket was inconceivable (Lynn 1975b).

Inconceivable or not, by March 1975, the Wallace campaign was going strong. The campaign had three dozen employees, a political scientist on staff and the resources of professional fundraiser Viguerie, who had raised 2.6 million dollars in the previous eighteen months. The Wallace staff had been working on the advertising campaign, drawing up position papers (Ayres 1975h), and appointing campaign chairmen in over twenty states (Ayres 1975f). Also on the scene was an ABW Movement, for Anyone But Wallace.

In the meantime, Governor Wallace had continued to appoint blacks to the Alabama payroll. He named William C. King as his administrative assistant (*New York Times* 1975v), and paid off a political debt to Jessie J. Lewis, the publisher of the black weekly *Birmingham Times,* who had endorsed Wallace for his third term as governor, by appointing Lewis coordinator of the Highway and Traffic Safety Office, a cabinet-level position (*New York Times* 1975w). A subsequent look at Lewis' status, however, revealed that his job was not fulltime, and a subcabinet position at best. In recompense Wallace had allowed Lewis to stay on as consultant to his son as publisher. (Brill 1975a).

Seizing every opportunity to work on his image, Wallace espoused his views to those at the National Governors' Conference. In a speech there, he "dismissed racial issues and his old racist reputation, saying that schools were better integrated in Alabama than in Boston" (Lydon 1975h). Warming to his subject, he said "I can relate more to the average black man than any other man who's thinking of running for president ... because we all grew up in the South where we were poverty-stricken together" (Lydon 1975i).

He also used the forum at the National Governors' Conference to advise on the issues of his upcoming presidential candidacy. He was concerned with taxes and law and order, and opposed further military spending in South Vietnam. His speech had many references to the middle class (Lydon 1975h), which Wallace maintained "were paying most of the freight for the very rich and the very poor, and they were sick of it and needed somebody to look after their interests" (Reston 1975b). Wallace insisted further that "the authority of the Federal Reserve Board over interest rates and high income taxes ... [is] leading to the 'radicalization of the middle class'" (Lydon 1975i). Wallace pledged to argue their case.

Attempts to Undercut Wallace Support

Meanwhile many activities were underway which would have the consequence of undercutting Wallace's support or stopping him in some way. In one of these instances, the Justice Department was investigating the question of whether Wallace's third term as governor had begun illegally. Under the Voting Rights Act of 1965, southern states were required to submit any "political changes that might affect minority voting rights"; it was unclear whether the law that had allowed Wallace to succeed himself had been approved under this act (*New York Times* 1975u). Justice soon dropped the inquiry, however; everything was in order (*New York Times* 1975p).

.Other activities centered on Wallace's fund-raising operations. In 1974 the General Accounting Office had ruled that federal funds for campaigning would be available only to Democratic and Republican candidates. If Wallace decided to run as a third-party candidate, he would not be eligible for a cut of the federal monies, because the rules read that any independent or third-party candidate must have gotten at least five percent of the total vote in the previous election in order to qualify for the funds (*New York Times* 1974n). As a Democrat, however, Wallace became the first candidate to qualify. He had met the eligibility requirements by raising $5000 from each of twenty states in contributions of $250 or less (*New York Times* 1975r).

The federal government was also deciding whether matching funds would be based on a candidate's gross or net receipts. If they decided on net receipts, the Wallace campaign would receive much less than expected (Lydon 1975d), for the cost of Wallace's direct mail appeal usually ran about half of what was collected (*New York Times* 1975k). But the Wallace staff was not particularly concerned about what the government's final decision might be. They said that they wanted to pass up the federal money and "make an issue of Wallace's independence." They thought that Viguerie could easily raise the $10 million allowed for preconvention campaigning by himself; the Wallace campaign had a list of over 600,000 regular contributors, and an average mailing brought in as much as $700,000 (Witcover 1975b). If Wallace refused the matching funds, he would thus be able to say that "he is the only one not running at the taxpayer's expense, that he is the only one not being subsidized by the federal government" (Witcover 1975b).

The staff was optimistic in other ways as well. They said that they were counting on Wallace to win the Democratic presidential nomination, perhaps even on the first ballot (Witcover 1975b). An all-out effort was planned.

One priority was a more comprehensive grass roots organization. Whenever Wallace was going to travel to a particular area, the Viguerie computers were used to alert a substantial number of supporters and would-be supporters that the candidate would be in town (Lydon 1975d). The list was also used to people organizational meetings.

1976 Campaign Strategy

In reviewing their strategy, the Wallace staff had decided not to enter the New Hampshire primary. They would leave that one to the liberals, they said, who would knock each other out. Elaborating further, Griffin remarked, "It's like a $1,000 hooker going to the bus station one night .... We don't have anything to gain there" (Witcover 1975b).

Wallace would, however, enter Florida. The plan was to make as big a splash as they had in 1972. As far as the rest of the campaign went, the staff planned to fly Wallace into one state a day. In each state he would hold a press conference and give perhaps one speech. The rest of the campaign would use advertising and television spots keyed to specific media markets corresponding to particular congressional districts. The television campaigning would consist of tapes of previous rallies or talks from the governor's desk in Montgomery (Witcover 1975b).

Wallace's issues were to be "the squeeze on the middle-income worker; big government that wastes and doesn't work; permissiveness in the street on TV and in the movies, and softness in foreign policy" (Witcover 1975b).

In less euphoric moments, the staff confided that they were not certain that Wallace would win the nomination but said that it looked like he would have a great deal of influence. Most discussion centered around his sharing the ticket. Some suggested that he might team up with Jackson (Witcover 1975b), and when a staff member was asked whether Wallace would take the vice presidential slot, he replied: "Wallace is less interested in the power than the glory, and Vice President to a little boy from Clio, Alabama would be a pretty high station. Rockefeller took it.... I would imagine Wallace would run with anybody" (Witcover 1975b).

The Democrats speculated that Wallace would go to the convention with thirty-five to forty percent of the delegates. This would make it almost impossible for any other candidate to get a majority (Apple 1975f); they were clearly worried. Democratic National Committee Chairman Robert Strauss said that there was a good chance that the convention might deadlock. In that situation, Strauss said, Kennedy and/or Wallace would be powerbrokers (*New York Times* 1975o).

Melvin Laird contended that a Wallace race would actually help Ford. Wallace would attract votes, Laird said, that might otherwise go to "an anti-Ford conservative in a Republican primary" (Lydon 1975e).

Most Democrats felt that they were over a barrel. "He has the power to tear this party to pieces," said one moderate southern governor, "and he'll do it if we don't give him what he wants—or figure out a way to beat him" (*Newsweek* 1975).

In several states, there was talk of doing away with primaries altogether. Wallace got wind of that and called it "antidemocratic"; the plans were abandoned. Another ploy was to run favorite sons in key primaries—any sizeable favorite son accolade could drown out Wallace support. Yet another idea was to pit only one or two candidates against Wallace in major primaries (Apple 1975f). The lesson of the 1972 Florida primary had been that the more candidates entering a primary, the more likely Wallace was to get a plurality and win by default. Terry Sanford and Jimmy Carter were most often mentioned as the likely candidates to take on Wallace in the South, but the fear was that they might split the moderate southern vote between them, leaving the door open for a Wallace sweep to victory. Neither was a clear choice for a solitary run against Wallace, for any Wallace opponent had to win by a respectable margin. The worse Wallace made other Democrats look in the primaries, the more influence he would wield at the convention (Wicker 1975b).

Another quandary for the party was the question of how to respond to Wallace and his demands. If the Democrats ignored him, Wallace might lead "a disastrous third-party bolt. And even if there were no bolt, enough

Wallace voters could sit out a two-candidate election, or cross to the Republicans, to defeat the Democratic ticket." If the Democrats did respond to Wallace's demands, they would risk crippling their ticket or their platform or both (Wicker 1975b).

A reporter observed yet another dilemma: "the basic problem for the Democrats today is not simply that Wallace refuses to abide by the conventions. It is, instead the unwillingness of any Democrats of real standing to take the risk of confronting him directly. They all believe he is not equipped to be President, either ideologically or practically, but they are afraid to say so" (Behn 1975).

Those who did try to do something about it threw Wallace straight into the briar patch. At the National Democratic Governors' Conference, Florida's Gov. Reuben Askew suggested a loyalty oath; it played into Wallace's hands. "How could they ask that of him," Wallace demanded, "when many of them were saying that they could not support a ticket which included him?" (Apple 1975f). With a loyalty oath all Democrats would be put into the position of having to say whether they would or would not support Wallace; they would lose votes either way. A "no" would give Wallace yet another advantage: "A simple no ... again plays right to Mr. Wallace's strength—his appeal to the people as an independent who speaks directly to and for them rather than through the usual party process" (Wicker 1975b).

All of this discussion was over a man who had not yet finally announced his candidacy. To date, Wallace had said only that he would be "involved in the 1976 campaign" (*New York Times* 1975l), and the word was that he would delay his announcement until the end of the year. Observers saw this as a ploy giving him more time to decide between the Democratic party and a third party (Lydon 1975c). His mailings meanwhile contended that he was running for the Democratic nomination (Apple 1975f).

There were many options. If Wallace ran as a Democrat, Snider and Griffin saw two convention scenarios, both tradeoffs: either Wallace would throw his votes to an opponent or an opponent would throw his to Wallace. They did not envision a stalemate, nor did they discuss a third party (Witcover 1975b). But Wallace himself had refused to rule anything out.

The question of a third party hovered in the background. The convention of the American party was scheduled for the week after the Democratic National Convention, and both the American party and the American Independent party had filed for ballot position in a number of states (Witcover 1975b). In addition, Helms' Committee on Conservative Alternatives was gathering information in all fifty states on how to put a third party candidate on the ballot (*New York Times* 1975m).

Meanwhile, William Rusher, publisher of *The National Review,* argued that those conservatives who constituted a minority of the Democratic party and a majority of the Republican party could band together and form a new majority party (Rusher 1975).

A move in this direction was already being made by Richard Viguerie, Wallace's fund raiser. Viguerie had extensive conservative political connections, having done work for the Committee for the Survival of a Free Congress, the National Conservative Political Action Committee and the Conservative Congressional Committee (Lydon 1975b). He had also started the Conservative Caucus. While not yet a party, the Conservative Caucus was talking about "a nationwide convention that could nominate Wallace and provide him ballot position in most or all the states in 1976" (Witcover 1975b). Viguerie was also reported to be very interested in Ronald Reagan (Lydon 1975d).

The Wallace people were interested in Reagan as well. When Mickey Griffin visited Boston in search of support for Wallace, he told reporters that "he couldn't think of an issue on which Reagan and Wallace seriously differed" (Behn 1975). Cornelia Wallace said in an interview that Wallace and Reagan were in "the same boat" and suggested that "it would be interesting to run a little poll and see what people think of a Wallace-Reagan ticket."

A Harris Poll asking this question found that a Reagan-Wallace ticket would receive twenty-three percent of the vote, the "highest that Lou Harris had ever recorded in a third-party vote."[1] That twenty-three percent would throw the election into the House of Representatives (*New York Times* 1975n).

In May 1975, Wallace met with Reagan in Alabama; the June *Wallace Stand* came out with a front page picture of the two of them conversing. Its accompanying headline read "Anything is Possible" (Ayres 1975d), but there were no announcements.

In the meantime, Wallace appeared to be backing off from the American Independent party. A staff member explained that "the American party had acquired 'too many kooks' for a candidate who [is] . . . trying to portray himself as a moderate" (Ayres 1975d).

Wallace seemed most interested in Helms' Committee on Conservative Alternatives, but he was being very cautious. Campaign Manager Charles Snider emphasized that the Wallace campaign was not providing money or manpower to the Committee on Conservative Alternatives "because we're determined to keep good faith with the Democrats as long as possible" (Ayres 1975d), but a staff member confided, "If we go the third party route, we'll go mainly through the new Washington group" (Ayres 1975d).

While things looked rosy, there was trouble brewing. Wallace had to deal with some very negative publicity about his tenure in Alabama politics. A reporter took a hard look at his record as governor and wrote that the Wallace years "have been marked by violent racial repression, political intimidation, rampart corruption, and indifferent attention to the daily details of state" (Ayres 1975e).

Further, the reporter noted that among all fifty states in 1975, Alabama was 50th in per pupil expenditures, 48th in percent of draftees passing the armed forces mental test; 49th in per capita income; 48th in percent of residents living above the poverty line; 48th in infant survivability, and 48th in the number of doctors per 100,000 residents (Ayres 1975e, *passim*).

In answer to the criticism, Wallace replied defiantly that "the people of Alabama would not have asked him to run the state three times if there was any merit to such accusations" (Ayres 1975e). The fault finding continued, however, and there were growing rumors that Wallace's popularity in Alabama had slipped since his reelection eight months earlier (Brill 1975a).

There were reports that Wallace's presidential backing was slipping as well. One reporter checked this out in the Florida panhandle, a bastion of Wallace support. A newspaper editor whom he interviewed said that Wallace support was still strong and still keyed into the segregation issue, but several citizens said that they were tired of Wallace. Their main complaint was that he had been on the political scene too long: "Nobody really expects him to be elected anymore," one said. Another put it this way: "You go to the same bar every Saturday night .... You see the same fight every Saturday night. After a while, it's not very entertaining" (Apple 1975e).

Neither the Democrats nor the Republicans were taking any chances. President Ford said cautiously that he and Wallace had "similar philosophies on domestic issues ... 'We do have, apparently, some significant differences on foreign policy,' the president added, but he did not enumerate them, and said that it would be 'inappropriate' at the outset of his own Presidential candidacy to 'get into a brawl' with the Alabama Democrat" (Naughton 1975).

In an effort to attract the Wallace constituency, Ford dispatched Vice President Rockefeller to the South, and in Columbia, South Carolina, Rockefeller gave lip service to Wallace's positions, speaking of the "dangers of bureaucracy and high government spending, especially in the form of welfare programs." He also spoke of "the cheats who are taking advantage of the situation," and proclaimed "his dedication to 'states' rights and states' responsibilities.'"

When Rockefeller arrived in Alabama to attend the National Conference of Lieutenant Governors, Wallace said that Rockefeller was an "old personal friend." The vice president responded in kind by recalling his "delightful association" with Mr. Wallace at the National Governors'

Conferences. "George and I didn't always agree on issues," he said, "but we always respected each other, and I must say that we were two who were able to stand up and say what we believe in." (Lelyveld 1975).

In the years since the assassination attempt, Wallace's health had continued to be of concern. The governor himself had insisted he was healthy and had diverted attention from his condition with humor:

> I may be sick on one end, but some of the folks that have been running the country in the last couple of years have been sick on the other end, and I don't know but what that's worse than being sick on the leg end, frankly. (Reston 1975a, p. 45)

Cornelia Wallace had also done her part to boost the doubtful. "It's possible that we could have a child even now with his accident," she had told a reporter. "His spinal cord wasn't completely severed, you know, so that his condition doesn't rule out having another child" (Shearer 1974). But most people were not concerned with Wallace's fertility. They were concerned with whether or not he was healthy enough to do the job.

In August 1975 the news media reported that Wallace had broken his leg, and the issue came up again (*New York Times* 1975j). An article in the *Village Voice* discussed Wallace's health in detail. The reporter listed all that was wrong with Wallace and discussed possibilities of illness as well as the medications which Wallace took regularly. The conclusion was that Wallace was strong enough to run for president or vice president, but given the constant demands of the job, he was not strong enough to serve (Pincus, 1975).

In September there was a second attempt on President Ford's life, and secret service protection was immediately requested for all presidential candidates qualified to receive federal campaign funds. Although Wallace had not yet formally announced, he was given protection (Hunter 1975), and accepted it without equivocation (Weaver 1975).

Other Attempts to Undercut Wallace Support

Meanwhile, the Democratic party was still struggling to find a rules strategy to eliminate Wallace as a threat. Dan Fowler, chairman of the South Carolina Democratic party, introduced a resolution to the Democratic National Committee that would abolish proportional primaries or caucuses and let state party organizations name one-quarter of the delegates to the national convention. The other three-quarters of the delegates would represent the outcome of the presidential primary (Lydon 1975b).

Both Wallace supporters and liberal reformers argued that the resolution would violate the party's efforts to make the convention reflect grass roots opinion (*New York Times* 1975i). The Wallace people were particularly concerned because the plan would prevent Wallace from picking up at-large delegates in states where he might sweep the popular primary. And Griffin warned that Wallace wanted to be treated fairly, and would reciprocate if he were not. Fowler withdrew the resolution.

In another move, New York State announced a plan whereby 219 delegates would be elected in the primary as individuals rather than as part of specific slates. The presidential preference of these individuals would not be identified on the ballot. "The remaining delegates from New York, a total of fifty-five, would be selected at large by the Democratic state committee and . . . divided proportionately among the presidential candidates depending on the percentage of congressional district delegates they won" (Lynn 1975a).

Wallace continued trying to upgrade his image as presidential material. He began to make foreign policy references in his speeches, and by September these references constituted at least half of his content (Ayres 1975c). His positions were conservative. "He warns of Soviet trickery, insists that Cuba must mend some of its Communist ways, and demands retention of the Panama Canal," said a reporter (Ayres 1975b).

The European Tour

To further enhance his reputation as a knowledgeable spokesperson, Wallace announced that he would visit at least five European countries on a fact-finding mission. Kissinger's office helped set up the trip (Ayres 1975c), and the cost was covered by the campaign organization. As if to soothe his Alabama constituency, Wallace also said that he would be seeking industry in Europe for Alabama (Ayres 1975b).

The trip received considerable press coverage. In London, Wallace was briefed by U.S. Ambassador Elliot L. Richardson and met with Prime Minister Harold Wilson (Semple 1975), as well as Conservative party leader Margaret Thatcher (*New York Times* 1975h). Wallace used the opportunity to speak of his primary issue, the middle class. "The United States was not alone in its shameful treatment of the middle class," Wallace said. The governments of the Western nations had also "acted with 'malice' toward the middle class and had squeezed them between 'inflation' and 'the tax structure'" (Semple 1975). Wallace said that "President Ford and 'every other prospective candidate' had come around to his point of view'" on the middle class (Semple 1975). The press reported that Wallace was being treated "very much like a man who might be the next President of the United States" (Wicker 1975a).

In a visit with NATO and Common Market officials, Wallace recited American worries about "imports of cheap cars, and said it was important for Western nations to cooperate on oil" (*New York Times* 1975g). In other statements he warned against "Soviet 'trickery,' pledged himself to a strong Atlantic partnership, and denounced government paternalism and bureaucracy" (Semple 1975).

In Germany, Wallace criticized past "American foreign policy, which he said had been too tough on the Germans after World War I and drove them to the 'despicable character' Adolf Hitler and, later, [it was] too weak against Communism in letting the Russians take over East Germany and East Berlin" (*New York Times* 1975f).

After the trip was over, the candidate told his touring party that Europeans "know where Alabama is" (*New York Times* 1975e), and said he had only one regret—that he didn't get to see the Pope. The Pope's calendar had apparently been overscheduled, and there was no opportunity to arrange for an audience.

A senior Wallace aide thought the trip most productive: "First, it has completely dispelled any remaining doubts about his physical well-being or his capacity to hold the office of president. Second, it has shown he is capable of meeting with heads of state and displaying a vast knowledge of foreign affairs" (*Montgomery Advertiser* 1975).

Back home it was also apparent that Wallace's candidacy was being taken seriously. For the first time in his long history of running for the presidency, Wallace was being judged as "a potential President rather than just a protest candidate" (*New York Times* 1975d).

The 1976 Announcement

On November 12, he finally announced that he would seek the 1976 Democratic nomination for president. At the same time, he refused to rule out the possibility of a third-party run, but he said that he would enter "most of the thirty or so primaries scheduled" (Ayres 1975a).

In his announcement, Wallace did not mention race relations, but handed out a statement on "forced busing" to the crowd. The key issue of his campaign, he said, would be the " 'survival' of the average, middle-class American in an ultra-liberal age." On the foreign scene, he promised to "make this nation strong so that we shall be respected throughout the length and breadth of the world" (Ayres 1975a), and recommended "a return to 'old moralities' and 'law and order' and condemned Government overspending, waste in welfare, and unfair tax burdens" (Ayres 1975a). He "called for an 'overhaul' of United States foreign policy because of the 'lesson of Vietnam' and because of what he termed 'false detente' with the Soviet Union" (Ayres 1975a).

Following the announcement there was considerable discussion about his health. Most doctors saw no reason why Wallace shouldn't run for the presidency, and (Altman 1975) Wallace took the opportunity to compare himself with President Franklin Delano Roosevelt (*New York Times* 1975c).

In an appearance on "Meet the Press," Wallace was asked about his segregationist views. His answer was the revisionist view which had marked all of his recollections since the 1972 campaign. "We never did have any segregation except in the schools. I never was against people because of color, but I was against big government" (*New York Times* 1975b). Wallace went on to say that if he was elected president, he would push a Constitutional amendment "to let people choose where their children go to school" (*New York Times* 1975b).

Shortly after his announcement, Wallace began attacking Jimmy Carter, contending that the "Democratic party higher-ups plan to bill Carter as a Southern Alternative to Wallace" (Lydon 1975a). The word was that Daley, in particular, felt that Carter had a good chance of beating Wallace in the Florida primary (Apple 1975a). Wallace complained further that some of the Democratic hierarchy were "ganging up on him," but he had praise for Democratic National Chairman Robert Strauss, whom he said treated him "fairly." At a subsequent news conference, Strauss "said similarly conciliatory things about Mr. Wallace" (Apple 1975c).

It was apparent, however, that some factions were trying to slow Wallace down. Governor Byrne of New Jersey signed a ban on crossover voting (Sullivan 1975), and Attorney General Louis Lefkowitz of New York filed a suit against the Viguerie Company. If the suit was successful, it would be used to block further mailings into New York by the Wallace campaign. Viguerie had made a practice of assuming heavy mailing expenses in his business dealings with Wallace; the campaign paid him later, but the question was whether or not this constituted a normal and allowable business practice or an illegal corporate loan to a presidential candidate (*New York Times* 1975a).

Terry Sanford urged that the Democrats take Wallace head-on. Wallace, Sanford said, "has fooled people who have believed in him by calling forth the easy fears and avoiding the complex and tough-minded situation," and he should be stopped. Sanford presented himself as the ideal challenger (King 1975). Lloyd Bentsen announced that he would run against Wallace in the Texas primary, and urged others to do the same. "I think that every one of the candidates has to take Wallace in their home state to be viable," he insisted (Kneeland 1975).

Gradually, a unified plan began to emerge. Carter would take on Wallace in Florida, and other Democrats would stay out of that contest.

The word was that the Democratic hierarchy expected Wallace to win (Apple 1975d). It was more likely, however, that the other candidates stayed out deliberately so as not to divide the vote. Birch Bayh said that he was purposely staying "out of the Florida primary to avoid taking votes away from Jimmy Carter," and Wallace charged that the other Democratic candidates were staying out for the same reason (Ayres 1976v). Wallace maintained that the others "considered him 'sort of a nuisance' and were making a concerted effort to defeat him . . . . 'It's very important for them to beat me somewhere along the line, '" he said. "They got together and said, 'you take him on here and I'll take him on there'" (*New York Times* 1976u).

Preparing for the Primaries

The other primary for which Wallace was geared up was Massachusetts, scheduled second after New Hampshire. In Massachusetts, Wallace hoped "to capitalize on antibusing sentiment growing out of the confrontation in South Boston and on general anti-government feeling" (Apple 1975b).

There were problems with this. A survey in Quincy had shown that those against busing did not necessarily support Wallace. As one auto mechanic put it: "I don't like busing, but I don't like what Wallace says against blacks" (Evans and Novak 1975). Further, half of the respondents said that "they would not vote for Wallace under any conditions." None cited his physical disability, rather they said that he was "extreme," "radical," "arrogant," "blowhard," "ignorant," "bigoted" (Evans and Novak 1975).

Wallace himself did not think that he would run well in Massachusetts (Ayres 1976w), but his initial forays into the state had seemed promising (Ayres 1976w). State Sen. William Bulger of Massachusetts observed that "Mr. Wallace 'may well be the one we end up with' because he [is] . . . willing to 'speak up loud and clear and offend those who have made themselves our enemies'" (Apple 1975b).

On the surface, Wallace's presidential candidacy looked very promising. Throughout the United States he was "the favorite of almost one-fifth of the electorate," and he had more money and better organization than ever before (Ayres 1976x). But there was considerable doubt about how well he would actually do. His health was an important issue, and although his opponents did not mention it (possibly because they thought it might backfire), the media frequently brought up the issue of his health and openly speculated about its consequences (Ayres 1976x).

Others felt that 1976 was one campaign too many. Wallace's appeal was beginning to wear thin, and some of his past issues had vanished. The rest of his issues had been copied by other candidates. In Florida, the ex-governor of Georgia, Jimmy Carter, in full command of the southern style, was echoing Wallace's anti-Washington/antiestablishment themes. Another problem in Florida was that Ronald Reagan was running against Gerald Ford on the Republican ticket, and if people wanted to, they could easily switch tickets and vote for Reagan rather than for Wallace.

As a serious candidate, Wallace's record as governor of Alabama came under close scrutiny again and again. Said one reporter: "Mr. Wallace's political enemies contend that he only talks about problems, [and] never offers real solutions" (Ayres 1976x). And in one unusual move, Federal Judge Frank Johnson of Alabama announced that he was holding Wallace responsible for the condition of the state prison system, and ordered the governor and other state officials to come up with a comprehensive set of minimum constitutional standards that had to be maintained for the system's operation (*New York Times* 1976v). Wallace's response was to retort that the "country has been run ... by thugs and federal judges" (Wicker 1976b).

There were other criticisms. A couple of University of Alabama law students provided extensive documentation of bureaucratic and fiscal burgeoning in the Wallace years in a pamphlet titled "The Alabama Message." From 1962 to 1974, federal government outlays had gone up 176.7 percent compared to 359.6 percent in Alabama state expenditures. During the same period, the federal bureaucracy had grown by 17.1 percent; in Alabama, state bureaucracy had expanded by 113.3 percent (Wicker 1976a).

Problems with delegate selection also continued to plague the Wallace campaign. Wisconsin had refused to alter its open primary, thus permitting crossover voting, but the vote would only be a popularity contest with no significant bearing on delegate selection. Further, a Ford-Reagan contest was scheduled on the Wisconsin Republican ticket, and some Wallace supporters were bound to cast their votes in that contest instead (Delaney 1975).

The Wallace campaign planned to run slates in every district in New York State except Harlem, the South Bronx, and the North Country. But delegates on the New York primary ballot would be listed by their own names and would not be identified as supporters of Wallace or any other candidate (Carroll 1976).

The complexity of other delegate selection arrangements were apparent in the Mississippi contest. In this first contest between Wallace and Carter, Wallace defeated Carter by three to one in the Democratic precinct caucuses. He won more than forty-five percent of the delegates elected to attend county conventions, delegates who would ultimately choose Mississippi's twenty-four delegates to the Democratic National Convention (*New York Times* 1976t). While the overall judgment was that Wallace would ultimately get at least half of these delegates, his showing in Mississippi was a weaker one than in 1968 when he had gotten sixty-three percent of the vote as the candidate of the American Independent party (Apple 1976g). Given the complexity of the rules, however, the forty-five percent was still impressive, and Carter issued a statement that said "the Wallace organization must be credited for the job it has done. They have demonstrated an ability to compete strongly and effectively in a caucus system. This new ability indicates that Governor Wallace will be even stronger in 1976 than some have predicted" (*New York Times* 1976t).

Meanwhile, the Wallace campaign had decided to accept federal campaign funds. But some of the funds were being delayed or withheld because the Wallace Campaign's "bookkeeping operation has been questioned by the Federal Election Commission—certain cash-flow records apparently were not kept" (Ayres 1976x).

Primary campaigning began to get off the ground in early February. At that time a reporter observed that "the 1976 Wallace campaign is like no other the Alabama governor has conducted. The campaign is an armed camp, with a bullet-proof lectern, searches of spectators and newsmen at rallies, and secret service agents and bodyguards near at hand" (Ayres 1976t).

Besides the security problem, it was extremely difficult to conduct a national campaign in a wheelchair. "It is impossible for a wheelchair man to get out into the crowd," Wallace explained (Ayres 1976t). The report was that he felt isolated and dissatisfied.

There were other problems as well. The candidate had to be lifted and carried on and off airplanes and in and out of cars and discreetly placed in the wheelchair out of sight of the crowd before he rolled onto a stage or into a room for an appearance. The mechanics of how he got in and out of that wheelchair were not a part of the public consciousness; that is, however, not until he was dropped by a security guard carrying him on an airplane in the Florida panhandle at the beginning of the Florida campaign. Although the initial reports were that he was not seriously hurt (*New York Times* 1976s) and he resumed the campaign the next day (*New York Times* 1976r), many saw the incident as a serious reminder that the candidate was just not as healthy as others (Griffin 1978).

In February a Harris poll showed some slippage, but Wallace was drawing large crowds (Ayres 1976s) and no one thought it particularly important. Jackson changed his strategy and began to attack Wallace openly (Charlton 1976).

Wallace had not personally campaigned in Oklahoma but staged a last-minute advertising blitz in Tulsa and Oklahoma City. Jimmy Carter won the Oklahoma contest, followed by Fred Harris (Apple 1976f). As fifteen percent was the minimum required to win delegates, and Wallace got less than that, he did not get any delegates (*New York Times* 1976q).

The Massachusetts Primary

In Massachusetts, Wallace was drawing overflowing crowds (Ayres 1976r). On his first two forays into Massachusetts, he had "mentioned the busing issue only in passing and talked mainly about the 'survival of the great middle class,'" but on his third trip he began to hit hard on the issue of busing. He attacked Judge W. Arthur Garrity, the federal judge involved in the Boston busing suit. Wallace said if elected president, he would "prohibit 'forced' busing. He said he favors 'freedom of choice,' that is, letting each child decide which school to attend. The governor also says that he has asked President Ford to send Justice Department lawyers before the Supreme Court with a demand that the court overturn decisions that authorize busing" (Ayres 1976u).

Wallace was careful to avoid the abortion issue publicly. He didn't bring it up in his speeches but used flyers to get the issue across and "explain his opposition to liberalized abortion laws" (Ayres 1976r).

In general, Wallace did not use inflammatory rhetoric, but called for a peaceful resolution of problems (Ayres 1976q). The following quote shows this calmer image:

> I pray for the American dream to come true for all citizens, black and white, regardless of race. You can win this battle eventually. It takes a little time. But the way to do it is in the peaceful context of the ballot box, peacefully. An attempt at any other solution destroys order. It is not the American way. (Ayres 1976q)

The colorful language was still there, however. Wallace denounced federal judges who "push little children around in sociological experiments," and exclaimed, "Let the people make their own decisions about busing" (Ayres 1976u). Many thought that Wallace had a good chance in Massachusetts (Kifner 1976b). His particular advantage was in the number of Democratic candidates running—twelve in all. Thus it appeared that Massachusetts could be the Florida of 1972, a primary in which other candidates would so splinter the vote that Wallace would walk away with a plurality (Ayres 1976r). Wallace therefore decided to take some of the time originally scheduled for Florida and spend it in Massachusetts instead (Ayres 1976p). Florida seemed relatively secure (Ayres 1976n), and a victory in Massachusetts would really be a coup.

In the New Hampshire primary Wallace got 1,109 write-in votes, one percent of the total vote cast (*New York Times* 1976p). In Oklahoma the final counts were fifty-one percent uncommitted, 28.3 percent Carter, and 6.7 percent Wallace (*New York Times* 1976o). Wallace won the South Carolina Democratic precinct caucuses. He got twenty-eight percent compared to Carter's twenty-three percent; forty-six percent of the delegates were uncommitted (*New York Times* 1976m), but the victory was not what it seemed.

In total, the South Carolina vote was anti-Wallace. Democratic party leaders and black leaders had "urged voters to go unpledged on the grounds that it would give them some bargaining power with candidates who emerged as forerunners in the coming months" (Franks 1976). Despite the fact that Wallace had outspent Carter two-to-one in the media coverage and campaigned five times to every two that Carter had campaigned, the second choice of most of the uncommitted was Carter (Franks 1976).

In Massachusetts Wallace limited his appearances to well-advertised evening rallies held in theaters and halls in blue-collar neighborhoods in and around Boston. He also used television advertising (Ayres 1976p). He was counting on the busing issue, but also hoped "to tap the deep well of citizen discontent over a sagging economy and an even larger Federal bureaucracy" (Ayres 1976p).

All in all, Wallace spent twenty-two days campaigning in Massachusetts and almost a quarter of a million dollars (Ayres 1976p). When the tally came in, he came in third statewide and carried the city of Boston.

"The victory was shocking to outsiders, who tend to view . . . [Boston] as a city of students and Beacon Hill Brahmins, but in reality it is largely a city of tight-knit ethnic neighborhoods intensely resentful of court-ordered busing for school desegregation" (Kifner 1976a).

The statewide results were Jackson twenty-three percent, Udall eighteen percent, Wallace seventeen percent, and Carter fourteen percent. In the delegate counts Jackson got thirty, Udall twenty, Wallace twenty-one, and Carter sixteen (Apple 1976e).

A CBS News/*New York Times* poll of Democratic primary voters in Massachusetts taken right after they left the voting booths revealed that fewer than half of the Wallace voters thought that their candidate could win the presidency. Further, "nearly two-thirds . . . refused to name a second Democratic choice, far more than among any other candidate's voters." "The poll suggested that the Wallace vote came heavily from disaffected voters who were four times more likely to distrust the government than were any other group of voters" (Reinhold 1976b).

Wallace was delighted with his Massachusetts vote. He considered it "a victory." Said Wallace, the Massachusetts vote "tells me that the American people are beginning to realize that big government cannot solve all their problems." He continued gleefully, "The Democratic establishment is shaken up tonight [because] I've run so well in an impossible state" (Kneeland 1976).

The candidate went on to predict that he would win the Florida primary. "I'm in the mainstream of the Democratic party now," he crowed (Ayres 1976o). The other Democrats were far from elated. Morris Udall said that he would leave the party if Wallace were the nominee (Ayres 1976o).

While Wallace had been giving the impression that he was totally committed to running as a Democrat, he was still playing with the idea of a third-party run. Ayres reported that "periodically, some of the Governor's top aides discuss the progress of the current petition effort with leaders of the American Independent Party and with leaders of other groups involved, among them the American Independent Party and the Committee for a New Majority" (Ayres 1976o).

The American party had actually gotten ballot position in twelve states, but the report was that Tom Anderson, the party's leader, thought Wallace too liberal. In an attempt to shut him out, Anderson proposed that the American party hold its convention before the Democratic convention instead of afterwards, as had been originally planned. A fight ensued, and a number of members left the American party in protest and formed the American Independence party (Ayres 1976o).

Other conservative groups were also circulating petitions in several states to get third-party lines. In most of these efforts the name of the candidate was deliberately left off (Ayres 1976o). Meanwhile, William Rusher had formed the Committee for a New Majority, and the word was that the Committee would like to see Wallace and/or Reagan on their ticket (Ayres 1976o).

The Florida Primary

The Florida run was next. The first harbinger of trouble appeared in the results of a poll conducted in seven southern states by Darden Research in Atlanta. The poll showed that although Wallace had been more popular than Carter several months earlier, Carter had edged ahead during February. The poll results over the previous six months were as follows:

	Wallace	Carter
September 1975	51.3	29.4
January 1976	41.6	34.6
February 1976	33.8	46.7

Darden's February poll had also indicated that Southerners liked both Ford and Reagan better than they liked Wallace (1976n).

In Florida, Wallace made extensive efforts to attract certain voting blocks. He made a concerted attempt to get the retirement vote as well as the condominium vote, demanding "a stronger Social Security system for the retired," and calling "for new laws to stop developers from hitting condominium dwellers with hidden charges" (Ayres 1976n). He also courted naturalized Cubans. In his speeches, he made known his "implacable opposition to Prime Minister Fidel Castro of Cuba" (Reed 1976b). *The Wallace Stand* contained an article written by his Latin campaign manager for Florida and was printed in a Spanish edition as well (Reed 1976b).

While other candidates concentrated on Florida's 300,000 Jews, Wallace wooed the state's 600,000 Catholics. He had his campaign workers call priests and bishops in an effort to attract Catholic voters. The callers stressed Wallace's stand on abortion, and emphasized that Wallace was "the only Democratic candidate favoring a Constitutional amendment to make abortion on demand illegal" (Reed 1976b).

He stressed antibusing, the issue which had won the primary for him in 1972, and which had worked so well in Boston (Reed 1976b), and "railed against welfare payments for 'those who won't work when there is work.'" He also called for "putting lawbreakers in prison 'until their hair turns white or they go to the electric chair'" (Ayres 1976n).

Despite the time Wallace had subtracted from Florida and added to Massachusetts, Wallace spent almost three weeks campaigning in Florida and spent more than $200,000, two-thirds of which went for television advertising (Ayres 1976n). Still Wallace lost Florida to Carter by three percentage points. The final totals were Carter thirty-four percent, Wallace thirty-one percent, and Jackson twenty-four percent. Carter got thirty-four delegates, Wallace twenty-six, and Jackson twenty-one (*New York Times* 1976l).

The CBS News/New York Times Poll of Florida voters after they left the polls indicated that Wallace's paralysis had affected the vote. "More than forty percent of all Democratic voters said that the governor's health would impair his performance if he were President (Apple 1976d). Further, it appeared that Wallace had also misread the Florida voters: "Mr. Wallace's positions, the poll results indicated, were simply too extreme for Florida voters this year, with busing far less a topic of debate than it was four years ago .... He lost to Mr. Carter because he was unable to score with the moderates, as he did four years ago" (Apple 1976d).

The loss in Florida was termed Wallace's "worst political setback since he was shot and seriously wounded by an assassin" (Reed 1976a). It also put the national Democrats on notice. Wallace had run about ten percentage points behind his 1972 total at forty-two percent, and "was soundly beaten by a fellow Southerner. Together with his failure to win in Massachusetts even with the busing issue at full flame, the Governor's defeat here suggests that his role at the Democratic National Convention may be smaller than some expected" (Apple 1976d).

Wallace's second place finish in Florida left him devastated, but the Illinois primary was a week away, and the candidate was determined to go on with the show.

The End of the Line

In the meantime, the New York State campaign had hit a snag. Wallace forces had filed delegate slates in twenty-four of New York's thirty-nine districts. Jackson's organization had challenged the slates, and subsequent investigation had showed that many had insufficient signatures; some of the signatures looked like they had been forged. By March 8, thirteen of these slates had been invalidated. The New York/New Jersey/Pennsylvania coordinator was unavailable for comment, and the New York City coordinator said "'It's just a matter of time' before the entire campaign collapses" (Lynn 1976b).

As Wallace began to campaign in Illinois, he conceded that his health had become a main issue (*New York Times* 1976k). Rather than avoid the topic, he emphasized that he was in good health (Ayres 1976m), and remarked, "as Alfred E. Smith used to say about Franklin Delano Roosevelt, 'you don't have to be an acrobat to be President.'" (Saipukas 1976b).

He also dropped the busing issue, and chose to stress "that he was in the race to have the Democratic Party adopt a platform and a candidate that would deal with the needs of workers, farmers, small businessmen, and the 'middle class that built this country.'" He emphasized that "he had already accomplished this in the campaign and that the party and other candidates were adopting many of the issues that he had been raising all along. 'That's already happened,' he said, 'that battle is already won'" (Salpukas 1976a).

The Illinois primary was the ideal primary for Wallace. It was a preference vote, or "beauty contest" (Farrell 1976c). But when it was all over, Wallace had come in second. Carter won with forty-eight percent of the vote and Wallace got twenty-eight percent; Shriver came in third with sixteen percent, and Harris received eight percent. Wallace's twenty-eight percent had actually been a much better performance than the 8.5 percent of the Illinois vote that he had gotten in 1968 as the American Independent party candidate (Farrell 1976b), but it didn't mean anything. And because the Illinois primary was a nonbinding preference primary, Wallace did not get twenty-eight percent of the delegates; in fact, he won only three delegates in all (*New York Times* 1976j).

The defeat in Illinois left the Wallace campaign in complete disarray. The *Times* reported that "the Alabama Governor and his aides are showing signs of desperation and retrenchment." Campaign workers were "sniping at one another with charges of political incompetence" as well (Ayres 1976l). Most of them felt that it had been a mistake to enter the Massachusetts and Illinois primaries. They said that time could have been more productively spent campaigning in Florida and North Carolina (Ayres 1976l).

The North Carolina primary offered one last chance. Earlier, North Carolina had seemed a cinch. But there had already been some indications that support had begun to slip; a poll had shown Wallace trailing Carter by more than ten points (Ayres 1976l).

Wallace was determined to do well in North Carolina. He went into action. He assembled his troops; more than a dozen Alabama state legislators went into North Carolina to help him campaign (*New York Times* 1976i). Wallace changed his tactics and began to attack Carter, calling him "a warmed-over-McGovern," "a liar" (Ayres 1976l), and a "welsher who had backed Mr. Jackson in 1972 after promising to support Mr. Wallace" (Apple 1976b).

Many observers thought that Wallace had more serious problems in North Carolina than Jimmy Carter. Besides the issue of his health, the racial climate in North Carolina had cooled considerably since 1972. He could not count on his old appeals (Apple 1976c).

In the final count Carter got fifty-four percent of the North Carolina vote and thirty-six delegates. Wallace won thirty-five percent and twenty-five delegates (*New York Times* 1976h). Carter carried every single Congressional district in the state (Apple 1976b). The race for the candidacy was over.

The CBS News/*New York Times* poll said that those emerging from ballot booths in North Carolina had had the same concerns of the Florida and Illinois voters: "about two of every five worried about the Governor's health. Most of them voted for Mr. Carter" (Ayres 1976k).

Most of the Wallace workers had thought it was all over after the Florida primary (Azbell 1978; Griffin 1978). Griffin, however, thought it had been all over before that:

> When they dropped him down there in the panhandle, it was over for us. That was the day the campaign should have folded up. You drop a guy running for President of the United States and break his leg and he doesn't even know it. It was over. The air started coming out of the whole deal ... the day George Wallace was dropped in the panhandle we threw our pencils down, because it was over.... Wallace started being perceived by the American public as a disabled person when he broke his leg and didn't know it .... All of a sudden it gave everybody the excuse to go out and say, "You see what I told you, Wallace isn't capable of ...." You know, it was the breakwater for us. And so it was out of our hands; it was in the grace of God ... and we slowly went downhill. (Griffin 1978)

The press knew it was over after North Carolina. A CBS News/ *New York Times* nationwide poll (see chapter fourteen) showed that Wallace had "lost more than half the support he had six weeks ago." The reporter commented that "the collapse of support for Mr. Wallace can be traced both to his crippled condition and to the relative unimportance of racial matters as issues. The governor's health seems to be the more important factor" (Reinhold 1976a).

Reporters traveling with him had "seen few signs that his health is slowing him down." Instead they said that "he has seldom seemed fatigued and frequently has chided aides and reporters for 'lagging.'" The voters, however, were focused on the issue of his health. "All they see," said Wallace, "is the spokes on my wheelchair. The television catches every one" (Ayres 1976k). In addition, Wallace believed that the other "candidates have stolen his best issues—big government, busing, welfare, crime. He has been left, as he sees it, with the one issue he does not want—his confinement to a wheelchair" (Ayres 1976k).

In an obituary-like tone, a reporter summed it all up:

> Mr. Wallace showed ... that a Southerner could do it. In the most conspicuous way he expunged the stigma that had clung to the Deep South since the Civil War—the notion that access to national politics was automatically foreclosed to a Southern candidate. The lesson was not lost on Jimmy Carter, who is perking along trails that Mr. Wallace surveyed, cleared, and made possible. In a special sense Mr. Carter is Adam's rib, or more precisely, Mr. Wallace's, and is prospering because there was a Wallace against whom to wage a counterpoint campaign .... A much larger irony is that had there been no Wallace in all those years past, there might well have been no Carter running for the Democratic Presidential Nomination in 1976. (Johnson 1976c)

Despite his loss in North Carolina, Wallace insisted that he would be a factor at the Democratic National Convention and said that he planned to campaign in the Wisconsin primary (Ayres 1976k).

There were some differences in his manner. He started referring to his candidacy in the past tense, and said to reporters, "I guess you will all forget about me" (Ayres 1976k). He no longer talked about winning the White House, but boasted of old campaign achievements (Ayres 1976k). There was yet another difference: "Nor does the governor seem to revel any longer in being 'the bad boy of American politics,' as he once put it. Rather, he talks of being in the mainstream of current American politics; of how 'all the other candidates are now saying what I've been saying all along'; of, respectability" (Ayres 1976k).

Reporters asked why, after North Carolina, Wallace was going to campaign in Wisconsin. Campaigning in the South might be more productive, they suggested. Wallace replied,"Well, we've got all those delegates slated up there. We can't let them down. We planned this thing this way from the start" (Ayres 1976k).

In Wisconsin, he was greeted by a group of people wearing Arthur Bremer masks and pushing wheelchairs (*New York Times* 1976g). Public officials offered a hasty apology and Wallace continued campaigning. His public appearances were few. Mostly, the Wisconsin campaign consisted of two dozen thirty minute political commercials, appearances on television and radio news shows and at news conferences. The campaign was completely different from his previous ones; a reporter remarked that Wallace "has stopped telling political jokes, has eliminated his self-deprecatory remarks and had given up baiting reporters" (Ayres 1976j).

Despite his previous losses, Wallace had expected trouble in Wisconsin; busing was not a key issue, and there were reports that even his hard-core supporters had doubts about his health. But Wisconsin had been a good state in previous campaigns (Ayres 1976j). In 1964, Wallace had gotten thirty-four percent of the primary vote, and in 1972 he had won twenty-two percent (Ayres 1976j), but when 1976 was over, Wallace's percentage had dropped to thirteen. Carter won with thirty-seven percent, followed by Udall with thirty-six percent. In all, Wallace picked up ten delegates (King, S. 1976).

Again, the CBS News/*New York Times* Poll showed that Wallace's health had played a role. "Sixty-two percent of the Democratic voters said his paralysis had been a factor in their deciding to vote for another of the Democratic candidates" (King, S. 1976). One out of every four of Wallace's old supporters had switched to Reagan (Ayres 1976c).

After Wisconsin, Wallace dismissed all but thirty employees, "cut off financing for some forty of his fifty national campaign offices and ... [tried] to sublease an airplane that cost him about $100,000 a month to operate" (*New York Times* 1976e).

"Despite four straight primary defeats and a shortage of campaign funds," Wallace said that he was continuing. "At this time in 1972," he said, "I had seventy-five delegates. Now I have 104." He was determined to carry a number of delegates to the convention, and explained, "if I don't stay involved, the other candidates will start to slip a little to the left as is their natural tendency" (Ayres 1976i).

A number of other contests washed right over him. In the Virginia contest, Carter won 30.3 percent of the vote; Udall was second with 4.1 percent; and Wallace got 3.2 percent. Sixty-two percent of the Virginia delegates remained uncommitted (*New York Times* 1976f).

In New York, the *Times* reported that "Governor Wallace was virtually eliminated as a factor in the New York primary when his amateur supporters failed to file valid designating petitions in most of the state's Congressional districts (Lynn 1976a). And, Bablin, the New York/New Jersey/Pennsylvania coordinator, was charged "with knowingly filing with the board 'a forged instrument'—the petitions" (Rohan 1976). In Arizona Wallace got seven percent of the vote and won one delegate (Lichtenstein 1976).

At the end of April he spent two weeks vigorously campaigning in Pennsylvania, Indiana, and Texas. Insisting that he was still viable, Wallace said that he would be a broker at the convention. His supporters, he contended "must be heard" (Ayres 1976i).

In the meantime, Wallace denied interest in any third party, saying "it will not be necessary to switch to a third-party candidacy this time, as in 1968, 'because the Democratic platform is obviously going to be one I can support'" (Ayres 1976h).

The most immediate problem was money (Ayres 1976h). The campaign decided to cut costs by eliminating television advertising. They felt that "since their man was a household word" (Griffin 1978), they could easily get media coverage by calling press conferences and arranging for television appearances and radio interviews (Ayres 1976i). They also sent out another mailing and raised $150,000, enough for three more weeks of campaigning (Ayres 1976c).

When the results of the Pennsylvania primary came in, Carter got thirty-six percent; Jackson won twenty-six percent; Udall received nineteen percent, and Wallace polled eleven percent (Wooten 1976c).

The Texas primary was a particularly bad defeat; Wallace fielded slates in all thirty-one districts and did not get a single delegate. In that contest Carter trounced Bentsen, and Reagan won over Ford (Sterba 1976).

In Georgia, Carter got eighty-four percent of the vote and all the Georgia delegates; Wallace got twelve percent (King, W. 1976). On the Republican ticket, Reagan defeated Ford (Farrell 1976a).

In Indiana, Carter won with sixty-eight percent; Wallace got fifteen percent and Jackson got twelve percent. Reagan defeated Ford. Ford's campaign manager, Rogers C.B. Morton, described Reagan's victory as the direct result of "crossover votes from Democratic backers of Gov. George Wallace of Alabama" (Farrell 1976a).

Back Home: The Alabama Primary

The Alabama contest was particularly poignant. In campaigning for the delegates of his home state, Wallace "openly used nostalgia as a political tool and ... asked voters to cast their ballot for him 'just one more time'" (Ayres 1976f).

There were twenty-seven delegates at stake. For them, Wallace waged a major campaign, spending much more time and twice as much money on advertising as Carter (Ayres 1976f; Ayres 1976e). Typical of the Wallace approach was this: "I want to thank you all for letting me speak for you, for letting me represent your viewpoint, which is now the viewpoint of the majority of Americans. Remember when we were looked down upon as some subculture? I am proud of you" (Ayres 1976f).

Interestingly, neither one of Alabama's two Democratic senators gave Wallace's candidacy an unqualified endorsement. "Apparently aware of the possibility that the Governor might one day seek a Senate seat, the two men issued a joint statement that spoke only of Mr. Wallace's 'courage'" (Ayres 1976f).

In the Republican contest, Reagan beat Ford two to one, (Ayres 1976d), and Wallace led in twenty of the twenty-five Democratic races (Ayres 1976e). There had to be a runoff. It was a clear indication that Wallace's political strength "was eroding not only nationally but also in his home state." (Ayres 1976d). Although most felt that he would probably command a majority of Alabama's thirty-five member delegation at the Democratic national convention (Ayres 1976d), the results showed that the candidate was in serious trouble. As Ayres analyzed the situation, "In many of the undecided races, the vote tended to be split three ways—Wallace, Carter, and 'uncommitted.' If the uncommitted vote, frequently black, swings over to Mr. Carter in the runoffs, he could win six to eight delegates, enough to embarrass Mr. Wallace politically" (Ayres 1976d).

In the runoffs, Wallace got a total of twenty-seven delegates; five were uncommitted and three were pledged to Carter (*New York Times* 1976d). The crisis was narrowly averted. After the initial results, Wallace had said that Carter "had a 'very good chance' of winning the nomination. Then, for the first time publicly, he had also said 'I could support him'" (Ayres 1976d).

Alabama was followed by Michigan. In the Republican primary, Ford defeated Reagan. In the Democratic contest, Carter got forty-four percent, Udall won forty-three percent and Wallace received seven percent and two delegates (Stevens 1976). Meanwhile, the rumbles of a third-party candidacy were continuing. The American Independent party splintered and resplintered into three distinct factions. The leaders of two of these factions were ready to join the Republican right in a new, "unified conservative cause. The Committee for a New Majority has a huge legal outline of steps needed to qualify for the ballot in every state, and the nucleus of a Wallacite party has done so in three dozen states. What the committee does not have is a potentially strong nominee. Mr. Wallace, by all accounts, lacks the enthusiasm for another third-party candidacy." Reagan, by all reports also didn't seem to be interested (Naughton 1976b).

Wallace was reported to have been "'satisfied'with the results of his four Presidential campaigns because 'everybody is now saying what I started out saying back in 1964.' He boasted that he had 'cleared' the way for a Southerner like Mr. Carter to be 'accepted' as a genuine Presidential contender. 'There are no longer any real regional differences'" (Ayres 1976c).

Carter and the Convention

By the end of May, Wallace had won 163 delegates in the Democratic primaries. *Time Magazine* reported that Carter had approached Wallace about securing these delegates, but had obtained no pledge. Carter denied the story, saying that he had spoken only to inactive candidates, and not to Wallace (*New York Times* 1976c).

What Wallace was planning to do with his delegates was unclear. Without exception, the draft of the Democratic platform reflected Carter's views, and representatives of Jackson, Udall, and Wallace had all endorsed it (Rosenbaum 1976).

A couple of weeks later Wallace telephoned Carter and said that he was ready to support him. Carter personally went to Montgomery to "express his sincere gratitude" (Wooten 1976b). There were immediate negative reactions, and Carter quickly assured all that he "had no intention of allowing Governor Wallace to dictate any part of any approach, strategic or rhetorical, to the general election campaign" (Wooten 1976b).

A month or so later Carter and Strauss invited Wallace to speak at the Democratic convention on government reform and business accountability. Wallace also let it be known that he did not plan to have his name placed in nomination at the convention (*New York Times* 1976b). All seemed to have been amicably settled. The more likely explanation was that Wallace "seemed to be saying, finally and publicly what he has never quite admitted at any time in his long and colorful political career—that he has been bested, beaten, and that he knows it" (Wooten 1976b).

At the convention, Wallace, described by reporters as a "forlorn and neglected figure," met with his delegates who still resented Carter "in an effort to persuade them to fall in line behind the Georgian" (Apple 1976a). Many pleaded with him to continue (Carlson 1976b).

In one incident during a roll call, Alabama Sen. Robert Wilson, chairman of the Alabama delegation, tried to say a few words in praise of Wallace. Before he could declare that Alabama was on the team, he was shouted down. There was so much noise raised in protest that many did not hear Wilson announce that all but a handful of the Alabama delegates had switched to Jimmy Carter. Some of the Alabama delegates walked out of the convention, and later DNC chairman Strauss declared from the podium that Wilson's remarks had been "seriously misinterpreted" (Ayres 1976b).

Wallace kept a low profile at the convention and stayed in his room most of the time (Carlson 1976b). Many of those present spoke of the "racial and regional harmony among delegates" and of a "deep political change that has swept the South in recent years, change that allowed a new-style politician like Jimmy Carter to rise and prevail in the South" (Ayres 1976b). Among the observers, Wallace was not touted as the trail blazer. Despite his new image, he was remembered as the segregationist who stood in the schoolhouse door in defiance of the new order.

Aftermath

Not long after the convention, a report hit the papers that Mrs. Wallace had tapped the governor's bedroom phone. The report said that she had "decided to tap her husband's phone to determine whether he was discussing her with other women, perhaps in disparaging terms" (Ayres 1976c). Wallace told the press that the matter was "purely domestic, involving me and my wife" (Ayres 1976a).

Both the Democratic and Republican nominees came through Alabama in search of the Wallace constituency. Campaigning in Birmingham with Wallace at his side, Carter hailed the South's basic conservatism (Wooten 1976a). Wallace also welcomed President Ford to Alabama, saying that he "did so as a reflection of the respect Alabamians have for the Presidency" (Naughton 1976a). "During your tenure in the presidency, however long that might be, the people of Alabama hope that you and pray that you are successful," Wallace said. "The President in turn praised Mr. Wallace as a governor interested in the welfare of his constituents, and said that despite the different party affiliations, he and Mr. Wallace had always maintained a good 'working relationship in trying to solve problems'" (Naughton 1976a).

In October 1976, Wallace quite suddenly switched the position of the flags flying on the top of the Alabama State Capitol. The Confederate flag had been flying from the top of the flagpole for years, and Wallace reordered the United States flag to the top position and the Confederate flag to the third position under the Alabama State flag. He gave no reason for his action, but Milo Howard, director of the Archives and History, explained that "Mr. Wallace was making 'a serious attempt to make a gesture of friendliness to twenty-five or thirty percent of our population'" (Jenkins 1976). Presumably Mr. Howard meant blacks.

In another startling gesture, Wallace pardoned Clarence Norris, the last of the Scottsboro Nine (a case in the 1930s in which nine blacks were accused of raping two white women on a freight train). "In pardoning Clarance Norris ... Wallace in effect acknowledged that Mr. Norris has never committed a crime," said a reporter (Johnson 1976b).

At Carter's victory in November, Wallace sent a congratulatory telegram, which pledged his cooperation. It read, "I look forward to working with you and the Carter administration during the forthcoming years" (*New York Times* 1976a). In return, Carter telephoned Wallace to thank him and Alabama voters for their support (*New York Times* 1976a).

In December, Wallace met with Mr. Norris, who had left the South long ago, and assured him that Alabama was "one of the best states in the country 'for white or black people.'" Onlookers saw the pardon, Norris' visit and the reestablished priority of the United States flag on the top of the capitol as "attempts to remain politically viable by assuring himself of at least a portion of the state's increasingly important black vote" (Johnson 1976a). The indefatigable campaigner, Wallace had his eye on the Senate in 1978 (*New York Times* 1976c).

Chapter Fourteen

Wallace Support in 1976: Into the Mainstream

Data on Wallace support are of two types and are drawn from 1976 CBS News/ *New York Times* polls. The first is three nationwide polls conducted by telephone in February, March, and April. Respondents selected within random households average approximately 1500 persons per monthly poll. The second type of data is from the Florida primary and consists of a systematic sample of 1680 voters interviewed as they left the voting booths.

Both sets of data are important and the decision to include them here stems from the fact that they provide two distinct perspectives. The nationwide data show general trends starting the month before the primaries and ending the month after Wallace's political demise in Florida, Illinois, and North Carolina. It also gives a sense of overall Wallace support relative to that of other candidates.

From July 1973 through September 1975, Wallace support had been running at sixteen percent. In November 1975, it was at a high of twenty-one percent, and a month later George Gallup showed that Wallace was first choice of twenty percent of Democrats and twenty-seven percent of Independents. In March 1976, at the beginning of the primaries, a CBS News/ *New York Times* poll showed Wallace support at eighteen percent. By April it was fourteen percent, and in May it dropped to seven percent.

The Florida primary is the key to this drop in support. Wallace's loss to Carter by three percentage points completely changed the Democratic scenario and marked the end of Wallace's political career. In addition, Carter's Democratic nomination was assured by his win in this primary— George Wallace had been beaten by a fellow Southerner in a southern state that also represented (in the diversity of its population) a microcosm of the

United States. Carter became the dragon slayer, the representative of a New South and a new order which had replaced the old. It gave the illusion of a clean slate, a fresh start, and brought hope to a country whose people felt ravaged by demogogues and Washington insiders.

Nationwide data from the months of February, March, and April will be discussed first. Percents for these polls are given in terms of range over the three month period, low to high.

Nationwide Data

Demographics

Wallace support in 1976 follows many of the same patterns as in previous years (see Table 14.1). Wallace is much less likely to have black support than are other Democratic candidates. Between February and April, the CBS News/*New York Times* nationwide poll shows Wallace's white support ranging between eighty-nine to ninety-one percent. For the first time, however, he does show some black support (2 to 3% in February and March; 8% in April). Carter's black support, meanwhile, averages fifteen percent.

In terms of age, Wallace support among those eighteen to twenty-nine years of age is proportionately much larger than that of other candidates. Forty-three percent of Wallace supporters in February and March are between eighteen and twenty-nine; Carter's proportion runs thirty percent. Among those sixty-five and over, Carter and Jackson predominate.

Males represent about fifty-one percent of the Wallace support in February, a big change from other years and a discrepancy from the 1976 data in general, in which even larger majorities of Wallace support than in the past are male.

Again, most Wallace supporters are from the South (40% in February), but Carter support in the South is equally strong (41%). Ford is concentrated in the Northeast (32%) and the Midwest (30%), and Reagan support is more evenly distributed across all regions: twenty-three percent in the Northeast; thirty percent in the Midwest; twenty-six percent in the South and twenty-two percent in the Far West.

Wallace has more Catholic support in 1976 than in recent years (it ranges from 23% to 34%); as previously, Wallace has little Jewish support. On political party, a majority of Wallace supporters say that they are Independents, or have no preference. Figures are fifty-five and fifty-seven percent in March and April. While this proportion seems quite large, it is no larger than the proportions of Ford (55–65%) and Reagan (58–65%) supporters who declare themselves Independents/no preference. Carter and Jackson supporters are more likely to be loyal party members.

When asked to describe their own views on most political matters, twenty-six percent of Carter supporters and twenty-three percent of Wallace supporters say that they are liberal, followed by twenty percent of Reagan supporters, nineteen percent of Jackson supporters, and seventeen percent of Ford supporters. On the other hand, about a third (31–39%) of the Wallace supporters consider themselves conservatives, and supporters of the two Republicans, Ford (33–36%) and Reagan (42–46%) are also more likely to identify themselves as conservatives.

When asked to identify the politics of their candidate, forty-four percent of the Reagan supporters identify him as a conservative, twenty-four percent label Reagan a moderate, and nine percent say that he is a liberal. Wallace, however is considered a liberal by twenty-one to twenty-seven percent of his supporters, a moderate by thirteen to twenty-five percent, and a conservative by thirty-one to thirty-five percent.

Affective Issues

When asked how they personally feel about the candidates they prefer (see Table 14.2), supporters of Wallace are far more likely than are supporters of other candidates to say "I strongly favor him" (53% with an epsilon of +22 from the nearest group). In contrast, forty percent of Carter's supporters and thirty-eight percent of Jackson's supporters admit that they have some reservations about their particular candidates.

Reagan supporters are more likely to have a favorable opinion of Wallace than are supporters of other candidates. A majority of Ford supporters have an unfavorable opinion of Wallace, and even larger proportions of Carter and Jackson supporters dislike Wallace. In fact, a majority in each supporter group (except for Wallace supporters) say that George Wallace is too extreme on the issues. Those having this opinion range from fifty-five percent of Reagan supporters to seventy-one percent of Jackson supporters.

When asked their opinion of Wallace's health, a majority of all groups say that his health would have little or no effect on his ability to do the job. As expected, those most likely to say that support Wallace: specific percentages are eighty-two percent Wallace supporters, sixty-four percent Reagan supporters, sixty-one percent Jackson supporters and fifty-nine percent both Carter and Ford supporters.

Campaign Issues

Respondents were asked which three of five political issues were most important to them in choosing the candidates they support (see Table 14.3). Majorities in all groups say that the first most important issue is the state of

TABLE 14.1
Selected Demographic Characteristics*

	Carter	Wallace	Jackson	Ford	Reagan
Race					
White					
February	83	89	96	92	93
March	85	91	85	91	94
April	83	89	83	93	93
Black					
February	17	2	3	6	2
March	13	3	12	5	3
April	14	8	10	6	4
Spanish-speaking, Oriental					
February	0	9	2	2	4
March	2	5	2	3	2
April	3	3	6	1	3
Refused					
February	0	0	0	0	0
March	1	1	1	1	0
April	0	0	0	0	0
Age					
18-29					
February	31	43	27	32	29
March	30	43	23	37	29
April	29	38	26	37	29
30-44					
February	22	26	14	26	30
March	30	28	16	26	31
April	28	25	18	28	29
45-64					
February	22	23	49	26	27
March	29	24	38	23	31
April	29	26	38	22	31
65 and over					
February	25	8	11	17	13
March	11	4	22	13	10
April	15	10	18	13	12
Refused					
February	0	0	0	-	1
March	1	1	1	1	0
April	-	-	-	0	0

Table 14.1 (Continued)

	Carter	Wallace	Jackson	Ford	Reagan
Sex					
Male (February)	62	51	63	49	52
Female (February)	38	49	37	51	48
Region					
Northeast (February)	19	24	38	32	23
Midwest (February)	19	24	31	30	30
South (February)	41	40	16	26	26
Far West (February)	21	13	16	11	22
Religion					
Protestant					
February	52	56	49	70	65
March	56	61	47	60	64
April	66	66	53	73	65
Catholic					
February	22	34	34	22	26
March	33	30	35	27	28
April	29	23	29	20	27
Jewish					
February	10	1	9	1	0
March	2	0	4	1	0
April	1	0	10	1	1
Other					
February	5	8	2	5	5
March	5	5	9	6	4
April	2	7	2	3	3
None					
February	12	1	6	2	3
March	2	3	3	4	4
April	1	3	4	3	3
Refused					
February	0	0	0	0	1
March	1	2	2	2	0
April	1	0	1	1	2
Party Identification					
Democrat/Republican					
February	74	62	74	52	43
March	57	38	64	40	32
April	53	39	60	33	39
Independent, no preference					
February	25	31	25	44	53
March	41	55	34	55	65
April	45	57	37	65	58

Table 14.1 (Continued)

	Carter	Wallace	Jackson	Ford	Reagan
Personal Political Philosophy					
Liberal (February)	26	23	19	17	20
Very liberal					
March	6	2	3	4	3
April	5	13	8	7	5
Somewhat liberal					
March	24	13	20	19	11
April	21	15	21	16	14
Moderate					
February	51	35	60	39	34
March	38	39	42	38	34
April	36	31	34	36	29
Conservative (February)	19	31	18	36	42
Somewhat conservative					
March	23	26	15	26	31
April	25	28	27	32	39
Very conservative					
March	5	13	12	7	15
April	7	8	5	4	7
Don't know					
February	2	9	3	7	4
March	3	5	6	4	6
April	6	5	4	5	6
No answer, refused					
February	2	1	0	2	0
March	1	2	2	2	0
April	1	2	1	1	0

	Wallace	Reagan
Candidate's Political Philosophy**		
Liberal		
February	27	9
March	24	
April	21	
Moderate		
February	24	24
March	13	
April	25	
Conservative		
February	31	44
March	35	
April	31	
Don't know		
February	16	7
March	16	
April	17	

Table 14.1 (Continued)

	Wallace	Reagan
Refused, no answer		
February	2	2
March	0	
April	2	

* Percentages add vertically by columns within months to 100 percent, except for rounding errors.

** February figures add vertically by columns to 100 percent with the addition of respondents who were omitted because they said they didn't have enough data on the candidate to have a clear impression.

the economy. Sixty-two percent of Ford supporters are so concerned, compared to fifty-nine percent of Carter supporters and fifty-four, fifty-three, and fifty percent of Jackson, Reagan, and Wallace supporters respectively. The second most frequently mentioned issue as a first choice item is relations with Russia. Next is a government guaranteed job program, closely followed by the issue of the size of the federal government. Treatment of blacks and other minorities is of least importance to those in every supporter group.

When questioned more closely about the economy, a majority in each supporter group say they are dissatisfied with the way things are going. Seventy-two to seventy-five percent of Wallace supporters state that they are dissatisfied with the present economy, closely followed by supporters of Jackson (68–76%) and Reagan (72–72%). Slightly less of those for Carter (62–66%) are dissatisfied; Ford supporters are the least dissatisfied (55–58%).

Wallace's supporters are somewhat more pessimistic than are others, with over one-third evaluating the state of the economy as deteriorating. One-fourth to one-fifth of the supporters of other candidates also share this perception.

Respondents were asked if they think that the federal government should have a more balanced budget even if it means spending less money on programs and services for such things as health and education. A plurality of most groups agree, with Republican supporters in the lead (Ford 44–56%; Reagan 49–58%). Wallace supporters are next with forty-two to fifty-one percent, followed by Carter supporters (38–54%) showing more inconsistency over the three month period. Jackson voters (38%) are the least likely to agree with this conservative position.

At the same time, and in contradiction, a majority of all groups, with the exception of Reagan supporters at forty-eight percent, say that govern-

TABLE 14.2
Affective Issues*

	Carter	Wallace	Jackson	Ford	Reagan
Feelings About Candidates**					
I strongly favor him	31	53	26	18	17
I have some reservations about him	40	26	38	27	18
I would prefer a candidate not running	21	15	26	8	15
Don't know	8	7	9	5	5
Refused	0	0	0	-	-
Opinion of George Wallace					
Favorable					
February	24	82	28	27	41
March	26	80	13	30	45
April	18	83	14	27	34
Unfavorable					
February	58	11	55	51	41
March	61	9	69	51	39
April	62	10	70	52	48
Undecided					
March	-	-	-	-	-
April	5	2	5	4	7
Don't know enough					
March	11	11	15	17	13
April	15	5	11	17	10
Don't know (February)	14	4	17	21	15
No answer, refused					
February	4	3	0	2	2
March	2	1	3	3	3
April	0	0	0	0	1
"If George Wallace were president, do you think his health would...."					
(March only)					
Severely limit his ability to do the job	10	0	6	9	7
Have some effect on his ability to do the job	28	14	27	26	22
Have little effect on his ability to do the job	24	27	20	27	26
Have no effect at all	35	55	41	32	38
Don't know	3	3	7	4	6
No answer, refused	0	0	0	1	0

*Percentages add vertically by columns within months to 100 percent, except for rounding errors.

**Percentages for Ford and Reagan add to 100 percent when Republican sentiment is added (only Democrats and Independents were asked this question).

ment spending for health, education, and programs for the poor should be increased. Ford supporters are proportionately less likely to favor increases in such spending (54–57% when compared to supporters of Democrats: Carter 61–67%; Jackson 63–67%; and Wallace 56–61%).

Another means of cutting the budget would be to eliminate welfare programs. But when asked whether such programs should actually be eliminated, most respondents disagree, but only by slight margins. In March, a plurality of Wallace supporters think that welfare programs should be eliminated; in April, however, their positions reverse. On yet another issue, a majority of all supporters contend that the social security system should be strengthened even if it means higher taxes. Here, larger proportions of Carter and Jackson supporters more often agree than do those in the other three groups, all of whom run about fifty-one to fifty-six percent on agreement.

On federal job guarantees, majorities in each group think that the federal government should see to it that every person who wants to work has a job. As might be expected, supporters of Democrats are more likely to agree: totals range from sixty-four to seventy-two percent for Carter's supporters, sixty-seven to seventy-two percent for Wallace supporters and seventy-three to seventy-eight percent for Jackson supporters.

On domestic policy issues, supporters of Democratic candidates also follow the traditional pattern of being more liberal than supporters of Republican candidates. While following the expected pattern, Wallace supporters tend to fall in the middle, somewhere between the more liberal supporters of other Democrats and the more conservative supporters of Republicans.

Foreign policy is another area in which supporters' views differ (see Table 14.4). With the single exception of Ford supporters, a majority of all the candidate groups think that Secretary of State Henry Kissinger has made too many concessions which have hurt America's position in the world. Agreement with that statement ranges from fifty-one percent of Jackson's supporters to fifty-eight percent of Wallace's supporters. In contrast, thirty-nine percent of Ford supporters agree with the statement; most support Kissinger's efforts.

Opinions about our relations with Russia generally reflect the attitudes of the candidates themselves. A majority in each group do not think it is in our best interests to be so friendly to Russia, stating that we are not getting enough in return. While the differences among supporter groups are small, a larger proportion of those with negative attitudes are found among Wallace, Jackson, and Reagan supporters.

On our relationships with other countries, less than one-quarter of any

TABLE 14.3
Campaign Issues — Domestic Policy*

	Carter	Wallace	Jackson	Ford	Reagan
First Most Important Issue in Supporting Candidate (March)					
Our relations with Russia	10	14	9	9	12
A government guaranteed job program	18	18	20	15	16
The size of the federal government	5	5	7	5	11
The treatment of blacks and other minorities	3	7	6	6	4
The state of the economy	59	50	54	62	53
Satisfaction With the Economy					
Satisfied					
March	30	18	20	35	21
April	30	21	28	40	23
Dissatisfied					
March	62	75	76	58	72
April	66	72	68	55	72
Don't know					
March	7	7	3	6	6
April	4	7	4	4	4
No answer					
March	1	0	1	1	1
April	0	0	0	1	1
Perception of the State of the Economy					
Improving rapidly					
March	4	1	3	4	2
April	2	2	6	4	3
Improving slowly					
March	43	27	30	42	39
April	39	22	46	42	41
Staying about the same					
March	29	34	36	31	32
April	31	35	22	31	25
Getting worse					
March	22	36	26	20	24
April	25	36	24	21	25
Don't know					
March	2	2	4	2	4
April	3	5	3	2	6
Balanced Budget/Less Spending for Health and Education					
Agree					
February	54	45	38	56	58
March	38	42	38	44	49
April	43	51	38	49	50
Disagree					
February	40	45	59	37	35
March	56	52	49	48	41
April	51	40	53	45	44

Table 14.3 (Continued)

	Carter	Wallace	Jackson	Ford	Reagan
Don't know, depends, mixed feelings					
February	4	10	2	6	7
March	6	5	12	8	11
April	6	8	9	6	6
Reduce/Increase Government Spending for Health/Education/Poor					
Reduce					
March	19	21	14	23	26
April	19	25	13	23	35
Increase					
March	61	61	67	54	48
April	67	56	63	57	48
Keep at same level					
March	8	4	9	11	8
April	8	11	17	13	9
Don't know					
March	8	12	10	11	14
April	4	7	6	6	8
No answer					
March	3	3	0	1	3
April	1	1	1	1	0
Eliminate Welfare Programs					
Agree					
March	40	49	36	40	41
April	38	39	35	35	43
Disagree					
March	49	36	52	47	42
April	51	44	56	54	44
Don't know, depends, mixed					
March	11	14	12	13	17
April	10	16	9	11	11
Strengthen Social Security, Higher Taxes					
Agree					
March	61	53	64	54	50
April	65	51	69	56	52
Disagree					
March	31	34	27	36	37
April	28	40	23	34	36
Don't know, depends, mixed					
March	7	13	9	9	12
April	7	9	8	10	11
Federal Job Guarantees					
Agree					
February	68	72	78	65	63
March	64	67	73	63	60
April	72	71	73	62	60

Table 14.3 (Continued)

	Carter	Wallace	Jackson	Ford	Reagan
Disagree					
February	27	27	21	32	31
March	33	28	19	33	35
April	23	28	25	33	36
Don't know, depends, mixed					
February	5	1	1	4	6
March	3	4	8	4	4
April	5	2	2	5	4

*Percentages add vertically by columns within months to 100 percent, except for rounding errors.

supporter group feels that we should sell arms to Egypt as well as to Israel in order to play a more even-handed role in the Middle East. Those disagreeing with the idea range from fifty-seven percent (Carter and Ford supporters) to sixty-five percent (Wallace supporters).

When asked whether government spending for military defense should be reduced, a majority in each group disagree. Most think that it should be kept at the same level or increased. There is little difference among groups.

On another aspect of military defense, respondents are asked whether we should try harder to reach agreement with the Russians to control the arms race rather than build up our own armaments. In answer, fifty-two percent of the supporters of Wallace and Reagan opt for building up armaments. Supporters of other candidates most often think that agreement is more important.

On foreign policy matters, then, most supporter groups are the same, with a few differences. Ford supporters are more likely to support current foreign policy than others, and both Reagan and Wallace supporters are toughminded when it comes to the arms race, promoting peace through superior firepower.

Racial Attitudes

On issues of racial politics (see Table 14.5), a majority in each supporter group agree with the statement that nonwhites should be able to move into any white neighborhood if they want to. The agrees range from a low of sixty-two percent of Wallace supporters to a high of eighty-four percent of Jackson supporters.

When asked whether the government has paid too much attention to the problems of blacks and other minorities, a majority of both Wallace (51–57%) and Reagan (53–57%) supporters agree. Opinion is split about fifty-fifty among Carter and Ford supporters, and Jackson supporters move back and forth between agreeing and disagreeing over the three month period.

TABLE 14.4
Campaign Issues — Foreign Policy*

	Carter	Wallace	Jackson	Ford	Reagan
Kissinger Hurt America With Too Many Concessions					
Agree	54	58	51	39	55
Disagree	34	32	39	47	34
Don't know, depends, mixed	12	10	10	14	11
Caution Advised With Russia					
Agree					
February	50	59	58	51	55
March	75	82	76	75	80
April	58	61	68	54	64
Disagree					
February	35	27	31	35	30
March	15	6	13	15	8
April	27	28	25	33	21
Don't know, depends, mixed					
February	13	13	11	13	15
March	10	11	10	9	12
April	14	10	7	12	14
Military Aid to Israel and Arms to Egypt (April)					
Agree	23	17	20	23	20
Disagree	57	65	64	57	62
Don't know, depends, mixed	19	17	13	18	16
No answer	1	1	3	1	2
Reduce Defense Spending					
Agree, reduced (February)	34	31	40	31	31
Should be reduced					
March	33	26	34	32	30
April	38	36	29	39	32
Disagree with reduced (February)	55	58	54	57	59
Should be increased					
March	45	49	51	46	45
April	46	52	50	42	48
Kept at same level					
March	12	18	7	14	18
April	8	7	13	12	9
Don't know, depends					
February	11	10	6	11	9
March	9	6	9	7	6
April	7	5	8	7	10
Agreement With Russia to Control Arms Rather than Build Armaments					
Agree	48	36	47	55	40
Disagree	42	52	45	35	52
Don't know, depends, mixed	9	11	8	9	7
No answer	1	1	0	1	0

*Percentages add vertically by columns within months to 100 percent, except for rounding errors.

In all groups a majority disagree that racial integration of the schools should be achieved even if it requires busing. Those disagreeing range from fifty-nine percent of Carter supporters to eighty-two percent of Jackson supporters. Wallace supporters are in the middle with seventy-four percent disagreeing.

It is apparent from these results that the negative attitudes expressed in the busing question are more likely disapproval of busing rather than disapproval of integration, given the majorities who say that blacks should live anywhere they please.

The finding that emerges from the answers to these questions is that Wallace supporters no longer stand out as being so different from supporters of other candidates on their racial attitudes. While being on the more vehement edge, they are closely followed by Reagan supporters, who in turn are not that different from the others. In general, Ford supporters tend to be more liberal in their racial attitudes, followed by Jackson supporters, with supporters of Carter somewhere in the middle. On the question of busing to achieve integration, however, Carter supporters show larger proportions who agree that integration should be achieved even if it requires busing.

Authoritarian Personality

Here again there are no F scale items with which to measure authoritarian personality tendencies of Wallace supporters. One could make a case, however, for valuing increased armament over reaching agreement on the question of the arms race as indicating a preoccupation with strength. In that case, however, both Wallace and Reagan supporters are equally preoccupied.

Marginal Voter Theory

In these polls, Wallace supporters have more often not voted in the 1972 election than have other supporters of other candidates (see Table 14.6). Thirty to thirty-one percent of them say that they did not vote or were not registered to vote for the 1972 election; seventeen to twenty-seven percent of Reagan voters also did not vote, followed by twenty-one to twenty-five percent of Ford supporters. Figures for other candidate supporter groups are twelve to twenty-five percent of Jackson supporters and ten to twenty-one percent of Carter supporters.

In addition, respondents were asked to indicate how closely they have followed the primary elections (see Table 14.6). In comparison with others, Wallace supporters more often reply only a little or not at all; sixty-seven percent of them have little interest in the primaries. A majority of both

TABLE 14.5
Racial Attitudes*

	Carter	Wallace	Jackson	Ford	Reagan
Non-whites Should Be Able To Move Into Any White Neighborhood					
Agree	73	62	84	80	67
Disagree	19	30	10	14	23
Don't know, depends, mixed	6	5	5	5	9
No answer, refused	2	2	1	1	2
Government Has Paid Too Much Attention to Problems of Blacks and Other Minorities					
Agree					
February	46	51	54	43	57
March	46	55	48	45	57
April	47	57	42	43	53
Disagree					
February	46	38	39	47	33
March	45	35	39	46	31
April	44	35	48	47	37
Don't know, depends, mixed					
February	8	11	7	9	10
March	6	9	12	8	12
April	10	5	9	9	9
Integration Should Be Achieved Even If It Requires Busing					
Agree	33	24	14	20	18
Disagree	59	74	82	74	78
Don't know, depends, mixed	8	2	0	4	5

*Percentages add vertically by columns within months to 100 percent, except for rounding errors.

Ford (54%) and Reagan (52%) supporters feel the same. In contrast, a majority of both Carter supporters (67%) and Jackson supporters (69%) say that they are following the primaries somewhat closely or very closely.

In terms of labor union memberships, Democrats more often belong to unions or have someone in their household who belongs to a union than do Republicans. Twenty-six to thirty percent of Carter supporters belong to a labor union compared to twenty-five to thirty-five percent of Wallace supporters and thirty-five percent of Jackson supporters. Nineteen to twenty-five percent of Ford supporters also belong to a labor union, as do twenty-one to twenty-seven percent of Reagan supporters.

It is important to note that this sample includes nonvoters as well as voters. All other samples in this book (except for the 1964 data) are of voters only. While there is some evidence that a proportion of Wallace supporters are habitual nonvoters, we are not concerned with them in this study. Those who effect election outcomes have been of central interest because they are the people who constitute the Wallace threat. In other words, in an election it doesn't matter if habitual nonvoters support one particular candidate or another, for the nonvoters are of no consequence. Further, nonvoters are marginal voters by definition. Thus the argument is tautological.

TABLE 14.6
Marginal Voter Measures*

	Carter	Wallace	Jackson	Ford	Reagan
Vote in 1972 Presidential Election					
Voted					
February	88	68	87	77	72
March	77	64	70	71	76
April	76	63	83	73	78
Didn't Vote					
February	10	30	14	21	27
March	19	30	25	25	21
April	21	31	12	25	17
Don't know, no answer, refused					
February	3	2	0	2	2
March	3	5	5	4	4
April	3	7	5	3	7
Following of Primary Elections					
(February)					
Very closely	35	6	22	7	13
Somewhat	32	25	47	38	33
Only a little	28	50	20	39	40
Not at all	5	17	10	15	12
Don't know	0	1	2	1	1
No answer, refused	0	2	0	–	1
Union Member in Household					
Yes					
February	30	25	35	19	21
March	26	35	35	24	25
April	30	27	35	25	27
No					
February	70	69	50	80	78
March	71	64	63	74	73
April	70	69	59	73	72
Don't know					
February	0	5	6	0	–
March	0	0	0	0	2
April	0	4	5	2	0
Refused, no answer					
February	0	1	8	1	1
March	2	1	2	2	1
April	0	0	1	0	1

*Percentages add vertically by columns within months to 100 percent, except for rounding errors.

Status Theories

SES scores were not calculated, so status demographics will be given instead (see Table 14.7). As in previous years, Wallace supporters are less well-educated than are supporters of other Democrats and of Republicans. Only five to seven percent of Wallace supporters have graduated from college, compared to an average of sixteen percent of both Carter and Reagan supporters, fourteen percent of Ford supporters, and twelve percent of Jackson supporters.

Occupational positions also differ for Wallace supporters. A majority are blue collar (48–59%), compared to thirty-one to forty-six percent of Carter supporters, thirty-one to forty percent of Ford supporters, and thirty-three to thirty-eight percent of Reagan supporters. The largest proportions of professional and technical white-collar workers are found among Ford (28–45%) and Reagan (28–42%) supporters as well as among Carter (21–51%) supporters.

Income structure also differentiates Wallace supporters from supporters of other candidates. While approximately one-third of all groups have incomes between $12,000 and $20,000, smaller proportions of Wallace supporters (9–14%) have incomes over $20,000.

These findings differ from others in this study and may well be a reflection of the inclusion of nonvoters, as the Florida primary data does not show such variation. At any rate, the status theory cannot be adequately tested with the data available.

The Power Theory

These surveys include several questions about people's attitudes toward government (see Table 14.8). When asked to agree or disagree with the statement, my vote doesn't count because it doesn't really matter who is elected president, most respondents disagree, ranging from a low of seventy-six percent of Wallace supporters to a high of eighty-four percent of Jackson supporters. On the surface then, most people believe that it really does matter who is elected president.

Another related issue, that of trust in government, involves answers to the question, how much of the time do you think you can trust the government to do what's right—just about always, most of the time, only some of the time, or none of the time? Less than ten percent of any group reply just about always. Wallace, Reagan and Jackson supporters are more pessimistic; fifty-five percent of Wallace supporters, sixty-three percent of Reagan supporters, and sixty-six percent of the Jackson supporters reply only some of the time. Supporters of Ford are generally more optimistic than the others.

TABLE 14.7
Selected Status Variables*

	Carter	Wallace	Jackson	Ford	Reagan
Education					
Less than high school					
February	37	51	33	31	24
March	33	34	47	31	32
April	43	40	35	28	34
Completed high school					
February	25	32	32	40	45
March	38	45	32	36	38
April	34	45	38	40	35
Some college/trade/business school					
February	15	10	18	15	14
March	15	13	9	17	14
April	13	10	17	16	15
College graduate/post graduate					
February	24	5	16	13	17
March	14	7	9	14	15
April	10	6	11	16	15
Refused, don't know					
February	0	2	2	0	0
March	1	1	3	2	0
April	–	–	–	0	0
Occupation					
Blue collar					
February	31	59	27	30	33
March	42	52	48	42	36
April	46	48	40	40	38
White collar (professional, technical)					
February	51	27	50	45	42
March	30	12	21	28	29
April	21	21	21	30	28
Other white collar (clerical, sales)					
February	3	3	5	3	5
March	11	11	5	9	14
April	13	11	11	11	9
Farming					
February	16	8	17	18	16
March	5	7	3	4	5
April	4	5	6	3	9
Miscellaneous					
February	0	3	0	1	2
March	11	11	18	14	13
April	14	11	21	14	12
Unemployed					
February	–	–	–	–	–
March	1	5	3	2	3
April	3	2	1	1	3
Don't know					
February	–	–	–	–	–
March	–	–	–	–	–
April	–	2	–	1	–

Table 14.7 (Continued)

	Carter	Wallace	Jackson	Ford	Reagan
Occupation - continued					
No answer, refused					
February	-	-	1	2	1
March	1	2	2	1	1
April	-	-	-	-	-
Income					
Under $8000					
March	22	17	25	18	21
April	25	22	19	18	21
Over $8000, under $12,000					
March	18	18	19	20	16
April	19	23	19	19	16
Under $12,000, unspecified					
March	1	5	2	2	3
April	3	2	-	2	1
Over $12,000, unspecified					
March	2	4	2	3	4
April	1	-	3	3	1
Between $12,000 and $20,000					
March	32	38	34	33	32
April	28	32	34	30	31
Over $20,000					
March	23	9	12	20	20
April	18	14	21	22	24
Refused					
March	2	9	7	5	4
April	7	7	5	6	4

*Percentages add vertically by columns within months to 100 percent, except for rounding errors.

A majority in each group (except Ford supporters at 49%) agree that even when most people want something done on important matters, the government usually fails to act. The percent agreeing constitute sixty-nine percent of Jackson supporters, sixty-two percent of Wallace supporters, sixty-one percent of Reagan supporters, and fifty-two percent of Carter supporters.

Another issue in the campaign is the size of the federal government. Respondents were read this statement: "In general, government grows bigger as it provides more services. If you had to choose, would you rather have a small government providing less services, or a bigger government providing more services?" Republicans in general opt for a smaller government providing less services (Ford 46%; Reagan 50%). Supporters of Democratic candidates, however, Wallace included, vote for a bigger government providing more services (Carter 52%, Jackson 49%, and Wallace supporters by a plurality of 45%).

There is also a question on states' rights. The statement reads: "The federal government now runs many programs for health, education and the poor. It would be better if these were run instead by the states, agree or disagree?" In answer, a majority of those in each supporter group agree. Reagan supporters lead the list at eighty percent, followed by Jackson supporters at seventy-three percent, Carter supporters at sixty-nine percent, and supporters of Wallace and Ford with sixty-seven percent and sixty-five percent respectively. Those who agreed were asked further if the states should be free to run such programs without federal controls or regulations. Replies range from thirty-one percent of Ford supporters agreeing to forty-eight percent of Jackson supporters agreeing. Wallace supporters are in the middle with thirty-eight percent.

There is widespread distrust of government and a general feeling of powerlessness. Both Democrats and Republicans show their traditional colors on the issues of government services and federal regulation. The most interesting finding is that Wallace supporters in 1976 are no longer distinguished from others in terms of their attitudes toward government. All queried feel equally distrustful.

Florida Primary

The 1976 Florida primary is a key primary in Wallace's political demise. After a showing of seventeen percent in the state of Massachusetts and carrying the city of Boston, Wallace campaigned in Florida with high hopes of replaying his 1972 victory. He had two Democratic opponents, and a victory in Florida would have made him invincible.

The result was an upset unexpected by the Wallace camp, but it was exactly what the Democrats had hoped for. Jimmy Carter, a fellow southerner from a neighboring state, had been pitted against Wallace, and Carter had won. Wallace lost to Carter by three percentage points (31–34%); the CBS News/*New York Times* poll results reported here show why.

Summary of the Data

Demographics in the 1976 Florida campaign show the traditional patterns. Wallace voters are more often male and more often Protestant than are other voters. On status variables, they are not very different, however. While Wallace voters have slightly more blue-collar workers in

TABLE 14.8
Selected Power Variables*

	Carter	Wallace	Jackson	Ford	Reagan
"My vote doesn't count because it doesn't really matter who is elected president." (April)					
Agree	16	20	15	15	16
Disagree	79	76	84	81	82
Don't know, depends, mixed	4	4	1	4	2
No answer	0	1	0	-	-
"How much of the time do you think you can trust the government to do what's right?" (February)					
Just about always	4	7	8	10	3
Most of the time	41	28	26	39	25
Some of the time	50	55	66	46	63
None of the time	3	7	1	2	7
Don't know	3	2	0	2	2
No answer, refused	0	0	0	0	0
"Even when most people want something done on important matters the government usually fails to act." (February)					
Agree	52	62	69	49	61
Disagree	36	24	19	33	29
Don't know, depends, mixed	12	14	12	16	10
"In general, government grows bigger as it provides more services. If you had to choose, would you rather have...." (April)					
A smaller government providing less services	34	43	40	46	50
A bigger government providing more services	52	45	49	39	38
Don't know, depends	12	9	11	13	12
Refused, no answer	1	3	1	1	0
"The federal government now runs many programs for health, education and the poor. It would be better if these were run instead by the states."					
Agree	69	67	73	65	80
Disagree	20	20	17	24	13
Don't know, depends, mixed	10	13	10	10	6
"Each state should be free to run these programs without any federal control or regulation."					
Agree	39	38	48	31	45
Disagree	30	21	18	2	27
Don't know, depends, mixed	0	7	6	5	8

*Percentages add vertically by columns to 100 percent, except for rounding errors.

their ranks than do other voters, they have proportions almost equal to others in the professional/managerial category. In addition, Wallace voters'incomes are similar to others. They do, however, tend to be less well-educated than other voters.

A majority (58%) declare themselves Democrats. Those who call themselves Independents constitute twenty-one percent, compared to twenty-five percent of the Reagan voters, nineteen percent each of the Carter and Jackson voters, and thirteen percent of the Ford voters.

On nonvoting, Wallace voters are squarely in the middle. Those who did not vote in the 1972 general election consist of fourteen percent of Carter voters, twelve percent of Jackson voters, eleven percent of Wallace voters, and seven and four percent of Ford and Reagan voters, respectively.

Patterns of opinion on the issues which appear in the national data are also present in Florida. On the matter of a balanced budget and a cut in governmental spending for social service programs, Wallace voters take the most conservative positions, but Reagan voters are close behind, within two or three percentage points. On the question of military spending, Wallace voters are somewhere in the middle, with Reagan voters taking the most conservative position.

Affective Issues

When respondents are asked why they voted for their candidates, the qualities most often mentioned by Wallace voters are Wallace's "position on the issues" (27%), and the feeling that "he is honest and has integrity" (21%) (see Table 14.9).

Carter and Ford voters most often mention "honest and has integrity," while "strong qualities of leadership" is most important for Reagan and Jackson voters. Although "position on the issues" is important for all voter groups, the largest proportion mentioning it are Wallace voters.

TABLE 14.9
Which of These Qualities Best Describe Why You Voted for Your Candidate Today?*

	Carter	Wallace	Jackson	Ford	Reagan
Doesn't say one thing, another tomorrow	6	13	11	8	6
Best chance to win in November	9	5	12	18	5
Not part of the crowd running things now	14	17	3	3	18
Honest and has integrity	35	21	21	44	18
Position on the issues	16	27	21	17	24
Strong qualities of leadership	23	16	23	16	32
Would be a competent president	16	13	18	14	19
Just issues, not qualities	5	6	6	5	6

*Percentages add vertically by columns to more than 100 percent because more than one quality could be mentioned.

When queried as to those issues which were most important in deciding for whom to vote, Wallace voters answer as follows (up to two issues could be mentioned):

Size of the federal government	22%
State vs. federal control of domestic programs	20%
Welfare	19%
Crime and drug abuse	15%
Power of big business and corporations	13%
Racial matters	10%

Size of federal government is also most important for Carter voters (22%), as well as for Ford (31%) and Reagan (30%) voters. Jackson voters see relations with Russia (21%) as paramount (see Table 14.10).

State vs. federal control of domestic programs is the second most important issue among Ford and Reagan voters (both 20%) as well, and the fourth most important issue among Carter voters (15%). Welfare is also significant to Reagan voters (20%), Carter voters (19%), and Ford voters (15%). Jackson voters have decidedly different priorities from the rest of the voter groups, with the power of big business and corporations as a second interest and spending for military defense a third.

Crime and drug abuse is of interest to few except Wallace voters, but twenty percent of Carter voters are interested in the power of big business and corporations. Racial matters, an issue of very high priority in the 1972 primary, is of little consequence in 1976 in deciding which person to support (Carter and Jackson 6%; Ford and Reagan 1%).

Looking at the listing of issues, it is immediately apparent that most voters are concerned about the same things. These are issues which have traditionally been Wallace's—mistrust of government, the position that people cannot get what they need from government, and general mistrust of government social service programs. By 1976 they are no longer the purview of Wallace only; they have come to concern everyone.

Wallace's initial reaction was that the other candidates had stolen his issues. Later he becomes more philosophical:

> Nearly every candidate now drinks from the same well and the same dipper as I have [for] a long time.... All of them are saying the same things, and as a consequence that may have diluted the strength that I have, but it hasn't diluted the strength of the positions that I have taken. ("Meet the Press" 1976)

A detailed look at one question shows that not only were people interested in the same issues, they generally had the same positions on those

TABLE 14.10
Which Issues Were Most Important in Deciding
Which Person to Vote For?*

	Carter	Wallace	Jackson	Ford	Reagan
Enviroment and pollution	7	2	10	8	4
Welfare	19	19	13	15	20
Size of the federal government	22	22	11	31	30
Abortion	1	1	1	1	2
Relations with Russia	4	5	21	8	15
Crime and drug abuse	10	15	6	10	8
Spending for military defense	12	8	16	20	16
State vs. federal control of domestic programs	15	20	11	20	20
Racial matters	6	10	6	1	1
Power of big business and corporations	20	13	19	7	9
Just qualities, no issues	16	14	16	11	9

*Percentages add vertically by columns to more than 100 percent, because more than one issue could be mentioned.

issues (see Table 14.11). When asked if the government usually fails to act even when most people want it to, a statement we would expect to appeal most to Wallace voters, we find that sixty-seven percent of Wallace voters agree, closely followed by sixty-five percent of Reagan voters, sixty-four percent of Jackson voters, and fifty-nine percent of Carter voters. President Ford's voters are more optimistic, probably reflecting the fact that their candidate *is* the government. Forty-one percent of them agree with the statement and forty-eight percent disagree.

In spite of the fact that racial issues are not important to voters in terms of their choice of candidate, racial politics continues to distinguish Wallace voters from others (see Table 14.11). In Florida, Wallace voters, more than any others (70%), say that the government has paid too much attention to the problems of blacks and other minorities. A smaller majority of Reagan voters also agree (64%). Carter voters are equally split on the issue, with forty-six percent agreeing and forty-six percent disagreeing; Ford voters show similar results (46 to 47% disagreeing). Only Jackson voters are more liberal on the question (40 to 50% disagreeing). Thus the issue is still present, and divides the population. Its relative importance, however, has diminished, and with it interest in Wallace has also diminished.

Beyond the issues are two other considerations that greatly influence the primary's outcome. The first is the issue of Wallace's health (see Table 14.11). Loyal to the last, eighty-one percent of Wallace voters say that the candidate's health would not affect his ability to function as president. Others, however, think it would affect his ability to run things properly. Fifty-eight percent of Jackson voters, forty-nine percent of Carter voters, forty-six percent of Ford voters, thirty-three percent of Reagan voters, and fourteen percent of Wallace voters think that Wallace's ability to function as president would be affected. Whether or not and how this consideration has affected the decision of whom to support for president is unclear.

What is clear, however, is that for whatever reason, a majority of the Wallace voters do not think that their candidate can win (see Table 14.11). When asked what chance the candidate they voted for has to be elected president, Wallace voters are the least likely to say that he has a very good chance. Forty-five percent of the Wallace voters say he has a very good chance and thirty-two percent think he has some chance. Other candidates' voters are more optimistic. Seventy-three percent of the Ford voters, sixty-one percent of the Jackson voters, fifty-eight percent of the Carter voters, and forty-nine percent of the Reagan voters say that their candidate has a very good chance.

While there is no way of determining exactly why Wallace voters think that their candidate doesn't have much of a chance of winning the presidency, that sentiment has most likely played a part in other voters' decisions to support someone else.

Quite a large number choose to support someone other than Wallace. In

TABLE 14.11
Selected Campaign Issues

	Carter	Wallace	Jackson	Ford	Reagan
"The government usually fails to act even when most people want something done."					
Agree	59	67	64	41	65
Disagree	33	21	22	48	28
No answer	8	12	13	12	7
"The government has paid too much attention to the problems of blacks and other minorities."					
Agree	46	70	40	46	64
Disagree	46	23	50	47	29
No answer	9	7	10	7	7
"George Wallace's health would not affect his ability to function as president."					
Agree	46	81	31	45	59
Disagree	49	14	58	46	33
No answer	5	5	11	8	8
Perceptions of Candidate's Chance To Be President					
Very good chance	58	45	61	73	49
Some chance	31	32	26	6	26
Little chance	6	8	2	-	4
No chance	2	5	1	-	-

*Percentages add vertically by columns to 100 percent, except for rounding errors.

a great many cases, however, Wallace is their second choice. The following percents in each voting group say that Wallace is their second choice: twenty-four percent of the Carter voters, twenty percent of the Reagan voters, eleven percent of the Jackson voters, and eleven percent of the Ford voters.

In summary, Wallace's loss in Florida was due to four factors:

1. His issues were used successfully by other candidates.
2. Racial issues had diminished in importance.
3. Other candidates were perceived as more likely to win.
4. He was paralyzed below the waist and confined to a wheelchair.

It is quite possible that Wallace's health was the most important factor in his demise. As Griffin (1978) put it:

> It started when they dropped him. You know, a man doesn't know he's got a broken leg! He didn't feel it. You know, people say hum . . . hurmph, hello? It's weird, you know, how a trend will set in. I'll give you an example: the Legionnaire's Disease. Destroyed an otherwise nice hotel in Philadelphia, because of public panic, public perception. That's what happened to us after he was dropped. All of a sudden it gave everybody the excuse to go out and say, "you see what I told you, Wallace isn't capable of . . ." (Griffin 1978)

If Carter and Reagan had not run in the 1976 Florida primary, Wallace might well have won. And if he had won, there might not have been a President Wallace, but there would have definitely been no President Carter.

Chapter Fifteen

Analysis of 1976 Speeches: "Trust the People"

Once again in 1976, Wallace's campaign speeches resound with populist intonations describing the plight of a powerless people. This time, however, he is not alone, a voice in the wilderness crying out against an unheeding, unresponsive government. There are others with him, and they are all using the same appeals.

Wallace complains that "they" have stolen his issues, and that is true. References to "the people" come from the mouths of Carter, Jackson, Udall, Brown, and Reagan as well as President Ford. Jimmy Carter uses the same antiestablishment theme. Jerry Brown talks of government responsibility and the importance of meeting people's needs and balancing the budget at the same time. Ronald Reagan is perceived as so much like Wallace that many people cross over party lines and vote for him rather than for Wallace because Reagan can stand on his own two feet and somehow seems a bit more respectable.

Wallace is right; he has brought the Democratic party back to the "center," to a more conservative position. His issues have worked and others are embracing them. Witness this passage from Carter's presentation to the platform committee of the Democratic party in June 1976. It is titled "A New Beginning."

> Our party and the platform should emphasize three themes—(1) The need for an *open, responsive, honest government,* at home and abroad. (2) The need to restore a *compassionate government* in Washington, which cares about people and deals with their problems.... (3) The need for a *streamlined, efficient* government, without the incredible red tape, duplication, and overlapping of functions which has hamstrung the effectiveness of government and deprived the American people of the benefits of many of its programs. (Carter 1976)

As do other politicians, Wallace talks of a spiritual crisis in the country, but there is one important difference: Watergate is not in evidence, nor is it mentioned. For Wallace the spiritual crisis is an old story, resulting from the discrepency between what people expect and need from their government and what their government actually gives to them. Once again, Wallace uses everything he can to turn his appeal into an issue of power. The scenario is the same—the government ignores the needs of those whom Wallace represents and gives freely to others at their expense. Once again the problem is an unresponsive federal government that has robbed people of their dreams and has run over their rights:

> We've got a whole lot of people in this country who've been beat on and stomped on and hit on so long by the Government that they just don't know what to think. It's a spiritual problem. Americans are down-in-the mouth. They've lost their faith in the country. (Wooten 1976)

> The great mass of middle-class America is probably in the greatest state of anguish and discontent they've ever been in. These people have been the supporters of this system, and they are losing their influence, and they cannot make ends meet. People on one end are looked after and people on the other end are looked after, but those in the middle have been looking after everybody. (Reston 1975)

As in 1972, the solution is to stand fast with Wallace against the trends of the time. A public affirmation of nonsupport will in itself effect changes in governmental policy. And Wallace himself is the only person who can lead the people in this endeavor; he is the only person who genuinely understands and can champion their cause.

Somehow, however, in the ensuing four years, the zeal has gone out of his appeal. It is too bland. Wallace no longer inspires confidence or exudes certainty. In his attempt to create a more respectable image, Wallace has become less defiant; the passion is no longer there.

> I want a new day for my country and my people. We can only achieve this new day by trusting the people, by having the courage to stand up for what we believe, by being wise and acting with deliberation in all we do. (Wallace 1975)

Powerlessness in the post-Watergate age is a common phenomenon (Caddell and Shrum 1974; Gans 1972; House & Mason 1975a). People everywhere are disaffected, but the crucial ingredient in Wallace's version of powerlessness is making people feel so relative to others—to blacks in particular. As part of his campaign in 1976 to broaden his appeal, however, Wallace drops his references to blacks as the enemy, and in doing so loses the fire and guts of his appeal. He replaces them with others—those on welfare, the poor, the disaffected, immigrants who come to the cities in search of a better life, but none of these are organized groups, only amorphous enemies, incapable of inspiring fear or passion. There is simply no danger of these people usurping goods and services meant for Wallace supporters. Few have any fear that the poor or the children of the poor will take their places on the job or their children's places in the schools.

With the racial issue blunted (except in a few selected situations like the Boston campaign), busing as an issue is little more than an intellectual exercise. Wallace denounces busing for all children, black and white, but no longer goes into long-winded explanations as to why it is wrong. Instead he presents his position as a matter of civil rights, an interesting twist for a man who has spent so much time denying the existence of civil rights. Busing in Wallace's argument is a denial of a person's basic rights, and he calls for a constitutional amendment to bring it to an end:

> I am not surprised at anything that this Court does—not at all. But whenever you talk about it's legal to bus little children from one section of the city to another, one section of the country to another, in order to achieve something that some social planner thinks is best for your child and my child, then the basic civil rights of that family, whether it be black or white, has been violated. (Wallace 1976)

> I support a Constitutional amendment to outlaw forced busing. There is only one answer to forced busing. Stop it and stop it now. We must return to local control of schools without discrimination of any type and with freedom of choice. The social schemers who dreamed up forced busing admit it's a failure and eighty percent of our people oppose it. We should end it and never again tamper with our children's lives in such a ridiculous social scheme. (Wallace 1976)

In 1976, Wallace again returns to the issue of states' rights, but it has been updated. As before, state government is more responsive to people's needs than is federal bureaucracy. But in the revamping of his philosophy to fit the order of a new day and to expand his appeal, Wallace talks about states' rights in terms that are synonymous with civil rights:

> States' Rights are the backbone of our Constitution. They are a check against the massive power of the federal government's uncaring bureaucracy. Rights of the state are sacred to the states and should not be tampered with by a federal bureaucracy as we have witnessed in recent years. The states remain closer and more responsive to the people than the Washington bureaucracy. State governments reflect the wishes of the majority of the people of the state and any interference in states' rights by the federal government is a violation of the rights of the people. (Wallace 1976)

In the 1976 campaign, the beautician, the barber, and the blue-collar worker have all dropped from sight, and in their place is the great middle class, a catchall which presumably includes the Wallace cadres of yesteryear as well as everyone else. Using the term "middle class" rather than working class as in 1968 upgrades the campaign and makes it more respectable. The candidate thinks he has a chance for the presidency this time and his appeals show it, from the toned down rhetoric to the more general phrasing and the more respectable manner.

He chooses issues that are safe and that concern everyone. The most frequently mentioned issue of this type is taxes. Taxes are the mode of exploitation whereby the federal government fleeces the middle class in order to pay favors to the poor. Wallace talks about equitable taxes for all, but his message is aimed primarily toward those who feel that they are left footing the bill, caught between the rich with their tax shelters, the tax-free foundations, and the poor who do not pay taxes. In a rather long and formal statement distributed as a position paper, the candidate affirms the free enterprise system, calls for curbs to inflation, urges efficiency in government spending and promotes a balanced budget:

> We will work toward a reduction in the tax burden for all our citizens, using as our tools efficiency and economy in the operation of government, the elimination of unnecessary and wasteful programs and reduction in government expenditures at home and abroad .... to achieve these goals and objectives, we would use government for the strengthening of the free enterprise rather than the replacement of the free enterprise system by government .... We feel little is done to curb inflationary trends in the nation's economy merely by taking from the taxpayer in order to enrich the spending programs of big government. We propose, rather, a stabilized and equitable tax base affording fair treatment to those of small income and designed to cause all persons, organizations and foundations to assume their rightful financial responsibility for government coupled with selective and prudent reductions in the wasteful expenditures of government .... We commit to the American people a return to fiscal responsibility and a conscientious and diligent effort toward a balancing of the federal budget, now operating at a record deficit, and a reduction of the huge national debt with which the nation is burdened. Fiscal sanity must be restored. (Wallace 1976)

Other problems that Wallace is concerned with are crime and welfare. He is particularly dramatic when he speaks about crime; it is a safe issue on which to show fervor. This passage, therefore, sounds like an excerpt from an earlier time:

> Crime rides America. Streets and entire sections in cities across our land are unsafe day or night. Our police officials are handcuffed by court decisions so that they feel alone and helpless as they seek to control the situation. Millions of our citizens are locked behind closed doors at night, captives in their own

homes, because they are not safe on the streets of American cities. Muggings, murders, sex crimes, holdups, and bank robberies are so common they get mention on a back page ... Motorists lock their doors, day and night, as they ride the streets of our cities. Guards have to escort some employees to their homes so that they will not be harmed. (*The Wallace Stand* 1975)

Crime and welfare are problems for all citizens, but particularly for the middle class. Wallace is not at all sympathetic with those who have been shortchanged by social injustice. His sympathies lie with those who have been shortchanged financially because of these social injustices— the middle class who has been left footing the bill for social problems in America:

A chief contributing cause to problems of metropolitan areas has been uncontrolled growth. In many instances, foreign workers have moved into urban areas in addition to the migration of millions from rural America. New ghettos have been created. Crime has grown out of proportion until today many cities have areas where it is not safe to walk on the streets night or day. Welfare rolls have become bloated with these new thousands who came in search of a better life. Heavy taxes on average citizens in the inner city have become a burden to carry. (Wallace 1976)

Although Wallace's foreign policy statements are more in evidence than in previous campaigns, Wallace in his new role as self-appointed statesman (and therefore presidential material) concentrates on the same issues as before: Vietnam was a mistake, he says; we should have taken a hard line and stuck to it. The refrain is a familiar one with a couple of new twists— Wallace says that the Vietnam War was a bad investment; it cost too much in terms of lives and money, and it only proved what we have always known—that you can't trust a Communist. In the last few campaigns Wallace utters few anti-Communist statements; this is a throwback straight to 1964:

Sure, we should have bombed Cambodia. We should have bombed Hanoi. We should have bombed the docks. And if we were afraid to bomb them because we were going to start another war with somebody else, we should never have been over there in the first place. What I'm saying is, this country has wasted 50,000 lives, hundreds of billions of dollars, and the country is wound up being taken over. And we pulled out and they [the Communists] didn't keep a single agreement they made. They lied and they cheated like they've always lied and cheated. (*New York Times* 1975)

His basic philosophy on foreign policy remains unchanged. It is a matter of having a full store of weapons and of adopting the right pose. It is a matter of being tough and convincing people that you mean what you say.

Wallace is suspicious of détente. Peace comes only through strength, through superior firepower:

> Peace is the most sought after product of our times. Each of us wants peace. The answer to achieving peace is in a strong military, second to none. History teaches us that we can only achieve peace through strength. We must be superior militarily so that when we talk of peace, our enemies will listen. (Wallace 1975)

Peace also comes through friendship, but it must be the right kind of friendship. Wallace advocates "affirmative action" in searching for friends. He cautions that we should choose our friends wisely and demand reciprocity in the form of loyalty and shared responsibility. In Wallace's mind foreign policy is but a reflection of domestic social relations, and he uses the image of welfare to denote the failures of foreign aid:

> We must have affirmative action to go out across the world in search of friends because they believe in and desire peace and freedom. We must learn the difference between the hand of friendship and the hand of welfare for international relations built on a welfare dole will never produce lasting friends. (Wallace 1975)

In general, the Wallace issues in 1976 are essentially repetitions of his most successful themes in earlier campaigns. They are, however, new to the national political arena. As Wallace puts it, he was first, a harbinger of things to come:

> All of them are saying the same things, and as a consequence that may have diluted the strength that I have, but it hasn't diluted the strength of the positions that I have taken. ("Meet the Press" 1976)

These issues are important ones. Others approach them cautiously, coinciding surprisingly with Wallace's approach, which in the interest of attracting a broader constituency has been flattened out, made more general, and phrased in a less offensive manner.

In becoming more respectable, Wallace has become indistinguishable from everybody else. The problem is twofold—not only do they have his issues, he is trying to be like the others and succeeding. In such a contest, in which the issues and the manner of all candidates are the same, voters will choose one candidate as well as another. In such a contest, why would anyone vote for a man in a wheelchair?

Chapter Sixteen

Wallace Support: Demographic and Attitudinal Changes, 1964 to 1976

In previous chapters the demographic and attitudinal attributes of Wallace supporters have been presented campaign by campaign. A comparison of these data, as well as the addition of some other samples and figures allows for observations of change in the Wallace constituency from 1964 through 1976.

In summary, we will find that the basis of the Wallace appeal remains the same throughout the twelve year period. In every campaign Wallace supporters continue to measure differently from others on authoritarianism, racial prejudice, and political powerlessness. Further, despite contentions by Wallace's chief aides (Snider 1974; Griffin 1974) that the class basis of the Wallace support changed over the years, a review of the data shows no such changes.

The samples used here are as follows:

The 1964 sample is comprised of 230 Wallace supporters (discussed in detail in Chapter Five) and is the only group which includes nonvoters.

Two samples from 1968 are employed. The first consists of 114 voters for Wallace as candidate of the American Independent party in the general election (analyzed extensively in Chapter Eight). The second is devised by the author. Respondents in the American National Election Study are asked to designate their sentiments for Wallace on an attitude scale ranging from zero to one hundred, with fifty being neutral. The group labeled here as pro-Wallace (149 respondents in 1968) is comprised of those who reflect *very* positive feelings toward Wallace, with scores ranging from seventy to one hundred. Those who have *very* negative feelings toward Wallace, with scores ranging from zero to thirty, are labeled anti-Wallace (588 respondents). Those who are considered neutral (between thirty to seventy) are disregarded.

Identical pro and anti-Wallace samples are drawn from the 1972 and 1976 American National Election Studies. Pro and anti-Wallace respondents number 342 and 330 respectively in 1972 and 254 and 457 in 1976. Most discussions will focus on those who are pro-Wallace, but there will be occasional comparisons with those who are anti-Wallace.

While the 1968 pro-Wallace group differs from the sample of actual voters for Wallace in the 1968 general election, a comparison of the two in this chapter shows that they are very similar. Thus the validity of using groups described as pro-Wallace in 1972 and 1976 to discern the qualities of those who might have voted for Wallace had he run in the general elections of 1972 and 1976 is assured. While not a replacement for data on actual voters (voters in the 1972 and 1976 Florida primaries are discussed in Chapter Eleven and Fourteen), this kind of data provides information on Wallace sentiment nationally and enables us to explore changes over time. (Other nationwide data on Wallace support in 1976 is discussed in Chapter Fourteen; the sample includes nonvoters and was not chosen to be presented here as it has limited comparative usefulness.)

It must be remembered that the 1968 pro-Wallace group includes people who did not vote for Wallace in 1968. Likewise, the pro-Wallace sample of 1972 and 1976 includes those who might not have voted for Wallace in 1972 and 1976 had he been on the ballot. As support for this warning, note the 1968, 1972, and 1976 pro-Wallace voting shown in Table 16.1.

Only 61.7 percent of the 1968 pro-Wallace group actually voted for Wallace in the general election. Fully one-fourth of the sample vote for Nixon (25.5%) and 12.8 percent vote for Humphrey.

In 1972, only 2.4 percent of the pro-Wallace group vote for John Schmitz, Wallace's replacement on the American Independent party ticket. Over three-quarters vote for Nixon (78.5%), while 19.1 percent cast their ballots for McGovern.

In 1976 the pro-Wallace group gives a majority of their votes to Carter over Ford (53.2% to 46.8%).

Thus one should keep in mind that these data are not an exact replica of what might have been, and that their use is primarily heuristic.

In summary, the 1964 statistics do not reflect Wallace voters—only those who prefer him in contrast to Goldwater and Johnson. The sample includes eventual voters as well as nonvoters and differs from other groups in that respect. Thus, its comparability in the other groups is incomplete. Its usefulness, however, is unquestionable, as it serves as a rough estimate of support in the beginning.

TABLE 16.1
Actual Vote of Those Who Are Pro-Wallace in 1968, 1972, and 1976

1968		1972		1976	
Humphrey	12.8	McGovern	19.1	Carter	53.2
Nixon	25.5	Nixon	78.5	Ford	46.8
Wallace	61.7	Schmitz	2.4		100.0%
	100.0%		100.0%		

The other samples are all from the same kind of data base, taken from the Center for Political Studies' American National Election Studies. They include only those who have voted in that year's general election and are completely comparable.

Table 16.2 presents the distribution of Wallace sentiment in the pro and anti-Wallace samples in 1968, 1972, and 1976. Between 1968 and 1972 there is a decided change. Negative sentiment drops drastically, by 36.7 percentage points. Those who have strongly positive feelings for him increase only slightly (6.8%) over the same time period, but a much larger proportion can be described as coming to feel relatively neutral (a change of 29.9%). The changes are in the opposite direction over the next four year period, and are as drastic as between 1968 and 1972: from 1972 to 1976 pro-Wallace sentiment drops 3.2 percent, the neutral category decreases by 25.1 percent, and those who are anti-Wallace increase by 28.2 percent. Such changes seem enigmatic until one remembers that the 1972 data was gathered in September and November—a few months after Wallace was shot in May, 1972. Thus, the figures most likely document positive sentiment for the candidate as a victim of an assassination attempt rather than reflect any real change in Wallace acceptability.

TABLE 16.2
Pro/Anti-Wallace Samples

	1968	1972	1976
Pro-Wallace	14.6	21.4	18.2
Neutral	28.0	57.9	32.8
Anti-Wallace	57.4	20.7	48.9
	100.0%	100.0%	100.0%

This conclusion is supported by the following data, which shows that positive sentiment for Wallace after he was shot increased steadily until 1974, after which it began to decline again.

Harris Polls July 1, 1974 and June 16, 1975
Statements About Gov. Wallace

Positive	1972	1974	1975
He is a man of high integrity	40	61	49
He sincerely wants to help working people by relieving their tax burden	37	54	48
He would keep law and order the way it should be kept	30	50	41
Negative			
He is an extremist	57	37	53
He is a racist, stirring up trouble	48	29	46
If elected president, he would divide the country and could not rule	53	33	41

Had the general election been held in 1974, the outcome of the presidential race might have been different.

The net change from 1968 to 1976 shown in Table 16.2 is thus a more accurate indicator of fluctuation in Wallace sentiment. In reality, there has not been very much change over the eight year period. From 1968 to 1976, there is a gain of 3.6 percent among the pro-Wallace group, a decrease of 8.5 percent among the anti-Wallace group, and an increase of 4.8 percent among those who are essentially neutral. There is little to indicate that Wallace's popularity or acceptability increased over the years.

This finding is supported by several other sources of data as well. A tracing of Harris and Gallup polls show that Wallace support varies between nine and twenty-seven points over the twelve year period that he is a presidential candidate. These figures parallel the findings in Table 16.2, and seem to indicate that although the Wallace strength remained constant and the candidate attracted almost a fifth of the voting population at any given time, he did not really amass a majority of support at any time. Thus, it seems unlikely that Wallace would have ever been able to capture the public imagination to the extent that he would have been voted the designee of a major party. More than in other ways, Wallace's strength came from his role as a possible third-party candidate (*New York Times* 1975n). While it is unlikely that he would have won the presidency in such a capacity, he certainly would have been able to amass enough support to throw the election into the House of Representatives, or at the very least to gain concessions from the major parties.

Demographics

Have those who have supported Wallace changed over the years? There is some evidence of such change (see Table 16.3).

Throughout his four presidential campaigns, Wallace appeals to very few blacks. As would be expected, Wallace support is almost one hundred percent white until 1976, the year he drops his overt racist appeals. In dropping his pose as a die-hard segregationist, Wallace picks up 3.4 percent black support.

Over the years the Wallace support shifts in terms of sex. In 1964 there is a slight majority of males (50.4%) among Wallace supporters. In 1968 males constitute 57.9 percent among the voters in the general election and 56.4 percent among those who are pro-Wallace. By 1972 the male support drops significantly to 49.7 percent. In the 1976 election period, the Wallace support more nearly reflects the distribution of sex in the general population, with 47.2 percent males and 52.8 percent females showing strongly positive feelings for Wallace.

Age distributions show a slight increase among those in the youngest category (18–24) in 1972. This is likely due to the fact that eighteen-year-olds are included as voters for the first time in 1972. There is also an increase in the proportions of those between 24–44 and 45–59 in 1968. As 1968 is the heyday of Wallace's racist appeals, it is conceivable that those in these age groups might be particularly susceptible to Wallace's racial appeals and intonations of powerlessness because they have the most to lose from the rising power of blacks in Wallace's formulation.

The regional distribution of Wallace support shifts most between 1964 and 1968. In 1964, Wallace support is primarily a southern phenomenon; three-quarters of all of his supporters are from the South. By 1968 he shows inroads into the Midwest and has gained friends in the Northeast as well. From 1968 to 1976, there is a trend of growing support for Wallace outside of the South. In that eight year period there is a gain of three percent in midwestern support and almost six percent in support from the Northeast.

There are a declining proportion of Protestants in relation to an increasing number of Catholics over the twelve years. Between 1968 and 1972 Wallace shows a nine percent Catholic gain. Few Jews are ever attracted to Wallace.

Between 1968 and 1972, however, the candidate almost doubles his Republican support, but given the large proportion of Republicans supporting him in 1964, the overall pattern of party affiliation shows a steady decline in organized party members and an increase of Indepen-dents. Nineteen sixty-eight is an anomoly in itself in the fact that Wallace is the candidate of a third party and on the ballot in all fifty states. This might very well explain why there is such a large proportion of Independents among both 1968 voters and 1968 pro-Wallace respondents.

In summary, there is some change in Wallace support over the years reflecting a broadening of appeal. Wallace begins to attract more women and more Catholics. In the twelve year period the proportion of Catholics supporting Wallace increases by ten percentage points.

The most notable changes are in Wallace support in different parts of the United States. Largely confined to the South in 1964, inroads are first made in the Midwest and then in the Northeast. By 1976, however, Wallace does not appeal equally well throughout the United States. His support remains concentrated in the South (46.1% in 1976). Despite the fact that over one-quarter is in the Midwest (27.2%), the heavily populated Northeast constitutes only 17.3 percent of his total support and his far West support never reaches ten percent. This is quite different from the more evenly distributed Carter and Reagan support shown in Chapter Fourteen, and it suggests that Wallace never really moved away from being a regional candidate despite his occasional successes in states like Wisconsin, Michigan, and Massachusetts. It is unlikely, therefore, that he would have ever been able to mobilize the national support needed to win the nomination for the presidency.

Ideological Variables

A comparison of Wallace supporters' attributes on a liberal/conserva-tive continuum (see Table 16.4) demonstrates that those who feel very positive toward Wallace are more likely to call themselves conservatives than are those who dislike Wallace intensely. Although the poll results shown here span a period of twelve years, the answers of Wallace supporters are remarkably consistent and do not differ over that time period. The anti-Wallace sample, however, is markedly different from those who favor Wallace; they are more likely to call themselves liberals, especially in 1972.

Among those who favor Wallace in 1976, one-fifth call him a liberal, an increase of almost seven percent since 1972. The majority, however, continue to label Wallace a conservative (63.2–66.7%). Among those who dislike Wallace, there is also a change in how he is perceived ideologically over the four year period. Twenty-five percent, compared to 14.6 percent in 1972, call him a liberal. The majority however (68.3%), continue to label him conservative.

TABLE 16.3
Selected Demographic Characteristics*

	1964 Supporters	1968 Voters	1968 Pro-W	1972 Pro-W	1976 Pro-W
Race					
White	99.1	100.0	99.3	99.1	96.6
Black	0.9	0.0	0.7	0.9	3.4
Sex					
Male	50.4	57.9	56.4	49.7	47.2
Female	49.6	42.1	43.6	50.3	52.8
Age					
21-24**	5.7	5.3	4.7	9.7	5.1
25-44	37.3	43.9	42.3	35.5	32.3
45-59	30.9	35.0	36.2	28.1	30.7
60 and over	26.1	15.8	16.8	26.7	31.9
Region					
Northeast	7.4	9.6	11.4	14.7	17.3
Midwest	9.2	25.4	24.2	26.9	27.2
South	74.7	56.2	56.4	48.5	46.1
Far West	8.7	8.8	8.0	9.9	9.4
Religion					
Protestant	84.4	79.8	81.2	72.9	74.0
Catholic	10.0	14.9	14.8	23.8	21.7
Jewish	0.0	0.9	0.0	0.0	0.4
Other or none	5.6	4.4	4.0	2.3	4.0
Party Affiliation					
Republican	32.3	13.1	16.8	30.0	25.7
Democrat	52.7	46.5	41.6	42.1	39.8
Independent	15.0	40.4	41.6	27.9	28.5
No preference	0.0	0.0	0.0	0.0	6.0

*Percentages add vertically by columns to 100 percent, except for rounding errors.

**1972 and 1976 percentages include 18-20 age group.

Racial Politics

While there has been a definite trend toward moderation on racial issues, Wallace supporters remain distinctly different from others in having larger proportions with negative attitudes toward blacks (see Table 16.5). For instance, when respondents are asked in 1972 whether they agree or disagree with the statement "It's really a matter of some people not trying hard enough; if blacks would only try harder they could be just as well-off as whites," a large proportion agree (75.3%, compared to 40.9% of those who dislike Wallace).

TABLE 16.4
Ideological Positions*

	Liberal	Moderate	Conservative
Self-proclaimed			
1964 supporters	11.8	34.3	53.9
1972 pro-Wallace	9.7	36.2	54.1
1972 anti-Wallace	57.0	23.8	19.2
1976 pro-Wallace	14.3	32.0	53.7
1976 anti-Wallace	36.3	29.8	33.9
Views of Wallace			
1972 pro-Wallace	13.5	23.3	63.2
1972 anti-Wallace	14.6	3.6	81.8
1976 pro-Wallace	20.3	13.1	66.7
1976 anti-Wallace	25.0	6.7	68.3

*Percentages add horizontally by rows to 100 percent, except for rounding errors.

Wallace supporters, more than others, choose to view individual blacks as being at fault rather than blame the system of perpetuating racism. A surprisingly large number of persons (even among the anti-Wallace group at 40.9%) place a premium on individual effort. The American Dream, with rewards expected to follow efforts, is very much alive.

Whenever views on racial issues of the pro-Wallace group are compared to those who are against Wallace, a larger proportion of the pro-Wallace group gives racist responses. However, a trend toward moderation is apparent in the answers to a number of questions on the American National Election Studies.

When asked, "Are you in favor of desegregation, strict segregation or something in between," Wallace supporters saying they are in favor of segregation number 37.5 percent of Wallace voters in 1968, 30.1 percent in 1968, 24.1 percent in 1972, and 19.1 percent in 1976. Over the same time period, commitment to desegregation increases from 13.4 percent to 26.4 percent. In all, the biggest gains occur between 1968 and 1972.

Another question asks the respondent's perception of the speed of the civil rights movement. Those in the pro-Wallace group who say that civil rights leaders are trying to push too fast drop from 93.5 percent in 1968 to

71.4 percent in 1972 and 65.0 percent in 1976, a difference of 28.5 percentages points over the eight year period.

An equal change is noted among those who agree that whites have a right to keep blacks out of their neighborhoods if they want to: 47.8 percent of the pro-Wallace group agree with this position in 1968; by 1976 only 19.4 percent agree. Again, on both of these questions, the most change occurs between 1968 and 1972.

The busing issue is a different matter. There is little change among those

TABLE 16.5
Selected Racial Attitudes

"It's Really a Matter of Some People Not Trying Hard Enough; That If Blacks Would Only Try Harder They Could Be Just As Well-Off As Whites."*	Pro-Wallace	Anti-Wallace
Agree	75.3	40.9
Disagree	24.7	59.1

"Are You In Favor of Desegregation, Strict Segregation, or Something-In-Between?"*	1968 Voters	1968 Pro-W	1972 Pro-W	1976 Pro-W
Desegregation	13.4	17.8	25.4	26.4
In-between	49.1	52.1	50.5	54.5
Segregation	37.5	30.1	24.1	19.1

Those Saying That "Civil Rights Leaders Are Trying to Push Too Fast."**	
1968 voters	90.0
1968 pro-Wallace	93.5
1972 pro-Wallace	71.4
1976 pro-Wallace	65.0

Those Agreeing That "White People Have a Right To Keep Black People Out Of Their Neighborhoods If They Want To."**	
1968 voters	46.1
1968 pro-Wallace	47.8
1972 pro-Wallace	33.2
1976 pro-Wallace	19.4

"Some People Think Achieving Racial Integration Is So Important That It Justifies Busing Children to Schools Out of Their Neighborhoods. Others Think Letting Children Go To Their Neighborhood School Is So Important That They Oppose Busing. Where Would You Place Yourself in This Scale?"***	Bus To Achieve Integration	Neutral	Keep Children in Neighborhood Schools
1972 pro-Wallace	0.6	4.4	95.0
1972 anti-Wallace	20.3	24.7	55.0
1976 pro-Wallace	2.1	5.8	92.2
1976 anti-Wallace	11.0	24.2	64.8

*Percentages add vertically by columns to 100 percent, except for rounding errors.

**Adding those disagreeing with the statement brings the total in each category to 100 percent.

***Percentages add horizontally by rows to 100 percent, except for rounding errors.

who are pro-Wallace; they are overwhelmingly against busing and want to keep children in neighborhood schools. (The range is from 92.2 to 95%.) A majority of those who dislike Wallace are also against busing, but they are generally less adamant. In 1972, 55 percent want to keep children in neighborhood schools; by 1976 the proportion feeling this way increases to 64.8 percent. In general, the public is against busing.

Marginal Voter Theories

Earlier analyses of Wallace voters and supporters (see Chapters 5, 8, 11, and 14) show no differences between them and supporters for other candidates on measures of marginal voting. They are as much in the mainstream as are others in voting regularly and in participating as members of various organizations and interest groups. The same is true in comparisons between pro and anti-Wallace groups (see Table 16.6).

There are few changes over time on measures of marginal voting. The drop noted in percent not voting between 1964 and 1968 occurs primarily because the 1964 sample contains a number of nonvoters. All of the other groups consist only of voters; thus, 1964 is not comparable to other years.

Another apparent change is noted among those in 1972, meaning that a larger proportion voted in the 1968 election. Because these people are pro-Wallace, it is very likely that they were more motivated than others to vote for third-party candidate Wallace in 1968. Otherwise, the proportion remains generally the same over the years.

Membership in interest groups is most often represented in these surveys by labor union affiliations. There has been a slight decrease of 4.9 percent among Wallace supporters who belong to labor unions since 1968. The deviant tally in 1964 is most likely due to the fact that that sample contains many nonvoters who are usually nonjoiners as well.

Authoritarian Personality

Although there are few questions on the schedules which permit comparison with Adorno's F Scale, there have been some that indicate that Wallace supporters might be somewhat more authoritarian than the rest of the population. On the 1972 survey are a number of questions which, while not part of the F Scale, are very similar to those items. These questions elicit attitudes which indicate rigidity and a concern with toughness that can be said to indicate authoritarianism (see Table 16.7). Differences between the pro-Wallace group and the anti-Wallace group on these questions is particularly marked—those who are pro-Wallace are much more likely to give responses which could be labeled authoritarian.

TABLE 16.6
Measures of Political Marginality

Those Who Did Not Vote
in the Previous Election*

1964 supporters	34.3
1968 voters	11.9
1968 pro-Wallace	10.7
1972 pro-Wallace	5.0
1976 pro-Wallace	10.9

Those Belonging to Labor Unions**

1964 supporters	19.1
1968 voters	29.8
1968 pro-Wallace	29.5
1972 pro-Wallace	26.8
1976 pro-Wallace	24.6

*Adding those who did vote brings the total in each group to 100 percent.

**Adding those who do not belong to labor unions brings the total in each group to 100 percent.

For instance, 87.1 percent of the pro-Wallace group, compared to 53.1 percent of the anti-Wallace group, agree that what young people need most is strict discipline by their parents. And those saying "I prefer the practical man anytime to the man of ideas" constitute 70.4 percent of the pro-Wallace group and 43.7 percent of those in the anti-Wallace group.

Those who disagree with the statement, "The findings of science may someday show that many of our most deeply held beliefs are wrong," run 55.2 percent of persons who are pro-Wallace and 38.5 percent of those who are anti-Wallace.

In responding to the following question, those who are pro-Wallace are more adamant than those who don't like him: "Some people are primarily concerned with doing everything possible to protect the legal rights of those now accused of committing crimes. Others feel that it is more important to stop criminal activity even at the risk of reducing the rights of the accused. Where would you place yourself in this scale?" In 1972, 48.3 to 11.2 percent and in 1976, 45.2 to 22.7 percent say that we should stop crime regardless of the rights of the accused.

On all such measures Wallace supporters are proportionately more adamant than are those who dislike him. This suggests that they are distinguishable by their authoritarianism.

Status Theories

In comparison with supporters of other candidates in earlier chapters, we found no indication that Wallace supporters differ significantly on status measures. The same is true when they are compared to those who are anti-Wallace. In both 1968 and 1972, in fact, the pro-Wallace people have larger proportions in middle and high SES statuses than those who are anti-Wallace.

While Wallace's chief aides (Griffin 1974; Snider 1974) maintain that the

TABLE 16.7
Selected Authoritarian Measures

Those Agreeing That "What Young People Need Most of All Is Strict Discipline by Their Parents."*

Pro-Wallace	87.1
Anti-Wallace	53.1

Those Agreeing That "I Prefer the Practical Man Anytime to the Man of Ideas."*

Pro-Wallace	70.4
Anti-Wallace	43.7

Those Disagreeing That "The Findings of Science May Someday Show that Many of Our Most Deeply Held Beliefs Are Wrong."**

Pro-Wallace	55.2
Anti-Wallace	38.5

"Some People Are Primarily Concerned With Doing Everything Possible to Protect the Legal Rights of Those Now Accused of Committing Crimes. Others Feel That It Is More Important To Stop Criminal Activity Even At the Risk of Reducing the Rights of the Accused. Where Would You Place Yourself in This Scale?"***

	Protect Rights of Accused	Neutral	Stop Crime Regardless of Rights of Accused
1972 pro-Wallace	16.3	35.4	38.3
1972 anti-Wallace	49.0	39.8	11.2
1976 pro-Wallace	24.4	30.3	45.2
1976 anti-Wallace	30.5	46.8	22.7

*Adding those disagreeing with the statement brings the total in each category to 100 percent.

**Adding those agreeing with the statement brings the total in each category to 100 percent.

***Percentages add horizontally by rows to 100 percent, except for rounding errors.

Wallace support changed over the twelve year period and the candidate declared himself the spokesman of the middle class in 1976, there is little evidence that the class basis of the Wallace vote changed very much (see Table 16.8).

Ascribed status (race and religion combined—see Appendix) shows only slight change. No longer are all of those who support Wallace both white and Protestant. The changes noted among those with one ascribed status (plus almost ten percent from 1968 to 1972) most likely result from the growing presence of white Catholics.

Moving to the components of achieved status, we note an increase in the percentage of Wallace supporters who have some college education. There is quite a big difference in the percent of those who have some college education between the 1968 voters (17.5%) and those who are pro-Wallace in 1968 (26.2%). It is unclear what this means. Perhaps more college educated people are attracted to Wallace than actually vote for him. Since 1968 the proportion of those pro-Wallace people who are college educated has remained constant, ranging from 24.9 to 29.1 percent.

Income shows a mixed picture. The income distribution among supporters in 1964 is not as evenly distributed as it is among the 1968 voters and the 1972 pro-Wallace group. In 1976 the income distribution among supporters is similar to what it is in 1964. What this means is unclear, but it does show that the income status of Wallace supporters relative to that of the general population has not improved over time.

Achieved status, a combination of education and income, shows that in 1968 more Wallace supporters of high achieved status like him than choose to vote for him. From 1964 to 1972 there is a drop in proportions among those with low achieved status accompanied by a rise in those with high achieved status. Things change abruptly in 1976; fully one-third of those who are pro-Wallace have low achieved status in that year.

When ascribed and achieved statuses are combined into a socioeconomic status (SES) score (see Appendix), we note that a slightly larger proportion of those with high SES in 1968 like Wallace than voted for him.

In general, Wallace supporters are concentrated in the middle two SES categories. SES fluctuates at both extremes but not enough so to warrant the claims of the Wallace staff that the status of Wallace supporters has changed drastically over the years.

In terms of subjective measures of SES, most respondents identify themselves as working class or having been born to working-class parents. The figures show some increase among those who describe themselves as middle class in 1972; the picture changes again in 1976.

Status components of Wallace support remain much the same over the twelve year period.

TABLE 16.8
Selected Status Attributes*

	1964 Supporters	1968 Voters	1968 Pro-W	1972 Pro-W	1976 Pro-W
Ascribed Status					
None	0.0	0.9	0.7	0.0	2.0
One	16.5	19.3	18.8	28.1	26.4
Both	83.5	79.8	80.5	71.9	71.7
Education					
Grade school	36.5	24.6	22.8	19.0	18.9
High school	55.7	57.9	51.0	56.1	52.0
College	7.8	17.5	26.2	24.9	29.1
Income					
Lowest third	38.6	33.9	29.9	27.2	34.9
Middle third	37.2	33.9	26.7	39.6	35.3
Highest third	24.2	32.2	33.4	33.2	29.8
Achieved Status					
Low	50.7	39.3	34.7	29.0	33.6
Working	26.4	22.3	25.2	32.0	29.4
Middle	19.8	28.6	24.5	26.9	22.3
High	3.1	9.8	15.6	12.1	14.7
SES					
Low	13.0	8.8	8.8	16.7	18.6
Working	45.7	46.5	40.9	33.6	35.6
Middle	38.3	38.6	38.9	41.5	35.6
High	3.0	6.1	11.4	8.2	10.3

	1968 Pro-Wallace	1972 Pro-Wallace	1976 Pro-Wallace
Subjective Social Class			
Working	61.1	56.9	60.2
Middle	38.9	43.1	39.8
Status of Family of Origin (Subjective)			
Low	1.4	0.0	0.8
Working	74.1	66.6	69.9
Middle	25.5	33.4	29.3

*Percentages add vertically by columns to 100 percent except for rounding errors.

The Power Theory

There are differences between the pro and anti-Wallace groups on all the power variables (see Table 16.9). On personal anomie, pro-Wallace people show higher proportions with high personal anomie in 1968 and in 1976. In 1972, however, the two groups are almost identical.

Readings on low personal power are practically the same in 1968 and 1972; there is very little difference between the two groups. In 1968 about one-quarter show low personal power. In 1972 this drops to almost no one feeling low personal power; by 1976 low personal power is up again, with a larger proportion of the pro-Wallace group (30.9%) and 22.5 percent of the anti-Wallace group showing little personal power.

The pattern also exists among those with high political anomie. In 1968 the pro-Wallace group with high political anomie outnumbers the anti-Wallace group by two to one, with majorities of 57.6 percent among pro-Wallace people and 61.1 percent among Wallace voters showing high political anomie. In 1972, however, the anti-Wallace group shows 60.9 percent with high political anomie, doubling since 1968 and 3.5 percentage points more than those who are pro-Wallace. By 1976 the pro-Wallace group and anti-Wallace group have switched back, but they are up by eight to fifteen percentage points over 1972; 72.9 percent among the pro-Wallace group and 68.8 percent of the anti-Wallace group show high political anomie.

On measures of political power, the pro-Wallace group consistently outnumbers the anti-Wallace group. Voters in 1968 show even higher levels of political powerlessness. In 1968, 52.4 percent of the voters, 46.9 percent of the pro-Wallace group, and 32.7 percent of the anti-Wallace group reflect low political power. The percentage of the pro-Wallace group who feel politically powerless continues at that level over the years, while the proportion of those among the anti-Wallace group continues to fall. In 1976 the difference between the two groups is 17.2 percentage points.

Those with low institutional power show the same pattern. Voters in 1968 (33.9%) have higher proportions with low institutional power than those who are pro-Wallace (24.4%). The anti-Wallace group has 13.9 percent. The two groups drop in 1972 and come within three percentage points of each other with 13.8 percent of the pro-Wallace group and 10.4 percent of the anti-Wallace group showing low institutional power. In 1976 the two groups show higher proportions with low institutional power. Of the pro-Wallace group, 20.6 percent shows low institutional power and 11.4 percent of the anti-Wallace group demonstrates that same reading. In 1968 those who feel positive about Wallace and those who feel negative about him are relatively close together on measures of personal powerlessness and personal anomie; but they are quite different from each other on measures of political anomie and both kinds of political powerlessness. The most consistently noted difference is in the measure of political powerlessness. From 1968 through 1976, pro-Wallace persons outnumber anti-Wallace persons by epsilons of 14.2 to 19.1.

Over the years Wallace supporters exhibit a combination of characteristics that continue to distinguish them from persons who dislike Wallace.

TABLE 16.9
Selected Power Measures

	1968	1972	1976
High Personal Anomie*			
Voters	40.8	no sample	no sample
Pro-Wallace	35.0	40.8	41.9
Anti-Wallace	27.5	40.1	26.8
Low Personal Power**			
Voters	25.8	no sample	no sample
Pro-Wallace	26.3	0.7	30.9
Anti-Wallace	24.4	2.7	22.5
Political Anomie*			
Voters	61.1	no sample	no sample
Pro-Wallace	57.6	57.4	72.9
Anti-Wallace	30.0	60.9	68.8
Low Political Power**			
Voters	52.4	no sample	no sample
Pro-Wallace	46.9	48.8	45.3
Anti-Wallace	32.7	29.7	28.1
Low Institutional Power**			
Voters	33.9	no sample	no sample
Pro-Wallace	24.4	13.8	20.6
Anti-Wallace	13.9	10.4	11.4

*Adding proportions of persons with low and middle levels brings the total to 100 percent in each category.

**Adding proportions of persons with middle and high levels brings the total to 100 percent in each category.

Those who are pro-Wallace are more authoritarian and more prejudiced against blacks. They are also clearly distinguished from others on the power measures. In particular, they show greater proportions of persons with high political anomie and low political power.

Epilogue

In an appearance on "Good Morning, America," in May, 1977, George Wallace announced that he intended to run for the Senate seat of Alabama Senator John Sparkman (*New York Times* 1977g). About a month later he reiterated this pledge during a speech at the annual meeting of the Alabama Associated Press Broadcasters' Association. He was the logical choice, Wallace said, "because of his involvement in national politics, he had come to know many people in national government, including President Carter, and, 'I'd like to use that for the people of Alabama'" (*New York Times* 1977e). He said that he thought he might use "the issue of higher electricity rates to generate support" for his candidacy (*New York Times* 1977f).

Over the next six months Wallace's personal life changed drastically. A copy of a divorce petition on his behalf found its way into the offices of Alabama's newspapers, radio and television stations, and wire services offices. Reporters found that the document had not been filed in court. Wallace's office disclaimed any knowledge and said there was nothing to it (*New York Times* 1977d).

A month later, Cornelia Wallace moved out of the governor's mansion (*New York Times* 1977c), and George Wallace filed for divorce after six years of marriage. The grounds were incompatibility. Mrs. Wallace said that she could "no longer endure the vulgarity, threats, and abuse," (*New York Times* 1977b) and said that the reason for the breakup "was not incompatibility, but the commission of actual violence and cruelty by the governor." She further maintained that "Wallace had beaten her and caused her to fear for her life" (*New York Times* 1977a).

The rumor was that Wallace "thought his wife neglected him, traveling frequently while he stayed at home." There was gossip that she had had affairs with other men as well, and she reputedly tapped his telephone "to find out who was spreading [these] destructive rumors about her, and accused Mr. Wallace's brother Gerald of making her husband suspicious of her" (*New York Times* 1978a).

After seven years of marriage, the Wallaces were divorced in January 1978. Although Wallace insisted that he was not worried, he was reported to be very uneasy about the effect that the divorce might have on his Senate campaign. He insisted that his chief concern was the disclosure of "private, personal affairs between me and my family." But when reporters "asked if he thought Mrs. Wallace's allegation of 'physical cruelty and actual violence' might be used in the campaign, he said, 'In a political campaign, everything is used'" (*New York Times* 1978g).

The Question of the Senate Race

In April, Wallace asked the legislature to pass a bill guaranteeing police protection to him after he left office in January (*New York Times* 1978f). He warned that he might have to drop the Senate race if the state dropped his bodyguards (*New York Times* 1978f). The legislature guaranteed protection (*New York Times* 1978e).

In May, Wallace announced quite suddenly that he would not run for the Senate. It was a curious decision. As Wallace was "barred by law from succeeding himself in 1978," his stepping out of the Senate race was seen as a most significant gesture. "He is generally considered to have brought his political career to an end." (Raines 1978). He said that he felt that he could win, but had decided not to run for personal reasons. He did not indicate what those reasons were.

Although the divorce had seemed to be personally troubling, there was no indication that it had hurt Wallace politically. He also insisted that the decision was not health related. It was known, however, that he did not relish the prospect of conducting a statewide campaign in a wheelchair (*New York Times* 1978e). In addition, his hearing had deteriorated over a period of time, and it was getting worse (*New York Times* 1978d).

A Senate campaign would have cost around one million dollars. While not a large sum in terms of what Wallace had raised for previous campaigns, the source of funds for a Senate run would be mainly from Alabama, and not from all over the United States as before. The truth was that Wallace's popularity ratings in Alabama had slipped (Raines 1978), and it was not certain that he could raise the money (*New York Times* 1978e).

It is entirely possible that Wallace had lost so much support that he could not have won such a race. Howell Heflin, one of the more probable candidates for that seat, touted "poll results by Peter Hart of Washington 'which are said to document' a steady decline of Mr. Wallace's support" in Alabama (Raines 1978).[1]

There was another rumor that Helfin had "bought Wallace out" of the Senate race (Raines 1978). Just how this was supposed to have been done was unclear. Heflin's office refused to comment.[2] The only reference the *Times* had was to John M. Herbert III, a Birmingham businessman with ties to both Heflin and Wallace. Herbert apparently wanted to raise money to endow a chair for Wallace on the faculty of one of the state universities (Raines 1978). Wallace would teach law, political science, or government and was reportedly interested in the prospect (*New York Times* 1978f).

Gerald Wallace said that the truth of the matter was that his brother "just didn't want to go to Washington" (Raines 1978). Griffin (1978) and Azbell (1978) agreed. And Wallace himself insisted that the "ultimate factor was his unwillingness to live in the capital" (*New York Times* 1978c).

Later Wallace said he could have won, but, he said: "I decided after a long thought about the matter that to live in Washington—paralyzed—was something that mentally I didn't know I could take, especially living alone" (*Daily Argus* 1978).

Wallace refused to endorse any Senate candidate; nor would he endorse any of those who hoped to succeed him as governor (Raines 1978). In the meantime, Heflin raised over $300,000 in the first three months of 1978 for his run. And Mike House, Heflin's campaign manager, said that when Wallace saw Heflin's list of contributors, he was upset "because a lot of his people were on it" (Raines 1978).

The report was that Wallace was "brooding over his failing grip on both state government and the loyalty of the voters." A survey had shown his popularity "at a ceiling of about one-third of the projected Democratic primary vote. Unable to expand on that hard-core support . . . Mr. Wallace would inevitably be defeated in the runoff by whomever he opposed" (Raines 1978).

In June, Sen. James B. Allen of Alabama died unexpectedly (Jenkins 1978). The governor's office was flooded with telephone calls, letters, and telegrams asking Wallace to reconsider. "The reason most of them gave . . . is that unless Mr. Wallace is elected, Alabama will be without an experienced name in the Senate (*New York Times* 1978b). Wallace reportedly gave consideration to resigning the governorship and having Jere Beasley, the lieutenant governor who would succeed him, appoint him to fill Allen's unexpired term (Allen 1979).

But Beasley and Wallace did not get along, and Maryon Allen, Senator Allen's widow, contended that Wallace could not be sure that Beasley would appoint him to the seat if he did resign. So Wallace named the Senator's widow to fill the unexpired term. Apparently during their telephone conversation in which Wallace informed Mrs. Allen of his decision to appoint her, he made it clear that he was expecting her to vacate the seat for his run when the term expired in 1978. Mrs. Allen refused to say that she would not run at the end of the term (Allen 1979).

Publicly, Wallace ruled out his own race for either Senate seat and assured his followers that "he would remain politically active" (*New York Times* 1978a). He did not give details of how he would do that. Meanwhile, the firm which had handled the advertising for his gubernatorial campaigns started to work on Heflin's senate campaign (Elliott, 1978).

The Beautification of the Record

In the meantime Wallace attended to state business. Occasionally he reminisced to reporters: "Many have said that had I come along at a later time, as President Carter did, after the racial problems had been more or less resolved, and the stigma of being a Southern governor was not scaring, my quest for the presidency would have been different" (Roberson 1978). He said that he thought he would have been on the Democratic national ticket if he had not been shot. He also contended that the "Democratic Party hierarchy [had] used his paralysis as an excuse to stop his Presidential ambitions" (Roberson 1978).

In October, Wallace accepted an offer to be director of development for rehabilitation resources of the University of Alabama in Birmingham and for the University of Alabama systems. The appointment was effective January 16, 1979; his duties were "expected to include fund raising, consulting in rehabilitation, working with federal grant agencies and lecturing" (*Alabama Journal* 1978). Arrangements were made for him to do most of his work in Montgomery (Raines 1979b); negotiations had apparently been underway for eighteen months (*Alabama Journal* 1978).

It was the end of an era. In January, Wallace would go out of office sixteen years after he first took the governor's oath. In an end of term interview, he referred "to the wheelchair as symbolizing the price he paid to spread a popular message that he said reshaped American politics and made possible the election of a fellow Southerner, Jimmy Carter, as President. 'I would do it all over again even if I knew this would happen,' he said with a gesture toward his paralyzed legs. 'I would do it all over again because I get a lot of satisfaction out of hearing a President or a Governor at a governors' conference sound like I did in 1963'" (Raines 1979c).

In the interview, Wallace conceded that "Alabama was better off without the segregation he once pledged to preserve." The reporter said further that "Wallace veered even closer to public apology for his resistance to the civil rights movement of the 1960s, saying that racial killings in Alabama during his three terms as Governor 'broke my heart.'" He also said, apparently for the first time, that the commander of the Alabama state troopers, now dead, defied his direct orders by attacking civil rights marchers in Selma on the "Bloody Sunday" protest of March 7, 1965. But his deepest regret, he made clear, was allowing what he described as "philosophical opposition to federal intervention to be taken as an indication that he personally hated blacks." Explained Wallace, "we were fighting against politicians, not black people" (Raines 1979c).

A final mailing went out to his political supporters; each was asked to send in donations of between five and one hundred dollars to buy the governor a farewell gift—a new Lincoln Continental (Raines 1979c).

Gossip had it that he would run for governor in 1982 (Raines 1979c), but no one seemed particularly interested. As Joe Azbell put it (Azbell 1978), "a setting sun gives off no heat."

At the inauguration of Fob James as the new governor of Alabama, James promised to "bury forever the negative prejudices of the past." Wallace sat on the platform, but James acknowledged him only perfunctorily, and twice praised Martin Luther King, Jr. (Raines 1979b).

In his first month as governor, James abruptly ended the adversary relationship that the governor's office had had with Federal District Judge Frank M. Johnson. Agreeing to correct the nightmarish "prison conditions that Judge Johnson ruled unconstitutional in 1976," James sent a petition to Johnson which "acknowledged 'indefensible conditions in Alabama prisons' and placed the blame on 'inadequate and inefficient management' in the Wallace years." As one reporter (Raines 1979a) put it, James' petition was "a stunning repudiation of the Wallace legacy."

Notes

1. I spoke to Peter Hart's office and was referred to Senator Heflin. Heflin's chief aide, Mike House (formerly his campaign manager), refused to release the poll in question but said that Wallace had run his own polls and found that "a lot of his old guard was going with us."
2. House said "We weren't involved in anything," and laughed that "if we did everything we were accused of doing . . . ."

Conclusion

Throughout this book, Wallace supporters are distinguished from others by their authoritarianism, feelings of political powerlessness, and racial prejudice. Another thing about them stands out as well; they are not a social movement. Although they are an important bloc of voters, in the end they were only a loose collectivity attracted to Wallace and to the sentiments he expressed, more like a fan club than anything else.

Wallace was a one-man phenomenon. The New Mexico Wallace chairman reported that Wallace supporters in his state would not work for a Wallace-sponsored slate, but only for Wallace as a lone individual (Kraft 1976). The candidacy of Schmitz in 1972 clearly demonstrates that the beliefs of Wallace were not transferable to others. This was partly due to the fact that Wallace ran his campaigns like a petit bourgeois business. Further, Wallace did not share his power with anyone, nor did he groom a successor. When Wallace was gone from the scene, the Wallace vote disintegrated, with his supporters voting for Ford or for Carter in nearly equal proportions in the 1976 general election. The Wallace "movement" disappeared as quickly as it had appeared. And it is not likely to coalesce around anyone else, for Wallace represented no discernable ideological politics, only a position, a stance.

The Wallace politics were essentially expressive rather than instrumental (Gusfield 1963). They were not designed to move in any productive way toward getting more power for the people, but to make them feel more powerless instead. As the *New York Times* noted, "compromise and conciliation are not in his interest. He and his kind of protest politics thrive on turmoil, excitement, discord. He is interested in exploiting issues, not solving problems" (*New York Times* 1972r).

Much of Wallace's powerlessness ploy was based in a particular historical moment and in a particular subculture. Over the last century the white South had been in a unique position vis-a-vis the federal government in relation to the rest of the United States. The South lost the Civil War, and from that time on did not share proportionately in the power distribution meted out to the rest of the United States (Havard 1972, ch. 1). There were trade-offs in Congress, in which positions of titular and distributory power went regularly to Southern congressmen in return for tacit agreements that the federal government would leave the power relationship between blacks and whites in the South untouched. The South suffered in the deal, however, and remained poor and relatively under-developed. This history had certain cultural consequences for southern whites, aptly described by Wallace. There had been suffering: "Both national parties, the Republicans and the Democrats, have used the State of Alabama and the South as a doormat for the last hundred years" (House 1969, p. 109).

Wallace's sense of history and of his own destiny in leading the South in saving "this nation from the left-wing trend it has gone on" (House 1969, p. 104) reflect both shame and a sense of having been victimized. There is tremendous anger at having been made to feel powerless:

> One hundred years ago, the spirit of the South became passive as this spirit was subdued by violent means—yet remained undimmed. For the flame of our passion burned within us as an arc of our covenant—a covenant of our heritage of liberty under law with no surrender to those who would destroy us. (Wallace 1971b)

With a burning fury like this, neither the white South nor Wallace was about to accept integration, particularly from a government that told them that they had no recourse in the matter. Thus there was a dynamic of both personal and cultural powerlessness associated with this issue.

Wallace was aware of the potential of this long-buried rage; he stoked it carefully, keeping it under control and fueling his candidacy with it. He became aware that feelings of anger can be loosed when the fact of people's powerlessness is brought to their attention, and he set about engendering that sense of powerlessness nationwide. He knew that his possible constituency was not limited to the South: ". . . my campaign in the North has convinced me that there are Southerners in every state of the Union" (House 1969, p. 104).

This rage at being made to feel powerless was very skillfully directed by Wallace toward the target of the federal government as proclaimed enemy. The old laissez-faire cry resounds throughout his speeches: "We want big government to get out of our lives and leave us alone!" ("Wallace Campaign" 1972b). His contentions that he was "ahead of his time" are nonsense. Because he understood discontent, he knew how to capitalize upon people's deepest feelings. That makes him an opportunist rather than a savior.

There was another historical and cultural element at work in Wallace's candidacy. In the beginning (1964) Wallace spoke primarily of the South; at issue was a struggle over political power. The situation in the South was that blacks were being assured rights under the auspices of federal government sponsorship they had not enjoyed before—the permission to go to an "all-white" school, encouragement and help in registering to vote, being allowed to purchase services and property for which one can pay. However, these gains were not themselves the issue. The gains became highly significant when viewed from two directions. First, the whites in the South were being told by the federal government that this is the way things will be and there was no room for debate, holding actions, or resistance on the part of whites. Second, and more important, the Southern white imagination was kindled by an understanding of the changes in power relations that would occur if all blacks exercised such rights. To label the latter as the fear of loss of status is to totally misunderstand the power relationships between blacks and whites which existed in the early 1960s and before in the South.

Whites in the South had maintained their superiority only by maintaining control over the power structure. Things had been relatively peaceful only because they had successfully controlled blacks' thoughts of going against the established system through the threat of force. The sheriff and his deputies, the Klan and other vigilante groups appeared "when necessary." In quieter times an authoritarian posture and moral and social outrage on the part of dominant whites could all be brought to bear. Economic pressures also kept blacks under control.

It was only when the federal government opened up the possibility of blacks getting legitimate political power that the southern whites really had something to fear. The possibility of blacks gaining power through the ballot and attaining even more such power under the auspices of the Civil Rights Bill, such as the power to buy property which whites do not wish to sell, or to attain personal services which whites might not care to render, opened a Pandora's Box for the southern white world.

The prize at hand in this struggle was power. The unwillingness of Wallace and the people he represented to share power with blacks seemed to be rooted in a particular understanding of power as a zero-sum entity (Wilhoit 1973). Wallace and his followers seemed convinced that there was only so much power to go around, and only so many rewards available in terms of governmental resources to meet the needs of people. If blacks began to get their needs met, then the constituency which Wallace represented would begin to lose out.

Television played an important role in creating such consciousness. If southern blacks were politicized through television, as Matthews and Prothro (1966: 237) have suggested, then it is certain that southern whites were politicized as well. One watched George Wallace stand in the schoolhouse door on television, saw blacks demonstrating and war protestors marching, and watched representatives of the federal government intervene in the interests of one group or another on television, every night.

Further, the press functioned as Wallace's own public relations mechanism. Not only did the media bring George Wallace to the attention of the public, they also publicized his issues: Vietnam and the civil rights struggle were brought into millions of living rooms.

The press saw Wallace as good copy, and played right into his hands. They bought his role and pictured him as an underdog, a pitiful and powerless figure struggling against great odds and the opposition of the federal government, and people could see it on TV. Presented this way, Wallace also appeared, despite his ideological abberations, as brave and undaunted, a hero.

While others ranted and raved against him, Wallace was silent. He did not presume to tell anyone what to do, he said. He insisted over and over that he only wanted local communities to have the right to make their own decisions. What he was protesting was being told what to do by the federal government. And people could see that on TV.

The establishment tried to stop Wallace, especially as he became a threat to their own power structure, but they played into his hands, too. The more they fought him, the more they gave validity to his pose. As Chester, Hodgsen, and Page (1969, p. 271) have described it, Wallace's style was to "invite punishment by defiance, slyly avoid real unpleasant consequences, then advertise your martyrdom." If Wallace had been ignored by the press and the establishment, few would have paid him any attention.

Wallace had little to offer. Despite the fact that he is a man who has traveled many miles in his thirteen years of campaigning for the presidency, and who has talked to so many people, he shows no evidence of truly understanding the magnitude of problems which exist among the populace. His remarks are never detailed; they are shallow. The only thing which Wallace does know and which he knows intimately, is how to feel out and to exploit the discontent which he hears around him. His own duplicity is seen in the "Stand in the Schoolhouse Door."

While Wallace gave dramatic expression to the grievances of white people of Alabama and to the values and goals which they stood for in the stand in the schoolhouse door, after delivering his proclamation of protest, Wallace stepped aside and let the two black students enter to register.

But there was no public outcry, and few noticed that Wallace had silently sold them out. His unyielding resistance was only a pretense. In effect, it hastened the passage of the 1964 Civil Rights Bill as well as the integration of southern schools.

One question remains unanswered. Is the Wallace support, which accounts for twenty percent of the voting populace and with which, as one major party strategist put it "all the liberal Democratic presidents from Roosevelt on were elected" (Newsweek 4/21/75), there for mobilization by any politician of great charisma who might come along?

The answer is no. The Wallace vote was a particular configuration of attitudes which will not reappear in exactly that same form again. But there is plenty of discontent to be capitalized upon, and people are ripe for appeals by unprincipled but charismatic politicians.

Appendix: Methods

This appendix supplements the methodological explanations appearing in the body of the book. In particular it explains how the scales are constructed and why certain intellectual decisions were made. All data sources are noted within the chapters, or in the notes following those chapters, and this appendix does not repeat any of that information.

SPSS (Statistical Package for the Social Sciences) (Nie, *et al.* 1975) computer programs are used throughout for the data analysis, with the exception of the 1976 CBS News/*New York Times* polls.[1] The subprograms used most often are Frequencies and Crosstabs, with accompanying statistics. As noted in each chapter, support for Wallace is compared with support for other candidates. The data was grouped into subfiles as defined previous to computer runs, thus candidate choice cannot be used as a dependent variable. This makes statistical testing by computer of the differences among candidates of any given variable impossible. Instead of resorting to extensive hand calculation to make such comparisons, I have chosen to rely on epsilon (the difference among percentages) as a means of demonstrating differences among candidate supporter groups on any particular variable. A quick eye comparison among percents is sufficient for determining differences. Where crosstabulation is involved, a comparison of the appropriate statistics gives a clear indication of the strength of the relationship between the variables in each candidate supporter group.

That the data are aggregated by states may have hidden some distinguishing factors. Janowitz and Miller (1952) and Campbell and Stokes (1959) contend that national samples gloss over differences which are found among people of different demographic characteristics when they are examined in specific geographical units. An analysis of the 1976 Massachusetts, Florida, Illinois, and Wisconsin primaries CBS News/*New York Times* polls lends credence to this observation. In general, most of the samples used are representative only of the four basic regions of the United

States. It is conceded, however, that Wallace supporters from one state may be different from Wallace supporters from another state.

All demographic and attitudinal variables are held constant by region for each candidate group, but only findings of great importance are reported here. While sectional differences are very important (Stouffer 1963), it is not the central focus of this study.

Construction of Measures

Wherever there is a scale of seven intervals (Likert-type) used to pinpoint attitudes, I have collapsed the scale into three categories to provide a clearer and more concise contrast. In doing so, I have combined scores one and two; three, four, and five; and six and seven. The collapsed one and two and six and seven represent the extremes of an attitude and three, four, and five are considered an average or neutral position on issues.

Each data chapter details variables used to explore the theories considered here. Measures of status and power created to explore the 1968, 1972, and 1976 election data are explained below.

Construction of SES Measures

SES measures are calculated following the suggestions of Olsen and Tully (1972). Only those variables found throughout all of the studies are used, however, as comparability is essential. Olsen and Tully created measures of ascribed and achieved statuses and then combined these measures into a score of socioeconomic status.

In creating ascribed status, they make use of parental nativity and ethnic identification, neither of which is included in all of the studies. Here I have used only race and religion to create a measure of ascribed status. Each is scored separately. For race, a score of three is given for the answer white and a score of zero, representing no status, is given for black and other, as adjacent numbers would not provide enough separation. For religion, the respondent receives a score of three only if the respondent is a Protestant. If the respondent is Catholic, Jewish, or answered nothing, the respondent is scored as zero, denoting low religious status. Olsen and Tully classify a "no answer" as a three along with Protestant. I decided not to do that. Thus the possible range of scores for ascribed status (religion and race added together) is from six (both white and Protestant); to three, only one ascribed status; to zero, having no ascribed status.

Two variables are used to calculate a measure of achieved status. Education of the respondent is arranged into three categories in ascending order; a score of one is given for grade school education, ranging from no schooling to completion of the eighth grade; two signifies a high school education, covering everything from ninth grade through a high school diploma, including the designation technical school; and three is the score given for a college education, ranging from a few months of college through all advanced degrees.

The other component of achieved status, income, is family income for the year. Wattenberg's (1974) figures on income distribution show a radical change between 1964 and 1972. And it is certain that inflation since 1972 has also made the meaning of a specific income in 1964 quite different from the same income in 1976. Because there is no way of adjusting income to allow for such changes (figures for income are coded, and the codes used for each of the surveys are not comparable), I decided to divide income distribution into rough thirds. I reasoned that status vis-a-vis income distribution (buying power) would remain relatively constant, and assumed that being in the lowest third income level, whatever that range happened to be in numbers, would have the same meaning and the same status in 1964 as in 1976. This enables the comparison of income levels as well as achieved status over the years with some assurance.

In using income, therefore, to calculate achieved status, the lowest third is given a score of one, the middle third a score of two, and the highest third a score of three. Scores for education and income are then added together for each respondent and recoded into a measure of achieved status as follows:

New Code	Name	Initial integer scores resulting from addition of income and education
1	Lowest	2, 3
2	Working	4
3	Middle	5
4	Upper	6

An SES score is then created by adding the integer scores for achieved status and the integer scores of zero, three, and six for ascribed status. The variable SES is then recoded and classified as:

SES Code	Name	Integer totals and description of possibilities
4	High	10 only: white, Protestant, college, highest third of income.
3	Middle	8 or 9: off on either education or income by one point, but not off on race or religion; could be off on two achieved scores.
2	Working	6 or 7: 7 could be off on race or religion but not education or income—or possibly off on 3 achieved points.
1	Low	5 or below: many combinations possible.

It should be noted that this scoring does not allow for a black middle class or a Catholic middle class. While it overrepresents whites and Protestants in the upper two classes, it strictly follows Olsen and Tully's basic classification scheme and is similar to previous measures of socioeconomic status. It also affects all candidate groups equally and does not affect comparativeness. It should be noted, however, that the whole concept of SES needs reconsidering. Status attributes are perceived differently than they were ten or fifteen years ago. Moves toward egalitarianism in the 1970s and wider ethnic and religious acceptance are realities which are not reflected in such scales.

The SES calculation described above is used consistently throughout the data chapters so that changes in SES can be compared across the years. The score used is somewhat limited in that it does not incorporate an occupational prestige score. This score is not generally included because the data is unavailable or classified differently in different studies.

Calculations of mobility in chapter eight are made from Duncan Occupational Status Scores. For simplicity's sake, these scores are arranged in deciles (a low of 02 becomes 0; a high of 94 become 9) and housewives, students, and those with no answer as to occupation are omitted from the calculations. Mobility for the respondents is then measured by the difference in status between the occupation of the respondent's father, and the occupation of the head of the respondent's household.

Five possibilities are determined. If the two occupations have the same first digit, they are considered equal in status. That individual is then considered stable or immobile, remaining at the same level as the individual's father. If, however, there is a five digit difference between the two numbers (such as the difference between a zero and a five, or a four and a nine), then the respondent (even though it might be the head of the household's occupation which was being tabulated and not the respondent's) is considered either very upwardly mobile or very downwardly mobile, depending on position relative to that of the father. A simple upward or downward designation lies in between the categories of "same" and "very" mobile. Thus a crosstabulation of the two Duncan SES decile scores yields a measure of difference.

Power Variables

The questions used in constructing the power variables are listed in chapter eight, and are the same in the 1968, 1972, and 1976 American National Election Studies. The measure of personal anomie results from a tabulation of the answers to three questions, each of which has two extreme answers. A positive answer, showing trust in people is given a value of one; all negative answers are given a value of five. All responses of "don't know," "no answer," or any ambiguous responses are omitted. Any respondent who does not answer all three questions is eliminated from the sample. The scores for the three questions are then added, yielding possible combinations from three to fifteen. A score of three is assigned the value low personal anomie, as it reflects three positive answers. Seven is considered average and eleven or fifteen is considered high. Two negative responses are enough to classify an individual as high; this decision was made from my understanding of the inherent meaning of the scores.

The value of personal powerlessness is constructed in the same manner, except that four questions are involved. Values from four to twenty are possible, scores of four and eight are labeled high personal power, twelve is average, and sixteen and twenty are classified as low.

The value of political anomie is constructed from five questions. Two of the questions have two categories with values of one and five, one being positive and five being negative. Three questions have three values, a score of three given to the in-between response. Thus the possibilities for scores range from five to twenty-five. Five to nine are classified low political anomie, as they represent positive answers; eleven to sixteen are classified as average, and scores of seventeen to twenty-five are classified as high political anomie.

The value of political power consists of four questions, scored in the same way as described above. All four questions have only two answers, the negative score getting a value of one and the positive a value of five. Thus the range runs from four to twenty and scores are classified as four, eight: low political power; twelve, average; and sixteen and twenty, high political power.

The value of institutional power is more complicated, as it consists of four components. Three are individually scored in the following way prior to combining them with the fourth in a measure of institutional power. Faith in Congress, faith in political parties, and faith in the federal government are all measures that consist of crosstabulating one question with two answers and one question with three answers. The crosstabulation looks like this:

		Two-Answer Question	
		Negative	Positive
	Positive	—	high, both answers optimistic
Three-Answer Question	Average	—	—
	Negative	low, both answers pessimistic	—

Those persons falling into the two extreme cells are classified as shown; those in the other cells are labeled average. A low gets a score of one, average a score of two and high a score of three.

A single question is the fourth component of the variable of institutional power. The question is, "How much does having elections make the government pay attention to what people think?" This question has three answers, which are given the following scores: five, a good deal (positive); three, some (average); and one, not much (negative). The answers for all four components are then added together and recoded as follows into a measure of institutional power: a score of four, five, or six is labeled low power; seven, eight, and nine are labeled average; ten, eleven, and twelve are labeled high institutional power.

Statistics Used

The use of epsilon has already been discussed. In a few cases, two coded variables are correlated. Since they are coded, it was impossible to utilize a Pearsonian correlation coefficient because that statistic is only appropriate for interval level data. Since it was certain that there would be a larger number of ties of rank because the codes are so few (three for each variable), Kendall's tau is used as the statistic. This is far more suited to data in which there are a small number of categories than is a Spearman's rank correlation coefficient (rho) (Nie 1970, p. 153; Blalock 1960, p. 317).

Cramer's V is used as a measure of association whenever there are two nominal level variables involved, and gamma is used as an associative measure between two ordinal scales. If the variables are nominal, but mirror each other and are arranged in the same order, gamma is used as the test statistic. Gamma shows direction by sign; zero represents no association, and one shows complete dependence. Means are used only with interval level data (Blalock 1960).

Notes

1. The 1976 CBS News/ *New York Times* data were accessed through the use of a terminal at CBS. Their system language was used to generate the tables.

Bibliography

Abcarian, Gilbert and Stanage, Sherman M. 1965. "Alienation and the Radical Right." *Journal of Politics* 27 (November): pp. 776–96.

Aberbach, Joel D. 1977. "Power Consciousness: A Comparative Analysis." *American Political Science Review* 71 (December): pp. 1544–60.

———. 1973. "Power and Consciousness: A Comparative Analysis." Paper delivered at American Political Science Association (September 4–8) at New Orleans, Louisiana.

———. 1969. "Alienation and Political Behavior." *American Political Science Review* 63 (March): pp. 86–99.

Adams, Val. 1968. "ABC Charges Wallace Aide Seized Film of Shelton Greeting." *New York Times*, June 28, p. 83.

Adorno, T.W.; Frenkel-Brunswick, Else; Levinson, Daniel J.; and Sanford, R. Nevitt. 1950. *The Authoritarian Personality*. New York: W.W. Norton & Co.

Alabama Journal. 1978. "Wallace Accepts UAB Post as Consultant." October 9, p.1.

———. 1964. "The Line in the Dust." March 16.

Alabama Political Research Group. 1976. *The Alabama Message: A View From Within*. Tuscaloosa, Ala.: Alabama Political Research Group.

Albright, Joseph P. 1974. "The Price of Purity." *New York Times Magazine*, September 1, p. 12.

Allen, Maryon. 1979. "Free at Last!" *Washington Post Magazine*, January 21, p. 7.

Almond, Gabriel A. and Verba, Sidney. 1965. *The Civic Culture, Political Attitudes and Democracy in Five Nations*. Boston: Little, Brown.

Alsop, Stewart. 1967. "George Wallace for President." *The Saturday Evening Post* (March 25): 18.

Altman, Lawrence K. 1975. "Wallace Opens 1976 White House Drive; Health Assayed." *New York Times*, November 13, p. 1.

Apple, R.W., Jr. 1976a. "Democrats Meet, Strauss Asks an End of 'Years of Nixon, Ford,' Beame and Carey Join in Attack." *New York Times*, July 13, p. 1.

———. 1976b. "Reagan Tops Ford in North Carolina for First Triumph in a Primary; Carter Easily Defeats Wallace." *New York Times*, March 24, p. 1.

———. 1976c. "Reagan, Wallace Facing Key Tests." *New York Times*, March 21, p. 1.

———. 1976d. "Impact of Florida Vote." *New York Times,* March 10, p. 1.

———. 1976e. "Bayh and Shriver Expected to Quit Democratic Race." *New York Times,* March 4, p. 1.

———. 1976f. "Carter Apparent Winner in Oklahoma's Caucuses." *New York Times,* February 8, p. 44.

———. 1976g. "Wallace Defeats Carter Three-to-One in Mississippi Test." *New York Times,* January 26, p. 1.

———. 1975a. "Daley Again Has a Key Role as King Maker." *New York Times,* December 25, p. 26.

———. 1975b. "Outlook is Good in Massachusetts for Reagan and Wallace Camps." *New York Times,* December 20, p. 28.

———. 1975c. "Carey Maps Plans for Convention." *New York Times,* December 4, p. 27.

———. 1975d. "Reagan is Termed Florida Favorite." *New York Times,* November 17, p. 1.

———. 1975e. "Florida Panhandle Still Wallace's, but Slippage is Seen." *New York Times,* August 3, p. 32.

———. 1975f. "Democratic Governor Discussions of 1976 are Haunted by Thoughts of Wallace." *New York Times,* June 12, p. 17.

———. 1975g. "Study of 3D Party for '76 Approved by Conservatives." *New York Times,* February 17, p. 1.

———. 1975h. "Jackson Enters 1976 Bid; Vows Aid to 'Little People.'" *New York Times,* February 7, p. 1.

———. 1975i. "Complex Rules on Picking Delegates Alter Shape of Democrats' '76 Nomination Drive." *New York Times,* January 21, p. 17.

———. 1973. "Kennedy Speaks at Wallace Fete." *New York Times,* July 5, p. 1.

———. 1972a. "McGovern Shy 130 Votes as Delegate Choice Ends." *New York Times,* June 26, p. 1.

———. 1972b. "'Ghost' Candidates a Factor in Oregon." *New York Times,* May 23, p. 26.

———. 1972c. "Michigan Race: Key Was Busing." *New York Times,* May 18, p. 36.

———. 1972d. "Wallace Campaign is Expected to Peak in Tuesday's Races." *New York Times,* May 14, p. 1.

———. 1972e. "8 Primaries in 2 Weeks Aims at Blue-Collar Vote." *New York Times,* April 23, p. 1.

———. 1972f. "McGovern Winner in Wisconsin; Wallace, Humphrey Vie for 2D; Lindsay, Trailing, Gives Up Race." *New York Times,* April 5, p. 1.

———. 1972g. "When You Put Your Finger in the Air." *New York Times,* March 26, sec. IV, p. 3.

———. 1972h. "Wallace Gain Emerging as Key Campaign Figure." *New York Times,* February 20, p. 1.

———. 1972i. "Two Key Election Issues." *New York Times,* February 18, p. 18.

———. 1972j. "O'Brien Says Vote for Wallace is Vote for the Republican Ticket." *New York Times,* January 15, p. 14.

———. 1972k. "Wallace's Move: A Threat to Muskie, Possible End of Jackson." *New York Times,* January 5, p. 23.

———. 1971a. "Wallace Drive Grows, But Race is in Doubt." *New York Times,* June 25, p. 36.

———. 1971b. "1968 Political Campaigns Set $300-Million Record." *New York Times,* June 20, p. 1.

————. 1971c. "Nixon Said to Favor San Diego in '72." *New York Times,* June 3, p. 28.

————. 1971d. "Nixon Planning to Clarify Calley Case Intervention." *New York Times,* April 9, p. 10.

————. 1970a. "Elections 1: Wallace Victory May Affect '72 Race." *New York Times,* June 7, sec. IV, p. 1.

————. 1970b. "Wallace Defeats Brewer in Runoff for Governorship." *New York Times,* June 3, p. 1.

————. 1970c. "Wallace-Brewer Race Close But Mild." *New York Times,* May 29, p. 27.

————. 1970d. "Neither Wallace, with Ad Blitz, Nor Gov. Brewer is Expected to Win Alabama Majority Tomorrow." *New York Times,* May 4, p. 29.

————. 1970e. "Wallace Battles For His Political Life." *New York Times,* May 3, sec. IV, p. 4.

————. 1968. "Rockefeller Wary of Reagan Ticket." *New York Times,* June 25, p. 1.

Apter, David E., ed. 1964. *Ideology and Discontent.* London: Free Press of Glencoe.

Armstrong, Forrest Harrell. 1970. "George C. Wallace: Insurgent on the Right." Ph.D. dissertation, The University of Michigan.

Ash, Roberta. 1972. *Social Movements in America.* Chicago, Markham.

Augusta Courier. (Augusta, Georgia) 1973. "Wallace Vote is the Wild Card of U.S. Presidential Politics." January 8, p. 1.

Ayres, B. Drummond, Jr. 1976a. "Mrs. Wallace's Wiretap Spurs Questions on Marriage." *New York Times,* September 11, p. 8.

————. 1976b. "Democratic Unity Reflects Changes in South." *New York Times,* July 16, p. 1.

————. 1976c. "Wallace At the End of a Long Trail." *New York Times,* June 7, p. 1.

————. 1976d. "Results in Alabama Show Wallace Strength Fading." *New York Times,* May 6, p. 43.

————. 1976e. "Wallace Takes an Early Lead in Alabama." *New York Times,* May 5, p. 27.

————. 1976f. "Carter a Threat to Wallace in Home State Tomorrow." *New York Times,* May 3, p. 10.

————. 1976g. "Wallace, Running Low on Cash, Prepares for Drive in Ga." *New York Times,* April 28, p. 20.

————. 1976h. "For Wallace, It Is All Over But the Exit." *New York Times,* April 11, sec. IV, p. 1.

————. 1976i. "Wallace, Despite Four Defeats, Vows to Continue His Campaign." *New York Times,* April 8, p. 31.

————. 1976j. "Wallace Trims Wisconsin Drive." *New York Times,* April 3, p. 12.

————. 1976k. "Wallace Openly Despairs About His Political Future." *New York Times,* March 25, p. 30.

————. 1976l. "Wallace Drive in Disarray; Aides Decide to Retrench." *New York Times,* March 18, p. 1.

————. 1976m. "'Phony Health Issue' Blamed by. Wallace." *New York Times,* March 11, p. 32.

————. 1976n. "Wallace Pushing Hard For Wide Florida Vote." *New York Times,* March 9, p. 22.

————. 1976o. "Wallace Tactics Appear to Indicate Possible Acceptance of a Role in a Third Party." *New York Times,* March 7, p. 41.

————. 1976p. "A Confident Wallace Ends Drive With Busing Attack." *New York Times,* March 2, p. 20.

————. 1976q. "Wallace Cheered in South Boston." *New York Times,* February 22, p. 45.

————. 1976r. "Wallace Hopes Splintered Votes Will Aid Him in Massachusetts." *New York Times,* February 19, p. 24.

————. 1976s. "Wallace is Regaining Cockiness and Drawing Overflow Crowds." *New York Times,* February 10, p. 29.

————. 1976t. "Wallace Isolated by Tight Security." *New York Times,* February 1, p. 34.

————. 1976u. "Wallace Begins Attack on Busing." *New York Times,* January 30, p. 26.

————. 1976v. "Shooting Inquiry Asked by Wallace." *New York Times,* January 12, p. 18.

————. 1976w. "'Exotic liberals,' 'Ultra-Elitists' Are Wallace Targets in Boston." *New York Times,* January 10, p. 17.

————. 1976x. "Doubts Rise on Wallace's '76 Strength; Some Pet Issues Have Lost Their Magic." *New York Times,* January 2, p. 1.

————. 1975a. "Wallace Opens 1976 White House Drive." *New York Times,* November 13, p. 1.

————. 1975b. "Wallace Prepares for European Trip to Show He is Fit." *New York Times,* October 11, p. 1.

————. 1975c. "Wallace Assails Foreign Policy." *New York Times,* September 17, p. 13.

————. 1975d. "Wallace is Close to GOP Oriented Group." *New York Times,* June 22, p. 34.

————. 1975e. "Wallace, Critics and Statistics Differ on Alabama Achievements Since 1963." *New York Times,* May 5, p. 22.

————. 1975f. "Wallace Can't Win, But Can't be Ignored Either." *New York Times,* April 20, sec. IV, p. 5.

————. 1975g. "Wallace Sees Halting of Some State Primaries as Party Chiefs' Plot Against Him." *New York Times,* April 10, p. 33.

————. 1975h. "Wallace Aides Organize All Over U.S." *New York Times,* March 30, p. 27.

————. 1975i. "Governor Wallace, Offering Lessons in Racial Harmony, Is Sworn In for His Third Term." *New York Times,* January 21, p. 14.

————. 1974a. "Julian Bond to Enter Presidential Primaries in '76." *New York Times,* October 8, p. 30.

————. 1974b. "And George Wallace Will Probably Be in It." *New York Times,* September 29, sec. IV, p. 3.

————. 1974c. "Wallace Accused on Hiring of Blacks." *New York Times,* September 27, p. 37.

————. 1974d. "Alabama Primary Won by Wallace." *New York Times,* May 8, p. 41.

————. 1974e. "Wallace Likely to Win Primary Today; Seeks Black Support for National Bid." *New York Times,* May 7, p. 30.

————. 1974f. "Black Clubbed in Selma Assails Blacks Aiding Wallace." *New York Times,* April 24, p. 22.

———. 1974g. "Nixon to Visit Huntsville on 'Honor America' Day." *New York Times,* February 18, p. 18

———. 1973a. "A Highway Funds Scandal Threatens Wallace's Political Future." *New York Times,* November 30, p. 24.

———. 1973b. "Southern Black Mayors Give Wallace Standing Ovation at a Conference." *New York Times,* November 19, p. 25.

———. 1972. "Agnew Censures Muskie's Attack." *New York Times,* March 16, p. 31.

Azbell, Joe (Director of Public Relations, Wallace Campaign). 1978. Interviews with J. Carlson. 29 November, at Montgomery, Alabama.

———. 1974a. Interview with J. Carlson. 23 January at Montgomery, Alabama.

———. 1974b. Interview with J. Carlson. 22 January at Montgomery, Alabama.

———. 1974c. Interview with J. Carlson. 21 January at Montgomery, Alabama.

Bablin, Mark (New York/New Jersey/Pennsylvania Coordinator, 1976 Wallace Campaign). 1975. Interview with J. Carlson. 27 October at New York, N.Y.

Barnicle, Mike. 1974. "Busing Puts Burden on Working Class, Black and White." *Boston Globe,* October 15.

Bass, Jack and Walter DeVries. *The Transformation of Southern Politics; Social Change and Political Consequence Since 1945.* New York: Basic Books.

Bauer, Raymond A., ed. 1966. *Social Indicators.* Cambridge, Mass.: M.I.T. Press.

Behn, Dick. 1975. "Swinging with Reagan and Wallace; an Odyssey." *Ripon Forum* 11 (May 15): 1–3.

Bell, Daniel, ed. 1963. *The Radical Right.* Garden City, N.Y.: Anchor Books, Doubleday.

———. 1955. *The New American Right.* New York: Criterion Books.

Bendix, Reinhard and Lipset, Seymour Martin. 1966. *Class, Status, and Power: Social Stratification in Comparative Perspective,* 2nd ed. New York: The Free Press.

Berelson, Bernard R.; Lazarsfeld, Paul F.; and McPhee, William N. 1954. *Voting: A Study of Opinion Formation in a Presidential Campaign.* Chicago: University of Chicago Press.

Bernard, Bina. 1974. "Wallace: The Healing Power of Politics and His Cornelia." *People,* May 6, pp. 5–9.

Bierstedt, Robert. 1950. "An Analysis of Social Power." *American Sociological Review* 15 (December): pp. 730–38.

Bigart, Homer. 1969. "Wallace Has No 'Political Plans,' But His Staff in Alabama is Larger Than That of National Democrats." *New York Times,* June 22, p. 34.

———. 1968. "Nominee is Heard on TV in South." *New York Times,* October 4, p. 50.

Birmingham News. 1957. "Wallace Plays 'Government by Contempt.'" January 8.

Black, Earl. 1976. *Southern Governors and Civil Rights; Racial Segregation as a Campaign Issue in the Second Reconstruction.* Cambridge, Mass.: Harvard University Press.

Blalock, Hubert M., Jr. 1960. *Social Statistics.* New York: McGraw-Hill.

Blau, Peter. 1969. "Differentiation of Power." In *Political Power: A Reader in Theory and Research,* ed. Roderick Bell, David V. Edwards, R. Harrison Wagner. New York: Free Press.

Blauner, Robert. 1972. *Racial Oppression in America.* New York: Harper and Row.

Bone, Hugh A. 1967. "American Party Politics, Elections and Voting Behavior."

Annals of the American Academy of Political and Social Science 372 (July): 124–37.

Boorstin, Daniel J. 1953. *The Genius of American Politics.* Chicago: University of Chicago Press.

Borders, William. 1968. "Wallace Turns to Connecticut." *New York Times,* August 4, p. 49.

Brill, Steven. 1975a. "The Wallace Watch." *New York Magazine* 8 (June 30): 8–9.

———. 1975b. "George Wallace Is Even Worse Than You Think He Is." *New York Magazine* 8 (March 17): 37.

Broder, David S. 1966. "Romney Bars 'Blank Check' Backing on Vietnam." *New York Times,* July 5, p. 18.

Brown, W. Aggrey. 1971. "Theories of Racism and Strategies of New World African Liberation." in Vernon J. Dixon and Badi G. Foster, eds. *Beyond Black or White: An Alternate America.* Boston: Little, Brown.

Burdick, Eugene and Brodbeck, Arthur J., eds. 1959. *American Voting Behavior.* Glencoe, Ill.: Free Press.

Burnham, Walter Dean. 1968. "Election 1968—The Abortive Landslide." *Transaction* 6 (December): 18–24.

Caddell, Patrick and Robert Shrum. "White Horse Pale Rider." *Rolling Stone,* October 24, p. 42.

Camp, Billy Joe (Press Secretary to Governor Wallace). 1974. Interview with J. Carlson. 25 January at Montgomery, Ala.

Campbell, Angus. 1968. "How We Voted—and Why." *The Nation* 207 (November 25): 550–53.

———. 1964. "Voters and Elections: Past and Present." *Journal of Politics* 26 (November): 745–57.

Campbell, Angus; Converse, Philip E.; Miller, Warren E.; and Stokes, Donald E. 1966. *Elections and the Political Order.* New York: John Wiley.

———. 1964. *The American Voter: An Abridgement.* New York: John Wiley.

———. 1960. *The American Voter.* New York: John Wiley.

Campbell, Angus; Gurin, Gerald; and Miller, Warren E. 1954. *The Voter Decides.* Evanston, Ill.: Row, Peterson.

Campbell, Angus and Kahn, Robert L. 1952. *The People Elect a President.* Ann Arbor, Mich.: Survey Research Center, pamphlet.

Campbell, Angus and Stokes, Donald E. 1959. "Partisan Attitudes and the Presidential Vote." In *American Voting Behavior,* ed. Eugene Burdick and Arthur J. Brodbeck. Glencoe, Ill.: Free Press.

Campbell, James E. 1976. "Sincere and Sophisticated Voting: The Wallace Vote." Paper delivered at American Political Science Association (September 2–5) at Chicago, Illinois.

Carlson, Jody. 1976a. "Racism Among Wallace Supporters: 1964–1972." Paper delivered at Society for the Study of Social Problems (August 27–30) at New York, N.Y.

———. 1976b. Observations at Democratic National Convention (July) at New York, N.Y.

———. 1976c. "The Politics of Powerlessness: The Wallace Campaigns of 1964, 1968 and 1972." Ph.D. dissertation, Rutgers University.

Carroll, Maurice. 1976. "Wallace Driving for Delegates in All But 3 of State's Districts." *New York Times,* January 16, p. 58.

Carter, Jimmy. 1976. "'A New Beginning;' Presentation by Jimmy Carter to the Platform Committee of the Democratic Party." June 16.

Carter, Luther J. 1968. "George C. Wallace: He's Not Just Whistling Dixie." *Science* 162 (October 25): 436–40.

Cash, W.F. 1957. *The Mind of the South.* New York: Alfred A. Knopf.

Charlton, Linda. 1976. "Jackson Attacks Wallace in a Change of Strategy." *New York Times,* February 12, p. 28.

———. 1972. "Sanford Future Unclear After Defeat in Carolina." *New York Times,* May 8, p. 42.

———. 1970. "Wallace, in City Says U.S. Suffers." *New York Times,* December 5, p. 23.

Chester, Lewis; Hodgson, Godfrey; and Page, Bruce. 1969. *An American Melodrama; The Presidential Campaign of 1968.* New York: Viking Press.

Cleghorn, Reese. 1968. "Radicalism: Southern Style; a Commentary on Regional Extremism of the Right." Pamphlet for the Southern Regional Council and the American Jewish Committee Institute of Human Relations.

Coleman, James S. 1973. "Loss of Power." *American Sociological Review* 38 (February): 1–17.

Commager, Henry Steele. 1950. *The American Mind: An Interpretation of American Thought and Character Since the 1880's.* New Haven: Yale University Press.

Converse, Philip E. 1967. "Information Flow and the Stability of Partisan Attitudes." In *Elections and the Political Order,* ed. Angus Campbell, Philip E. Converse, and Warren E. Miller. New York: John Wiley.

Converse, Philip E.; Miller, Warren E.; Rusk, Jerrold G.; and Wolfe, Arthur C. 1969. "Continuity and Change in American Politics: Parties and Issues in the 1968 Elections." *American Political Science Review* 63 (December): 1083–1105.

Converse, Philip E.; Clausen, Aage R.; and Miller, Warren E. 1965. "Electoral Myth and Reality: The 1964 Election." *American Political Science Review* 59 (June): 321–36.

Conway, M. Margaret. 1968. "The White Backlash Re-examined: Wallace and the 1964 Primaries." *Social Science Quarterly* 49 (December): 710–19.

Cramer, M. Richard. 1963. "School Desegregation and New Industry: The Southern Community Leaders Viewpoints." *Social Forces* 41: 384.

Crass, Philip. 1976. *The Wallace Factor.* New York: Mason/Charter.

Crewdson, John M. 1974. "Dates From House Panel Tell of Political Moves." *New York Times,* July 12, p. 22.

———. 1973. "Sabotage by Segretti: Network of Amateurs." *New York Times,* July 10, p. 1.

Crouse, Timothy. 1972. *The Boys on the Bus.* New York: Random House.

Dahl, Robert A. 1956. *Preface to Democratic Theory.* Chicago: University of Chicago Press.

Dahl, Robert A. and Tufte, Edward R. 1973. *Size and Democracy.* Stanford, Calif.: Stanford University Press.

Daily Argus (Mt. Vernon, N.Y.). 1978. "Wallace: As his Career Nears its End, the Voice of the Old South Says it's Better Like it is Now." December 7.

Dauphin, Alton (Assistant Campaign Director and Financial Director, Wallace Campaign). 1974. Interview with J. Carlson. 25 January at Montgomery, Alabama.

Davidowicz, Lucy. 1964. "The Politics of Prejudice: Wallace in the Presidential Primaries in Wisconsin, Indiana and Maryland." American Jewish Committee, Mimeographed.

Delaney, Paul. 1975. "G.O.P. May Suffer in Wisconsin Vote." *New York Times,* December 29, p. 17.

———. 1972. "Maryland Delegates May Quit Wallace." *New York Times,* May 9, p. 24.

Dorman, Michael. 1976. *The George Wallace Myth.* New York: Bantam Books.

Edelman, Murray. 1967. *The Symbolic Uses of Politics.* Urbana, Ill.: University of Illinois Press.

Egerton, John. 1974. *The Americanization of Dixie: The Southernization of America.* New York: Harper's Magazine Press.

Eitzen, D. Stanley. 1970. "Status Inconsistency and Wallace Supporters in a Midwestern City." *Social Forces* 48 (June): 493–98.

Elazar, Daniel J. 1972. *American Federalism: A View From the States.* 2nd ed. New York: Thomas Y. Crowell.

Eldersveld, Samuel J. 1951. "Theory and Method in Voting Behavior Research." *Journal of Politics* 13 (February): 70–87.

Ellerin, Milton. 1972. "The George Wallace Candidacy—An Interim Report." Report of Trend Analyses Division, The American Jewish Committee (March), Mimeographed.

———. 1968. "The Wallace Movement—A Post Election Appraisal." Prepared for Trends Analyses, Division Report, The American Jewish Committee (December), Mimeographed.

Elliott, Lou. 1978. "Advertising Agency for Wallace Switches to Foe for Senate Race." *Alabama Journal,* March 2, p. 1.

Emerson, Richard M. 1962. "Power-Dependence Relations." *American Sociological Review* 27 (February): 31–41.

Epstein, Benjamin R. and Forster, Arnold. 1967. *The Radical Right. Report on the John Birch Society and Its Allies.* New York: Vintage.

Evans, Robert R., ed. 1973. *Social Movements: A Reader and Source Book.* Chicago: Rand McNally.

Evans, Roland and Robert Novak. 1975. "Wallace's Big Issue." *New York Post Magazine.* October 24, p. 39.

"Face the Nation." 1964. Transcript of telecast, 19 July 1964. CBS-TV Network.

Fackre, Gabriel. 1969. "The Blue-Collar White and the Far Right." *Christian Century* 86 (May 7): 645–48.

Faris, Robert E.L., ed. 1964. *Handbook of Modern Sociology.* Chicago, Rand McNally.

Farrell, William E. 1976a. "Reagan Defeats Ford in Indiana and Also Wins Georgia Primary; Carter is Victor in Both States." *New York Times,* May 5, p. 1.

———. 1976b. "Ford Decisively Defeats Reagan in Illinois Voting; Carter is a Solid Winner." *New York Times,* March 17, p. 1.

———. 1976c. "President Expected to Win Illinois Primary Tuesday." *New York Times,* March 14, p. 14.

———. 1973. "Kennedy Censured by SCLC for Appearance with Wallace." *New York Times,* August 18, p. 28.

Farris, Charles D. 1956. "'Authoritarianism' as a Political Behavior Variable." *Journal of Politics* 18 (February): 61–82.

Fenton, John H. 1968a. "Wallace Enlists Aid of Students." *New York Times,* July 12, p. 34.

———. 1968b. "Wallace Stumps in Massachusetts." *New York Times,* June 30, p. 37.

Ferkiss, Victor C. 1962. "Political and Intellectual Origins of American Radicalism, Right and Left." *Annals of the American Academy of Political and Social
Science* 344 (November): 1–12.

Finifter, Ada W. 1970. "Dimensions of Political Alienation." *American Political
Science Review* 64 (June): 389–410.

Fischer, Claude S. 1973. "On Urban Alienation and Anomie: Powerlessness and
Social Isolation." *American Sociological Review* 38 (June): 311–26.

Flanigan, William H. 1972. *Political Behavior of the American Electorate*. 2nd ed.
Boston: Allyn and Bacon, Inc.

Flanigan, William H. and Nancy H. Zingale. 1979. *Political Behavior of the
American Electorate*. 4th ed. Boston: Allyn and Bacon, Inc.

Flint, Jerry M. 1972a. "Michigan Democrats Avoid Split." *New York Times*,
June 12, p. 30.

———. 1972b. "Wallace Rebuked on TV by Michigan Democrats." *New York
Times*, May 15, p. 30.

———. 1968. "Wallace Wins Over Humphrey in Auto Union Poll." *New York
Times*, October 6, p. 75.

Florida. 1972. *Laws of Florida*. 72–3: p. 115.

Forster, Arnold and Epstein, Benjamin R. 1964. *Danger on the Right*. New York:
Random House.

Fox, Al. 1964. "Wallace Receives Rousing Reception." *Birmingham News*,
April 2, p. 1.

Frady, Marshall. 1975. "The Return of George Wallace." *New York Review of
Books* 22 (October 30): 16–26.

———. 1968. *Wallace*. New York: Meridian Books, World Publishing Company.

———. 1967. "Governor and Mister Wallace." *Atlantic Monthly* 220 (August):
35–40.

Frankel, Max. 1972a. "Nixon Elected In Landslide." *New York Times*, November 8, p. 1.

———. 1972b. "Humphrey and Muskie Yield to McGovern." *New York Times*,
July 12, p. 1.

———. 1970. "The President and His Action in the Latest 'Crisis.'" *New York
Times*, April 11, p. 16.

———. 1968a. "Nixon Wins By a Thin Margin, Pleads for Reunited Nation." *New
York Times*, November 7, p. 1.

———. 1968b. "Humphrey Terms Campaign a Poll of Human Rights." *New York
Times*, September 9, p. 1.

———. 1968c. "Across the Land, Wallace Insists a Vote For Him Won't Be
Wasted." *New York Times*, July 30, p. 27.

Franklin, Ben A. 1973. "$100 for Wallace is Called Illegal." *New York Times*,
October 31, p. 22.

———. 1972. "Kennedy Guarded by Secret Service." *New York Times*, May 16,
p. 1.

———. 1968a. "Was It The Last Hurrah of George Corley Wallace?" *New York
Times*, November 10, p. 2.

———. 1968b. "'Wallace Phenomenon' Appears Contained in South." *New York
Times*, November 6, p. 23.

———. 1968c. "To the Polls." *New York Times*, November 3, Sec. IV, p. 2.

———. 1968d. "Agnew Makes Bid for 'Protest' Vote." *New York Times*, October 8, p. 33.

————. 1968e. "Agnew in Alaska on One-Stop Visit." *New York Times*, October 6, p. 77.

————. 1968f. "The New Wallace is a 'National Candidate.'" *New York Times*, September 15, Sec. IV, p. 2.

————. 1968g. "Wallace Defends Chicago's Police." *New York Times*, August 30, p. 15.

————. 1968h. "Wallace Says He Influenced GOP on Agnew." *New York Times*, August 10, p. 11.

————. 1968i. "Wallace Showered with Donations—Big and Little." *New York Times*, February 27, p. 28.

————. 1968j. "Wallace in Race; Will 'Run to Win.'" *New York Times*, February 9, p. 1.

————. 1968k. "Wallace Campaign Will Move North This Week." *New York Times*, January 29, p. 20.

————. 1967a. "Alabamians Go West to Help Wallace." *New York Times*, December 3, p. 70.

————. 1967b. "Wallace Accepts Support of Klan." *New York Times*, October 1, p. 41.

————. 1965. "Wallace Seeking Statesman Image." *New York Times*, September 6, p. 7.

————. 1964a. "Wallace Renews Maryland Drive." *New York Times*, October 20, p. 26.

————. 1964b. "Wallace Renews Appeal to North." *New York Times*, September 17, p. 27.

————. 1964c. "Wallace Weighs His Candidacy in View of Goldwater's Victory." *New York Times*, July 19, p. 51.

————. 1964d. "Maryland's Vote Held Anti Negro." *New York Times*, May 21, p. 1.

————. 1964e. "Brewster Victor, Wallace Has 43% in Maryland Vote." *New York Times*, May 20, p. 1.

————. 1964f. "Wallace Foes Bid for Union Votes." *New York Times*, May 18, p. 16.

————. 1964g. "Wallace Impugns Negroes' Motives." *New York Times*, May 16, p. 10.

————. 1964h. "'Hate' Groups Back Wallace Bid." *New York Times*, May 14, p. 27.

————. 1964i. "8 in House Back Wallace's Drive." *New York Times*, May 13, p. 21.

————. 1964j. "Cambridge, Md. Negroes Routed By Tear Gas After Wallace Talk." *New York Times*, May 12, p. 1.

————. 1964k. "Collegians Treat Wallace Kindly." *New York Times*, May 10, p. 69.

————. 1964l. "Brewster Attack, Johnson Visit Bolster Drive Against Wallace." *New York Times*, May 8, p. 18.

————. 1964m. "Wallace Making a Costly Effort." *New York Times*, May 3, p. 73.

————. 1964n. "Democrats Move to Stop Wallace." *New York Times*, April 26, p. 76.

————. 1964o. "Wallace Enters Maryland Race With Attack On Civil Rights Bill." *New York Times*, March 10, p. 29.

Franks, Lucinda. 1976. "Wallace's Victory in Carolina is Narrow." *New York Times*, March 1, p. 32.

Frost, David. 1978. *I Gave Them a Sword: Behind the Scenes of the Nixon Interviews.* New York: Ballentine.

Gabriel, Ralph H. 1963. *Traditional Values in American Life.* New York: Harcourt, Brace and World.

Gans, Herbert J. 1972. "The American Malaise." *The New York Times Magazine,* February 6, p. 16.

George C. Wallace Newsletter. 1970. 2, no. 3 (May 1970).

Geschwender, James A., ed. 1971. *Black Revolt.* Englewood Cliffs, N.J.: Prentice-Hall.

———. 1967. "Continuities in Theories of Status Consistency and Cognitive Dissonance." *Social Forces* 46 (December): 160–71.

Goldhamer, Herbert and Shils, Edward A. 1939. "Types of Power and Status." *American Journal of Sociology* 45 (September): 171–82.

Goldwin, Robert A., ed. 1967. *Left, Right and Center: Essays on Liberalism and Conservatism in the United States.* Chicago: Rand McNally.

Graham, Fred P. 1968. "Wallace Placed on Ballot in Ohio." *New York Times,* October 16, p. 1.

Grasmick, Harold George. 1973. "Social Change and the Wallace Movement in the South." Ph.D. dissertation, University of North Carolina.

Greenhaw, Wayne. 1976. *Watch Out For George Wallace.* Englewood Cliffs, N.J.: Prentice Hall.

Gregor, A. James. 1969. *The Ideology of Fascism: the Rationale of Totalitarianism.* New York: Free Press.

———. 1968. *Contemporary Radical Ideologies: Totalitarian Thought in the Twentieth Century.* New York: Random House.

Griffin, Michael (Campaign Aide, Liaison between Democratic National Committee and Wallace Campaign). 1978. Interviews with J. Carlson, 30 November–1 December, at Montgomery, Ala.

———. 1974. Interview with J. Carlson, 22 January at Montgomery, Ala.

Grupp, Fred W., Jr. 1969. "The Political Perspectives of Birch Society Members." In *The American Right Wing: Readings in Political Behavior,* ed. Robert A. Schoenberger. New York: Holt, Rinehart and Winston.

Guest, Avery M. 1975. "Comment on House and Mason." *American Sociological Review* 40 (April): 365–67.

———. 1974. "Subjective Powerlessness in the United States: Some Longtitudinal Trends." *Social Science Quarterly* 54: 827–42.

Gusfield, Joseph R. 1963. *Symbolic Crusade; Status Politics and the American Temperance Movement.* Urbana: University of Illinois Press.

———. 1962. "Mass Society and Extremist Politics." *American Sociological Review* 27 (February): 19–30.

Hamilton, Richard F. 1972. *Class and Politics in the United States.* New York: John Wiley & Sons.

Harris, Louis. 1964a. "Wallace's Candidacy More Costly to Goldwater than to Johnson." *Washington Post,* July 10.

———. 1964b. "Indiana Governor's Unpopularity May Give 30% of Vote to Wallace." *Washington Post,* May 4.

———. 1964c. "Poll Gives Wallace Three Votes Out of Ten." *Indianapolis News,* May 4.

Harris, Patricia Ann. 1971. "Socio-Economic Status, Political Alienation and Right Wing Extremism as Determinants of the Wallace Vote in 1968: a Multivariate Analysis." Ph.D. dissertation, Louisiana State University and Agricultural and Mechanical College.

Hartz, Louis. 1955. *The Liberal Tradition in America: an Interpretation of American Political Thought Since the Revolution.* New York: Harcourt, Brace.

Havard, William C., ed. 1972. *The Changing Politics of the South.* Baton Rouge, La.: Louisiana State University Press.

Hendrickson, Frances. 1976. Telephone interview with J. Carlson. 1 April in Oklahoma City, Oklahoma.

Herbers, John A. 1974. "Nixon Assails 'Distorted View that America is Sick!'" *New York Times,* February 19, p. 1.

———. 1972a. "Wallace's Platform Proposals Rejected." *New York Times,* July 12, p. 1.

———. 1972b. "Democrats Assured of a Platform Fight." *New York Times,* June 28, p. 1.

———. 1972c. "Democrats Vote Pro-Busing Plan." *New York Times,* June 27, p. 1.

———. 1972d. "Liberal Democrats Picked to Draft Party's Platform." *New York Times,* June 24, p. 12.

———. 1970. "Nixon Aides Vow Wide Integration." *New York Times,* June 5, p. 1.

———. 1968. "Nixon Holds Most of Support in South by Promising Conservative Stand on Rights." *New York Times,* August 8, p. 24.

———. 1965. "Gov. Wallace Presses for Second Term." *New York Times,* October 3, p. 5.

———. 1964a. "Election Called Blow to Wallace." *New York Times,* November 8, p. 84.

———. 1964b. "Elector Victory Buoys Wallace." *New York Times,* May 7, p. 20.

Hersh, Seymour M. 1973a. "Anti-Wallace Aid Laid to Kalmbach." *New York Times,* May 29, p. 1.

———. 1973b. "Investigators Term GOP Spying a Widespread Attempt to Insure Weak Democratic Nominee in 1972." *New York Times,* May 3, p. 1.

Hill, Gladwin. 1968. "Wallace Buoyed by Coast Backing." *New York Times,* January 4, p. 20.

———. 1967. "Wallace Group on Coast Opens Campaign for 1968." *New York Times,* June 21, p. 28.

Hoffman, Victor and Strietelmeier, John. 1964. "Gary's Rank and File Reaction." *The Reporter* 31 (September 10): 28–9.

Hofstadter, Richard. 1955. "The Pseudo-Conservative Revolt." In *The Radical Right,* ed. Daniel Bell. Garden City, N.Y.: Anchor Books.

Hollingsworth, J. Rogers. 1965. "Populism: The Problem of Rhetoric and Reality." *Agricultural History* 39 (April): 81–85.

Horowitz, Irving Louis. 1968a. *Professing Sociology: Studies in the Life Cycle of Social Science.* Chicago: Aldine.

———. 1968b. "Radicalism and Americanism: A critique of Daniel Bell's Thesis of the Radical Right Based upon a Content Analysis of *American Opinion.*" Mimeographed.

House, Jack, ed. 1969. *George Wallace Tells It Like It Is.* Selma, Ala.: Dallas Publishing Co.

House, Jack. 1969. *Lady of Courage.* Montgomery, Alabama: League Press.

House, James S. and William M. Mason. 1975a. "Political Alienation in America, 1952–1968." *American Sociological Review* 40 (April): 123–47.

————. 1975b. "Reply to Guest." *American Sociological Review* 40 (April): 367–76.

Howard, Milo (Director, Archives and History, State of Alabama). 1974. Interview with J. Carlson. 27 January at Montgomery, Ala.

Huber, Joan and Form, William H. 1973. *Income and Ideology: An Analysis of the American Political Formula.* New York: Free Press.

Huie, William Bradford. 1976. "The Truth About the Lie that Made George Wallace Famous." *Village Voice* 21 (January 12): 1.

————. 1968. "Alabamians Against Wallace." *Look* 32 (April 30): 50–57.

Hunter, Marjorie. 1975. "Guard for '76 Candidates Urged." *New York Times,* September 24, p. 1.

————. 1972. "Nixon's Plan Splits Rivals; Ervin Leads Busing Attack." *New York Times,* March 18, p. 1.

Husbands, C.T. 1972. "The Campaign Organizations and Patterns of Popular Support of George C. Wallace in Wisconsin and Indiana in 1964 and 1968." Ph.D. dissertation, University of Chicago.

Hynson, Lawrence McKee, Jr. 1972. "Status Inconsistency, Classification and the George Wallace Support in the 1968 Presidential Elections." Ph.D. dissertation, University of Tennessee.

Indianapolis Star. 1964. "Letters on Race Issue Run 3–1 Against Welsh." April 21.

Ingalls, Leonard. 1964. "Poll Calls Lodge GOP's Top Hope." *New York Times,* April 7, p. 20.

Janowitz, Morris and Marvick, Dwaine. 1953. "Authoritarianism and Political Behavior." *Public Opinion Quarterly* 17 (Summer): 185–201.

Janowitz, Morris and Miller, Warren E. 1952. "The Index of Political Predisposition in the 1948 Election." *Journal of Politics* 14: 710–27.

Janson, Donald. 1972a. "Humphrey Tops McGovern in Vote in Pennsylvania: McGovern Wins Bay State." *New York Times,* April 26, p. 1.

————. 1972b. "Pennsylvania Bill Begun by Wallace." *New York Times,* April 18, p. 38.

————. 1969. "Wallace Endorses the Work of Christian Crusade." *New York Times,* August 3, p. 48.

Jenkins, Roy. 1978. "Allen's Death Rails Politics in Alabama." *New York Times,* June 3, p. 8.

————. 1976. "U.S. Flag Back on Top in Alabama." *New York Times,* October 14, p. 1.

————. 1975. "Often-Embattled Southern Judge is Honored." *New York Times,* April 21, p. 20.

————. 1974. "Black Vote for Wallace is Put at 20–25% in Alabama Primary." *New York Times,* May 9, p. 50.

————. 1966. "Mr. and Mrs. Wallace Run for Governor of Alabama." *New York Times Magazine,* April 24, p. 28.

Jennings, M. Kent and Zeigler, L. Harmon, eds. 1966. *The Electoral Process.* Englewood Cliffs, N.J.: Prentice-Hall.

Johnson, Thomas A. 1976a. "Wallace Assures Scottsboro Survivor Alabama is One of the Best States." *New York Times,* December 2, p. 30.

————. 1976b. "Last of Scottsboro 9 is Pardoned; He Draws a Lesson for Everybody." *New York Times,* October 26, p. 1.

————. 1976c. "Into the Ring and Just About Out." *New York Times,* March 28.

Jones, Bill. 1966. *The Wallace Story.* Northport, Ala.: American Southern Publishing Co.

Kelly, Dennis K. and Chambliss, William J. 1966. "Status Consistency and Political Attitudes." *American Sociological Review* 31 (June): 375–82.

Kendall, Robert (former Alabama State Senator). 1974. Interview with J. Carlson. 27 January at Montgomery, Alabama.

Kenkel, William F. 1956. "The Relationship Between Status Consistency and Politico-Economic Attitudes." *American Sociological Review* 21 (June): 365–69.

Kenworthy, E.W. 1968. "Nixon Strategy in South." *New York Times,* October 5, p. 20.

———. 1964a. "Alabama Rejects Loyalty Oath; Democrats Begin Session Today, Pledge Foreign Policy Restraint." *New York Times,* August 24, p. 1.

———. 1964b. "Mississippi Factions Clash Before Convention Panel." *New York Times,* August 23, p. 1.

———. 1964c. "Senators Doubt Wallace Impact on Rights Action." *New York Times,* May 21, p. 1.

Key, V.O., Jr. 1949. *Southern Politics in State and Nation.* New York: Vintage Books.

Kifner, John. 1978. "Busing Complicates Massachusetts Race." *New York Times,* February 27, p. 10.

———. 1976. "Strong Organization Held Key to Jackson's Victory." *New York Times,* March 4, p. 18.

Killian, Lewis M. 1970. *White Southerners.* New York: Random House.

———. 1964. "Social Movements." In *Handbook of Modern Sociology,* ed. Robert E.L. Faris. Chicago: Rand McNally.

King, Seth S. 1976. "Jackson First in Delegate Race in N.Y.; Udall in Second Place; Carter Tops Udall in Wisconsin." *New York Times,* April 7, p. 1.

———. 1973. "Wallace to Stay in Political Ring." *New York Times,* June 6, p. 27.

———. 1972a. "Indiana Blacks Aided Humphrey." *New York Times,* May 4, p. 30.

———. 1972b. "Humphrey Indiana Victor; Jackson Quits Primaries." *New York Times,* May 3, p. 1.

King, Wayne. 1976. "Georgians Back Carter, Reagan." *New York Times,* May 5, p. 76.

———. 1975. "Sanford Pins Victory Hope on His Non-Political Stance." *New York Times,* December 29, p. 1.

Klein, Joe. 1974. "The Ministry of George C. Wallace." *Rolling Stone,* October 24, pp. 32–41.

Kneeland, Douglas E. 1976. "Jackson Lays Result to Coalition." *New York Times,* March 3, p. 16.

———. 1975. "Bentsen Problem A Lack of National Recognition." *New York Times,* December 25, p. 1.

———. 1972a. "Wallace Write-Ins Pushed in California." *New York Times,* June 3, p. 12.

———. 1972b. "McGovern Gains 54 of Delegates in Wisconsin Race." *New York Times,* April 6, p. 1.

———. 1972c. "Wallace Runs a Close 4th in Wisconsin Voter Survey." *New York Times,* March 29, p. 24.

———. 1972d. "Wallace Wisconsin Plea Emphasizes Tax Reform." *New York Times,* March 24, p. 22.

Kornhauser, William. 1959. *The Politics of Mass Society.* Glencoe, Ill.: Free Press.

Kovach, Bill. 1972. "Wallace is Victor in Tennessee Vote." *New York Times,* May 5, p. 27.

Kraft, Joseph. 1974. "The Cast." *New York Times Magazine,* November 17, p. 32.

Krock, Arthur. 1964. "Johnson's Performance." *New York Times,* August 30, sec. IV, p. 11.

Lamott, Kenneth. 1968. "'It Isn't a Mirage They're Seeing,' Says George Wallace." *New York Times Magazine,* September 22, p. 32.

Lasswell, Harold D. 1936. *Politics: Who Gets What, When, How.* New York: McGraw-Hill.

Lasswell, Harold D. and Kaplan, Abraham. 1950. *Power and Society: A Framework for Political Inquiry.* New Haven: Yale University Press.

Lazarsfeld, Paul F.; Berelson, B.R.; and Gaudet, Hazel. 1948. *The People's Choice.* 2nd ed. New York: Columbia University Press.

Lelyveld, Joseph. 1975. "Rockefeller, in South, Denounces Government Spending." *New York Times,* August 28, p. 14.

Lenski, Gerhard E. 1966. *Power and Privilege: A Theory of Social Stratification.* New York: McGraw Hill.

———. 1954. "Status Crystallization: A Non-Vertical Dimension of Social Status." *American Sociological Review* 19 (August): 405–13.

Lesher, Stephan. 1972. "John Schmitz is no George Wallace." *New York Times Magazine,* November 5, p. 6.

Lewis, Anthony. 1976. "Reading Jimmy Carter." *New York Times,* April 1, p. 31.

Lichtenstein, Grace. 1976. "Arizona Primary is Won by Udall." *New York Times,* April 26, p. 21.

Lipset, Seymour Martin. 1968. "George Wallace and the U.S. New Right." *New Society* 12 (October 3): 477–83.

———. 1964. "Beyond the Backlash." *Encounter* 23 (November): 11–24.

———. 1963. "Three Decades of the Radical Right: Coughlinites, McCarthyites and Birchers." In *The Radical Right,* ed. Daniel Bell. Garden City, N.Y.: Anchor Books.

———. 1963. *Political Man: The Social Bases of Politics.* Garden City, N.Y.: Anchor Books.

Lipset, Seymour Martin and Raab, Earl. 1970. *The Politics of Unreason: Right-Wing Extremism in America, 1790–1970.* New York: Harper & Row.

———. 1969. "The Wallace Whitelash." *Transaction* 7 (December): 23–35.

Loftus, Joseph A. 1968. "Labor Found Split on the Election." *New York Times,* September 14, p. 16.

Lutterman, Kenneth G. and Middleton, Russell. 1970. "Authoritarianism, Anomie and Prejudice." *Social Forces* 48 (June): 485–92.

Lydon, Christopher. 1975a. "Wallace Guide a Rightist Writer." *New York Times,* December 1, p. 24.

———. 1975b. "Fund Raiser Quits Group of Rightists." October 6, p. 17.

———. 1975c. "Wallace Delays Entry in '76 Race." *New York Times,* June 13, p. 17.

———. 1975d. "Credit System Fuels Wallace Fund Drive." *New York Times,* May 23, p. 1.

———. 1975e. "Laird Expects a Challenge to Rockefeller." *New York Times,* May 14, p. 10.

———. 1975f. "G.O.P. Donors are Shunning $1,000-a-Plate Dinner." *New York Times,* April 14, p. 26.

———. 1975g. "Conservative Challenge to Ford is Forming in New Hampshire." *New York Times,* March 13, p. 30.

———. 1975h. "Political Fights in 1972 Pose a Knotty Issue." *New York Times,* February 24, p. 15.

———. 1975i. "28 Governors Oppose Ford Oil Tariff." *New York Times,* February 21, p. 8.

———. 1974a. "Democratic Regular Controlling Selection of Delegates to Mini-Convention." *New York Times,* May 23, p. 24.

———. 1974b. "Wallace Faction Works to Elect Delegates to Party Convention." *New York Times,* February 12, p. 10.

———. 1974c. "Despite a Big Constituency Across the Country, Wallace Keeps a Low Profile on Current National Issues." *New York Times,* February 11, p. 21.

Lyman, Stanford M. 1972. *The Black American in Sociological Thought.* New York: G.P. Putnam.

Lynn, Frank. 1976a. "Jackson First in Delegate Race in N.Y.; Udall in Second Place; Carter Tops Udall in Wisconsin; Georgian is Third." *New York Times,* April 7, p. 1.

———. 1976b. "Slates for Wallace Facing Elimination from State Ballot." *New York Times,* March 9, p. 1.

———. 1975a. "3 or 4 Candidates Expected to Remain in April Presidential Primary Here." October 12, p. 61.

———. 1975b. "Carter Hunts for Backing Here as an 'Alternative to Wallace.'" *New York Times,* March 13, p. 25.

———. 1975c. "Sanford Draws 250 Well-Wishers to His Presidential Coming-Out Party Here." *New York Times,* February 27, p. 18.

McClosky, Herbert. 1969. "Consensus and Ideology in American Politics." In *Power and Change in the United States,* ed. Kenneth M. Dolbeare. New York: John Wiley.

———. 1958. "Conservatism and Personality." *American Political Science Review* 52 (March): 27–45.

McEvoy, James III. 1971. *Radicals or Conservatives? The Contemporary American Right.* Chicago: Rand McNally.

McKinney, John C. and Thompson, Edgar T., eds. 1965. *The South in Continuity and Change.* Durham, N.C.: Duke University Press.

Mannheim, Karl. 1936. *Ideology and Utopia: An Introduction to the Sociology of Knowledge.* New York: Harcourt, Brace and World.

Mathews, Pete (House of Representatives, State of Alabama). 1974. Interview with J. Carlson. 23 January at Montgomery, Ala.

Mazo, Earl. 1976a. "Wallace to Push Presidency Race." *New York Times,* June 8, p. 1.

———. 1964b. "Wisconsin's Meanings." *New York Times,* April 9, p. 1.

"Meet the Press." 1976. Transcript of telecast 28 March. vol. 20, no. 13. NBC-TV News. Washington, D.C.: Merkle Press.

———. 1972a. Transcript of telecast 26 November. vol. 16, no. 47. NBC-TV News. Washington, D.C.: Merkle Press.

———. 1972b. Transcript of telecast 19 March. vol. 16, no. 12. NBC-TV News. Washington, D.C.: Merkle Press.

———. 1971. Transcript of telecast 22 August. vol. 15, no. 33. NBC-TV News. Washington, D.C.: Merkle Press.

———. 1969. Transcript of telecast 30 November. vol. 13, no. 46. NBC-TV News. Washington, D.C.: Merkle Press.

————. 1963. Transcript of telecast 2 June. vol. 7, no. 21. NBC-TV News. Washington, D.C.: Merkle Press.

Meyer, Frank S. 1967. "Principles and Heresies: the Populism of George Wallace." *National Review* 19 (May 16): 527.

Middleton, Neil, ed. 1973. *The I.F. Stone's Weekly Reader.* New York: Vintage Books.

Miller, Arthur H.; Miller, Warren E.; Raine, Alden S.; and Brown, Thad A. 1976. "A Majority Party in Disarray: Policy Polarization in the 1972 Election." *American Political Science Review* 70 (September): 753–78.

Miller, Arthur H.; Brown, Thad A.; and Raine, Alden S. 1973. "Social Conflict and Political Estrangement, 1958-1972." Mimeographed. Paper delivered at Midwest Political Science Association (May), Chicago.

Mills, C. Wright. 1959. *The Sociological Imagination.* New York: Grove Press.

Mohr, Charles. 1964. "Arizonian Presses Wallace to Yield." *New York Times,* July 13, p. 18.

Montgomery Advertiser. 1964. "New Debate Dare Issued by Wallace." April 25.

————. 1956a. "Grand Jury Backs Wallace's Decision." February 9.

————. 1956b. "State Circuit Judge Ready to Order Arrest of 'Invading' U.S. Officers." February 7.

Morris, John D. 1964. "Johnson Doubts Gain by Wallace." *New York Times,* May 7, p. 19.

Mueller, Samuel A. 1972. "Busing, School Prayer, and Wallace: Some Notes on Right Wing Populism." *Christian Century* 89 (April 19): 451–54.

Mulcahy, Kevin V. and Katz, Richard S. 1976. *America Votes; What You Should Know About Elections Today.* Englewood Cliffs, N.J.: Prentice-Hall, Inc.

Naughton, James M. 1976a. "Ford Tells South He Opposes Firearm Regulation." *New York Times,* September 27, p. 36.

————. 1976b. "Some Republicans Fearful Party is on its Last Legs." *New York Times,* May 31, p. 1.

————. 1975. "Ford Sums Up First Year in 'Different White House.'"*New York Times,* July 25, p. 1.

————. 1973. "Haldeman Says He and Nixon had No Watergate Knowledge; Heard Tapes Played Recently." *New York Times,* July 31, p. 1.

————. 1972a. "McGovern, Praising Two Rivals, Turns to Task of Party Unity." *New York Times,* July 12, p. 18.

————. 1972b. "McGovern, in the South, Lays 'Racist' Tactics to Nixon." *New York Times,* June 28, p. 35.

————. 1972c. "McGovern to Help Wallace Be Heard." *New York Times,* May 21, p. 41.

New York Times. 1978a. "Wallace Rules Out Race for Either Senate Seat." June 22, p. 20.

————. 1978b. "Wallace is Weighing Race for Senator Allen's Post." June 8, p. 13.

————. 1978c. "Notes on People." May 23, p. C4.

————. 1978d. "Wallace Says It Himself: He'll Quit." May 21, sec. IV, p. 4.

————. 1978e. "Wallace Won't Run for a Senate Seat." May 17, p. 16.

————. 1978f. "Wallace May Drop Senate Race if State Drops Bodyguards." April 21, p. 11.

————. 1978g. "Wallace Divorced After Seven Years; Suit Settled Before Trial Starts." January 10, sec. II, p. 10.

————. 1978h. "Divorce Trial is Set for the Wallaces." January 1, p. 25.

————. 1977a. "Notes on People." September 16, p. B8.

————. 1977b. "Notes on People." September 13, p. 24.

————. 1977c. "Notes on People." September 7, p. C2.

————. 1977d. "Notes on People." August 3, p. C2.

————. 1977e. "Wallace Says He'll Run for Seat in Senate Now Held by Sparkman." June 19, p. 30.

————. 1977f. "Alabama Legislature in Final Hours Votes Funds to Keep Courts Going." June 11, p. 8.

————. 1977g. "Notes on People." May 17, p. 65.

————. 1976a. "Carter and Ford Hailed in Message by Wallace." November 4, p. 24.

————. 1976b. "Wallace Will Address Convention on Tuesday." July 8, p. 21.

————. 1976c. "Wallace Denies Any Talks on Releasing His Delegates." *New York Times,* June 1, p. 42.

————. 1976d. "Wallace Gets 27 Delegates." May 29, p. 9.

————. 1976e. "Dwindling Funds Force Wallace Campaign Cuts." April 7, p. 22.

————. 1976f. "Carter is Victor in 2 State Races." April 4, p. 1.

————. 1976g. "Heckling Flares at Madison, Wisconsin." April 1, p. 22.

————. 1976h. "Vote Totals in North Carolina." March 25, p. 30.

————. 1976i. "Wallace Busy in Carolina." March 19, p. 19.

————. 1976j. "Late Vote Totals in Illinois Races." March 18, p. 34.

————. 1976k. "Wallace at Rallies." March 16, p. 24.

————. 1976l. "Final Totals in Florida Primary." March 11, p. 33.

————. 1976m. "Uncommitted Block Ahead in Carolina Democratic Vote." March 9, p. 20.

————. 1976n. "Carter Leads Wallace in the South; Poll Indicates." March 3, p. 17.

————. 1976o. "Carter Leads in Oklahoma." February 29, p. 43.

————. 1976p. "NH Vote: Results at a Glance." February 26, p. 18.

————. 1976q. "Oklahoma Voting is Won by Carter." February 17, p. 22.

————. 1976r. "Primary Ballot in Texas." February 4, p. 53.

————. 1976s. "Wallace's Right Leg Put in Cast After Accident Aboard Plane." February 3, p. 52.

————. 1976t. "Wallace Does Well in Mississippi Test; Carter and 3 Trail." January 25, p. 1.

————. 1976u. "Wallace Charges 'Plot'" January 21, p. 29.

————. 1976v. "Candidates Split on Oil Money." January 14, p. 51.

————. 1975a. "NY Seeks to Ban Wallace's Fund-Raiser." December 22, p. 17.

————. 1975b. "School Amendment Urged by Wallace." November 17, p. 20.

————. 1975c. "Mr. Wallace's Powerful Announcement." November 16, sec. 4, p. 3.

————. 1975d. "Fool's Errand." November 12, p. 42.

————. 1975e. "Wallace Says Europeans 'Know Where Alabama Is.'" October 27, p. 18.

————. 1975f. "Wallace Asserts He is a Berliner." October 23, p. 15.

————. 1975g. "Wallace sees NATO and Market Aides." October 17, p. 16.

————. 1975h. "Notes on People." October 15, p. 34.

————. 1975i. "Democrats Seek Calm 1976 Parley." October 14, p. 17.

————. 1975j. "Notes on People." August 1, p. 9.

————. 1975k. "Wallace Raises $1.3 Million, Widening Fund Lead." July 15, p. 17.

————. 1975l. "Wallace to be 'Involved' in '76 Drive." June 19, p. 24.

———. 1975m. "Conservatives Move to Get Third Party on Ballots for 1976." June 11, p. 46.

———. 1975n. "'76 Kennedy-Glenn Ticket Rated as Leader in Poll." May 13, p. 36.

———. 1975o. "Strauss Foresees Deadlock in Party." May 5, p. 16.

———. 1975p. "State Law on Second Term for Wallace is Approved." April 25, p. 32.

———. 1975q. "Support is Found for a Third Party." April 20, p. 39.

———. 1975r. "Indiana Primary Petition." April 8, p. 7.

———. 1975s. "Third Party Intimations." March 8, p. 30.

———. 1975t. "Reagan Urges Party Unity." February 16, p. 49.

———. 1975u. "Wallace 2D Term Under U.S. Scrutiny." February 7, p. 9.

———. 1975v. "Notes on People." February 1, p. 21.

———. 1975w. "Wallace Selects Black Alabamian." January 10, p. 25.

———. 1974a. "Wallace Aides See a Total Campaign." November 24, p. 23.

———. 1974b. "Notes on People." November 8, p. 45.

———. 1974c. "Gov. Wallace Wins a 3D Term: Senator Allen is Also Re-elected." November 6, p. 38.

———. 1974d. "Kennedy Rules Out Support for Wallace on 1976 Ticket." October 5, p. 37.

———. 1974e. "Wallace Backers to Poll Voters on Third Party Bid." October 1, p. 69.

———. 1974f. "Mrs. Mitchell Sees Nixon Tied to Bremer." September 22, p. 34.

———. 1974g. "Wallace Accused of Bias on Blacks." August 20, p. 16.

———. 1974h. "Wallace to Push His '72 Program." July 28, p. 40.

———. 1974i. "Evers Says He Could Back Wallace for Vice-President." June 10, p. 24.

———. 1974j. "At the Polls." May 10, p. 36.

———. 1974k. "Black Paper Backs Wallace Saying He has 'Softened.'" April 26, p. 33.

———. 1974l. "Tuskegee's Black Mayor Backs Wallace in Bid for Re-election." April 12, p. 12.

———. 1974m. "Meany and Wallace Meet for an Hour." February 16, p. 18.

———. 1974n. "Federal Aid in '76 Barred to Wallace 3D Party Race." February 14, p. 9.

———. 1974o. "Wallace Seeking a Key Party Role." January 6, p. 34.

———. 1973a. "Wallace is Said to Plan 3D Term Race." December 9, p. 38.

———. 1973b. "Plumbers' Inquiry Urged by Ellsberg." October 24, p. 28.

———. 1973c. "Excerpts From Haldeman's Testimony Before the Select Panel on Watergate." July 31, p. 24.

———. 1973d. "Wallace Sees Liberal Shift." July 17, p. 13.

———. 1973e. "Wallace and Bond to Speak." July 15, p. 28.

———. 1973f. "G.O.P. Fund Used to Undermine Wallace." June 7, p. 34.

———. 1973g. "Schmitz Vote Tops One Million." January 14, p. 44.

———. 1972a. "Strauss Journeys to Meet Wallace on Unity in Party." December 22, p. 13.

———. 1972b. "Wallace Tells Democrats, 'Listen to the People.'" December 5, p. 40.

———. 1972c. "American Party Chiefs Bar a 1976 Drive for Wallace." December 4, p. 51.

———. 1972d. "American Party Elects." December 3, p. 85.

———. 1972e. "Wallace Office Opened." November 21, p. 22.

———. 1972f. "Wallace Seeks Changes." November 15, p. 28.

———. 1972g. "Excerpts From McGovern Interview on Election Reaction." November 14, p. 36.

———. 1972h. "Wallace is Hoping to Reshape His Party." November 8, p. 30.

———. 1972i. "A Nonspeaking Wallace Helps House Candidate." October 7, p. 40.

———. 1972j. "Candidate Scores Kissinger." October 4, p. 93.

———. 1972k "Kennedy, Wallace Discuss Campaign." September 23, p. 15.

———. 1972l. "Ex-Aide to Wallace is Guilty of Evading U.S. Tax on Bribes." September 16, p. 13.

———. 1972m. "Candidate Protests Abortions Here." August 29, p. 21.

———. 1972n. "Wallace to Get Platform." August 25, p. 19.

———. 1972o. "Wallace Asserts He's Out of Race." July 30, p. 38.

———. 1972p. "Wallace Aide Says Governor Will Skip Parley of 3D Party." July 21, p. 18.

———. 1972q. "Wallace 3D-Party Draft Due." July 15, p. 11.

———. 1972r. "The Poisoned Cup." July 6, p. 36.

———. 1972s. "Courage Party in State Wants Wallace on Ballot." June 18, p. 36.

———. 1972t. "Wisconsin Unit for Wallace." June 14, p. 16.

———. 1972u. "Old-Time Wallace Campaign Has Modern Touches." April 9, p. 64.

———. 1972v. "Aide to Wallace Quits Post Amid Fund Drive Reports." March 31, p. 18.

———. 1972w. "Writer to Head Panel of Blacks for Wallace." March 30, p. 32.

———. 1972x. "Newly Elected Negro Delegate to Quit Wallace's Florida Bloc." March 27, p. 24.

———. 1972y. "Considers Third Party Candidacy." March 20, p. 30.

———. 1972z. "Wallace Gets Convention Space." January 28, p. 16.

———. 1972aa. "AFL-CIO Opposes Nixon Re-Election." January 26, p. 16.

———. 1972bb. "Wallace Gets Spot on Florida Ballot; Rep. Mills Omitted." January 19, p. 43.

———. 1971a. "Calley Attorney is Seeking American Party Nomination." December 5, p. 42.

———. 1971b. "Democrats in Florida Drop Proposal to Pledge Wallace." November 6, p. 62.

———. 1971c. "Senate Unit Backs Wallace." September 15, p. 22.

———. 1971d. "Alabama House Passes Antibusing Bill." September 3, p. 9.

———. 1971e. "Wallace Plans to Issue New Edicts on Busing." August 23, p. 16.

———. 1971f. "Wallace Tells Local Board to Defy Court and Reopen School." August 14, p. 22.

———. 1971g. "Wallace Defies Court on Busing Plan." August 13, p. 15.

———. 1971h. "Alabama Adding Police for School Reopening." July 1, p. 59.

———. 1970a. "Wallace Elected Governor in Alabama Landslide Vote." November 4, p. 31.

———. 1970b. "Wallace Urges Defiance of Integration Order." September 8, p. 20.

———. 1970c. "Negro Democrats Put Up a Slate of 169 for Elections in Alabama." September 2, p. 22.

———. 1970d. "Black Party Backs a Candidate to Face Wallace for Governor." August 2, p. 38.

———. 1970e. "Lose a Thurmond, Gain a Young." July 21, p. 34.

———. 1970f. "Wallace is Official Winner." June 10, p. 72.

———. 1970g. "Brochure Backs Wallace." May 22, p. 46.

——. 1970h. "Two Rivals Woo Alabama Loser." May 17, p. 71.

——. 1970i. "Brewer Leads by 5,908." May 12, p. 16.

——. 1970j. "Wallace Brother Assails Newsman." April 16, p. 25.

——. 1970k. "Calley Meets with Wallace and Receives Sympathy." February 21, p. 1.

——. 1970l. "Brewer Will Run in Alabama for a Full Term as Governor." February 11, p. 29.

——. 1969a. "Independents Criticize Wallace But Urge Him to Run in 1972." December 8, p. 38.

——. 1969b. "Wallace Ties War to Nixon's Future." December 1, p. 11.

——. 1969c. "Andrews is Backed by Wallace Party." July 20, p. 44.

——. 1969d. "Democrats Seek Unity in Alabama." June 22, p. 35.

——. 1969e. "American Party is Granted Official Sanction by Wallace." May 27, p. 17.

——. 1969f. "Wallace Party Merges with Several Others." May 5, p. 22.

——. 1969g. "Wallace Returns to Campaign Trail." March 19, p. 16.

——. 1968a. "Wallace Dissidents Form National Unit." November 17, p. 66.

——. 1968b. "Suit Says Wallace Loots Fund." October 11, p. 53.

——. 1968c. "Wallace Support by Labor Denied." October 11, p. 32.

——. 1968d. "Humphrey Wins Backing of Santa Barbara Paper" [Meridian, Miss. dateline]. October 5, p. 20.

——. 1968e. "Bogus Notice Angers Democrats." October 3, p. 32.

——. 1968f. "Unions Plan Drive Opposing Wallace Among Members." September 21, p. 17.

——. 1968g. "Wallace to File Ohio Suit to Gain Place on Ballot." July 21, p. 47.

——. 1968h. "Wallace Target of Election Plan." July 18, p. 23.

——. 1967a. "9-Day Wallace Trip Begins in the West; Preparations Broad." October 27, p. 41.

——. 1967b. "Wallace Supporters Open Headquarters Near Capitol." April 6, p. 27.

——. 1965. "Alabama's Senate Kills Wallace Plan for a Second Term." October 23, p. 1.

——. 1964a. "Wallace Defied on Elector Plea." September 1, p. 24.

——. 1964b. "Opinion of the Week: At Home and Abroad." August 30, sec. IV. p. 11.

——. 1964c. "Wallace Assails National Party's 'Alien Philosophy.'" August 22, p. 6.

——. 1964d. "Wallace Releases Alabama Delegates." July 24, p. 10.

——. 1964e. "Wallace Drops Presidency Bid; Denies Any Deals." July 20, p. 1.

——. 1964f. "Wallace May Lose His 3 Indiana Votes." June 12, p. 39.

——. 1964g. "Maryland Unit Vote Voided in Primaries." May 26, p. 28.

——. 1964h. "Wallace is Assailed by Maryland Bishop." May 6, p. 20.

——. 1964i. "Alabama Expected to Choose Electors Backed by Wallace." May 3, p. 73.

——. 1964j. "Alabama Scored by Wallace's Foes." April 22, p. 35.

——. 1964k. "Wallace Got 33.7% of Vote of Wisconsin Democrats." April 21, p. 21.

——. 1964l. "Wallace Predicts Victory in Indiana." April 21, p. 25.

——. 1964m. "Maryland Democrats Concerned Over Signs of Wallace Strength." April 19, p. 82.

——. 1964n. "Political Straws." April 12, sec. IV. p. 1.

————. 1964o. "Writer Discloses Alabama Threats." April 7, p. 19.

————. 1964p. "Wisconsin Governor Praised by Johnson." April 6, p. 44.

————. 1964q. "Wallace Widens His Grip at Home." April 5, p. 41.

————. 1964r. "Wallace, Stassen Certified in Indiana." March 31, p. 16.

————. 1964s. "Wallace Answers Catholics on Racism." March 24, p. 71.

————. 1964t. "Wallace Faces Fight in Wisconsin." March 8, p. 76.

————. 1964u. "Wallace Considers Primaries in North." January 11, p. 11.

————. 1963a. "Wallace in Maryland for Talk." September 13, p. 34.

————. 1963b. "Wallace Backed on Moves for '64." August 25, p. 63.

Newsweek. 1975. "Wallace Starts to Roll." April 21, pp. 43–4.

————. 1974. "Wallace Lives." February 18, p. 31.

Nie, Norman H.; Hull, C. Hadlai; Jenkins, Jean G.; Steinbrenner, Karin; and Bent. Dale H. 1975. *SPSS: Statistical Package for the Social Sciences.* 2nd ed. New York: McGraw-Hill.

Nie, Norman; Bent, Dale H.; and Hull, C. Hadlai. 1970. *SPSS: Statistical Package for the Social Sciences.* New York: McGraw-Hill.

Nordheimer, Jon. 1973. "Wallace Rebounds from Despair." *New York Times,* May 14, p. 1.

————. 1972a. "Wallace Recovery: Battling Self-Doubt as Well as Wounds." *New York Times,* October 30, p. 1.

————. 1972b. "Foes of Wallace in Alabama Hurt." *New York Times,* May 4, p. 30.

————. 1972c. "Alabamians Ask Wallace to Come Home." *New York Times,* April 23, p. 40.

————. 1972d. "Wallace is Cautious on Wisconsin Race." *New York Times,* March 25, p. 14.

————. 1972e. "Askew Raises $25,000 for TV Time to Continue to Fight on Antibusing Referendum." *New York Times,* March 5, p. 53.

————. 1972f. "Busing on Florida Ballot as Key Issue in Primary." *New York Times,* February 16, p. 1.

Olsen, Marvin E. and Tully, Judy Corden. 1972. "Socioeconomic-Ethnic Inconsistency and Preference for Political Change." *American Sociological Review* 37 (October): 560–74.

Osgood, Charles E.; Suci, George J.; and Tannebaum, Percy H. 1957. *The Measurement of Meaning.* Urbana, Ill.: University of Illinois Press.

Parker, Richard. 1972. "Those Blue-Collar Worker Blues." *The New Republic* 67 (September 23): 16–21.

Parsons, Talcott. 1967. *Sociological Theory and Modern Society.* New York: Free Press.

————. 1962. "Social Strains in America: A Postscript." In *The Radical Right,* ed. Daniel Bell. Garden City, N.Y.; Anchor Books.

Pateman, Carole. 1970. *Participation and Democratic Theory.* London: Cambridge University Press.

Peirce, Neal R. 1974. *The Deep South States of America; People, Politics and Power in the Seven Deep South States.* New York: W.W. Norton and Company.

Pettigrew, Thomas F. 1971. *Racially Separate or Together?* New York: McGraw-Hill.

Pettigrew, Thomas F.; Riley, Robert T.; and Vanneman, Reeve D. 1972. "George Wallace's Constitutents." *Psychology Today* 5 (February): 47–49, 92.

Phelps, Robert H. 1968. "O'Brien Attacks Role by Agnew." *New York Times,* September 12, p. 42.

Pincus, Ann. 1975. "George Wallace Couldn't Function as President—Even if Elected." *Village Voice,* August 4, pp. 6–7.

Pirtle, Mabel (Director of Mail Services, Wallace Campaign). 1974. Interview with J. Carlson, 23 January at Montgomery, Ala.

Polsby, Nelson W. 1963. "Toward an Explanation of McCarthyism." In *Politics and Social Life,* ed. Nelson W. Polsby, Robert A. Dentler and Paul Smith. Boston: Houghton Mifflin.

Pomper, Gerald M. 1975. *Voter's Choice: Varieties of American Electoral Behavior.* New York: Dodd, Mead and Company.

————. 1971. *Elections in America: Control and Influence in Democratic Politics.* New York: Dodd, Mead and Co.

Porter, Kirk H. and Johnson, Donald Bruce. 1969. *National Party Platforms, 1840-1964; Supplement 1968.* Urbana, Illinois: University of Illinois Press.

Pranger, Robert J. 1968. *Action, Symbolism and Order: The Existential Dimensions of Politics in Modern Citizenship.* Nashville, Tenn.: Vanderbilt University Press.

Prothro, James W. and Griff, Charles E. 1960. "Fundamental Principles of Democracy: Bases of Agreement and Disagreement." *Journal of Politics* 22: 276–94.

Raines, Howell. 1979a. "Governor Ends Alabama's Rift With Judge." *New York Times,* February 12, p. A14.

————. 1979b. "Forrest James Is Sworn In As Successor to Wallace." *New York Times,* January 16, p. A12.

————. 1979c. "Wallace, at the Last, Tries to Erase 'Unfair' Verdict." January 7, p. 26.

————. 1978. "Wallace Withdrawal Sets Off Power Struggle in Alabama." *New York Times,* May 18, sec. II, p. 11.

Range, Peter Ross. 1974. "A Wallace is a Wallace is a Wallace." *New Times* 3 (December 13): 18-23.

Ransford, H. Edward. 1972. "Blue Collar Anger: Reactions to Student and Black Protest." *American Sociological Review* 37 (June): 333-46.

————. 1968. "Isolation, Powerlessness and Violence: A Study of Attitudes and Participation in the Watts Riots." *American Journal of Sociology* 73 (March): 581-91.

Rawls, Wendell, Jr. 1978. "Panel Convinced Bounty Induced Ray to Kill King." *New York Times,* November 17, p. 1.

Reed, John Shelton, 1972. *The Enduring South.* Lexington, Massachusetts: Lexington Books.

Reed, Roy. 1976a. "Ford Defeats Reagan in Florida: Carter is Winner Over Wallace in Demo Vote, Jackson 3D." *New York Times,* March 10, p. 1.

————. 1976b. "Wallace Pressing the Abortion Issue." *New York Times,* March 3, p. 17.

————. 1974. "Wallace to Seek A Third Term; Bars Decision on Plans for 1976." *New York Times,* February 23, p. 25.

————. 1973. "Nixon Popularity Reviving in South." *New York Times,* November 22, p. 1.

————. 1972. "Southern Governors Elect Wallace as Chairman." *New York Times,* September 7, p. 36.

————. 1971. "Wallace, at Inauguration, Hints a New Race in 1972." *New York Times,* January 19, p. 16.

————. 1970. "McKeithen Says He is Ready to Lead Third Party." *New York Times,* March 27, p. 15.

————. 1968a. "Wallace Loses Some Momentum." *New York Times,* October 20, p. 2.

————. 1968b. "Wallace Issues Platform Urging Tougher Policies." *New York Times,* October 14, p. 1.

————. 1968c. "Wallace Offers Foreign Policy." *New York Times,* October 8, p. 50.

————. 1968d. "Wallace Baits Hecklers to Rouse Backers." *New York Times,* October 4, p. 50.

————. 1968e. "Wallace Taunts Nixon to Debate." *New York Times,* September 19, p. 38.

————. 1968f. "Wallace Studies #2 Prospects." *New York Times,* September 17, p. 38.

————. 1968g. "Wallace Race a Traveling Show: Songs, Spiels, Fun and Prospect of Violence." *New York Times,* September 16, p. 43.

————. 1968h. "Maddox Praises Wallace Courage." *New York Times,* September 15, p. 76.

————. 1966a. "Wallace Doubts Reagan's Beliefs." *New York Times,* November 10, p. 30.

————. 1966b. "Wallace Talking About Presidency." *New York Times,* September 20, p. 30.

Reich, Kenneth. 1972. "George Wallace, Fake Populist." *The Nation* 214 (May 1): 550–52.

Reinhold, Robert. 1976a. "Surge by Carter on National Basis Indicated in Poll." *New York Times,* March 29, p. 1.

————. 1976b. "Mass Poll Hints Deep Democratic Rifts." *New York Times,* March 4, p. 1.

Reston, James. 1975a. "A Talk with George Wallace." *New York Times Magazine,* April 27, p. 45–48.

————. 1975b. "The Wallace Spirit." *New York Times,* February 26, p. 39.

————. 1974a. "What Makes Jerry Run." *New York Times,* November 20, p. 43.

————. 1974b. "Hobgoblins Right and Left." *New York Times,* October 30, p. 45.

————. 1968. "'New Coalition': A Nixon Gamble." *New York Times,* August 10, p. 12.

Ripley, Anthony. 1974. "Research Study Finds More Than $24 Million is in the Hands of Political Candidates and Committees." *New York Times,* February 13, p. 21.

Robbins, William. 1972. "Nixon Backs Death Penalty for Kidnapping, Hijacking." *New York Times,* June 30, p. 1.

Roberts, Gene. 1967a. "Says George Wallace in Awe: 'They Like Me!'" *New York Times,* November 12, sec. IV, p. 3.

————. 1967b. "Wallace is Lagging in California Ballot Drive." *New York Times,* November 2, p. 40.

————. 1967c. "Wallace Developing an Informal Campaign Style." *New York Times,* September 24, p. 66.

————. 1966. "Grenier is Chosen by Alabama GOP." *New York Times,* July 31, p. 56.

Roberts, Steven V. 1973. "Nazi Party Linked to G.O.P. Anti-Wallace Move." *New York Times,* June 8, p. 17.

Roberson, Peggy. 1978. "Wallace Believes Bullet Cost Him Spot on Democratic National Ticket." *Alabama Journal,* June 5, p. 1.

Robertson, Wilmot, 1973. *The Dispossessed Majority.* Cape Canaveral, Fla.: Howard Allen.

Robinson, J.P. and Shaver, P.R. 1969. *Measures of Social Psychological Attitudes.* Ann Arbor, Mich.: Institute for Social Research.

Rogin, Michael Paul. 1969. "Politics, Emotion and the Wallace Vote." *British Journal of Sociology* 20 (March): 27–49.

———. 1968. "Wallace as Catharsis." *Commonweal* 89 (November 29): 310–12.

———. 1967. *The Intellectuals and McCarthy: The Radical Spectre.* Cambridge: MIT Press.

———. 1966. "Wallace and the Middle Class: The White Backlash in Wisconsin." *Public Opinion Quarterly* 30 (Spring): 98–108.

Rohter, Ira S. 1969. "Social and Psychological Determinants of Radical Rightism." In *The American Right Wing: Readings in Political Behavior,* ed. Robert A. Schoenberger. New York: Holt, Rinehart and Winston.

Ronan, Thomas P. 1976. "Election Board Alleges Flaws in Wallace's Primary Petitions." *New York Times,* April 8, p. 31.

Rosenbaum, David E. 1973. "Kalmback Says Strangers Got $400,000 From Him." *New York Times,* July 18, p. 1.

———. 1970. "3 White Districts Choose Negroes for House Seats." *New York Times,* November 5, p. 28.

Rosenberg, Morris. 1956. "Misanthropy and Political Ideology." *American Sociological Review* 21 (December): 690–95.

Rosenthal, Jack. 1972a. "Times Study Finds Wallace Could Cut Votes for Nixon." *New York Times,* May 18, p. 1.

———. 1972b. "Survey Ties Issues, Not Shooting, to Wallace Victory." *New York Times,* May 17, p. 30.

———. 1972c. "Times Study Finds Voters Liked McGovern on Taxes." *New York Times,* April 6, p. 1.

Rosow, Jerome M. 1970. "The Problem of the Blue Collar Worker." Memorandum for the Secretary of Labor prepared for President Richard M. Nixon (April 16) Mimeographed.

Rotter, J.B. 1966. "Generalized Expectancies for Internal Versus External Control of Reinforcements." *Psychological Monographs* Whole No. 609.

Rugaber, Walter. 1972. "Threat of Delegate Defection Perils Wallace's 2 Victories." *New York Times,* May 18, p. 36.

———. 1968a. "Wallace Is Left With Nostalgia." *New York Times,* December 8, p. 48.

———. 1968b. "Gen. LeMay Joins Wallace's Ticket as Running Mate." *New York Times,* October 4, p. 1.

———. 1968c. "Wallace is Hailed in South But Fund Sources Stay Closed." *New York Times,* June 16, p. 23.

———. 1967. "Wallace Pushes Presidency Bid." *New York Times,* April 30, p. 49.

Runyon, John H.; Verdini, Jennefer; and Runyon, Sally S., eds. 1971. *Source Book of American Presidential Campaign and Election Statistics 1948–1968.* New York: Frederick Ungar.

Rush, Gary B. 1967. "Status Consistency and Right-Wing Extremism." *American Sociological Review* 32 (February): 86–92.

Rusher, William A. 1975. "A Marriage of Conservatives." *New York Times,* June 23, p. 27.

Safire, William. 1973. "A Cap Over the Wall." *New York Times,* July 5, p. 29.

Salpukas, Agis. 1976a. "Wallace Strategists Divided on Key Issues." *New York Times*, March 15, p. 36.

———. 1976b. "Wallace Presses the Health Issue." *New York Times*, March 13, p. 11.

Sartori, Giovanni. 1972. "Politics, Ideology and Belief Systems." In *Political Attitudes and Public Opinion*, ed. Dan D. Nimmo and Charles M. Bonjean. New York: David McKay, Inc.

Satori, G. 1962. *Democratic Theory*. Detroit: Wayne State University Press.

Scammon, Richard M. 1973. *America Votes 10: A Handbook of Contemporary American Election Statistics (1972)*. Washington: Government Affairs Institute, Congressional Quarterly.

———. 1970. *America Votes 8; a Handbook of Contemporary Election Statistics (1968)*. Washington: Congressional Quarterly.

Schanberg, Sydney H. 1968. "O'Dwyer Seeks to Counter Wallace Sentiment in Labor Ranks." *New York Times*, October 11, p. 31.

Schoenberger, Robert A., ed. 1969. *The American Right Wing: Readings in Political Behavior*. New York: Holt, Rinehard and Winston.

———. 1968. "Conservatism, Personality and Political Extremism." *American Political Science Review* 62 (September): 868–77.

Seeman, M. 1972. "Alienation and Engagement." In *The Human Meaning of Social Change*, ed. A. Campbell and P.E. Converse. New York: Russell Sage.

———. 1959. "On the Meaning of Alienation." *American Sociological Review* 24 (December): 783–91.

Semple, Robert B., Jr. 1975. "Wallace, Starting European Tour, Meets With Wilson." *New York Times*, October 14, p. 1.

———. 1968a. "Wallace Shadow Causes Nixon to Consider a 3D Party Appeal." *New York Times*, September 21, p. 16.

———. 1968b. "Nixon Sees a Plot by Rivals in South." *New York Times*, September 18, p. 1.

———. 1968c. "Nixon Starts Off Smoothly." *New York Times*, September 8, sec. IV, p. 2.

———. 1968d. "Nixon Repudiates Any Wallace Tie." *New York Times*, June 27, p. 21.

Sennett, Richard and Cobb, Jonathan. 1972. *The Hidden Injuries of Class*. New York: Vintage Books.

Shabecoff, Philip. 1974. "AFL-CIO Council, by Vote of 31–1, Calls Impeachment Trial 'Only Way' to 'Get at Truth.'" *New York Times*, February 19, p. 13.

Shanahan, Eileen. 1974. "Nixon Asked Data on Wallace Tax, Panel Was Told." *New York Times*, July 17, p. 1.

———. 1968. "Wallace Backed by Small Donors." *New York Times*, October 30, p. 30.

Shannon, William. 1974. "Mr. Wallace Again." *New York Times*, July 9, p. 37.

Shearer, Lloyd. 1974. "Is the White House Ready for George Wallace? (Because He is Ready for It)." *Parade Magazine*, June 9, p. 4–6.

Sherif, Muzafer. 1953. "Reference Groups in Human Relations." In *Groups in Harmony and Tension: An Integration of Studies in Intergroup Relations*. New York: Harper and Row.

Sherrill, Robert. 1968. *Gothic Politics in the Deep South; Stars of the New Confederacy*. New York: Grossman Publishers.

Shils, Edward. 1968. "The Concept and Function of Ideology." In *International*

Encyclopedia of the Social Sciences, ed. David L. Sills. New York: Crowell, Collier and Macmillan.

Sievers, Harry J. 1968. "George Wallace, The Potential Spoiler." *America* 118 (April 6): 431.

Sindler, Allan P., ed. 1963. *Change in the Contemporary South.* Durham, N.C.: Duke University Press.

Sitton, Claude, 1964a. "Alabamians Quit Over Party Oath." *New York Times,* August 27, p. 1.

———. 1964b. "Wallace Called Reluctant in Dropping Campaign." *New York Times,* July 30, p. 10.

———. 1964c. "Goldwater Finds North is Uneasy." *New York Times,* May 2, p. 22.

———. 1964d. "Johnson Prestige on Line in Indiana." *New York Times,* April 19, p. 83.

———. 1964e. "Wallace Pleased by Indiana Drive." *New York Times,* April 16, p. 30.

———. 1964f. "Wallace Presses Wisconsin Drive." *New York Times,* March 22, p. 52.

———. 1964g. "Clerics Hostile to Gov. Wallace." *New York Times,* March 19, p. 17.

———. 1963a. "Wallace Staging Oratorical Tour." *New York Times,* October 11, p. 24.

———. 1963b. "Alabama Admits Negro Students; Wallace Bows to Federal Force; Kennedy Sees 'Moral Crisis' in U.S." *New York Times,* June 12, p. 1.

Skolnick, Jerome H. 1969. *The Politics of Protest.* New York: Simon and Schuster.

Smelser, Neil J. 1963. *Theory of Collective Behavior.* New York: Free Press of Glencoe.

Smith, Anita. 1969. *The Intimate Story of Lurleen Wallace; Her Crusade of Courage.* Montgomery, Ala.: Communications Unlimited, Inc.

Snider, Charles (National Campaign Director, the Wallace Campaign). 1978. Interview with J. Carlson. 30 November at Montgomery, Ala.

———. 1974. Interview with J. Carlson. 23 January at Montgomery, Ala.

Sokol, Robert. 1967. "Power Orientation and McCarthyism." *American Journal of Sociology* 73 (November): 443–52.

Srole, Leo. 1956. "Social Integration and Certain Corollaries: An Explanatory Study." *American Sociological Review* 22 (December): 709–16.

Steel Labor. 1964. "McDonald Nails Down Lies About Civil Rights Bill in Message Sent to All Steelworker Local Unions." June, p. 2.

Sterba, James P. 1976. "Reagan Victor Over Ford by Huge Margin in Texas; Carter Trouses Bentsen." *New York Times,* May 2, p. 1.

Stevens, William K. 1976. "Ford Beats Reagan in Michigan and Maryland; Carter Defeated by Brown, Challenged by Udall." *New York Times,* May 19, p. 1.

Stone, Richard. 1972. "Tabulation of Official Votes Cast, Presidential Preference Primary Election, March 14, 1972." Office of the Secretary of State, State of Florida.

Stouffer, Samuel. 1963. *Communism, Conformity and Civil Liberties.* Gloucester, Mass.: Peter Smith.

Sullivan, Joseph F. 1975. "Byrne Signs a Ban on Crossover Voting." *New York Times,* December 13, p. 57.

Sunday Bulletin [Philadelphia]. 1972. "Gov. Wallace Quizzed by Reporters at the Bulletin." April 23, sec. 1, p. 3.

Synon, John J., ed. 1968. *George Wallace: Profile of a Presidential Candidate.* Kilmarnock, Va.: MS, Inc.

Time. 1975. "And Then There Were Ten." November 24, p. 41.

Trieman, Donald J. 1966. "Status Discrepancy and Prejudice." *American Journal of Sociology* 71 (May): 651–64.

Trow, Martin. 1957. "Right-Wing Radicalism and Political Intolerance: A Study of Support for McCarthy in a New England Town." Ph.D. dissertation, Columbia University.

Turner, Ralph H. and Killian, Lewis M. 1972. *Collective Behavior.* 2nd ed. Englewood Cliffs, N.J.: Prentice-Hall.

Turner, Wallace. 1964. "Rightists Warn of Third Party Step." *New York Times,* July 9, p. 18.

Vecsey, George. 1972a. "Schmitz Details Theory on Plots." *New York Times,* August 6, p. 43.

———. 1972b. "Wallace Deters Backers: Californian Chosen Instead." *New York Times,* August 5, p. 12.

———. 1972c. "Third Party Delegates Hear Plea Not to Draft Wallace." *New York Times,* August 4, p. 37.

Vierick, Peter. 1962. *Conservatism Revisited.* New York: Free Press.

Waldron, Martin. 1972a. "McGovern Battles Drive by Foes in New Mexico." *New York Times,* June 6, p. 26.

———. 1972b. "Wallace Faces Mounting Criticism in Alabama Over His Record, His Brother and His Aides." *New York Times,* May 5, p. 26.

———. 1972c. "Wallace Gets 42%, Humphrey 2D, Jackson 3D, Muskie 4th in Florida; Lindsay Edges McGovern for 5th." *New York Times,* March 15, p. 1.

———. 1972d. "Florida Expects Record Turnout in Primary Today." *New York Times,* March 14, p. 1.

———. 1972e. "Wallace's Rivals Fight to Prevent Sweep in Florida." *New York Times,* March 12, p. 1.

———. 1972f. "Florida Unions Seek to Stop Wallace." *New York Times,* March 5, p. 52.

———. 1972g. "Senate Bus Votes Sharpen Issue in Florida's Primary." *New York Times,* March 1, p. 20.

———. 1971a. "People of Mobile Shun Wallace Pleas to Oppose Busing Actively." *New York Times,* September 9, p. 22.

———. 1971b. "Integration Foes Booming Wallace." *New York Times,* September 5, p. 37.

———. 1968. "Wallace Charges Polls are Rigged." *New York Times,* October 10, p. 50.

Wallace Campaign. 1976a. "Jobs, Prices and the Tax Load." Position Paper. Montgomery, Ala. The Wallace Campaign.

———. 1976b. "Only George Wallace Stands With the People of Illinois on the Eighteen Most Important Issues and Answers in the March 16 Democratic Primary." Newspaper Advertising in the Illinois Primary.

———. 1976c. "Problems of the Inner City." Position Paper. Montgomery, Ala. The Wallace Campaign.

———. 1976d. "States Rights and People's Rights." Position Paper. Montgomery Ala. The Wallace Campaign.

———. 1976e. *Wallace Labor Action.* Newspaper. Montgomery, Ala.: The Wallace Campaign.

———. 1972a. *The Earned Years.* Newspaper. Montgomery, Ala.: The Wallace Campaign.

———. 1972b. *Wallace Labor Action.* Newspaper. Montgomery, Ala.: The Wallace Campaign.

Wallace, Cornelia. 1976. *C'Nelia.* Philadelphia: A.J. Holman.

Wallace, George C. 1978a. Interview with J. Carlson. 1 December, at Montgomery, Alabama.

———. 1978b. "George Wallace's Valedictory." *The Washington Post,* June 4, p. B1.

———. 1976. *Stand Up for America.* Garden City, N.Y.: Doubleday and Company.

———. 1975. "'Trust the People'; Formal Announcement of Candidacy for President of the United States." 12 November, at Montgomery, Alabama.

———. 1975. Untitled Speech Used to Address Legislators, State Democratic Party Officials, in Effort to Change Delegate Selection Procedures. Obtained from Michael Griffin, December 1978, 4 pages.

———. 1974. Interview with J. Carlson. 25 January at Montgomery, Alabama.

———. 1972a. "Stand Up for America." Speech, used throughout 1972 campaign.

———. 1972b. "Governor George C. Wallace Declares Candidacy for Democratic Party Nomination and Florida Democratic Presidential Preferential Primary." Statement to the Press. 13 January at Tallahassee, Florida.

———. 1971a. "Speech by George C. Wallace, Governor of Alabama, to National Press Club." Speech 6 December at Washington, D.C.

———. 1971b. "Governor George C. Wallace, Inaugural Address, January 18, 1971." Speech, 18 January at Montgomery, Alabama.

———. 1968. *Hear Me Out.* Anderson, S.C.: Droke House.

———. 1964a. "Speech Prepared for Delivery by George C. Wallace, Governor of Alabama Before the United States Junior Chamber of Commerce." Speech, 23 June at Dallas, Texas.

———. 1964b. "Speech Prepared for Delivery by George C. Wallace, Governor of Alabama to Organization Against Communism." Speech, 11 June at Cleveland, Ohio.

———. 1964c. "Address to the National Press Club." Speech, 4 June at Washington, D.C.

———. 1964d. "Speech Prepared for Delivery by George C. Wallace, Governor of Alabama." Speech, used throughout 1964 campaign.

———. 1963a. "Statement and Proclamation of Governor George C. Wallace, University of Alabama, June 11, 1963." Speech, 11 June at Tuscaloosa, Alabama.

———. 1963b. "The Inaugural Address of Governor George C. Wallace." Speech, 14 January at Montgomery, Alabama.

Wallace, George C., Jr. 1975. *The Wallaces of Alabama.* Chicago: Follett Publishing Company.

The Wallace Stand. 1975. 5, no. 1 (March 1975).

———. 1972a. 2, no. 4 (November 1972).

———. 1972b. 2, no. 3 (Convention Issue).

———. 1971a. 1, no. 9 (December 1971).

———. 1971b. 1, no. 5 (July 1971).

———. 1971c. 1, no. 1 (March 1971).

Wattenberg, Ben J. 1974. *The Real America.* Garden City, N.Y.: Doubleday and Co.

Weaver, Warren, Jr. 1975. "Secret Service Guards Offered to Six Democratic Candidates." *New York Times,* September 30, p. 20.

————. 1968. "Bailey Will Let McCarthy Speak." *New York Times,* July 10, p. 1.

————. 1967a. "Wallace Planning California Race." *New York Times,* June 18, p. 45.

————. 1967b. "Johnson Strategists Bank on South in '68." *New York Times,* May 11, p. 1.

————. 1967c. "Wallace Refuses to Score Birchers." *New York Times,* April 28, p. 28.

Weber, Max. 1946. "Class, Status, Party." In *From Max Weber: Essays in Sociology,* ed. H.H. Gerth and C. Wright Mills. New York: Oxford University Press.

Wehrwein, Austin C. 1964a. "Democrats Hail Welsh Victory." *New York Times,* May 7, p. 20.

————. 1964b. "Wallace Gets 29% of Indiana Votes; Welsh is Winner." *New York Times,* May 6, p. 1.

————. 1964c. "Big Wallace Vote Likely in Indiana." *New York Times,* May 5, p. 35.

————. 1964d. "Wallace Ending Drive in Indiana." *New York Times,* May 4, p. 17.

————. 1964e. "Indiana Democrats Push Drive to Cut Wallace Primary Votes." *New York Times,* May 3, p. 73.

————. 1964f. "Indiana Publicity Drive Aimed Against Wallace." *New York Times,* April 25, p. 14.

————. 1964g. "Goldwater Aides Hail Illinois Vote." *New York Times,* April 16, p. 1.

————. 1964h. "Wallace's Vote Exceeds 200,000 in Wisconsin Test." *New York Times,* April 8, p. 1.

————. 1964i. "Heavy Vote Today Seen in Wisconsin." *New York Times,* April 7, p. 21.

————. 1964j. "Democratic Race Rouses Wisconsin." *New York Times,* March 29, p. 40.

Weiss, John. 1967. *The Fascist Tradition: Radical Right-Wing Extremism in Modern Europe.* New York: Harper and Row.

Wicker, Tom. 1976a. "Sending the Message." *New York Times,* February 27, p. 31.

————. 1976b. "Back in the Gutter." *New York Times,* January 18, p. 17.

————. 1975a. "Wallace on the Wing." *New York Times,* October 17, p. 35.

————. 1975b. "Playing to Wallace's Strength." *New York Times,* June 10, p. 39.

————. 1974a. "Blacks for Wallace(!)" *New York Times,* May 12, p. 19.

————. 1974b. "Looking Ahead to '76." *New York Times,* January 27, p. 15.

————. 1972a. "The Two Georges." *New York Times,* April 6, p. 43.

————. 1972b. "The Uses of Defiance." *New York Times,* March 26, sec. IV, p. 13.

————. 1972c. "Loud and Clear." *New York Times,* March 16, p. 47.

————. 1970. "In the Nation: Thank You, General Thurmond." *New York Times,* July 21, p. 34.

————. 1968. "In the Nation: No, No and Wallace." *New York Times,* July 25, p. 32.

————. 1967a. "In the Nation: Wallace's Powerful Medicine." *New York Times,* December 12, p. 46.

————. 1967b. "George Wallace: A Gross and Simple Heart." *Harper's Magazine* 234 (April): 41–49.

————. 1963. "Cheers for Kennedy in South Regarded as Good '64 Omen." *New York Times,* May 20, p. 1.

Wilhoit, Francis M. 1973. *The Politics of Massive Resistance.* New York: George Braziller.

Wills, Garry. 1975. "The Man the Democrats Need." *The New York Review of Books* 21 (January 23): 14–16.

———. 1971. *Nixon Agonistes.* New York: Signet, New American Library.

Wilson, Francis G. 1945. "Pessimism in American Politics." *Journal of Politics* 7 (May): 124–44.

Wirt, Frederick, M. 1970. *Politics of Southern Equality: Law and Social Change in a Mississippi County.* Chicago: Aldine.

Witcover, Jules. 1975a. "Public's Opinion of Wallace is Returning to the Negative." *Washington Post,* June 16, p. 1.

———. 1975b. "Wallace Machine: Well-Oiled for All-Out '76 Push." *Washington Post,* May 4, p. 1.

Wooten, James T. 1976a. "Carter, With Wallace at His Side, Hails South's Basic Conservatism." *New York Times,* September 14, p. 28.

———. 1976b. "Old South Bows to New as Wallace Meets Carter." *New York Times,* June 13, p. 34.

———. 1976c. "Carter is Victor in Pennsylvania, Beating Johnson in Pivotal Test; Udall is Next, Ahead of Wallace." *New York Times,* April 28, p. 1.

———. 1976d. "Wallace's Last Hurrah?" *New York Times Magazine,* January 11, p. 14.

———. 1974. "The Wallace Message." *New York Times Magazine,* March 17, p. 15.

———. 1972a. "Wallace Talks to Agnew, Shifts on Endorsement." *New York Times,* October 12, p. 40.

———. 1972b. "Schmitz Says U.S. Hides Data on Plot to Slay Wallace." *New York Times,* September 15, p. 24.

———. 1972c. "Wallace Likely to Bar Third-Party Draft." *New York Times,* July 28, p. 12.

———. 1972d. "Manager Insists Wallace May Run." *New York Times,* July 14, p. 12.

———. 1972e. "Wallace Tells Convention He Wants to Help Party." *New York Times,* July 12, p. 1.

———. 1972f. "Wallace Poised to Renew Fight." *New York Times,* July 11, p. 19.

———. 1972g. "Wallace Nears Test of Political Future." *New York Times,* July 4, p. 4.

———. 1972h. "Wallace Keeps Third-Party Option Open." *New York Times,* May 28, p. 45.

———. 1972i. "Again a Gun Alters the Politics of the Republic." *New York Times,* May 21, sec. IV, p. 1.

———. 1972j. "Wallace Receives Physical Therapy." *New York Times,* May 19, p. 43.

———. 1972k. "Wallace Buoyed by Pennsylvania." *New York Times,* April 29, p. 12.

———. 1972l. "Wallace Elated in Detroit by Double-Audience Rally." *New York Times,* April 17, p. 38.

———. 1972m. "Wallace's Drive Gathers Speed After Wisconsin." *New York Times,* April 8, p. 12.

———. 1972n. "Instead of Racial Appeals, Wallace Stresses Opposition to Busing." *New York Times,* February 26, p. 14.

———. 1971a. "Wallace Asserts He Holds U.S. Courts in 'Contempt.'" *New York Times,* August 27, p. 19.

————. 1971b. "Either Way, Mr. Wallace Gets What He Wants." *New York Times,* August 22, sec. IV, p. 3.

————. 1971c. "Wallace Bars Two More Integration Plans." *New York Times,* August 19, p. 28.

————. 1971d. "Wallace to Seek Ruling on Busing." *New York Times,* August 18, p. 11.

————. 1971e. "Judge Calls Wallace's Busing Stand 'Meaningless.'" *New York Times,* August 17, p. 13.

————. 1971f. "Busing for Desegregation to Affect 350,000 Pupils in the South." *New York Times,* August 15, p. 63:

————. 1971g. "Wallace Asserts He'll Run in '72." *New York Times,* August 6, p. 1.

————. 1970a. "Wallace Says Nixon Fails to Keep School Pledges." *New York Times,* June 4, p. 1.

————. 1970b. "Racial Issue Key to Brewer-Wallace Vote Tuesday." *New York Times,* May 31, p. 50.

————. 1970c. "Activism Arrives at University of Alabama." *New York Times,* May 24, p. 52.

————. 1970d. "Alabama Race: 'I Never Seen' One 'Like This Before.'" *New York Times,* May 3, p. 45.

————. 1970e. "Governor's Contest in Alabama is Likened to Gentlemanly Duel." *New York Times,* March 20, p. 22.

————. 1970f. "Confident Wallace Enters Race; Says Nixon Men Seek His Defeat." *New York Times,* February 27, p. 18.

————. 1970g. "Wallace Urges a Defiant South." *New York Times,* February 9, p. 1.

————. 1969a. "'Spirit of Wallace' Rules Southern Governors." *New York Times,* September 16, p. 30.

————. 1969b. "Wallace: Alive, Well, Thinking Big in Alabama." *New York Times,* September 7, sec. IV, p. 6.

————. 1969c. "Wallace Backed on School Stand." *New York Times,* September 5, p. 1.

————. 1969d. "Citizens Councils Hail Their Heroes." *New York Times,* August 31, p. 34.

Wolfinger, Raymond E.; Wolfinger, Barbara Kaye; Prewitt, Kenneth; and Rosenhack, Sehilah. 1964. "America's Radical Right: Politics and Ideology." In *Ideology and Discontent,* ed. David E. Apter. London: Free Press of Glencoe.

Woodward, C. Vann. 1966. *The Strange Career of Jim Crow.* 2nd ed. London: Oxford University Press.

————. 1959. "The Populist Heritage and the Intellectual." *The American Scholar* 29 (Winter): 55–72.

Woolf, S.J., ed. 1968. *The Nature of Fascism.* New York: Vintage Books.

Wright, Gerald C., Jr. 1977. "Contextual Models of Electoral Behavior: The Southern Wallace Vote." *American Political Science Review* 71 (June): 497–508.

Wrong, Dennis H. 1968. "Some Problems in Defining Social Power." *American Journal of Sociology* 73 (May): 673–81.

Index

Aberbach, Joel, 113, 114, 169; political efficacy, 114
Abernathy, Ralph, 182
Abortion, 208, 211, 244
Adorno, T. W., 10, 98, 170, 262; E scale, 170; F scale, 10, 11, 49, 97, 170, 234, 262
AFL-CIO, 187
Age. *See* Voting/political support, factors in
Agnew, Spiro, 81, 82, 135, 145, 149, 154; Wallace's influence on choice of Agnew as Nixon's running mate, 81
AIP. *See* American Independent Party
Alabama, 276, 278
Alabama Freedom March (Selma to Montgomery), 68–69
Alabama Labor Council, 189
"Alabama Message," 206
Alabama Movement, 131, 132, 136
Alabama, politics: black voting, 137, 184, 188, 190; congressional delegation, 35; Democratic Party, 67, 141, 147, 151; National Democratic Party, 137, 151, 190; 1964 general election, 33, 41, 42; 1972 general election, 146–47; 1976 general election, 216–17; 1958 gubernatorial election, 21–22; 1962 gubernatorial election, 24; 1966 gubernatorial election, 71; 1970 gubernatorial election, 134–37, 183; 1974 guber-

natorial election, 184, 187–90; Republicans, 68, 136; Senate election, 220; unpledged electors (1964), 33, 41, 43–44
Alabama, quality of life indicators, 200
Alabama, state of: Department of Public Safety, 190; legislature, 138; National Guard, 26; state troopers, 273
Alabama, University of: integration of, 62–63; student unrest, 136. *See also* Stand in the Schoolhouse Door
Alienation, political, 5
Allen, James B., 271
Allen, Maryon, 271–72
American Dream, 16, 18, 185, 208, 260
American Independent Party, 5, 72, 73, 74, 76, 77, 81, 85, 86, 127, 131, 133, 141–42, 172, 173, 183, 198, 199, 207, 210, 217, 253, 254; in Indiana, 194; in Kansas, 74; in New York, 74, 150; in Oklahoma, 77, 84n; platform, 127, 128; split (formed American Party), 141. *See also* American Party
American National Election Studies. *See* Center for Political Studies
American Nazi Party, 76, 183
American Party, 141–42, 153–54, 198, 199, 210, 212; in Texas, 152; 1972 convention, 152–53. *See also* American Independent Party
American Voter, The, 12

319

Anderson, Jack, 135
Anderson, Tom, 153, 154, 210
Andrews, T. Coleman, 141, 142, 153
Anomie, 113, 115. *See* Power/power-lessness, measures of; political anomie.
Anti-Defamation League, 76
Antiwar movement, 93, 95, 127, 130, 178, 278. *See also* Vietnam
Apple, R. W., Jr., 144
Arizona: 1976 Primary, 216
Arms race, 232, 233, 234
Askew, Reuben, 143, 144, 198
Assassination attempt. *See* Wallace, assassination attempt
Attitudes. *See* Voting/political support, factors in
Authoritarian personality, 9, 10, 11, 49–50, 57, 85, 96–97, 121, 163–64, 170, 234, 262–64. *See also* Authoritarianism
Authoritarianism, 253, 262, 264, 268, 275, 277; relationship to conservatism, 10; relationship to right wing attitudes, 10. *See Also* Authoritarian personality
Ayres, B. Drummond, 210, 217
Azbell, Joe, 7, 44n, 69, 75, 76, 139, 140, 155, 189–90, 271, 273

Bablin, Mark, 75, 139, 153, 216; charged with filing forged petitions, 216
Backlash, 14, 30, 33
Ballot position, 142, 198, 199, 258; (1964), 32, 39; (1968), 71–73, 75, 76, 77, 82
Barbour County, Alabama, 22
Barnett, Ross, 27, 40
Bayh, Birch, 32, 205
Beasley, Jere, 271
Bentsen, Lloyd, 204, 216
Birmingham News, 21, 40
Birmingham Times, 188, 194
Birthplace. *See* Voting/political support, factors in
Blacks, 64, 174, 248, 259, 260, 261, 268, 273, 276, 277, 278; protest/rebellion, 18, 33, 37, 127; reaction to black support for Wallace, 188, 208, 219; rising status of, 51, support for

Wallace, 188, 189, 190, 257; vote in 1964 Maryland primary, 37; voter registration, 22. *See also* Civil rights; Civil rights legislation; Civil rights movement; Racial attitudes
Bloc voting, 135, 136
Bloody Sunday. *See* Alabama Freedom March
Blount, Winton, 135, 152
Blue collar, 15, 36, 59n, 189, 209, 237, 238, 240, 242, 249
Blumer, Herbert, 13
Bond, Julian, 188
Branch, William M., 188
Bravado. *See* South, southern political style
Bremer, Arthur, 183, 188, 215
Brewer, Albert, 74, 134, 135, 136, 137
Brewster, Daniel B., 34, 35, 36
Brown, (Jerry) Edmund G., Jr., 247
Brown, Thad A. 114, 169
Bulger, William, 205
Bullock County, Alabama, 22
Bureaucracy, 174, 177, 182, 203, 206, 209, 249
Bureaucrats, 138, 144
Business, big/corporations, 243, 244
Busing, 5, 9, 17, 81, 134, 137, 138, 139, 143, 144, 145, 150, 158, 160–63, 164, 166, 169, 171, 175, 176, 179, 203, 204, 205, 208, 211, 212, 214, 215, 234, 235, 249, 261–62; antibusing activity, 9, 138, 139, 143, 144, 160; in Boston, 208; as factor in Wallace's 1976 Florida primary loss, 211
Byrd, Robert, 191
Byrne, Brendan, 204

California: 1964 primary, 39; 1972 primary, 149
Callaway, Bo, 80–81; suggested that Wallace become Republican, 80–81
Calley, William L., 134, 142, 153
Camp, Billy Joe, 29
Campaign. *See* Alabama, politics; General election; Wallace campaign
Campbell, Angus, 87, 114, 281
Carsdale, Harold, 134
Carter, Jimmy, 194, 197, 204, 205, 207 209, 210, 211, 212, 213, 214, 215, 216, 217, 218, 219, 220, 247, 258, 269, 272,

275; 1976 Florida primary, 240, 242–46; 1976 support, 221–40, 241; Wallace supporters' vote for Carter, 254, 255

Cashin, John, 137

Caucus system, 207

CBS News/ *New York Times* Poll, 209, 211, 213, 214, 215, 221, 222, 240, 281

Celler, Emmanuel, 21

Center for Political Studies, American National Election Studies, 253, 255, 260; (1964), 58n, 113; (1968), 85, 101, 103, 115, 124, 126, 284; (1972), 170, 172, 254, 284; (1976), 254, 284

Chandler, Happy, 83

Charisma, 279

Checkler, Bob, 28

Chester, Lewis, 44, 68, 80, 82, 83, 278

Chisholm, Shirley, 149

Christian Crusade, 133, 153

Citizens Council, 72, 133, 138

Civil disobedience, 94, 95, 124, 129

Civil rights, 33, 63, 64, 128, 129, 178, 249

Civil Rights Commission, 22, 23

Civil rights legislation, 28, 35, 129, 130, 277; 1964 Civil Rights Act, 3, 27, 29, 30, 32, 33, 35, 36, 37–38, 39, 48, 61, 279

Civil rights movement, 3, 24, 36, 62, 69, 93, 96, 98, 100, 119, 120 121, 122, 123, 126n, 127, 260, 261, 272–73, 278; demonstrations, 94, 95. *See also* Alabama Freedom March; Montgomery bus boycott; Voter registration

Civil War, 2, 276; fostered southern unity, 2

Class, 17, 105, 107, 108, 109, 110, 253, 265; middle class, 110, 176, 195, 196, 202, 203, 208, 212, 248, 249–50, 251, 265, 266; working class, 15, 17, 107, 109, 110, 120, 166, 169, 250, 265, 266. *See also* Blue collar; White collar

Clausen, Aage R., 39

Cobb County, Georgia: federal investigation of racial makeup of grand juries, 20, 21

Coles, Robert, 17

Committee for a New Majority, 210, 217

Committee for the Survival of a Free Congress, 199

Committee on Conservative Alternatives, 194, 198, 199

Committee to Re-Elect the President. *See* CREEP

Communism, 30, 48, 49, 65, 132n, 203

Communists, 40, 91, 128, 129, 130, 153, 176, 178, 202, 251

Congress. *See* United States, Congress

Connally, John, 42, 82

Conner, Eugene "Bull", 24, 42

Conservative Caucus, 199

Conservative Congressional Committee, 199

Conservative Party (Kansas AIP), 74

Conservatives, 39, 199

Constitution. *See* United States, Constitution

Converse, Philip E., 39

County-unit rule. *See* Primaries

Courage Party (New York AIP), 74, 150

Courts, 128. *See also* United States, Supreme Court

CPS. *See* Center for Political Studies

CREEP (Committee to Re-Elect the President), 182–83

Crime, 129, 159–60, 161, 170, 177, 178, 211, 214, 243, 244, 250–51, 263–64

Crossover voting, 28, 33, 38, 191, 204, 206, 216, 247

Dabbs, James McBride, 32

Daily Worker, 31

Daley, Richard J., 19, 204; organization, 186

Darden Poll, 210

Dauphin, Alton, 75, 139, 156

Dees, Morris, 190

Defiance, 3, 6, 80, 131, 137, 278; of court orders, 134, 137, 138, 139. *See also* Wallace, political style

De Graffenried, Ryan, 24

Delegate, 147, 149, 212, 218; direct delegate election convention system, 192; Michigan, 150; New York, 202; selection rules, 191–93, 201, 206; unit rule, 185. *See also* Democratic party, delegate selection procedures

Democratic party, 33, 43, 44, 67, 143, 147, 150, 152, 155, 156, 173, 174, 182, 185, 190, 193, 199, 247, 272; Credentials Committee, 42; delegate selection procedures, 185, 191–93; Democratic National Committee (DNC), 82, 151, 155–56, 185, 193; Executive Committee of Democratic National Committee, 151, 156; Florida, 143; McGovern-Fraser reforms, 192–93; Mikulski Commission, 185, 186; Mini-Convention (1974), 186–87, 189, 191; 1964 Democratic Convention, 42–43; 1968 Democratic Convention, 97, 100, 127; 1976 Democratic Convention, 198, 212, 214, 217, 218; platform, 41, 152, 218; Platform Committee, 150, 247; Policy Advisory Committee, 182; reaction to Wallace's candidacy, 143, 197–98, 204–05; rules, 185, 186, 201; Rules Committee, 151; Wallace representation on Democratic National Committee, 185, 186, 201; Wallace representation on Platform Committee, 150. See also Democrats

Democrats, 11, 28, 38, 86, 100, 131, 146, 183, 190, 191, 197, 276, 279; Maryland, 148; Michigan, 148; 1972 Florida Primary, 143, 157–72; North Carolina, 148

Demographics: change over time, 253, 257–58, 259; (1964), 45–47; (1968), 86–87, 124; (1972), 157–58, 159; (1976), 222–23, 240, 242. See also Voting/political support, factors in

Desegregation, 3, 18, 94, 96, 98, 133–34, 136, 137, 138, 144, 150, 156; University of Alabama, 24. See also Integration; Schools, integration of; Segregation

Détente, 252

Direct Delegate Election Convention System. See Delegate

Domestic issues, 223, 227–8, 230–31, 240

Duncan Occupational Status Score, 103, 284

E scale. See Adorno, E scale

Economic issues, 158–59, 161, 170, 209, 227, 230; (1968), 90; (1972), 176

Education. See Voting/political support, factors in

Election. See Alabama, politics; General election; Wallace campaign

Electoral College, 79, 148

Ellsberg, Daniel, 183

Environmental issues, 244

Ethnicity, 31, 35, 282

Ethnocentrism, 10, 170

Evers, Charles, 188, 189

Ewing, Ed, 74, 139

Expressive politics. See Wallace, political style

Extremism. See Right wing politics

F scale. See Adorno, F scale

Faith in political parties. See Power/powerlessness, measures of

Farm. See Voting/political support, factors in

Federal government, 16, 30, 37, 61, 62, 63, 65, 69, 99, 111, 113–16, 128, 129, 133, 134, 137, 138, 144, 169, 170, 171, 177, 179, 191, 196, 203, 237, 245, 247, 248, 250, 276, 277, 278; attitudes toward, 11, 112, 124, 205, 206, 209, 240, 243; campaign funding by, 195–96, 201, 207; as "central government," 30, 62, 63, 128, 185; guaranteed job program, 227, 228, 230, 231–32; ineffectiveness of, 244, 245; interference by, 17, 26, 273; permissiveness, 177; power of, 85, 96, 109, 111, 124, 175; regulation, 240, 241; responsibility of, 247; size of, 196, 204, 209, 214, 227, 230, 239–40, 241, 243, 244; spending, 3, 48, 177, 227, 228, 230, 231, 232, 240, 241, 242, 250; troops, 24; as unresponsive, 174

Florida primary: (1972), 141, 142, 143–45, 157–72; 1972 vote relative to 1968 General Election vote, 172; (1976), 196, 204, 205, 206, 210–12, 213, 221, 240–46, 281; 1976 Wallace loss analyzed, 246; Wallace dropped by aide, 207, 213. See also Democrats, 1972 Florida primary

Flowers, Walter, 190
Folsom, Jim, 19, 20, 24
Ford, Gerald, 197, 200, 202, 206, 208, 210, 216, 217, 219, 247, 276; assassination attempts, 201; attempts to attract Wallace constituency, 200, 219; 1976 election support, 221–40, 241; 1976 Florida primary vote, 240, 242–46; Wallace supporters vote for Ford, 254, 255
Ford, Johnny, 188
Foreign policy, 82, 91–93, 124, 130, 179, 197, 202, 203, 228, 232, 233, 251–52; foreign aid, 93, 176, 177; isolationism, 91; military aid, 232, 233; tough stance, 178, 251–52
Fowler, Dan, 201, 202
Frady, Marshall, 19, 20, 24, 28
Free enterprise system, 128, 131, 250
Freedom March. *See* Alabama Freedom March
Frost, David, 183, 190

Gallup Poll, 39, 45, 58n, 79, 194, 221, 256
Garrity, W. Arthur, 208
Georgia: 1976 primary, 216
General election: (1960), 39; (1964), 27–44; (1968), 5, 9, 11, 83–84, 254; (1972), 5, 9; (1976), 9, 187, 191, 203, 207, 232, 233, 242, 243, 244, 275. *See also* Demographics: names of individual candidates
George C. Wallace Newsletter, 139
Goldwater, Barry, 38, 39, 40, 41, 43, 44, 45–59, 68, 254
Goodell, Charles, 80
Government. *See* Federal government; State and local government; United States
Graham, Bryce, 75
Griffin, Marvin, 82, 84n
Griffin, (Mickey) Michael, 75, 149, 153, 156, 185, 186, 191, 193, 196, 198, 199, 202, 213, 246, 271
Gronouski, John A., 29
Gurin, Gerald, 114

Haldeman, H. R., 139, 183
Hargis, Billy James, 133

Harris, Fred, 207, 212
Harris, Lou, 45, 199
Harris Poll, 38, 45, 199, 207, 256
Hart, Peter, 270–71, 273n
Hartke, Vance, 32
Heflin, Howell, 270–71, 272, 273n; funding, 271
Helms, Jesse, 193, 198, 199
Herbert, John M., III, 271
Herbstreith, Dolores, 28, 29
Herbstreith, Lloyd, 28
Hodgson, Godfrey, 44, 68, 80, 82, 83, 278
Hood, Jimmy, 24
Hoover, J. Edgar, 82–83
Horowitz, Irving Louis, 16
House, Mike, 271, 273n
House Judiciary Committee. *See* United States, House Judiciary Committee
House of Representatives. *See* Wallace, possibility of throwing election into House
Howard, Milo, 29, 219
Huie, William Bradford, 29
Humphrey, Hubert, 12, 80, 81, 82, 83, 85–126, 145, 147, 148, 149, 172
Hunt, H. L., 68

Ideology, 90, 91, 223, 226, 258, 260, 275. *See also* Voting/political support, factors in
I-E scale. *See* Rotter
Illinois: 1964 primary, 38; 1976 primary, 212, 213, 221, 281
Income. *See* Voting/political support, factors in
Independents, 11, 50, 54, 56, 58, 86, 99, 101, 119, 222, 225, 242, 258
Independents for President Nixon movement, 152
Indiana: AFL-CIO, 32; Democratic Committee, 33; 1964 primary, 31–34, 36, 38, 45; 1972 primary, 147; 1976 primary, 216
Inflation, 177, 179, 202, 250
Inouye, David K., 36
Institutional power. *See* Power/powerlessness, measures of
Instrumental politics, 275

Integration, 38, 61, 98, 120–21, 124, 136, 145, 160–63, 164, 166, 167, 169, 171, 175, 234, 235, 276. *See* Alabama, University of, integration. *See also* Desegregation; Schools, integration of; Segregation
Internal Revenue Service, 135, 183; investigation of Gerald Wallace, 135; investigation of Wallace supporters, 135

Jackson, Cecil, 74, 139
Jackson, Henry, 9, 144, 187, 190, 194, 197, 207, 209, 211, 212, 213, 216, 218, 247; 1976 Florida primary, 240, 242–46; 1976 support, 221–40, 241
Jackson, Jesse, 191
Jackson, Maynard, 189
James, Fob, 273
Janowitz, Morris, 281
John Birch Society, 7, 9, 28, 29, 76, 132n, 133, 153
Johnson, Frank M., Jr., 22, 23, 206, 273
Johnson, Lyndon B., 29, 32, 33, 34, 37, 38, 39, 40, 41, 42, 44, 80, 254; 1964 support, 45–59
Jones, Bill, 22, 25, 27, 28, 32, 36, 37, 65, 68, 69, 74, 139
Jones, Norman F., 145
Justice Department. *See* United States, Justice Department

Katzenbach, Nicholas J., 25, 26
Kendall, Robert, 28, 29, 43
Kennedy, Edward M., 33, 36, 149, 154, 181, 182, 190, 197; appearance with Wallace at 1973 Spirit of America Festival, Decatur, Alabama, 181, 182, 189; stressed similarity to Wallace, 182
Kennedy, John F., 24, 25, 26, 31, 37
Kennedy, Robert F., 2, 24, 29, 34, 127
Kent State University, 136
Key, V.O., 2
King, Martin Luther, Jr., 24, 68, 127, 191, 273. *See also* Alabama Freedom March
King, William C., 194
Kissinger, Henry, 153, 202, 228, 233
Kohn, John, 19, 20, 188

Ku Klux Klan, 22, 69, 76, 132n, 135, 136, 277

Labor unions. *See* Unions
Laird, Melvin, 197
Law and order, 9, 82, 93–94, 95, 129, 136, 177, 179, 195, 203
Lefkowitz, Louis, 204
LeMay, Curtis, 83, 130
Lewis, Jessie J., 194
Liberty Amendment, 28
Life Magazine, 40
Lindsay, John, 144, 145
Lipset, Seymour Martin, 10, 13, 14
Local government. *See* State and local government
Lodge, Henry Cabot, 38
Loeb, William, 194
Loss of power. *See* Power/ powerlessness, loss of power
Loyalty oath, 42, 43, 143, 198

McCarthy, Joseph, 9, 10; McCarthyism, 114
McCary, Elvin, 190
McClosky, Herbert: anomie scale, 10
McDonald, David J., 35, 36
McEvoy, James III, 10, 11, 12, 14
McGovern, George, 146, 147, 148, 149, 150, 151, 154, 155, 172, 187, 191, 213, 254, 255; attempts to attract Wallace supporters, 149, 151
McGruder, J.E.B. Stuart, 183
McKay, Richard B., 142, 153
Maddox, Lester, 40, 80, 153
Malone, Vivian, 24
Marginal Voting, 9, 11, 12, 50–51, 57–58, 85, 97–101, 102, 121, 164–65, 170, 234–36, 262, 263
Martin, James D., 40
Maryland: county-unit rule, 37; Democratic organization, 34; Democratic party, 37; 1964 primary, 31, 34–37; 1972 primary, 148–49
Massachusetts, 258; Boston, 209, 249; 1976 primary, 205, 208–10, 211, 213, 240, 281
Mathews, Pete, 29, 78
Matthews, Donald R., 278
Meany, George: visit to Wallace, 187
Menominee County, Wisconsin, 31

Methodology, 281–86

Meyer, Philip: study of 1972 Florida primary, 157, 169, 172

Miami Herald, 144

Michigan, 258; Jefferson-Jackson Day Dinner (1972), 146; 1972 primary, 146, 148; 1976 primary, 217

Michigan Inter-University Consortium for Political Research. *See* Center for Political Studies

Middle class. *See* Class, middle

Mikulski Commission. *See* Democratic party, Mikulski Commission

Miller, Arthur H., 114, 169; political trust. *See* Power/powerlessness, measures

Miller, Warren E., 39, 114, 281

Miller, William E., 40

Mills, C. Wright, 7

Military. *See* Foreign policy

Minutemen, 153

Misanthropy scale. *See* Rosenberg, Morris

Mississippi: Democratic precinct caucuses, 206–07

Mitchell, Martha, 183

Mitchell, John N., 138, 143

Montgomery Advertiser, 140

Montgomery Bus Boycott, 187

Morton, Rogers C. B., 216

Muskie, Edmund S., 144, 145, 147, 149, 183

Myers, Del, 153

My Lai Massacre, 134

NAACP, 22

National Black Citizens Committee for Wallace, 145

National Committee of Autonomous State Parties, 142

National Conference of Lieutenant Governors, 200

National Conservative Council, 39

National Conservative Political Action Committee, 199

National Democratic Governors Conference, 198

National Democratic Party. *See* Alabama, politics

National Governors Conference, 195, 200–01

National Press Club, 82

National Review, The, 198

Nativity, 125–26n

NATO, 203

Nazi. *See* American Nazi Party

Nebraska: 1964 Republican primary, 38

Negro. *See* Blacks

New Hampshire: 1964 Republican primary, 38; 1976 primary, 196, 205, 208

New Mexico: 1972 primary, 149

New York: 1976 primary, 206, 212, 215–16

New York Times, 29, 34, 35, 38, 67, 68, 69, 212, 215, 275

Nixon, Richard M., 9, 80–82, 83, 84, 85, 133, 134, 136, 137, 138, 142, 143, 144, 145, 149, 150, 152, 154, 155, 172, 181, 183, 254; appeals to "forgotten Americans," 81; appeals to South, 80–81, 135, 136, appeals to Wallace supporters, 80–82; appearance with Wallace in 1974 at Honor America Day, Huntsville Alabama, 187; Committee to Re-Elect the President. *See* CREEP; 1968 election vote, 12, 85–126; 1973 inauguration, 181; put money into 1970 Alabama gubernatorial campaign to defeat Wallace, 134; resignation, 190; strategy against Wallace, 82; Wallace supporters' 1972 vote for Nixon, 254, 255

Nonvoting, 50, 57, 97, 99, 102, 164–65, 170, 172, 234, 235–36, 237, 242, 254, 262, 263

Normlessness. *See* Anomie

Norris, Clarance, 219–20

North Carolina: 1972 primary, 145; 1976 primary, 213, 214, 221

O'Brien, Larry, 81, 143

Occupation. *See* Voting/political support, factors in

Ohio: 1972 primary, 149

Oklahoma: 1976 primary, 207–09

"Old American," 125–26n

Olsen, Marvin E., 125n, 166, 282, 284

Orfield, Gary, 80

Page, Bruce, 44, 68, 80, 82, 83, 278
Panola County, Mississippi, 3
Parks, Rosa, 187
Participation. *See* Political participation
Party affiliation. *See* Political parties, affiliation
Pateman, Carole, 7
Patriotism. *See* Wallace, political style, appeals to patriotism
Patronage. *See* Wallace, patronage
Patterson, John, 20, 21, 22
Peace, 179, 252. *See also* Antiwar movement
Pennsylvania: 1972 primary, 147; 1976 primary, 216
Permissiveness, 196–97; *See also* Federal government, permissiveness
Personal anomie. *See* Power/powerlessness, measures of
Personal power/powerlessness. *See* Power/powerlessness, measures of
Pettigrew, Thomas F., 11, 13, 14, 167
Pointer, Sam C., Jr., 138
Political activity, 39, 101
Political anomie. *See* Power/powerlessness, measures of
Political efficacy. *See* Political trust
Political interest, 101, 234–35, 236. *See also* Political activity
Political intolerance, 10, 263–64. *See also* Racism
Political participation, 7, 8, 11. *See also* Marginal voting; Nonvoting; Political activity; Political interest
Political parties, 115; affiliation, 46, 47, 48, 49, 50, 54, 86, 87, 88, 99, 100, 102, 117, 222, 225, 242, 257–58, 259; change of affiliation, 100, 102, 125n; effectiveness, 56, 100, 103. *See also* American Party; American Independent Party; Democratic party; Democrats; Republican party; Republicans
Political power/powerlessness. *See* Power/powerlessness
Political support. *See* Voting/political support
Political trust. *See* Power/powerlessness, political trust
Political vengeance, 10
Politics of Southern Inequality, 3

Pollution. *See* Environmental issues
Poor/poverty, 249, 250
Popular vote, 147, 148, 149, 173; relationship of popular vote to delegate strength, 186, 192
Populism. *See* Wallace, as populist
Powell, Adam Clayton, 20
Power/powerlessness, 1, 5, 12, 16, 17, 18, 54, 56, 58, 62, 65, 66, 85, 101, 111, 113, 114, 115, 116, 117, 124, 167, 169, 170, 173, 174, 179, 240, 247, 248, 275, 276, 278; loss of power, 16, 17, 57, 58, 62, 64, 65–66; measure of faith in political parties, 115; measure of institutional power, 113, 115–16, 117, 118, 119–20, 121, 123, 124, 267, 268, 285–86; measure of personal anomie, 113, 116, 117, 118, 119, 120, 121, 122, 167, 266, 267, 268, 284–85; measure of personal power/powerlessness, 113, 116, 117, 118, 119, 120, 122, 266, 267, 268, 276, 285; measure of political anomie, 12, 113, 114, 115, 116, 117, 118, 119, 120, 121, 122, 124, 126n, 169, 170, 171, 267, 268, 285; measure of political power/powerlessness, 113, 114, 115, 116–17, 118, 119, 121, 123, 124, 126n, 253, 257, 267, 268, 275, 277, 285; measures, 111–16; political trust, 54, 113, 114, 237, 241; political trust scale (Miller, Brown & Raine), 169; relationship to racial attitudes, 119–21, 126n; theory, 14, 17, 54–57, 58, 66, 109–23, 169, 237–40, 241, 266–68, 276
Prayer: in public schools, 34, 145, 156n
Prejudice. *See* Racism
Preservationism, 13–14
Presidential campaigns. *See* General election
Presidential election. *See* General election
Primaries: county-unit rule, 37; presidential preference primary, 37, 192, 212; proportional primaries, 192, 201; winner-take-all primaries, 185, 192. *See also* General election; names of individual states
Progressive Baptist Mission and Education Convention, 190–91
Protest. *See* Antiwar movement; Civil

rights movement; Wallace, political style
Prothro, James W., 278
Public opinion, 39. *See also* Darden Poll; Gallup Poll; Harris Poll; Yankelovich Poll

Raab, Earl B., 14
Race. *See* Voting/political support, factors in
Racial attitudes, 14, 15, 94–101, 109, 119–21, 122, 123, 124, 169, 232, 234, 235, 243, 244, 245, 246, 261–62; relationship to power/powerlessness, 119–21, 126. *See also* Racial issues; Racial politics; Racism; Wallace, racial politics
Racial issues, 29, 33, 130, 143, 160, 249. *See also* Racial attitudes; Racial politics; Racial violence; Racism; Wallace, racial politics
Racial politics, 57, 58, 85, 96–101, 120, 160, 167, 169, 171, 259; role of federal government in, 96. *See also* Racial attitudes; Racial issues; Racial violence; Racism; Wallace, racial politics
Racial prejudice. *See* Racism
Racial violence, 36, 38, 129, 177. *See also* Civil rights movement
Racism, 5, 14, 17, 29, 57, 61, 65, 69, 96, 124, 129, 135, 139, 167, 169, 170, 197, 205, 213, 227, 230, 235, 244, 245, 253, 257, 260, 268, 272, 275; appeals to, 81, 82; lessening importance of racism in voting, 213, 214; *See also* Racial attitudes; Racial issues; Racial politics; Wallace, racial politics
Radical right. *See* Right-wing politics
Raine, Alden S., 114, 169
Ransford, H. Edward, 15
Reagan, Ronald, 191, 193, 194, 199, 206, 210, 215, 216, 217, 221–40, 241, 242–46, 247, 258; 1976 Florida primary vote, 240, 242–46; 1976 support, 221–40, 241
Reapportionment, 56, 57, 58
Reference group, 13, 17
Region. *See* Voting/political support, factors in
Relative deprivation, 13, 14, 54, 167, 169, 171

Religion. *See* Voting/political support, factors in
Republican party, 38, 43, 44, 174, 199; Alabama, 68; appeals to Wallace vote, 80–81, 151–52; 1968 Republican National Convention, 127; Platform Committee, 151, 152; right wing, 217
Republicans, 5, 11, 28, 33, 43, 86, 100, 131, 151, 157–72, 276
Reston, James, 81
Reuther, Walter, 83
Reynolds, John W., 29, 30
Richardson, Elliot L., 202
Right-wing politics, 3, 7, 9, 12, 14, 16, 28, 36, 39, 40, 76, 132n, 133; relationship to authoritarianism, 10
"Right Wing Radicalism and Political Intolerance," 126
Rights of the accused scale, 263–64
Riley, Robert T., 11, 13, 14, 167
Robinson, J. P., 113; faith in people scale, 113; trust scale, 113
Rockefeller, Nelson, 38, 81, 197, 200–01; lip service to Wallace's positions, 200
Roosevelt, Franklin Delano, 204, 212, 279
Rosenberg, Morris, 113; misanthropy scale, 112
Rosow, Jerome, 15
Rotter, J. B.: I-E scale, 114
Rusher, William, 198–99, 210
Russell, Richard B., 20
Russia. *See* Soviet Union

Safire, William, 182
Sanford, Terry, 145, 194, 197, 204
Schmitz, John J., 75, 152–53, 172, 275; did not attract Wallace support, 153; 1972 vote, 153, 254, 255
Schools: integration of, 96, 261–62, 277, 279; local control, 62, 175. *See also* Desegregation; Integration; Segregation
Scottsboro Nine, 220
Seeman, M., 16, 113, 114; individual powerlessness, 114
Segregation, 22, 38, 109, 110, 119, 120–21, 124, 160, 162–63, 164, 166, 168, 171, 175, 204, 219, 257, 260, 261,

272. *See also* Desegregation; Integration; Schools, integration of
Segretti, Donald, 183
Selma, Alabama, 273. *See also* Alabama Freedom March
Sex. *See* Voting/political support, factors in
Shaver, P. R., 113
Shearer, William K., 72, 141, 142, 153
Shelton, Robert, 76, 136
Shriver, R. Sargent, 212
Siegal, Marc A., 193
Snider, Charles, 75, 139, 142, 149, 150, 151, 152, 155, 156, 184, 187, 198, 199; overtures by Republicans to Snider, 152
Social movement, 275
Social security, 176, 228, 230, 231
Sokol, Robert, 114
South, 40, 41, 43, 136, 276, 277; New South, 222; one-party system, 2; race relations as power relations, 1, 2; resistance to federal intervention, 2; set apart from North, 1; social change, 29, 219, 277; Southern political style, 1, 2. *See also* Civil rights movement; Southerners
South Carolina: Democratic precinct caucuses, 209
Southern Committee to Help Elect the Next President of the United States, 34
Southern Democratic Conference of Birmingham, 188
Southern Governors' Conference, 154
Southerners, 276, 277, 278. *See also* South
Soviet Union, 202, 203, 227, 228, 230, 232, 233, 244
Sparkman, John, 69
Srole, Leo, 167
Stand in the Schoolhouse Door, 2, 24–26, 31, 37, 61, 62–63, 219, 278; proclamation, 25. *See also* Alabama, University of, integration
State and local government, 111, 112
States' Rights, 21, 29–30, 32, 61, 62, 65, 128, 138, 240, 241, 243, 244, 249, 278
Status/socioeconomic status (SES), 12, 14, 51–55, 58n, 59n, 101, 103,

104, 105, 109, 110, 117–18, 120, 121, 126n, 165, 166, 167, 168, 169, 170, 237, 240, 264, 265, 266, 282–84; achieved status, 52, 53, 58, 59n, 103, 104, 107, 165, 166, 167, 168, 265, 266, 282, 283; ascribed status, 51, 52, 53, 55, 58, 59n, 101, 103, 104, 107, 125n, 126n, 165, 167, 168, 170, 265, 266, 282; loss of status, 13, 14, 66, 277; measures of, 282–84; relationship to power/powerlessness, 117; relationship to racial attitudes, 109, 110; relationship to right-wing consciousness, 12; status anxiety/security, 12, 13, 14, 51, 52, 54, 58, 105, 107, 108, 109; status deprivation. *See* Relative deprivation; status discrepancy, 12, 14, 58, 107, 167, 170; status mobility, 103–04, 105, 106, 284; subjective status, 117, 118, 120, 124; theory, 9, 12–14, 51–55, 58, 85, 101–09, 120, 165–69, 264–66
Stokes, Donald E., 281
Stouffer, Samuel, 87
Strachan, Gordon C., 139
Strauss, Robert, 155, 156, 182, 185, 197, 204, 218, 219; 1973 appearance with Wallace at Spirit of America Festival, Decatur, Alabama, 182
Student movement. *See* Antiwar movement; Civil rights movement
Support. *See* Voting/political support
Sutton, Percy, 189

Tawes, J. Millard, 34, 36
Taxes, 15, 146, 176, 177, 179, 186, 187, 195, 202, 228, 231, 250, 251
Television, 29, 34, 42, 62, 278. *See also* Wallace, use of media
Tennessee: 1972 primary, 148
Texas: 1964 delegation to Democratic Convention, 42; 1964 Republican primary, 38; 1976 primary, 216
Thatcher, Margaret, 202
Third party, 11, 39, 41, 43, 81, 82, 132n, 141, 142, 148, 149, 150, 152, 155, 183, 185, 189, 190, 191, 193, 194, 195, 197, 198, 199, 203, 210, 216, 217, 256, 258, 262; cost of Wallace's 1968 third party run, 155; as "wasted vote," 82

Thurmond, Strom, 44, 81, 136
Time Magazine, 218
Trammell, Seymore, 68, 74, 77, 83, 139, 154
Trow, Martin, 126n
Trust in government. *See* Political trust
Tully, Judy Corden, 125n, 166, 282, 284
Turnipseed, Tom, 139

Udall, Morris, 80, 209, 210, 215, 216, 217, 218, 247
Union, 33, 35, 36, 83, 101, 144, 146, 186, 189; anti-Wallace activity, 83, 144, 146; membership, 51, 235, 236, 262, 263; support for Wallace in Alabama, 35
Union Leader, 194
Unit rule. *See* Delegate, unit rule
United States: Congress, 115, 116, 276; Constitution, 26, 61, 62, 63, 64, 80, 249; Constitutional rights, 26, 33; Federal Election Commission, 207; Federal Reserve Board, 195; General Accounting Office, 195; House Judiciary Committee, 183, 190; Justice Department, 195, 208; 1954 Supreme Court decision ending public school segregation, 21; Senate 37; Supreme Court, 56, 64, 65, 128, 129, 138, 208, 249; Tenth Amendment to Constitution, 61
United Steelworkers of America, 35

Vanneman, Reeve D., 13, 14, 167
Vietnam, 18, 48, 91, 92, 93, 97, 100, 124, 129–30, 133–34, 150, 153, 164, 167, 178, 195, 203, 251, 278; Wallace's fact-finding tour, 133–35. *See also* Antiwar movement
Viguerie, Richard A., 184, 194, 196, 199, 204
Virginia: 1976 primary, 215
Vote. *See* Popular vote
Voter Decides, The, 114
Voter registration, 51, 135, 137, 277
Voters' League of Ozark, 188
Voting: counts/doesn't count, 237, 241; (1960), 58; (1964), 102; voting history, 50. *See also* Nonvoting.

Voting/political support, factors in: affective issues, 223, 229, 242; age, 46, 47, 86, 88, 117, 158, 159, 166, 222, 224, 257, 259; attitudes, 87, 158–60, 253; attitudes toward civil rights, 48, 49, 52, 54, 55, 56, 57, 58; birthplace, 158, 159; education, 12, 52, 53, 59n, 103, 104, 107, 111, 112, 117, 118, 124, 165, 168, 170, 237, 238, 242, 265, 266, 282, 284; farmers/ farm residence, 59n, 87, 88; ideology (self-proclaimed), 49, 50; income, 12, 52, 53, 59n, 103, 104, 107, 117, 118, 126n, 165, 166, 168, 170, 172, 237, 239, 242, 265, 266, 283–84; occupation, 12, 58n, 59, 237, 239; occupational prestige, 284; race, 45, 46, 47, 59n, 86, 88, 102–03, 104, 117, 126n, 157, 159, 165, 222, 224, 257, 259, 265, 282–84; region, 46, 47, 48, 86, 87, 88, 222, 225, 257, 258, 259, 281–82; region of childhood residence, 86, 88; religion, 51, 52, 59n, 87, 89, 102, 104, 126n, 165, 167, 168, 222, 225, 240, 257, 258, 259, 265, 282–84; self-employment, 126n; sex, 46, 47, 86, 87, 88, 158, 159, 222, 225, 240, 257, 258, 259; size of place, 46, 47, 56, 87, 88. *See also* Class; Nativity; Political activity; Power/powerlessness; Racial attitudes; Status; Union
Voting Rights Act of 1965, 195

Wallace, Cornelia, 199, 201, 219, 269–70
Wallace, George C.: as Alabama assistant attorney general, 19; as Alabama state legislator, 19; as alternate delegate to 1948 Democratic convention, 20; appearance with Nixon in 1974 at Honor America Day, 187; appearance with Ted Kennedy at 1972 Spirit of America Festival in Decatur, Alabama, 181, 182, 189; appointment/nonappointment of blacks, 190, 194; assassination attempt, 148, 150, 181, 183, 273; attempts to change gubernatorial succession law, 70; attempts to stand, give appearance of walking, 181, 182, 187; changed gubernatorial

succession law, 70, 71; as circuit court judge, 20, 22–23; considered Senate run, 69–70, 269, 270, 271–72; considered turning Republican, 44; as crucial factor in Nixon's 1972 election, 154–55; as delegate to 1956 Democratic convention, 21; divorce, 269–70; fact-finding tour of Vietnam, 133–34; first candidate to qualify for federal campaign funds, 195; Florida primary as 1976 turning point, 211; gubernatorial campaigns, 133, 134, 187; health, 149, 150, 201, 203, 204, 205, 211, 212, 213, 214, 215, 223, 229, 244–45, 246, 270, 272; hiatus between first and second gubernatorial campaigns, 23; leaving office, 272; losing popularity in Alabama, 200, 270–71, 273; 1964 campaign speech, 63–64; 1976 announcement for president, 203, 207; no mechanism for successor, 75, 275; "out-nigguhed" statement, 23; patronage, 67, 68, 70, 140; as populist, 174, 176, 178, 247; possibility of throwing election into House, 37, 38, 80, 127, 183, 199, 257; press response to, 278; problems translating popular strength into delegate strength, 147, 185; prompted Nixon's decision to resign, 190; rebuilding political base in Alabama, 69, 71; received contributions after Stand in Schoolhouse Door, 26; record as governor, 184–85, 199–200, 206; record as governor (criticism), 147; relationship to Governor Lurleen Wallace, 71; respectability after assassination attempt, 154; "Segregation now, tomorrow, forever" speech, 24; speeches, 29, 78, 79; spoke at 1976 Democratic Convention, 218; testified against civil rights legislation, 21; as underdog, 278; use of media, 70, 77, 78, 140, 149, 196, 205, 209, 211, 215, 216; withdrawing from 1964 campaign, 41; won unprecedented third term as governor (1974), 190. See also Alabama Movement; Alabama politics, gubernatorial elections

Wallace, George C., campaign for president: advertising, 35; cost of 1968 third-party effort, 155; defeat in 1976 Illinois primary left organization in disarray, 212–13; finances, 40, 68, 77, 152, 184, 194, 207, 216; fragmentation in 1968, 74, 76; fundraising, 72, 77, 140, 141, 152, 184, 195–96; groundwork for 1976, 151; mailings, 72, 184, 196, 198, 204, 216; 1968 strategy, 71, 79–80; 1972 platform proposals, 150, 151; 1976 strategy, 196–97; organization, 74, 194, 207; as petit bourgeois business, 275; polling operations, 140; rallies, 73, 77, 78, 141, 146, 209; staff, 74, 139, 152, 194; staff attempts to influence delegate selection rules, 186, 192–93; staff involvement in changing Democratic party rules, 182; staff not understanding Democratic party rules, 151; staff representation on Democratic National Committee, 151, 185; use of state personnel to conduct campaigns, 70, 73, 74, 75. See Ballot position

Wallace, George C., 1976 defeat, factors in: dropped in primary, 207, 213; issues used by others, 214, 243, 246, 247, 252. See also Wallace, health

Wallace, George C., political style: 30, 41–42, 63, 65, 78–79, 193, 198, 275, 278; appeals to anger, dispair and/or discontent, 6, 127, 276, 278, 279; appeals to patriotism, 63, 64, 179; development of, 23, 43; enemy as essential, 7, 140, 248–49; expressive politics, 18, 275; protest politics, 275, 278; use of hecklers, 78. See also Defiance; Power/powerlessness

Wallace, George C., racial politics: changing position, 137, 144, 175, 184, 188, 191, 195, 204, 248–49; going after black votes, 188, 220; not originally racist, 19–20

Wallace, George C., support (attempts by others to undercut): 32, 36, 146, 183, 195, 201, 209; ABW Movement (Anyone But Wallace) 194; by clergy,

28, 32, 34, 35; delegate selection rules, 201–02; by Democratic party, 143, 197–98, 204–05; "dirty tricks," 82, 134, 135; by Nixon, 82, 134; by unions, 83, 144, 146

Wallace, George C., supporters: assessment of Wallace's chances to win presidency, 245, 246; attitudes toward government, 10–11, 15, 16, 17; black support, 185, 188, 189, 190, 257; delegates to 1972 convention, 150; as loose collectivity, 275; (1964), 7, 38, 45–59, 125; (1968), 10, 11, 12, 80, 85–125, 253–68; (1972), 157–72; 253–68; (1976), 221–40, 241, 242–46, 253–68; 1964 through 1976, 253–68; opinion of Wallace, 223, 229; perception of Wallace's ideology, 258, 260; support by Ku Klux Klan, 76; union, 35; where 1972 support went in general election, 153. *See also* Ku Klux Klan

Wallace, Gerald, 67, 68, 135, 139, 147, 183, 270, 271; investigated by IRS, 135

Wallace, Jack, 135

Wallace, Lurleen: death, 74; gubernatorial campaign, 70–71

Wallace Stand, The, 139, 199, 211

War protestors. *See* Antiwar movement; Vietnam

Watergate, 18, 135, 139, 169, 183, 187, 248; hearings, 182–84; White House Plumbers, 183

Wattenberg, Ben, 283

Welfare, 15, 18, 175, 176, 177, 211, 214, 228, 230, 243, 244, 249, 250, 251

Welsh, Matthew, 32, 33, 45

West, John C., 154

White backlash. *See* Backlash

White collar, 59n, 237, 238

White House, 183, 187, 214

Wicker, Tom, 80, 136, 185, 189

Williams, Hosea, 188

Wilson, Harold, 202

Wilson, Robert, 218, 219

Wirt, Frederick, M., 3

Wisconsin: AFL-CIO, 29; 1964 primary, 28, 30, 31, 34, 36, 38, 215; 1972 primary, 145–46, 147, 215; 1976 primary, 206, 214, 215, 281; University of, 28

Wisconsin Citizens for Wallace, 150

Wooten, James T., 138, 149

Working class. *See* Class, working

Yankelovich Poll, 146

Zero Sum, 7, 15, 17, 277